The Black Worker

The Black Worker

Race, Labor, and Civil Rights
since Emancipation

Edited by
Eric Arnesen

University of Illinois Press
Urbana and Chicago

∞ This book is printed on acid-free paper.

Library of Congress
Cataloging-in-Publication Data
The Black worker : race, labor,
and civil rights since emancipation /
edited by Eric Arnesen.
p.   cm.
Includes bibliographical references and index.
ISBN-13: 978-0-252-03145-8 (cloth : alk. paper)
ISBN-10: 0-252-03145-8 (cloth : alk. paper)
ISBN-13: 978-0-252-07380-9 (pbk. : alk. paper)
ISBN-10: 0-252-07380-0 (pbk. : alk. paper)
1. African-Americans—Employment—History.
2. Discrimination in employment—United States—History.
3. Labor—United States—History.
4. Race discrimination—United States—History.
5. United States—Race relations.
I. Arnesen, Eric.
HD8081.A65B57   2007
331.6 396073—dc22   2006025173

Contents

The Black Worker

Introduction

For centuries, the "hands of the black man . . . have turned the wheels of southern industries, have tilled the soil and builded [*sic*] the roads that led to progress," the African American weekly newspaper, the *Chicago Defender,* reminded its readers in the spring of 1919. "[T]his large section of the country owes what it is today to the faithfulness and integrity of the black man." Not only the South, but the North, East, and West, too, "owe him everlasting gratitude," although for different reasons. Without the aid of black Americans, "there would not have been today a flag of victory waving and the Mason and Dixon line would as clearly have separated the factions of the blue and the gray as does the Atlantic ocean separate us from the old world." But the contributions of African American women and men to building and sustaining the economy of the United States and patriotically defending the nation in its battle against the slaveholders' rebellion were not appreciated by whites. "WITH ALL OF THIS BEHIND US," the paper resentfully reported, "we are still obliged to knock at the door of opportunity; we are still having to battle for a chance to earn by the sweat of our brow, our daily bread; we are still denied by the people who have in the harbor of New York a symbol of the Goddess of Liberty holding a light with outstretched arms . . . the right to be a part and parcel of organized labor, when it is recognized that labor is the biggest factor in society."[1]

Whatever specific issues African Americans confronted, there were two constants: racial inequality, on the one hand, and challenges to that inequality, on the other. The *Defender* touched on the former in its eloquent bill of complaint in the spring of 1919, but in innumerable other articles it chronicled—and encouraged—the efforts of black women and men to undermine and overturn the system of Jim Crow that had taken firm root in the post-Reconstruction South and North. Long before the modern civil rights movement of the 1950s and 1960s frontally assaulted the segregationist order, ordinary African Americans not only struggled to survive that harsh racial climate, but to challenge or escape it, as well. At times (and often by necessity) those challenges were subtle, restrained, and calculated to shield the people engaged in making them from identification and harm. At other times, however, African Americans publicly revealed their dissatisfaction with the status quo and their desire for a new order. Their challenges, both quiet and overt, served as clear reminders to the supporters of white supremacy that, despite their best efforts through violence, fraud, and the law, as long as whites insisted on maintaining racial inequality, the "race question" would never be fully resolved.

For African American workers, the vast majority of the black population in the United States, the race question was invariably intertwined with the "labor question" that preoccupied countless Americans in the late nineteenth through mid-twentieth centuries. Together, they touched on such wide-ranging subjects as the transition from slavery to freedom, the consolidation of the sharecropping system in the agricultural South, black migration, and pervasive discrimination in the larger labor markets of the South and North. Their experiences in those labor markets were anything but benign; rather, they encountered low wages, harsh conditions, managerial abuse, and racially discriminatory treatment. Although some simply endured what they perceived as the inevitable, others registered their dissatisfaction with their feet, leaving their farms or other work sites for the promise of some improvement elsewhere. Still others demonstrated their discontent through individual protest or collective action, forming independent labor associations or joining unions affiliated with the Knights of Labor, the American Federation of Labor, the Industrial Workers of the World, and the Congress of Industrial Organizations.[2] From the start, their efforts to better their families' lives by questioning or challenging the racial or economic status quo met with numerous obstacles. However they chose to respond to their workplace inequities, their strategies often brought them into conflict with white employers, white workers, the trade union movement, and even the black middle class.

White employers and white employees, for very different reasons, had a stake in keeping blacks in a subordinate position. White rural landholders and urban employers insisted on a poorly paid, pliant, and obedient labor force that did not question their far-reaching managerial prerogatives; when challenged, they rarely hesitated to resort to violence to enforce their near-absolute control.[3] In some instances, the fear of black economic competition stoked white workers' hostility toward their African American counterparts. In others, whites' very conceptions of themselves prompted them to put as much distance between themselves and blacks as possible. Either way, white workers in many cases tended to exclude blacks from their definition of the working class in general and from their trade unions in particular, at least until the rise of the Congress of Industrial Organizations during the Great Depression of the 1930s.[4]

But opposition to black workers' independent initiatives came not just from whites. Across the class divide, black elites, accustomed to leading their communities, frequently disapproved of black working-class activism on pragmatic and ideological grounds through the 1930s. Pragmatic in that they feared that black workers' challenges might jeopardize the race's precarious economic standing, ideological in that however much they might resent the rising tide of Jim Crow, they believed in managerial prerogatives, the sanctity of private property, and the ultimate beneficence of industrial capitalism. Their advice to black workers involved counseling patience — some would term it *accommodationism* — as well as hard work, a rejection of trade unionism, and a strategic alliance with capital. To the extent that they advanced a conception of civil rights, it was a circumscribed one that sought legal improvements in blacks' status but left the workplace largely untouched. Black elites evinced remarkably little interest in, much less understanding of, the day-to-day indignities black workers endured on the job.[5]

Yet for black workers, those indignities mattered deeply. Power relations being what they were, endurance and survival were the best that many could hope for. Even during the height of the Jim Crow era, African Americans found ways — invisible and visible, individual and collective — to question, challenge, and resist the degradation, abuse, and inequality they suffered on the job. At times they proved remarkably successful, given what they were up against; at other times — most other times — their efforts were stalemated or met with defeat.

To highlight traditions of workplace and labor activism is not to romanticize or idealize working-class struggles. It is, rather, to insist that in many instances, black workers put forth a critique of racial inequality that was distinctive and not reducible to that of their "social betters." It is also to insist that the labor question was a central element of African American politics and the broader black experience. Black workers' workplace experiences, long ignored by African American and labor historians dealing with the post-slavery period, have slowly become an established and critical component of both the history of black Americans and the history of labor in the United States. This "quest for economic justice," in the words of Charles Payne and Adam Green, has "defined some of the most challenging, imaginative — and underappreciated — campaigns" engaged in by blacks to improve their "life conditions."[6] Although such connections between the race question and the labor question seem self-evident today, a brief examination of the historiography suggests that this has not always been the case and that our understanding of both over the past century has been limited at best.

One of the most significant developments in the fields of labor and African American history has been the flourishing of scholarship devoted to the experiences of African American workers in recent years.[7] From the vantage point of the early twenty-first century, it seems only natural that these two areas of study would overlap and complement each other. After all, both are interested in social, economic, and political hierarchies; systems of exploitation; the experiences of nonelites; and struggles for social justice. Throughout much of the nation's history, most African Americans constituted a significant portion of the nation's working classes. Yet what seems obvious today was long obscured by formal subdisciplinary boundaries in the academy, as well as historiographical and political bias. These two fields, with so much ostensibly in common, followed distinctive historiographical paths, developing along parallel and at times diverging trajectories through the early 1980s.

To the extent that so-called old labor history—the institutionally focused Commons school of the pre-1960 period—dealt with race, it expressed sympathy for union leaders who viewed nonwhites as a threat to organized white labor and viewed white workers' efforts to exclude them from membership as a natural, understandable response of job-conscious unionists. The new labor history that developed in the 1960s and 1970s eschewed an exclusive focus on trade unions for explorations of working-class communities, culture, and agency, but race and African American workers slipped from view. In its sometimes romantic portrayals of working-class communities and their resistance to industrial capitalism, this generation acknowledged ethnic tensions but tended to celebrate instances of solidarity; it was certainly slow to examine how white workers' racial attitudes might have undermined their universalist claims and tarnished their reputations for radicalism. The new labor historians initially focused heavily (if not entirely) on white, skilled, or industrial male workers or white immigrant or native-born communities, largely ignoring racial divisions and the experiences of nonwhite workers. The four million African American slaves in the South on the eve of the Civil War might abstractly have been viewed as workers or members of a broadly defined working class, but most labor historians ceded that subject to their counterparts in African American history.[8] Black workers in the postbellum era attracted the attention of few labor historians.

This absence did not go unnoticed. In 1968, Herbert Gutman, a pioneering leader of the new labor history whose work was anchored both in labor and black history, identified as a serious problem the "absence of detailed knowledge of the 'local world' inhabited by white and Negro workers."[9] Gutman issued a call to social historians to dig deep, reconstruct those local worlds, and rectify that absence of detailed knowledge. Over the course of the 1970s, only a small number of labor historians—Peter Gottlieb, Peter Rachleff, Stephen Brier, Dolores Janiewski, Nell Irvin Painter, and Paul Worthman, in particular[10]—took up that charge, producing a social history of working-class race relations based not on the proclamations of white union leaders and black elites, but on the careful, ground-level reconstruction of the daily experiences of black and white workers living in specific communities.

In contrast, students of the African American experience did produce a scholarly literature that addressed race and racial differences among workers and in the organizations of labor over the course of the twentieth century. By the late 1920s and 1930s, a group of scholars, many if not all of them black, sought to delineate the experiences of African American workers in a variety of trades and unions. Charles Wesley, Sterling Spero and Abram Harris, Lorenzo Greene and Carter G. Woodson, Horace R. Cayton, George Mitchell, and St. Clair Drake—and, in the 1940s, Herbert Northrup—offered harsh (and deserved) indictments of union racial policies.[11] Like their labor history counterparts in the Commons school, these scholars examined black labor from an institutional perspective. "Written from the vantage point of organized labor," Joe William Trotter Jr. concluded a decade ago, "black labor history largely ignored unorganized workers, lacked a convincing theoretical framework, and showed little creativity in the location and use of new sources."[12]

The renaissance of scholarship in African American history in the 1960s and 1970s contributed significantly to an understanding of the black urban experience but did relatively little to illuminate the experiences of African American workers outside the important realms of chattel slavery and postbellum southern agriculture. The numerous case studies of northern black communities during the decades after the Civil War paid close attention to occupational structures, residential segregation, white racism, party politics, and struggles for civil rights. But the cast of characters was drawn overwhelmingly from the ranks of the black elite, whose experiences could be more easily reconstructed from the paper trail they conveniently left behind. White trade unions were the agents of discrimination and black workers were their intended victims.[13] This is not to deny the truth of much of this portrait, but some of the actors in this drama—particularly black workers themselves—appeared one-dimensional, playing only bit parts in a drama dominated by elites. The eminent historian August Meier, in his enduring 1963 classic *Negro Thought in America,* concluded that "We have no direct evidence on what the [black] masses were thinking" during the late nineteenth and early twentieth centuries.[14] That, as it turns out, was an overstatement. Through the 1970s, labor history's race problem had its counterpart in African American history's class or labor problem as well.

All of this changed in the 1980s and 1990s. At the same time that critics of the new labor history directed their fire against the field's ostensible failure to make race central to their work[15] (there were no comparable charges against black history for its neglect of the distinctive experience of nonagricultural black workers), numerous labor and African American urban historians launched research projects on particular communities, occupations, and/or unions that focused on grassroots relations between whites and blacks; working-class identity, ideology, and culture; and the agency of black workers. Building on the pioneering work of August Meier, Elliot Rudwick, and Herbert Gutman, among others,[16] historians of labor and the African American experience uncovered a tremendous reservoir of evidence on precisely the subjects their respective subfields had slighted in earlier years.

Historians of both race and labor and African American workers have, over the past several decades, begun to effectively chart the tensions between the labor movement's ideals of solidarity and inclusion and its all-too-common failure to live up to those ideals. There can be no denying the veritable outpouring of scholarship on labor and race since the 1980s, and vigorous debates about race and American labor continue unabated.[17] This project has required the abandonment of certain cherished assumptions and the adoption of a sober stance toward a subject that appears, appropriately, far less romantic than it once did. Equally—and perhaps more importantly—scholars have finally recognized the centrality of black working-class experiences and activism in the shaping of both modern labor and modern African American communities and their politics.

The essays in *The Black Worker: Race, Labor, and Civil Rights since Emancipation* reflect the dramatic changes that have taken place in African American and labor history in their treatments of black workers, race, and labor. Their definition of *labor* is broad, covering such disparate groups as sharecroppers, strikebreakers, sex workers, Pullman porters, lumber workers, and public employees, among others. Their themes are equally diverse, encompassing gender relations, class tensions within black communities, wartime protest and white repression, agricultural and industrial union organizing, white trade union practices, and challenges of black union leadership. The authors are engaged in a broad, collective project of recasting labor and African American history by restoring race to the heart of labor history, class to the center of black history, and the humanity and agency of working-class black men and women to both; they explore the multiple ways that the labor question and the race question overlapped and defined each other. This volume aims to establish the richness of the African American working-class experience and the indisputable role of black workers in shaping the politics and history of labor and race in the United States.

Notes

1. "Marketing Our Labor," *Chicago Defender,* April 26, 1919.
2. For a small sample of the newer literature emphasizing black workers' trade union or workplace activism, see Tera Hunter, *To 'Joy My Freedom* (Cambridge, Mass.: Harvard University Press, 1997); Robert Rodgers Korstad, *Civil Rights Unionism: Tobacco Workers and the Struggle for Democracy in the Mid-Twentieth-Century South* (Chapel Hill: University of North Carolina Press, 2003); Eric Arnesen, "Following the Color Line of Labor: Black Workers and the Labor Movement before 1930," *Radical History Review* 55 (Winter 1993), 53–87; Eric Arnesen, *Brotherhoods of Color: African American Railroad Workers and the Struggle for Equality* (Cambridge, Mass.: Harvard University Press, 2001); Beth Tompkins Bates, *Pullman Porters and the Rise of Protest Politics in Black America, 1925–1945* (Chapel Hill: University of North Carolina Press, 2001); Rick Halpern, *Down on the Killing Floor: Black and White Workers in Chicago's Packinghouses, 1904–54* (Urbana: University of Illinois Press, 1997); Brian Kelly, *Race, Class, and Power in the Alabama Coalfields, 1908–21* (Urbana: University of Illinois Press, 2001); Nan Elizabeth Woodruff, *American Congo: The African American Freedom Struggle in the Delta* (Cambridge, Mass.: Harvard University Press, 2003); Kimberley L. Phillips, *AlabamaNorth: African-American Migrants, Community, and Working-Class Activism in Cleveland, 1915–45* (Urbana: University of Illinois Press, 1999).
3. Employer attitudes and practices toward black workers after Reconstruction have received less attention than have white workers' attitudes and practices. On employers and black workers, see Brian Kelly, "Policing the 'Negro Eden': Racial Paternalism in the Alabama Coalfields, 1908–1921," Part One, *Alabama Review* (July 1998), 163–83; and Part Two, *Alabama Review* (October 1998), 243–65; Eric Arnesen, "'What's on the Black Worker's Mind?': African-American Labor and the Union Tradition on the Gulf Coast," *Gulf Coast Historical Review* 10, no. 1 (Fall 1994), 7–30.
4. Michael K. Honey, *Southern Labor and Black Civil Rights: Organizing Memphis Workers* (Urbana: University of Illinois Press, 1993); Michael Keith Honey, *Black Workers Remember: An Oral History of Segregation, Unionism, and the Freedom Struggle* (Berkeley: University of California Press, 2000); Kenneth D. Durr, *Behind the Backlash: White*

Working-Class Politics in Baltimore, 1940–1980 (Chapel Hill: University of North Carolina Press, 2003); Eric Arnesen, "'Like Banquo's Ghost, It Will Not Down': The Race Question and the American Railroad Brotherhoods, 1880–1920," *American Historical Review* 99, no. 5 (December 1994), 1601–33.

5. On black elites' stance toward black workers and organized labor, see Brian Kelly, "Industrial Sentinels Confront the 'Rabid Faction': Black Elites, Black Workers, and the Labor Question in the Jim Crow South," chapter 4 in this volume; and Robin D. G. Kelley, *Hammer and Hoe: Alabama Communists during the Great Depression* (Chapel Hill: University of North Carolina Press, 1990). On the shift in black middle-class and elite opinion on black unionization, see Beth Tompkins Bates, "The Brotherhood," *Chicago History* (Fall 1996), 4–23; and Beth Tompkins Bates, "A New Crowd Challenges the Agenda of the Old Guard in the NAACP, 1933–1941," *American Historical Review* 102, no. 2 (April 1997), 340–77.

6. Charles M. Payne and Adam Green, "Introduction," in Payne and Green, eds., *Time Longer than Rope: A Century of African American Activism, 1850–1950* (New York: New York University Press, 2003), 2–3.

7. On the historiography of African American workers and race and labor, see James A. Gross, "Historians and the Literature of the Negro Worker," *Labor History* 10, no. 3 (Summer 1969), 536–46; Joe William Trotter Jr., "African-American Workers: New Directions in U.S. Labor Historiography," *Labor History* 35, no. 4 (Fall 1994), 495–523; and Rick Halpern, "Organized Labor, Black Workers, and the Twentieth Century South: The Emerging Revision," in Melvyn Stokes and Rick Halpern, eds., *Race and Class in the American South since 1890* (Oxford, England: Berg, 1994), 43–76; Eric Arnesen, "Up from Exclusion: Black and White Workers, Race, and the State of Labor History," in Lou Masur, ed., *The Challenge of American History* (Baltimore: Johns Hopkins University Press, 1999), 146–74; Daniel Letwin, "Labor Relations in the Industrializing South," in John B. Boles, ed., *A Companion to the American South* (Malden, Mass.: Blackwell, 2001); Francille Rusan Wilson, *The Segregated Scholars: Black Social Scientists and the Creation of Black Labor Studies, 1890–1950* (Charlottesville: University Press of Virginia, 2006).

8. Even within the historiography of slavery, the labor dimension of the black experience was not always a key priority of exploration. "So central was labor in the slaves' experience that it has often been taken for granted," concluded Ira Berlin and Philip Morgan. "Recent studies have instead focused on the slaves' social organization, domestic arrangements, religious beliefs, and medical practices. This emphasis has, however, obscured the activities that dominated slave life. After all, slavery was first and foremost an institution of coerced labor. Work necessarily engaged most slaves, most of the time." "Introduction: Labor and the Shaping of Slave Life in the Americas," in Ira Berlin and Philip D. Morgan, eds., *Cultivation and Culture: Labor and the Shaping of Slave Life in the Americas* (Charlottesville: University Press of Virginia, 1993), 1.

9. Herbert Gutman, "The Negro and the United Mine Workers of America: The Career and Letters of Richard L. Davis and Something of Their Meaning, 1890–1900," in Julius Jacobson, ed., *The Negro and the American Labor Movement* (New York: Anchor Books, 1968), 117.

10. Peter J. Rachleff, *Black Labor in Richmond, 1865–1890* (1984; rpt. Urbana: Uni-

versity of Illinois Press, 1988); Stephen Brier, "Interracial Organizing in the West Virginia Coal Industry: The Participation of Black Mine Workers in the Knights of Labor and the United Mine Workers, 1880–1894," in Gary Fink, ed., *Essays in Southern Labor History* (Westport, Conn.: Greenwood Press, 1977); Dolores E. Janiewski, *Sisterhood Denied: Race, Gender, and Class in a New South Community* (Philadelphia: Temple University Press, 1985); Nell Irvin Painter, *The Narrative of Hosea Hudson: His Life as a Negro Communist in the South* (Cambridge, Mass.: Harvard University Press, 1979); Paul B. Worthman, "Black Workers and Labor Unions in Birmingham, Alabama, 1897–1904," *Labor History* 10 (Summer 1969), 375–406; Peter Gottlieb, *Making Their Own Way: Southern Blacks' Migration to Pittsburgh, 1916–30* (Urbana: University of Illinois Press, 1987); and David A. Corbin, *Life, Work, and Rebellion in the Coal Fields: The Southwestern West Virginia Miners, 1880–1922* (Urbana: University of Illinois Press, 1981).

11. Charles H. Wesley, *Negro Labor in the United States, 1850–1925: A Study in American Economic History* (New York: Vanguard Press, 1927); Sterling D. Spero and Abram L. Harris, *The Black Worker: The Negro and the Labor Movement* (1931; rpt. New York: Atheneum, 1969); Lorenzo J. Greene and Carter G. Woodson, *The Negro Wage Earner* (New York: Association for the Study of Negro Life and History, 1930); Horace R. Cayton and George S. Mitchell, *Black Workers and the New Unions* (Chapel Hill: University of North Carolina Press, 1939); St. Clair Drake and Horace R. Cayton, *Black Metropolis: A Study of Negro Life in a Northern City* (New York: Harcourt, Brace, 1945); Herbert Northrup, *Organized Labor and the Negro* (New York: Harper and Brothers, 1944).

12. Trotter was summarizing the earlier findings of James A. Gross. Gross, "Historians and the Literature of the Negro Worker," 537–38; Joe William Trotter Jr., "African-American Workers," 495.

13. Eric Arnesen, "The African-American Working Class in the Jim Crow Era," *International Labor and Working-Class History* 41 (Spring 1992), 59–75.

14. August Meier, *Negro Thought in America, 1880–1915* (Ann Arbor: University of Michigan Press, 1963), 208.

15. On criticism of labor history for its treatment of race, see Herbert Hill, "The Importance of Race in American Labor History," *International Journal of Politics, Culture, and Society* 9 (1995), 317–43; Herbert Hill, "Myth-Making as Labor History: Herbert Gutman and the United Mine Workers of America," *International Journal of Politics, Culture, and Society* 2, no. 2 (Winter 1988), 132–33; Nell Irvin Painter, "The New Labor History and the Historical Moment," *International Journal of Politics, Culture, and Society* 2, no. 3 (Spring 1989), 369; David Roediger, "Race and the Working-Class Past in the United States: Multiple Identities and the Future of Labor History," *International Review of Social History* 38 (1993 Supplement), 129; Bruce Nelson, *Divided We Stand: American Workers and the Struggle for Black Equality* (Princeton, N.J.: Princeton University Press, 2001).

16. August Meier and Elliot Rudwick, *Black Detroit and the Rise of the UAW* (New York: Oxford University Press, 1979); Gutman, "The Negro and the United Mine Workers of America."

17. David R. Roediger, *The Wages of Whiteness: Race and the Making of the American Working Class* (1991; revised edition, New York: Routledge, 1999); David Roediger, *Colored White: Transcending the Racial Past* (Berkeley: University of California Press,

2002); Eric Arnesen, "Whiteness and the Historians' Imagination," *International Labor and Working-Class History,* no. 60 (Fall 2001), 3–32; Eric Arnesen, "Assessing Whiteness Scholarship: A Reply to James Barrett, David Brody, Eric Foner, Barbara Fields, Victoria Hattam, and Adolph Reed," *International Labor and Working-Class History,* no. 60 (Fall 2001), 81–92; Eric Arnesen, "A Paler Shade of White," *New Republic* (June 24, 2002), 33–38.

1   "Sweet Dreams of Freedom":
    Freedwomen's Reconstruction of Life
    and Labor in Lowcountry South Carolina

In his memoir of Civil War and Reconstruction, rice planter Charles Manigault offered what he regarded as some of the "leading Characteristicks
of *The NEGRO*, and . . . *The Times,* through *which we have recently passed.*"
For Manigault, those characteristics were exemplified by his former slave
Peggy, who offered ample evidence of how emancipation and Confederate
defeat had turned Manigault's world upside-down. Manigault noted that
as the war came to a close, former slaves plundered and destroyed planter
homes throughout his lowcountry South Carolina neighborhood. Peggy
"seized as *Her part* of the *spoils* my wife's Large & handsome Mahogany
Bedstead & Mattrass & arranged it in her own Negro House *on which she
slept* for some time" and in which Manigault bitterly imagined she enjoyed
"her Sweet Dreams of freedom." Peggy also confiscated from the Manigault
residence "some *Pink Ribands,* & tied in a dozen bows the woolly head of her
Daughter, to the admiration of the other Negroes." Lastly, Manigault noted
Peggy's response when he, joined by his son and a former overseer (and
Confederate officer), came onto the farm and "immediately began to pitch
the Negro Effects" into two wagons, intending to evict the freedpeople.
Only Peggy ("the lady of the *Big Mahogany Bed*") tried to intervene: "placing
her arms *akimbo,* [Peggy] said *She* would go off to the Provost Marshal in
town & *stop our unlawful proceedings with their property in their own homes.*"[1]

    Peggy's appropriation of her former mistress's furniture, her use of con-
traband ribbons to style her daughter's hair, and her public challenge to
Manigault's authority all signaled to Manigault that Peggy was pursuing her
freedom with a literal vengeance, or what Manigault described as "reck-
lessness and Ingratitude." In the actions of freedwomen such as Peggy,
and also in the responses that she and freedwomen like her provoked from
former owners and from the civilian and military agents of Reconstruc-

tion, lies one of the most underexplored dynamics of the South's transition from slavery to freedom and the subject of this essay: the influence of former slave women's defining acts of freedom on the South's transition to a free labor society.

———————

In the past fifteen years, historians have produced an impressive body of work reexamining the South's transition from slavery to freedom during and after the Civil War, work that has yielded new information and a richer understanding of the complex process, and implications, of American emancipation.[2] Yet much of this scholarship, despite its emphasis on the multifaceted involvement of former slaves in shaping the South's transition to a free labor society, has omitted the actions and experiences of half of the four million who passed from slavery to freedom. Too often the transition from slavery to freedom has been investigated and portrayed as though slave women did not share that experience or failed to contribute to the process; enslaved African American women like Peggy, it would seem, had little if any specific or general influence on the shape of the path slaves forged that led from slavery to freedom.[3]

Historians' failure to come to terms with freedwomen's role in the wartime and postbellum South has not been entirely a matter of omission. Despite the dearth of research, many scholars have characterized freedwomen's role in the postbellum conflict as allegedly withdrawing and retreating from the labor force, a conclusion that relies upon the infallibility of contemporary observations by northern and southern whites, and also on census-based estimates of freedwomen's labor-force participation.[4] Even with limited evidence, scholars have freely interpreted freedwomen's motivations and expectations based on their alleged withdrawal from the paid workforce. Some posit that freedwomen gladly yielded to the demands of their husbands that they withdraw from agricultural employment, that they voluntarily collaborated with their husbands' postemancipation claims to the privileges and prerogatives of a patriarchally ordered family and household. Others suggest that freedwomen were imitating white behavior, anxious to claim for themselves the privileges they perceived in elite white women's domesticity—not the least of which was an escape from the physical demands of field work and the demeaning labor of domestic service.[5] The work of Jacqueline Jones and Gerald Jaynes has offered a significant departure from speculation, given their more focused investigations into the actions of freedwomen in the postwar South. Both have turned their attention to freedwomen's creative attempts to choose productive and reproductive labor in their own and their families' best interests. Yet although Jones posits that "Only at home could [freedwomen] exercise considerable control over their own lives and those of their husbands and children and impose a semblance of order on the physical world," Jaynes has persuasively argued that freedwomen's actions must be evaluated in the context of specific postwar agricultural economies, offering an important challenge to the somewhat deterministic implication that all freedwomen acted alike.[6] The conclusion that freedwomen's refusal to work in the manner demanded or prescribed by southern or northern whites actually culminated in women's wholesale withdrawal from labor markets across the South is premature, and its acceptance as "common knowledge" has deterred closer investigation of freedwomen's influence over and participation in wartime and postbellum conflict.

With the themes of withdrawal and retreat used to characterize women's postbellum experience, freedwomen like Peggy have been easily ignored as actors on the public landscape, the landscape from which historians typically identify the "facts" of Reconstruction. Yet Peggy's actions were both public and, as this essay will argue, typical for lowcountry freedwomen. In the actions of freedwomen like Peggy we find clues to some of the many ways in which former slave women distinguished their freedom from their slavery—from the vengeful ransacking of their former owners' homes, to the significance of dress and hair style in claiming and asserting a new personal dignity, to "reckless" confrontations with the plantation whites who had defined the day-to-day nature of exploitation under slavery. Recent research suggests there were also other important arenas in which former slave women tried to give meaning and substance to their freedom. Sharon Holt has revealed how freedwomen's (and -men's) efforts to increase their autonomy and their resources were intertwined with their desire to build, staff, and sustain schools, churches, mutual and benevolent societies, and a host of other independent institutions.[7] Elsa Barkley Brown has reminded us that when Radical Reconstruction opened the political arena to freedmen, freedwomen also brought forward their own claims to citizenship, to political meetings and rallies, to voter registration, and to the polls.[8] Work, which had been so central to women's experience of slavery, was also critical to women's definition of freedom. In lowcountry South Carolina, freedwomen escalated the battle to define black freedom when they sought autonomous control over plantation lands, when they negotiated and reconstructed plantation and domestic labor, and when they defended the new autonomy of their families and household economies from exploitation by planters and unwelcome intervention by northern agents of Reconstruction. In seeking control over their field labor on lowcountry rice plantations, women sought to distance themselves from the power and control of former slave-owning whites *outside* of the rice fields as much as *in* them.

Determined to pursue freedom on their own terms, freedwomen who sought the means and the opportunity to live and subsist as free from white intervention as possible encountered considerable opposition from several sources. Opposition came from white vigilantes, planters, mistresses, and overseers, all anxious for the return of a reliable and subordinate labor force, and from U.S. soldiers and agents of the Freedmen's Bureau who were frustrated by former slaves' unwillingness to embrace the tenets of the free labor society many northerners envisioned for the postwar South. The letters, reports, complaints, and official responses generated by freedwomen's observers and antagonists offer a rich record of freedwomen's efforts to reconstruct life and labor in lowcountry South Carolina. They also reveal that an important part of the work of defining freedom lay in freedwomen's determined efforts to reveal and disrupt the relations of power and domination that had marked their lives as enslaved laborers in the rice fields and planter residences of lowcountry plantations.[9] When freedwomen insisted on working "in their own way and as such times as they think fit," they were articulating a politics of Reconstruction in which women's experience of gender, race, and a history of enslavement were inseparable. They made the issue of reconstructing work their own, an integral part of their desire and intent to secure black freedom.

The women who had been held in slavery in mainland lowcountry South Carolina were situated in a region marked by a specific geography, a unique African American culture, and a particular plantation setting organized around a single crop cultivated under a distinctive system of slave labor. African American women enslaved elsewhere in the South were faced with a very different set of circumstances before, during, and after the Civil War. The rice-planting region of lowcountry South Carolina contained some of the South's largest plantations and wealthiest planters and, before the war, some of its largest, most stable, and culturally autonomous slave communities.[10] On the eve of the war, rice agriculture rested squarely on the shoulders of slave women whose lives were spent in the fields and ditches that marked the distinctive lowcountry terrain. As in other advanced plantation regimes, slave women on rice plantations were a significant proportion of "prime" field hands. However, to paraphrase from the introduction to an anthology on slave labor in the Americas, it was the particulars of slaves' labor that "determined, in large measure, the course of their lives."[11] Slave labor in the rice fields was organized under the task system, so that the work of preparing fields, and cultivating and processing the rice crop, was assigned to women by the task—a portion of an acre for hoeing, a certain number of linear feet for ditch digging, a certain number of rice sheaves cut and tied. This distinguished slave women's task labor from women's dawn-to-dusk gang labor in almost every other plantation economy. The pace of task labor was often set by slaves, who—with considerable effort—could often complete their tasks by mid-afternoon. For slave women, this translated into more daylight hours for the labor of raising and caring for families and for a variety of activities related to independent production.

Slave women's work in the rice fields and the elaborate residences of rice planters not only shaped their experience of slavery, but also influenced their wartime struggle to escape or destroy slavery. The naval blockade of Southern ports and the subsequent disruption of trade, the withdrawal of white men from agriculture to military service, and demands by the Confederate military and state authorities for slave labor and slave-produced goods all disrupted the long-established patterns of plantation life and labor in the lowcountry.[12] The forced removal of lowcountry slaves to the state's more protected interior further undermined the traditional cycle of rice agriculture, as well as the local ties that for many generations had anchored lowcountry plantation production and slavery. With the occupation of Port Royal by Union forces so early in the war, the constant threat posed by the proximity of the enemy exacerbated the war's domestic interruptions in South Carolina.

For lowcountry slave men and women, these wartime conditions translated into incremental disruptions of the traditions, customary rights, social relations, and domestic networks that they had forged over several generations of struggle against slavery. Yet even as wartime shortages forced a deterioration in the standard of living in the slave quarters, slave women accelerated the wartime collapse of slavery by slowing plantation production, resisting the new forms of exploitation introduced during the war, and escaping lowcountry plantations in unprecedented numbers and making their way to the fleet of federal ships blockading the coast. When slave women seized the opportunities presented by the war to further weaken the institution of slavery or to secure their own freedom, it was not only slavery that they hoped to leave behind, but also the worsening conditions of life on lowcountry plantations. Long before emancipation became a part of Union policy, slave women were struggling to alter the conditions of life and labor on South Carolina plantations.

It bears stressing that war affected not only the material conditions of lowcountry slave life, but also the relationships of power that were integral to slavery. As planters became increasingly unable to purchase or afford the most basic necessities; as they became subject to impressment of their plantation products and slaves; as they, their overseers, and their sons became vulnerable to conscription; and as increasing numbers of plantation mistresses assumed unprecedented and unanticipated responsibility for plantation operations in light of the absence of husbands and sons, slaves watched the weakening of their masters' ability to dominate. Slave women not only observed, but tested and acted upon, the wartime crisis of plantation mastery. Overseers and planter families alike complained during the war of slave women disrupting the peaceful operation of their plantations, threatening to run away, and slowing the pace of work.[13] One rice plantation mistress complained early in the war of the "license" increasingly taken by slaves; they "all think this a crisis in their lives that must be taken advantage of. . . . [T]imes and slaves, have changed" since secession."[14] The weaknesses in the bedrock of slavery exposed by the war were seized upon and widened by slave women who were determined to make the war's trajectory toward emancipation irreversible.

Thousands of slave women fled lowcountry plantations during the war and made their way to the Union-occupied Sea Islands, beginning their transition from slavery to freedom under the dominion of northern missionaries, civilians, and military authorities. Unlike native Sea Islanders who staked out their own portion of plantation lands and continued to live in their slave quarters, slave women from the mainland rice plantations constituted a refugee population. They found living quarters in refugee camps, abandoned buildings, or temporary barracks, and pieced together a living from the employment they found in the Quartermaster's Department, as regimental laundresses or cooks, from the pay of their enlisted kin or husbands, or by marketing provisions to Union soldiers stationed on the Islands. Yet their appreciation for the protection, schooling, and charity offered by northern military and civilian authorities did not slow women's response when the freedom offered under northern tutelage was less than what they expected. Whether this meant shaming the northern missionary women who pointedly ignored the pressing needs of young "unmarried" slave mothers, challenging military authorities who tried to prevent their entry into soldiers' camps to sell provisions or to "see and be seen," or leading groups of women to protest unacceptably low wages, these refugees from mainland slavery were hardly content to await passively the redefinition of black life and labor by others. Before the war had ended, these contraband women were already engaged in the process of defining and defending their freedom.[15]

Women's pursuit of freedom gained momentum and breadth in the immediate aftermath of the war. The final destruction of lowcountry slavery in early 1865, coinciding with the chaotic closing weeks of war in the wake of Sherman's advance through the state, inspired newly freed slave women to attack former overseers, raid planter residences and storehouses, and confiscate or destroy planter property. From the smallest luxuries to the most expensive furnishings, freedwomen clothed themselves and their children in confiscated and previously forbidden finery "in pride of their freedom." In the chaotic aftermath of the war, former slave women's defining acts of freedom were also found in their common efforts to reunite their families, separated before or during the war; in the strategies they adopted to endure calamitous material conditions and to evade violent attacks by white reactionaries and northern soldiers; and in the ways they reorganized and reallocated their agricultural, domestic, and household labor.

For most lowcountry freedpeople, women and men, land was critical to the freedom and independence they sought for themselves, their families, and their communities. Lowcountry freedpeople shared a definition of freedom as their right not simply to survive, but to work and thrive without white intervention on the land they had worked as slaves and where generations of their ancestors had lived, worked, and died.[16] On the Sea Islands and on the mainland, from Georgetown to the Savannah River, freedpeople held public meetings, organized commissions, appointed delegations, and formed paramilitary guards to protest the accelerating process of restoration under the terms of Johnsonian Reconstruction, and to prevent returning white landowners from setting foot on the islands and usurping their own claims to the land.[17] As federal Reconstruction policy accelerated the restoration of so-called abandoned lands to white planters, freedpeople were forced either to relinquish their claims or defend them. Freedwomen figured in many of the conflicts that flared in defense of those claims. They physically forced planters or overseers off the plantation, threatened violent confrontations with bureau agents and armed guards of U.S. soldiers, and refused to cooperate with white landowners.[18]

Women's vigorous resistance to restoration was evident in a violent confrontation that developed on Keithfield plantation. In March 1865, former slaves had driven the white overseer off the plantation, and for the rest of the year a community of about 150 freedpeople lived on and independently worked the plantation, cultivating at least a partial crop of rice.[19] But early in 1866 Keithfield's absentee planter, a widow, asked a neighboring planter to help her retake control of Keithfield. She could not have chosen a figure more hated by local freedpeople, for this neighbor, Francis Parker Sr., had helped carry out the ritualized public execution of recaptured fugitive slaves during the war. Adding to the potential for conflict, Parker attempted (with the approval of the local bureau agent) to install as overseer Dennis Hazel, a former slave driver.[20]

In March 1866, according to Parker and Hazel's account of the conflict, Parker sent his son and Hazel to deliver work orders to the people at Keithfield, but the men's authority was repudiated by Abram, whom the freedpeople had appointed their foreman. Parker's son threatened to bring Abram before the local provost marshal and "break him" but left the plantation before doing so. Abram called the women and men in from the field. The work gang turned their tools—"Axes hatchets hoes and poles"—into weapons and attacked Hazel, threatening to kill him. Hazel escaped and that afternoon returned to the plantation with Parker's son and two soldiers. On their appearance, the freedpeople assaulted them with their tools and pelted them with bricks and stones. Sukey and Becky entered the fray armed with heavy clubs. Joined by Jim, they exhorted their fellow laborers to join the fight, "declaring that the time was come and they must yield their lives if necessary—that a life was lost but once, and they must try and kill" the intruders. The crowd was joined by eight or ten "infuriated women," including Charlotte Simons, Susan Lands, Clarrisa Simons, Sallie Mayzck, and Quashaba and Magdalen Moultrie, who were armed with heavy clubs and hoes, and backed by four or five men. The women made a point of their particular hatred for the former slave driver Hazel by focusing their attack on him; the soldiers' efforts to defend him from their blows were "entirely ineffectual." Parker pleaded with the women to let up their attack on Hazel, promising to leave and let Freedmen's Bureau authorities settle the matter, but, as he recalled, "the mob was not to be reasoned with." The freedmen encouraged the women: "kill him, now is your time, don't let him get away." Three times, Parker called on the freedmen to "exert themselves," to stop and force back what he described as "the maddened women." The freedmen replied to Parker that he "had no business over there anyhow—that no white man could control them now they were free." Sukey and Becky then turned their attack from Hazel to Parker. Sukey seized a hickory stick out of Parker's hands and beat him with it over his back; both she and Becky delivered a series of heavy blows to his head. One of the soldiers, "his face covered with blood" and apparently disarmed by the freedpeople, "beseeched his comrade to shoot" at the mob, but Parker insisted no shooting take place, "fearing such a measure might further madden the desperate mob." Parker and Hazel turned to make a hasty retreat, begging the men to keep the women back, but before Parker could escape he was "struck very heavily over my right eye with a club in the hands of a woman Becky—the blow bringing blood instantly, and making me stagger with blindness—[.]" He noted that "vigorous efforts to strike me again were continued by women among whom I recognized Sukey, Becky, Quashuba, Charlotte, Susan." Now fearing for his life, Parker (followed by Hazel) made the only escape he could, by jumping into the river and swimming out to their boat, "under a shower of missiles." Parker and Hazel left the soldiers to make their own escape by foot, bloodied and disarmed by the freedpeople.

Later, an armed guard of U.S. soldiers temporarily settled the incident by arresting several of the ringleaders. Three of the freedmen were charged with inciting the freedwomen to violence; five of the women served sentences in the local jail. Although the Freedmen's Bureau agent called the violence attending Keithfield's restoration "unusual," reports from across the lowcountry noted vigor of women's participation as freedpeople resisted rice planters who attempted to reclaim their plantations and to reinstate overseers and former slave drivers. The reports confirmed the fears of Freedmen's Bureau agents who knew that freedpeople were cultivating so-called abandoned lands "in anticipation of being left to enjoy the fruits of their labors"; agents anticipated that the return of planters would inevitably lead to "serious difficulties" but seemed surprised at the role played by freedwomen.[21]

Some freedwomen faced more immediate battles over the consequences of emancipation when former owners remained on the plantations at the close of the war. Freedwomen's involvement in the conflicts was noted by the overseers, former owners, and white elites who were as outraged at freedwomen's purposeful violation of antebellum rituals of deference and subordination as by the actual content of their demands. Although conflict and resistance had been part of the fabric of day-to-day life under slavery, by the late summer of 1865, freedwomen were clashing with former slaveowners and other whites in a new, more public, and openly declared arena. Freedwomen like Peggy had added a new public strategy of insubordination and direct confrontation to their antebellum repertoire of evasive tactics and deceptive appearances.[22] They challenged former slaveowners' and overseers' expectations of ritualized, deferential behavior as they set out in clear terms and with definitive action how they believed life and labor should differ in freedom from their experience under slavery.

In the fall and early winter of 1865, lowcountry planters complained with growing frequency that freedpeople left the plantations without permission, refused work orders, and made threats against planters. Planters complained that freedpeople "not only will not work now, but tell you so openly & plainly."[23] They accused former slaves of being saucy, insolent, intractable, disobedient, and dangerous. Even in this general climate of conflict and resistance, men and women of the lowcountry planter class, white overseers, soldiers, and agents of the Freedmen's Bureau all complained pointedly about the insubordinate behavior of former slave women. Freedwoman Jane, who rejected work orders and slapped her white mistress, was denounced by her employers as "an audacious creature."[24] Mary Ann "boldly [and] unblushingly" confronted her former owner in the field, refused his assignment of work unrelated to the present crop, and "frequently contradicted me and spoke to me as roughly and defiantly as if I had been the meanest old negro in the country." He was as alarmed by Mary Ann's defiant bearing toward him as by her insistence on determining for herself which work she would and would not perform.[25] Another planter characterized freedwomen as idle and insolent, vagrant, playing sick and doing no work; the driver's wife thought she was "too fine a lady to think of doing any work," and even Eve, while admittedly "an old woman," he described as "very impertinent."[26] It was the behavior of women like these that prompted the agent on one lowcountry plantation to complain that "[t]he more kindness offered to them the more ingratitude & abuse we receive," an unwitting admission that freedwomen were challenging the facade of reciprocal relations that had masked the abusive and exploitative nature of antebellum paternalism.

Beyond their insistence on bringing radical change to their relationships with lowcountry elites, lowcountry freedwomen's reputation for insubordination was in part a consequence of the specific kinds of demands they made in postwar labor arrangements. Freedpeople needed to innovate new family economies to cope with conditions of starvation and want; they sought a balance between their ties to specific communities and plantation lands and their need for cash, or food and basic goods. After the harvest, freedmen (husbands and fathers) left the plantations in pursuit of day labor, sold firewood or fruit to passing steamers or in nearby towns, or found other temporary avenues into the cash economy. Freedwomen—often wives and mothers—remained on the plantations and assumed a frontline role in ongoing plantation battles over the shape of postemancipation labor while caring for family and tending independent crops.[27] Some families on mainland plantations managed to plant "private crops of their own," and the men "hire[d] out now & then . . . to neighbors" while freedwomen and children remained on the plantation.[28] This strategy not only exacerbated planters' concern about securing essential postharvest labor from freedpeople, it also placed freedwomen in direct conflict with planters.

Freedwomen fueled the escalating labor conflict by their refusal to perform postharvest domestic chores for planters. Planters had customarily assigned female slaves a range of postharvest labor that included spinning and weaving, the manufacture of clothing, butchering and preserving meat, and other kinds of domestic production critical to the maintenance and support of plantation operations. That labor had eaten into the hours slave women might otherwise have spent with, and working for, their own families. In the fall of 1865, freedwomen who had contracted to work as field hands were no longer willing to perform "double duty" in domestic production for their employers. This included freedwoman Mary Ann, who "shewed the virago from the start," according to her former owner, "she has refused to rake[,] fence[,] or do any work," leading him to fear that her behavior "will poison the rest of the people of the place."[29] Freedwomen on one of the Allston plantations brought an end to the extra burden of postharvest wool production, first killing off the plantation sheep and then eating them. One planter's wife reported that to get former slaves to work even half tasks in the field, chores related to domestic production, such as spinning, had to be totally abandoned. Another planter's wife found herself reported to a local bureau agent for trying to compel female field hands to do her spinning and weaving. Even young women like sixteen-year-old Margaret Brown rejected "weaving after night" for her employer, who took her refusal as provocation enough to beat her with his bare hands and with a stick.[30]

Freedwomen's contributions to lowcountry labor conflicts did not go unnoticed or unanswered. According to bureau and military records, many freedwomen paid a dear price for the audacity of insisting on their right to define free labor on their own terms. Their experience of violence at the hands of an outraged employer was not unusual. Hagar Barnwell had been ordered by her former owner to go into the kitchen and work, but "she refused . . . as she had contracted to work in the field." When Barnwell insisted she would leave the plantation rather than work in his kitchen, he threatened her with his pistol, stated he would kill her if not for the need to get his crop in, and then took her to a shed and tied her up by her thumbs so that her feet barely touched the ground. Barnwell eventually escaped, but appealed to three different army officers as well as a local magistrate before she found someone willing to investigate her mistreatment.[31] In another instance, "a Woman named Sarah . . . was tied up by the thumbs" by a planter and two accomplices, as punishment for violating plantation rules; "Sarah was pregnant . . . and she was left suspended for nearly two hours," reported the agent, and "in consequence of this brutality the birth of the child was forced." The infant "was dead when delivered" and Sarah "has not been expected to live."[32] Their refusal to withdraw from disputes over the meaning of black freedom meant that freedwomen became targets for physical attack, resulting in a record of brutality that historians of the postbellum South are only beginning to plumb.[33]

Planters and overseers were so intent on regaining control of plantation lands (and bureau and military personnel so determined that this was in the best interests of all lowcountry residents) that many failed to anticipate what freedwomen soon demonstrated: Restoration was only an incremental concession, the beginning of a longer process of negotiation on lowcountry plantations.[34] Between 1865 and 1867, it was not unusual for planters, their land restored, to discover that freedpeople "were not willing to make any contracts, inasmuch as the contract system would tend to bring them into a state of slavery again."[35] Along the Santee River, a region the Georgetown bureau agent described as "in a very unsettled state," planters discovered how quickly freedpeople could render restoration a hollow victory for planters. Many planters simply found that they could not negotiate with freedpeople; "the word of the planters to the freedpeople has no weight." The apparent accidental burning of a Santee River planter residence, following restoration, dissuaded other planters from returning.[36]

The owner of two Waccamaw River plantations returned in early 1866, to discover that nearly sixty women and men, formerly his slaves, had resided on and worked the plantation in his absence, and now, "in a state of utter insubordination," refused to contract, "claiming the right to remain on the places." They insisted "they will only work in their own way & at such times as they think fit, without the supervision of an agent or any white man & insist upon renting the lands[,] they to fix the amount to be paid us according to their notions of justice."[37] Although ultimately forced by the course of Reconstruction politics and their determined northern benefactors to relinquish control over the plantations and instead work for planters under the labor contract system, freedwomen disregarded the terms of the contracts and persisted in laboring on their own terms, while also focusing debate and open conflict on the nature of plantation labor and their new relationships to overseers, former slave drivers, employers, and former owners. The responses of military and civilian agents of Reconstruction to freedwomen's actions similarly underwent a noticeable change. In 1865, observers viewed freedpeople's resistance to restoration and contract labor primarily as a threat to the immediate peace and good order of a region still recovering from war, posing an obstacle to the military's efforts to prevent further starvation and reduce the chaos of the southern countryside. But by 1866, their continued resistance to the restoration of the lowcountry plantation economy was construed by some of the military and civilian agents of Reconstruction as a conscious and ill-informed rejection of the tenets of free labor during the crucial first full year of freedom.[38]

Although both freedmen and freedwomen insisted on shaping the terms of their labor in accordance with their own ideas about what freedom meant, freedwomen's refusal to work as they had under slavery that planters and northern agents of Reconstruction commented on most frequently and most bitterly. More than one planter complained to the Freedmen's Bureau that he was "forced to discharge my freedwomen for neglect and refusal to do less than reasonable tasks."[39] Planter E. B. Heyward's complaints in 1867 were typical:

> The women have got rather lazy and try your patience severely. The work progresses very slowly and they seem perfectly indifferent. . . . The women appear most lazy, merely because they are allowed the opportunity. They wish to stay in the house, or in the garden all the time—If you chide them, they say "Eh ch! massa, aint I mus' mind de fowl, and look a' me young corn aint I mus watch um." And to do this, the best hand on the place will stay at home all day and every day.

Heyward also noted that the "men are scarcely much better"; men and women both seemed to "feel bound as a slave and work under constraint, are impudent, careless and altogether very provoking." As a consequence, Heyward was cautious in his interactions with former slaves, saying, "If the women get mad . . . they run in their holes like Fiddlers and won't come out. I therefore never quarrel. . . . I avoid all difficulties, and make a kind of retreating fight." The freedwomen working on his cousin's plantation were scarcely much better; they "come out on a kind of frolic and sow and cover his rice doing it of course abominably. All the work is badly done."[40]

John DeForest, a bureau agent in upcountry South Carolina, was among the first to label freedwomen's rejection of a "prime" hand's labor and seeming withdrawal from field labor as the "evil of female loaferism." DeForest—whose memoir is often cited by historians as contemporary evidence of women's universal withdrawal from field labor—noted that "myriads of women who once earned their own living now have aspirations to be like white ladies and, instead of using the hoe, pass the days in dawdling over their trivial housework, or gossiping among their neighbors." DeForest's characterization of women's social and reproductive labor as "trivial" was probably as firmly rooted in the devaluation of (white) women's unpaid housework in the North as in the judgment he was also making about freedwomen's unpaid labor in and connected to the support of their households. Both issues were important to the way northern and southern whites viewed the decisions freedwomen were making.

What was the extent of women's withdrawal from the lowcountry workforce? Even DeForest was careful to add that he "did not mean that all women were thus idle; the larger proportion were still laboring afield, as of old; rigid necessity held them up to it." The withdrawal of some women from the waged workforce, he concluded, was gaining popularity among freedpeople just as it had "among us white men and brethren."[41] Most contemporary observers commenting on freedwomen's seeming withdrawal from field labor failed to qualify its extent, as DeForest had; planters from across the state reported that freedwomen would simply stay in their cabins if starvation didn't drive them to work. Freedwomen "generally decline to work altogether and depend on their lords [husbands] for their support," reported one planter in 1866, although another nearby planter relied on a plantation labor force composed of two freedwomen to every freedman.[42]

Freedwomen's efforts to shape their labor on lowcountry rice plantations from within the contract labor system are partially documented in the surviving labor contracts filed by lowcountry planters with the Freedmen's Bureau between 1865 and 1868. Although labor contracts offer at best an incomplete record of labor arrangements in the postwar era, they do suggest some important trends in the labor force participation of men and women, trends that appear consistent with the descriptive examples from other sources provided so far.[43]

Freedwomen's enrollment on the labor contracts for Georgetown District (see Table 1) suggests that they were continuing to work in the lowcountry rice fields but increasingly rejected full-time field labor. From 1866 to 1868, freedwomen's names were consistently nearly half of those attached to the contracts—which was very close to the proportion of slave women who were working in the rice fields before the war. Nonetheless, their intent to decrease the amount of agricultural labor they performed for planters was demonstrated by contracting not as prime or full hands, but as three-quarter or half hands. In fact, according to their enrollment on the labor contracts, men as well as women insisted on working less than they had as slaves. While a significant proportion of contracting freedwomen continued to work as full hands, many insisted on working less than a full hand would. Drawing on a subset of the labor contracts (those where the workers were indicated as contracting as full or partial hands), we learn that the percentage of freedwomen contracting as full hands on Georgetown plantations had declined from nearly 69 percent of the women who contracted to work in the fields in 1866 to 34 percent in 1868. During the same years,

Table 1. Georgetown Labor Contracts, 1866–68

	1866			1867		1868
Number of contracts with rating (total number of contracts)	57 (171)			45 (88)		14 (38)
	Women	Men	Women	Men	Women	Men
Number of rated hands (total rated and unrated)	800 (2,088)	749 (2,267)	812 (1,461)	669 (1,409)	191 (586)	161 (601)
Percentage contracting as full hands	68.75	81	54.4	81.3	34	70
Percentage contracting as 3/4 hands	11	6	16.2	6.27	31.9	18
Percentage contracting as 2 hands	17.75	7.87	27	9.27	29.3	11
Percentage contracting as 1/4 hands	2.5	2.8	1.9	3.1	4.7	—

in this same subset of all contracted hands, the percentage of freedmen contracting as full hands also declined, but at a much lower rate—from 81 percent to 70 percent.[44]

Further evidence that lowcountry freedwomen had not retreated from the battle to transform plantation labor was seen in their refusal to labor under former slave drivers and overseers, and their insistence on selecting their own foremen—regardless of the fact that most of the bureau-approved labor contracts for 1866 and 1867 gave that prerogative to their employers. Planters anticipated former slaves' refusal to work under their former overseers; as one planter warned, "I suppose there is no doubt of the ill will of the slaves to him—and in any case I do not think you could expect to renew your relations there or elsewhere *through any overseer formerly employed*— . . . the petty despot who came between you & them will never be submitted to."[45] But the refusal of southern whites to admit the specific grounds for freedpeople's hatred of former overseers—overseers' exploitation of the productive and reproductive labor of slaves, their oftentimes sexually charged domination, coercion, and violence against slave women—was also a denial of the extent to which freedpeople now rejected the relations of domination so critical to their experience of slavery.[46] Although southern white men defended the sensitivities of white women to the wartime horrors so recently perpetrated by northern whites (southern white women "would be averse, for the present at least, to intimate social relations with those who have been . . . connected with the suffering which they have endured"), African American women were afforded no such protection.[47] When freedwomen claimed the right to live and work free from their former tormentors, whites responded with ridicule.

Freedwomen on El Dorado plantation secured the right to work under a foreman of their own choosing, but the plantation mistress ridiculed the fact that "the 'foreman' escorts the women with an air of gallantry" to the fields, directing their labor "in the most courteous manner," addressing them as "ladies" even as they wielded their hoes in the field.[48]

In fact, the fight against the reinstatement of antebellum overseers and slave drivers was a struggle in which freedwomen gained particular notoriety. Freedwomen explicitly challenged the power and authority of their former overseers, purposefully and publicly violating the ritualized behavior of subservience, obedience, and submission demanded from them while slaves, at the same time escalating the protracted battle over the terms and conditions of their labor. Some overseers found freedwomen's verbal attacks on their authority so sharp as to threaten "manhood and common sense." Even agents of the Freedmen's Bureau concurred, reporting that whereas freedmen were "tolerably civil" toward former masters, "the women, especially those advanced in age, are abusive, with remarkable aptitude at 'billingsgate,'" the vituperative verbal weaponry exercised by women in London's famous open-air fish market.[49] Edwin Tilton, twelve years the overseer on Waverly plantation, complained in January 1866 that he was "subject of the most gross abuse" by the freedwomen, formerly slaves on the plantation, who candidly expressed their feelings about his employment on the plantation. On another plantation, freedwomen rebuked the white overseer when he attempted to revoke privileges they had won in slavery, such as the right to the open range of their poultry and farm animals on the plantations; in addition, they had become fierce defenders of their right to perform their labor without his supervision. One freedwoman, he reported, "has used very abusive and somewhat threatening language to me for shooting hogs in the field," and a second freedwoman "has ordered me out of her task, saying if I come in her task again she would put me in the ditch." When the same overseer tried to take a seat in a boat being used to transport harvested rice, one of the freedwomen demanded to know, as he reported, "who told me to sit down in the boat." Daunted by freedwomen's determined efforts to undermine his authority on the plantation, this particular overseer appealed for the support of an armed guard from local military authorities.[50]

Freedwomen's challenges to the legitimacy of overseers' authority may have been prompted by reasons beyond their experiences of exploitation; freedwomen may also have been acting strategically on behalf of their communities, aware that sometimes the risks were different for freedmen and freedwomen who challenged whites. One overseer explained that while freedwomen challenged him, "I did not mind it so much, but when the men took to backing up the women by some of the same talk I asserted my rights as an American Citizen under abuse by at once knocking down and trouncing one of the abusers" (the same overseer suggested that the provost marshal would "be surprised" at the "actions and language" of the freedwomen and freed men). Still, overseers could and did take their revenge with freedwomen who spoke their minds.[51]

Freedwomen's opposition to the reinstatement of former overseers, like their opposition to the return of planters, may also have indicated their concerns about developments outside the rice fields. The symbolic violation of freedpeople's homes became one avenue by which planters and their agents attempted to circumscribe the consequences of emancipation, avenge freedpeople's depredations on planter residences at the close of the war, and reclaim some of their antebellum power over former slaves—both in and outside the rice fields. Former owners and overseers entered and searched freedpeople's homes ostensibly to reclaim stolen property. Of course, given the enthusiasm with which freedpeople had ransacked the planter residences at the close of the war, it was possible— even probable—that many planters actually were trying to recover stolen property. But no less important than the reclamation of that property was the significance of planters and overseers claiming the right to enter and search freedpeople's homes and even their persons. In the process of these searches, planters and their agents performed a ritualistic return to antebellum relations of power on lowcountry plantations, reclaiming their prerogative to violate, and denying freedpeople's claims to the privilege of an inviolable family sphere. One such search was decried by freedman George Singleton as "not only unlawful and cruel but also indecent." Despite his protests and those of the two midwives attending his wife in childbirth, her bed and her person were searched by two white men, allegedly looking for stolen cotton. In this instance and in many others, the search also served as an instrument of terror.[52]

Searches were sometimes accomplished with the assistance of an armed guard from a local military post, evoking the disappointment—and outrage—of lowcountry freedpeople who felt betrayed by soldiers' complicity in what freedpeople clearly regarded as an invasion and an undesirable return to the past.[53] When a search of this type occurred on Hagley Plantation early in 1866, there was trouble "when the freedpeople resisted the soldiers while the latter were making a search of the former's houses for furniture belonging to the estate[;] one of the men Corporal Freck was severely beaten by them, and later in the darkness of the evening missiles were thrown" at an officer and the planter.[54] On another plantation, a planter and a bureau agent made a search of the freedpeople's homes, removing property that the planter identified as stolen. They ordered the freedpeople to carry the items back to the planter residence, but the people refused, saying that their work was done for the day. According to the bureau agent, the freedpeople were "most unruly and impertinent"; they "acknowledged that they had no right in the furniture but wanted to be obstinate." Having accomplished the search on this plantation, the bureau agent then went to a neighboring plantation and performed the same service there.[55] It was not unusual for the bureau to approve planter and overseers' searches made of freedpeople's homes on the pretext of recovering supposedly stolen crops, or to approve labor contracts that included clauses permitting planters to freely enter and search the homes of contracting freedpeople.[56]

While field laborers endeavored to derail the patterns of invasion and exploitation that had been so common to antebellum life and threatened their freedom, freedwomen who worked in planter residences developed their own strategies to reshape life and labor. Just before the war, from one-third to one-half of the slave workforce on lowcountry rice plantations had consisted of domestic servants, artisans, and other slaves with specialized work assignments; these slaves, involved in plantation operations outside the rice fields or waiting on the families of planters or overseers, had an experience of slavery very different from that of field hands.[57] Without the apparent separation between "master's time" and their own time that the task system permitted, house servants faced a more personal and daily struggle to limit the demands made of them. Female house servants were subject to a forced intimacy with slaveowning families, including a degree of vulnerability to sexual exploitation.

With the arrival of Union troops, former slave women began to abandon the mask of subservience they had been forced to wear as domestic slaves, and in the immediate aftermath of war, female domestic servants, like field hands, first resorted to a work stoppage. Some servants preferred to leave their former owners and find new employers rather than fight with former owners over what they would and would not continue to do now that they were free. Planters' families frequently complained to each other of having to perform their own domestic labor, "their servants having all left them." Since planters viewed the training of new servants as burdensome, some forcibly prevented their former servants from seeking employment elsewhere. Fifteen-year-old Rebecca Jane Grant knew "we had been done freed," but still her uncle "stole me by night from my Missus," so that she could return to her own family.[58] Other planters asked ex-Confederate guerrillas to track down and punish or return house servants who fled their former owners.[59]

Some freedwomen who tried to exercise their new mobility suffered the painful consequences of a domestic slave's constant proximity to slaveowners. Mistresses who had treated the children of their domestic slaves as pets resisted separation from those children when freedwomen decided it was time to leave. Even worse, the children themselves may have resisted separation, having formed strong attachments to the white women, who undoubtedly had more time to spend with the children than did their enslaved mothers. Wartime diarist Mary Chesnut recorded the drama of a three-year-old child, "a great pet," who "did not wish to go even with his mother." The child was "torn" from the arms of the mistress by "ruthless Yanks" and turned over to his mother. The mother—whose torment and fury over slavery's interference with her child's loyalties and attachments can only be imagined—was described by the mistress as running away with her child, "whipping this screaming little rebel darky every foot of the way." Like other former slaves who found their freedom so quickly revoked, this mother and her child were soon forcibly returned by rebel pickets. The three-year-old was denied the opportunity to renew his confused attachments; both mother and child were banished from the house by the angry and jealous mistress.[60]

When house servants began to reappear voluntarily at planter residences during the summer and fall of 1865, they tried to implement important changes in their work and in their relations with the white women who now employed rather than owned them. Former mistresses complained (mostly to each other) that former slave women studiously transgressed the rituals of subservience; they "just drop down into a chair if they come to talk to you about anything & are as free as possible."[61] In attempting to distinguish their work as wage laborers from their experience of slavery, freedwomen focused many of their efforts on undermining the fundamental demand for the undivided attention and loyalties of domestic servants. Freedwomen challenged this expectation in two fundamental ways: by trying to focus their employment on the tasks to be performed rather than the people to be served, and by explicitly preferring labor arrangements designed to accommodate their own familial interests and responsibilities.

To the consternation of many women of the planter families, freedwomen insisted that domestic service be broken down into specific tasks or skills: washing, cooking, cleaning, and nursing became separate jobs. For example, Hagar, a former slave and house servant, insisted she "was not strong enough" to do the laundry and refused to wash "even a towel fit to look at." She could carry water and clean the rooms, but she would not do the laundry, nor would she turn and beat the mattresses. Months later, her employer still had not found a house servant who would agree to do washing as well as cooking.[62] Freedwomen also began to insist on their right to reject particularly arduous or demeaning labor, prompting complaints by women of one planter family when a domestic servant refused to wash her employer's "necessaries"—her menstrual rags.[63] Freedwomen may have gained considerable satisfaction not only from freeing themselves from what they felt was demeaning labor, but also from knowing that former slaveowning women were now forced to perform such labor on their own.

Making their family responsibilities an explicit consideration in their labor arrangements, some freedwomen insisted, for example, on bringing their children along to their employer's house, or limited the hours or days they worked, as they tried to balance the demands of wage work and child care.[64] Many white women began to view the families of domestic servants as encumbrances and distractions; they tried their best to employ servants without families, a "quality" some prospective employers valued above cleanliness, industry, and even deference.[65] Employers resented the demands of young children on their domestic servants ("her infant monopolizes her attentions," one plantation mistress complained) but welcomed the employment of mothers who were willing to put their older children to work, as well.[66]

Freedwomen in domestic service also challenged the very nature of their relationship to planter families, seeking a new level of dignity even as servants. "Have you noticed with the negroes at home," inquired one planter's wife to another, "that when you call they will never answer, every body up here finds it the case, they seem to think it is a sign of their freedom, heard one of them say, 'My Miss don't like it because I won't answer, but I ain't got no call to answer now.'" White employers sometimes faced the difficult choice of firing servants or finding a way to put up with the changes freedom was bringing into their households; others began what seemed like an endless search for the perfectly deferential and obedient servant, as promising servants proved themselves too assertive for the job ("she was too impudent for anything"). White women treasured those servants they could hire who still acted "humble & civil."[67]

When freedwomen employed as domestic servants attempted to define their own terms of labor, their efforts were made all the more difficult by the fact that plantation mistresses—no less than planters—were unwilling to concede the end of slavery and their loss of ownership and control over former slaves. When freedwomen struck at the core of the antebellum mythology of domestic servitude—that slave women had no lives, priorities, or identity outside their service to white families—former slaveowners-turned-employers planned and schemed to prevent the return of formerly enslaved servants to their family and friends. Freedwomen became the target of considerable hostility and bitter resentment when they chose to abandon their former owners in search of their own families and lives.[68] Setting new boundaries and new terms on their household labor, freedwomen in domestic service challenged their employers' presumptions of intimacy and mutual dependency with their former slaves, at the same time undermining the plantation mistress's veneer of authority in her ability to command and manage a household of servants.[69] Thus, the "servant problem" described by so many elite white South Carolinians in the postbellum period referred not only to the shrinking supply of labor, but also to the assertiveness of freedwomen in shaping the terms and conditions of their employment.

When freedwomen sought control over their paid and unpaid labor, they were driven not only by their determination to shape the meaning of free labor in lowcountry rice fields and planter residences, but also by the increased demands on their domestic production in households stripped of the most basic tools and necessities. White observers seemed convinced that it was a desire not to work that motivated freedwomen, rather than an effort to negotiate the terms of their contracted work, or the necessity of devoting more of their time and resources to the direct care and support of their families, households, and independent crops. But when Union troops moved through the lowcountry at the close of the war, they had laid waste to the region's plantation infrastructure. Union soldiers destroyed or stole the household possessions of innumerable lowcountry slaves. Soldiers confiscated what little reserve of food or farm animals and poultry remained; even pots, pans, bedding, and mattresses were stripped from slave quarters. For many freedwomen, the material condition of their households was worse than it had been in slavery, and military and bureau officials had quickly forgotten their own role in making this so. However, the physical devastation of the countryside, the shortage of food and clothing and the most basic necessities, and the poor crops of the 1860s all heavily increased freedwomen's labor in their own homes. With their own survival and that of their families in the balance, laziness or an escape from hard work were luxuries they could not easily afford.

Freedwomen's "sweet Dreams of freedom" may be difficult to recover from the historical record, but their impact on South Carolina's transition to a free labor society cannot be denied. Far from passive or retreating figures withdrawing to the shadows of southern life, freedwomen played a visible and instrumental role in the reconstruction of life and labor in the postbellum South. They fought for greater freedom of movement between their household and family economies and the plantation economy, for greater insularity from the supervision of overseers and other hated figures from their recent past, and for the freedom to make their own decisions about how best to allocate their time and their labor. In nearly every arena of postbellum conflict, freedwomen also struggled to replace the antebellum configuration of plantation power relations with a new autonomy for African American women, one that protected their freedom both in the rice fields and plantation residences and outside them. Freedwomen assumed both the right to define black freedom and the responsibility for defending it, and our histories of slavery, war, and Reconstruction have yet to acknowledge their bold lessons about the meaning of freedom in America.

Notes

This essay first appeared in the *Journal of Women's History* 9 (Spring 1997): 9–38. Reprinted by permission of Indiana University Press.

1. Charles Manigault, "The Close of the War—The Negro, etc.," Manigault Family Papers, *Records of Ante-Bellum Southern Plantations,* Series (Ser.) J, Pt. 4, Reel (R) 1.

2. See, for example, Ira Berlin, Joseph P. Reidy, and Leslie S. Rowland, eds., *Freedom: A Documentary History of Emancipation, 1861–1867,* Ser. II: *The Black Military Experience* (Cambridge, England: Cambridge University Press, 1982); Ira Berlin, Barbara J. Fields, Thavolia Glymph, Joseph P. Reidy, and Leslie S. Rowland, eds., *Freedom: A Documentary History of Emancipation, 1861–1867,* Ser. I, vol. 1, *The Destruction of Slavery* (Cambridge, England: Cambridge University Press, 1985); Ira Berlin, Thavolia Glymph, Steven F. Miller, Joseph P. Reidy, Leslie S. Rowland, and Jule Saville, eds., *Freedom: A Documentary History of Emancipation, 1861–1867,* Ser. I, vol. 3: *The Wartime Genesis of Free Labor: The Lower South* (Cambridge, England: Cambridge University Press, 1990); Barbara Jeanne Fields, *Slavery and Freedom on the Middle Ground: Maryland during the Nineteenth Century* (New Haven, Conn.: Yale University Press, 1985); Eric Foner, *Nothing but Freedom: Emancipation and Its Legacy* (Baton Rouge: Louisiana State University Press, 1983) and *Reconstruction: America's Unfinished Revolution, 1863–1877* (New York: Harper & Row, 1988); Thavolia Glymph and John J. Kushma, eds., *Essays on the Postbellum Southern Economy* (Arlington: University of Texas Press, 1985).

3. The conflicts and alliances among and between southern and northern participants in Reconstruction also continue to be described as though women were not a part of the social landscape and as though gender were peripheral to the expression of power and domination in American cultures. The important exceptions include Jacqueline Jones, *Labor of Love, Labor of Sorrow: Black Women, Work, and the Family from Slavery to the Present* (New York: Basic Books, 1985); Susan A. Mann, "Slavery, Sharecropping, and Sexual Inequality," *Signs: A Journal of Women in Culture and Society*

14, no. 4 (1989): 774–98; Noralee Frankel, "The Southern Side of 'Glory': Mississippi African-American Women During the Civil War," in *"We Specialize in the Wholly Impossible": A Reader in Black Women's History,* Darlene Clark Hine, Wilma King, and Linda Reed, eds. (Brooklyn, N.Y.: Carlson, 1995), 335–42; Laura F. Edwards, "Sexual Violence, Gender, Reconstruction, and the Extension of Patriarchy in Granville County, North Carolina," *North Carolina Historical Review* 68, no. 3 (1991), 237–60; Catherine Clinton, "Reconstructing Freedwomen," in *Divided Houses: Gender and the Civil War,* Catherine Clinton and Nina Silber, eds. (New York: Oxford University Press, 1992), 306–19; Victoria E. Bynum, *Unruly Women: The Politics of Social and Sexual Control in the Old South, 1840–1865* (Chapel Hill: University of North Carolina Press, 1992); and Elsa Barkley Brown, "Negotiating and Transforming the Public Sphere: African American Political Life in the Transition from Slavery to Freedom," *Public Culture* 7 (1994), 107–46. See also Drew Gilpin Faust, "'Trying to Do a Man's Business': Slavery, Violence, and Gender in the American Civil War," *Gender & History* 4, no. 2 (1992): 197–214.

4. See Roger L. Ransom and Richard Sutch, *One Kind of Freedom: The Economic Consequences of Emancipation* (Cambridge, England: Cambridge University Press, 1977), 44–47 and 232–36, for their estimate of the extent of freedwomen's retreat from the paid workforce in select districts of the Cotton South. Their study is often used to support assertions about the prevalence of women's withdrawal, despite the inherent and explicit limitations of their estimates. Ransom and Sutch did not address, for example, how variations in family size and household makeup, plantation size, or the process and organization of agricultural production affected the amount of work performed by women in slavery or freedom, nor did they examine the propagandistic intent of such sources as Freedman's Bureau estimates of work.

Historians have tended to overlook the limitations of Ransom and Sutch's findings. Jacqueline Jones uses *One Kind of Freedom* as the basis for her assertion about the prevalence of withdrawal (in *Labor of Love, Labor of Sorrow*) but also emphasizes that firsthand observations about withdrawal were common (58–63). Both Lawrence Powell (*New Masters: Northern Planters during the Civil War and Reconstruction* [New Haven: Yale University Press, 1980], 108–9) and Jones attempt to contextualize women's withdrawal in terms of the exploitation and oppression they encountered in the postbellum organization of free labor.

5. See, for example, William Cohen, *At Freedom's Edge: Black Mobility and the Southern White Quest for Racial Control, 1861–1875* (Baton Rouge: Louisiana State University Press, 1991), 14, and Herbert G. Gutman, *The Black Family in Slavery and Freedom, 1750–1925* (New York: Pantheon Press, 1976), 167–68. Leon F. Litwack suggests that by insisting on the withdrawal of their wives from the workforce, freedmen attempted to "reinforce their position as the head of the family in accordance with the accepted norms of the dominant society" (*Been in the Storm So Long,* 245), but in a following paragraph he also portrays withdrawal as a strategy by which freedwomen gained control over the allocation and conditions of their paid labor.

6. Jones, *Labor of Love, Labor of Sorrow,* 58; see also Ira Berlin, Steven F. Miller, and Leslie S. Rowland, "Afro-American Families in the Transition from Slavery to Freedom," *Radical History Review* 42 (1988), 89–121. In his work *Branches without Roots: Genesis of the Black Working Class in the American South* (New York: Oxford University Press, 1986), Gerald Jaynes challenges the presumption of universality by historians

who have described freedwomen's work choices. He contrasts the rate of women's participation in different plantation systems and finds significantly less participation by women in postbellum sugar, as opposed to cotton, plantation agriculture (228–33). Jaynes also argues that the purchasing power of women's wage work lagged behind the value of women's unpaid social and reproductive labor, making "withdrawal" from the wage labor force and increased work in independent gardens and cash crops a logical and rational choice.

7. Sharon Ann Holt, "Making Freedom Pay: Freedpeople Working for Themselves, North Carolina, 1865–1900," in *The Journal of Southern History* 60, no. 2 (1994): 228–62.

8. Elsa Barkley Brown, "Negotiating and Transforming the Public Sphere: African American Political Life in the Transition from Slavery to Freedom," *Public Culture* 7 (1994): 107–46. See also Geo. E. Pingree to Maj. Edw. Deane, 31 Aug. 1867, R35, National Archives Microfilm Publication (M)869, and "Recent Election in South Carolina: Testimony Taken by the Select Committee on the Recent Election in South Carolina," House Miscellaneous Document No. 31, 44th Congress, 2nd Session (Washington, D.C.: Government Printing Office, 1877), 15, 19, 24, 27, 35, 38, 40, 55, 63.

9. See Leslie A. Schwalm, "The Meaning of Freedom: African-American Women and Their Transition from Slavery to Freedom in Lowcountry South Carolina," Ph.D., University of Wisconsin, 1991.

10. On emancipation and Reconstruction in lowcountry South Carolina, see Willie Lee Rose, *Rehearsal for Reconstruction: The Port Royal Experiment* (Indianapolis: Bobbs-Merrill, 1976); Joel Williamson, *After Slavery: The Negro in South Carolina during Reconstruction, 1861–1877* (Chapel Hill: University of North Carolina Press, 1965); Thomas C. Holt, *Black over White: Negro Political Leadership in South Carolina during Reconstruction* (Urbana: University of Illinois Press, 1977); Charles Joyner, *Down by the Riverside: A South Carolina Slave Community* (Urbana: University of Illinois Press, 1984); John Scott Strickland, "Traditional Culture and Moral Economy: Social and Economic Change in the South Carolina Lowcountry, 1865–1910," in Steven Hahn and Jonathon Prude, eds., *The Countryside in the Age of Capitalist Transformation* (Chapel Hill: University of North Carolina Press, 1985), 141–78, and "'No More Mudwork': The Struggle for the Control of Labor and Production in Low Country South Carolina, 1863–1880," in Walter J. Fraser Jr. and Winfred B. Moore Jr., eds., *The Southern Enigma: Essays on Race, Class, and Folk Culture* (Westport, Conn.: Greenwood Press, 1983), 43–62; Philip Morgan, "Work and Culture: The Task System and the World of Lowcountry Blacks, 1700 to 1880," *William and Mary Quarterly,* 3rd Ser., 39 (1982): 563–99; and Julie Saville, *The Work of Reconstruction: From Slave to Wage Laborer in South Carolina, 1860–1870* (Cambridge, England: Cambridge University Press, 1994).

11. Ira Berlin and Philip D. Morgan, "Labor and the Shaping of Slave Life in the Americas," in Ira Berlin and Philip D. Morgan, eds., *Cultivation and Culture: Labor and the Shaping of Slave Life in the Americas* (Charlottesville: University Press of Virginia, 1993), 1.

12. See Richard H. Sewell, *A House Divided: Sectionalism and Civil War, 1848–1865* (Baltimore: Johns Hopkins University Press, 1988), 101–25; Paul W. Gates, *Agriculture and the Civil War* (New York: Knopf, 1965), 3–45; Emory M. Thomas, *The Confeder-*

ate Nation, 1861–1865 (New York: Harper & Row, 1979), 236–42; and James L. Roark, *Masters without Slaves: Southern Planters in the Civil War and Reconstruction* (New York: Norton, 1977).

13. J. H. Easterby, ed., *The South Carolina Rice Plantation as Revealed in the Papers of Robert F. W. Allston* (Chicago: University of Chicago Press, 1945), 291–92, 309, 312, 314, 316; Adele Petigru Allston to Charles Allston, 8 July 1863, and Adele Petigru Allston to Benjamin Allston, 30 June 1864, both in R. F. W. Allston Family Papers, South Caroliniana Library (SCL); William Capers to Louis Manigault, 20 August and 24 September 1863, Louis Manigault Papers, Ser. F, Part (Pt.) II, R6, *Records of Ante-Bellum Southern Plantations*.

14. James M. Clifton, ed., *Life and Labor on Argyle Island: Letters and Documents of a Savannah River Rice Plantation, 1833–1867* (Savannah, Ga.: The Beehive Press, 1978), 320; C. Vann Woodward, ed., *Mary Chesnut's Civil War* (New Haven, Conn.: Yale University Press, 1981), 48, 78, 234, 464; Mary Elliott Johnstone to Mamma [Mrs. William Elliott], 1861 or 1862, Elliott and Gonzales Family Papers [Ser. 1.7, Folder 67], Southern Historical Collection, University of North Carolina (SHC).

15. Elizabeth Hyde Botume, *First Days amongst the Contrabands* (1893; reprint, New York: Arno Press, 1968), 124–27; Ira Berlin et al., eds., *The Wartime Genesis of Free Labor*, 316–19; Virginia M. Adams, ed., *On the Altar of Freedom: Black Soldiers' Civil War Letters from the Front: Corporal James Henry Gooding* (Amherst: University of Massachusetts Press, 1991), 110–11; Rupert Sargent Holland, ed., *Letters and Diaries of Laura M. Towne* (1912; reprint, New York: Negro Universities Press, 1969), 20–22, 56, 140, 144–45; Elizabeth Ware Pearson, ed., *Letters and Diaries from Port Royal, 1862–1866* (1906; reprint New York: Arno Press, 1979), 250, 303–4; see also Leslie A. Schwalm, *A Hard Fight for We: Women's Transition from Slavery to Freedom in South Carolina* (Urbana: University of Illinois Press, 1997).

16. *Charleston Daily Courier*, 31 May 1866.

17. Following Johnson's February 1866 veto of the Freedmen's Bureau Bill, including the bill's three-year extension on the possessory titles freedpeople held to Sea Island lands, the bureau and the military department in the state yielded to the inevitability of restoration. By March 1866, the possessory titles to Sea Island land held by freedpeople were subject to closer scrutiny, and those who held no title or who had settled on land other than that specified in the title were subject to eviction. See Martin Abbott, *The Freedmen's Bureau in South Carolina, 1865–1872* (Chapel Hill: University of North Carolina Press, 1967), 60–62; Foner, *Reconstruction*, 161–63; and Williamson, *After Slavery*, 84–86.

18. Lt. Col. B. F. Smith to Maj. Genl. Devens, 20 Jan. 1866, Letters Received, Ser. 2392, 4th Subdist., Mil. Dist. of Charleston SC, National Archives Record Group (RG) 393, Pt. II, No. 142; and George C. Fox to Lt. Col. A. J. Willard, 2 Nov. 1865, Registered Letters Received, Ser. 3202, Georgetown SC Subasst. Comr., RG 105.

19. W. C. Munnerlyn to Maj. Genl. Saxton, 29 Dec. 1865, Unregistered Letters Received, R21 M869; Geo. C. Fox, Monthly Land Report for the State of South Carolina, 31 Oct. 1865, Misc. Records, Ser. 3212, Georgetown SC Subasst. Comr., RG 105.

20. George C. Rogers Jr., *The History of Georgetown County, South Carolina* (Columbia: University of South Carolina Press, 1970), 407; testimony of Job Mayzeck, 11 Mar.

1873, and testimony of Dennis Hazel, 12 Mar. 1873, both in claim of Job Mayzeck, Disallowed Claims, RG 233; and testimony of Dennis Hazell, 18 Mar. 1873, claim of Alonzo Jackson, Southern Claims Commission, RG 217.

21. Testimony of Dennis Hazel, 4 April 1866; Statement of Francis S. Parker Jr., 4 April 1866; Charges and Specifications against Jim, Job, & Stewart, 2 April 1866; Charges against Sukey, 1 April 1866; Charges against Becky, 1 April 1866; Francis S. Parker Jr., to Col. Smith, 31 Mar. 1866, and undated, unsigned list of fourteen names, all in Letters Received, Ser. 2392, 4th Subdist., Mil. Dist. of Charleston SC, RG 393 Pt. 2 No. 142 [C-1606]. See also Lt. Col. Smith to Capt. M. N. Rice, 7 April 1866, vol. 156 Department of the South (DS), pp. 62–63, Letters Sent, Ser. 2389, 4th Subdist., Mil. Dist. of Charleston SC, RG 393 Pt. 2 No. 142; Capt. B. F. Smith to Major H. W. Smith, 6 April 1866, Reports of Conditions and Operations, Georgetown, R34 M869; and Capt. B. F. Smith, "Semi-Monthly Report of Persons Arrested," 15 May 1866, Reports of Arrests of Civilians, Ser. 4161, Department of the Carolinas, RG 393 Pt. I; Lt. Col. A. J. Willard to Capt. Geo. W. Hooker, 20 Oct. 1865, Vol. 156 DS, pp. 8–10, Letters Sent, Ser. 2389, 4th Subdist., Mil. Dist. of Charleston SC, RG 393 Pt. II No. 142 [C-1614]. Bracketed letters and numbers (e.g., [C-1614]) refer to file numbers assigned to the documents copied from the National Archives by the editors of the Freedmen and Southern Society Project at the University of Maryland, source of the multivolume history *Freedom: A Documentary History of Emancipation, 1861–1867.*

22. James C. Scott, *Domination and the Arts of Resistance: Hidden Transcripts* (New Haven, Conn.: Yale University Press, 1990), offers a theory of confrontations between dominant and subordinate groups that is helpful to understanding the changing relations between former slaveowners and former slaves in the postbellum South.

23. Williams Middleton to J. Frances Fisher, 17 Nov. 1865, Middleton Family Papers, South Carolina Historical Society (SCHS).

24. Entry for 24 Aug. 1865, James Chaplin Beecher Memorandum Book, 1865–66, James Chaplin Beecher Papers, Perkins Library, Duke University (PL).

25. Wm. G. Robert to Captain [Upham], 20 Nov. 1865, Ser. 2384, Letters Received, Subdistrict of Coosawatchie, RG 393 Pt. 2 No. 141 [C-1581].

26. Statement by W. W. Robertson, 15 Sept. 1865, and "List of Negroes with their Characters . . . ," undated, both enclosed in Lt. W. Wood to Lieut. S. Baker, 16 Sept. 1865, Letters Received, Ser. 2384, Subdistrict of Coosawatchie SC, RG 393 DS Pt. II no. 141 [C-1593].

27. One planter complained to military authorities that "All male hands but two have left the place. . . . So I have my houses, filled with women and children, 12 (twelve) women who are full hands, but will not work, 6 (six) half hands, 4 (four) old and crippled 21 (twenty one) children fit for no work of any kind, 43 (forty three) in all" (Benj. R. Bostick to Capt. Upham, 17 Oct. 1865, Letters Received, Ser. 2384, Subdistrict of Coosawatchie SC, RG 393 DS Pt. 2 No. 141 [C-1585]).

28. J. S. Bostick to Capt., n.d. [Sept. 1865?], Letters Received, Ser. 2384, Subdistrict of Coosawatchie SC, RG 393 DS Pt. 2 No. 141 [C-1588].

29. William Robert to Capt. Upham, 13 and 28 Sept. 1865, and to Captain [Upham], 20 Nov. 1865, all in Letters Received, Ser. 2384, Subdistrict of Coosawatchie, RG 393 Pt. 2 No. 141 [C-1581].

30. Elizabeth Catherine Porcher to Philip Edward Porcher, 23 Mar. 1865, typed

transcript, Folder 19, Palmer Family Papers, SCL; Easterby, ed., *The South Carolina Rice Plantation*, 208; Col. James C. Beecher to Gilbert Pillsbury, 11 Aug. 1865, and G. Pillsbury to Col. James C. Beecher, 16 Aug. 1865, both in R34, M869; entry for 10 Aug. 1865, James Chaplin Beecher Memorandum Book, 1865–66, James Chaplin Beecher Papers, PL.

31. G. G. Batchelder to Maj. Genl. R. Saxton, 10 Oct. 1865, R20 M869.

32. G. Pillsbury to Maj. H. W. Smith, 30 Dec. 1865, Unregistered Letters Received, R20 M869.

33. This question has been explored by Catherine Clinton, "Reconstructing Freed-women," in Clinton and Silber, eds., *Divided Houses*, 306–19, and by Laura F. Edwards in "Sexual Violence," 237–60. For an example of violence against lowcountry freed-women, see Lt. Col. Garrett Nagle, Report of Outrages Committed, 31 July 1866, Colleton District, Ser. 3353, RG 105.

34. Planters' exaggerated hopes for what restoration could accomplish are well documented in Daniel E. Huger Smith, Alice R. Huger Smith, and Arney R. Childs, eds., *Mason Smith Family Letters, 1860–1868* (Columbia: University of South Carolina Press, 1950).

35. Major James P. Roy to Lt. Col. W. L. M. Burger, 9 Dec. 1865 and 1 Feb. 1866, both in Letters Received, Ser. 4109, Dept. of SC, RG 393 Pt. 1.

36. *Charleston Daily Courier,* 24 Jan. 1866; William Bull Pringle to Gen. Sickles, 18 Jan. 1866, RG 98; Bvt. Lt. Col. B. F. Smith to 1st Lt. M. N. Rice, 21 Jan. 1866, vol. 156 DS, pp. 40–41, Letters Sent, Ser. 2389, 4th Subdist., Military Dist. of Charleston, RG 393 Pt. 2 No. 142 [C-1616]; Bvt. Lt. Col. B. F. Smith to 1st Lt. M. N. Rice, 21 Jan. 1866, vol. 156 DS, pp. 40–41, Letters Sent, Ser. 2389, 4th Subdistrict, Military Dist. of Charleston, RG 393 Pt. 2 No. 142 [C-1616]; Wm. R. Maxwell to Genl. Sickles and Genl. Bennet, 1 March 1866, Letters Received, Ser. 2392, RG 393 Pt. 2 No. 142.

37. W. St. J. Mazyck to Col. Smith, 4 Feb. 1866, Letters Received, Ser. 2392, 4th Subdist., Mil. Dist. of Charleston, SC, RG 393 Pt. 2 No. 142.

38. Maj. Gen. D. E. Sickles to James L. Orr, 17 Dec. 1865, South Carolina Governors' Papers; Capt. D. T. Corbin to Maj. H. W. Smith, 28 Feb. 1866, Mt. Pleasant, Reports of Conditions and Operations, R34 M869; Gen. R. K. Scott, Circular Letter to the Landlords and Laborers of the State of South Carolina, 26 Dec. 1866, *Charleston Daily Courier,* 5 Jan. 1867; Gen. R. K. Scott to Maj. Gen. O. O. Howard, 21 Feb. 1866, re-printed in U.S. Senate, *Senate Executive Documents,* 39th Cong., 1st Sess., No. 27, p. 25.

39. [?] McKim to Capt. F. W. Liedtke, 25 June 1866, and J. Calhoun Cain to Capt. F. W. Liedtke, 11 August 1866, both in Letters Received, Ser. 3277, Moncks Corner SC Subasst. Comr., RG 105.

40. Barney [Edward Barnwell Heyward] to Tab [Catherine Heyward], 5 May 1867, Heyward Family Papers, SCL.

41. John William DeForest, *A Union Officer in the Reconstruction* (New Haven, Conn.: Yale University Press, 1948), 94.

42. *Charleston Daily Courier,* 25 May 1866; Olney Harleston to General R. K. Scott, 21 Jan. 1867, Testimony, Reports, and Other Records Relating to Court Cases and Complaints, Ser. 3284, Moncks Corner SC Subasst. Comr., RG 105.

43. The labor contracts discussed here are located in Ser. 3210 and 3211, Labor Contracts, Georgetown SC Subasst. Comr., RG 105. Information from additional

contracts that are not themselves extant can be found in the Reports of Contracts Approved in the Subdistricts, Ser. 2930, SC Assistant Commissioner, RG 105, reproduced in R42 M869. The problems associated with this particular kind of evidence include the casual enforcement of contract terms and constant efforts by both employers and employees to overturn the contract terms; whether the contracts were representative of labor arrangements, given the likelihood that many plantations operated without contracts; and difficulties in transcribing the documents, in particular identifying the assignees by sex.

44. The data represented here are an imperfect and incomplete representation of postbellum labor arrangements. Judging from the total number of contracts that are extant for Georgetown District, there were more plantations operating without labor contracts than operating with. For these and other reasons, the contracts can only be considered a closed universe, rather than representative of all plantation labor in this particular lowcountry district.

45. E. Francis Fischer to Williams Middleton, 10 Feb. 1866, Middleton Family Papers, SCHS.

46. On rape, violence, and women's experience of slavery, see Catherine Clinton, "'Southern Dishonor': Flesh, Blood, Race, and Bondage," in Carol Blesser, ed., *In Joy and in Sorrow: Women, Family, and Marriage in the Victorian South* (New York: Oxford University Press, 1991), 52–68.

47. Rev. C. W. Howard, "Conditions and Resources of Georgia," in the *Report of the Commissioner of Agriculture for the Year 1866* (Washington, D.C.: 1867), 567–80.

48. C. P. [illeg.] to Mary Elliott Johnstone, 2 March 1868, Ser. 1.8, Elliott-Gonzales Papers, SHC.

49. Edwin M. Tilton to Col. Smith, 18 Jan. 1866, vol. 156 DS, Letters Sent, Ser. 2392, Post of Georgetown SC, RG 393 Pt. 2 No. 142; and Gen. James C. Beecher to Lieut. M. N. Rice, 21 Jan. 1866, Letters and Reports Received, Ser. 4112, Department of SC, RG 393 Pt. 1.

50. B. H. Pinners to Col. Smith, 1 May 1866, Letters Received, Ser. 2392, Post of Georgetown SC, RG 393 Pt. 2 No. 142.

51. Edwin M. Tilton to Col. Smith, 16 Jan. 1866, and B. H. Pinners to Col. Smith, 1 May 1866, both in Letters Received, Ser. 2392, Post of Georgetown SC, RG 393 Pt. 2 No. 142.

52. See *George Singleton v. John Henry Porcher & Samuel Ravenel,* Proceedings of Provost Courts, Military Tribunals, and Post Court-Martial Cases Tried in North and South Carolina, Ser. 4257A, Judge Advocate, RG 393. For another example of how white men used the pretense of searching freedpeople's homes as a means of terrorizing freedpeople, see freedman Austin Elmore's charges against Peter Bird, who entered the Elmore home, beat Austin, his wife, and his mother with a pistol and an iron, and smashed earthenware, provisions, and other property in the cabin; see Affidavit by Austin Elmore, 24 Dec. 1866, Misc. Records, Ser. 3353, Summerville SC Subasst. Comr., RG 105. E. C. P. to Hattie, 25 Oct. 1865, Palmer Family Papers, SCL.

53. For an example of the violence that accompanied these searches, see Affidavit of Austin Elmore, 24 Sept. 1866, Colleton Dist., Ser. 3353, RG 105.

54. Lt. Col. B. F. Smith to Lt. M. N. Rice, 20 Feb. 1866, vol. 156 DS, pp. 53–54,

Letters Sent, ser 2389, 4th Subdist., Mil. Dist. of Charleston, RG 393 Pt. 2 No. 142 [C-1616].

55. C. V. Wilson to Major O'Brien, 18 July 1866, Testimony, Reports, and Other Records Relating to Court Cases and Complaints, Ser. 3284, Moncks Corner SC Subasst. Comr., RG 105.

56. Entry for 10 Oct. 1866, vol. 239, Register of Complaints, Ser. 3283, Moncks Corner SC Subasst. Comr., RG 105; Smith et al., eds., *Mason Smith Family Letters*, 264–65; Contract between A. G. Heriot and Freedmen, 1 Feb. 1866, Labor Contracts, Ser. 3211, Georgetown SC Subasst. Commr., RG 105.

57. Based on slave lists from plantations belonging to Charles Manigault in 1845 (Clifton, ed., *Life and Labor on Argyle Island*, 31–32) and plantations belonging to James R. Sparkman in 1847 and 1858 ("Task Hands 1847 June," in MS vol. bd., 1827–1845, and "Dirleton 1858" and "Task Hands Birdfield Jany. 1 1858," both in MS vol. bd. 1857–1859, James Ritchie Sparkman Papers, Ser. A, Pt. 2, R 6, *Records of Ante-Bellum Southern Plantations*).

58. George P. Rawick, ed., *The American Slave: A Composite Autobiography* (Westport, Conn.: Greenwood Press, 1972), South Carolina, vol. 2, Pt. 2, 177–182. In Virginia Ingraham Burr, ed., *The Secret Eye: The Journal of Ella Gertrude Clanton Thomas, 1848–1889* (Chapel Hill: University of North Carolina Press, 1990), Thomas describes a very similar postwar scenario in which a young girl, a house servant and previously her slave, conspires with her mother—sold away for bad behavior—and "escaped" from the Thomas household, much to Thomas's disappointment (267–68).

59. Susan R. Jervey and Charlotte St. J. Ravenel, *Two Diaries from Middle St. John's, Berkeley, South Carolina, February–May 1865* (Charleston, S.C.: St. John's Hunting Club, 1921), 42.

60. C. Vann Woodward and Elisabeth Muhlenfeld, eds., *The Private Mary Chesnut: The Unpublished Civil War Diaries* (New York: Oxford University Press, 1984), 246.

61. Elizabeth Catherine Porcher to Hattie, 25 Oct. 1865, Palmer Family Papers, SCL.

62. Alice A. Palmer to Hattie, 20 July 1865, Folder 19, Palmer Family Papers, SCL.

63. Alice A. Palmer to Hattie, 17 Oct. 1866, and Elizabeth Catherine Porcher to Hattie, 25 Oct. 1865, both in Palmer Family Papers, SCL. See also Major Jos. Totten to Inspector General, 9 May 1866, T-19 1866, Letters Received, Ser. 15, RG 159 [J-51], for a description of the changes freedwomen made in domestic service.

64. Elizabeth Catherine Porcher to [My Dear Hattie], 5 Aug. [1866], and E. L. Porcher to Harriet [?], [1870], Palmer Family Papers, SCL; Meta M. Grimball to J. B. Grimball, Jan. 5 1866, John Berkeley Grimball Family Papers, PL.

65. Hattie [Harriet Rutledge Elliott Gonzales to Mama [Ann Hutchinson Smith Elliott], Monday 11th [1867–68], Ser. 1.8, Elliott-Gonzales Papers, SHC.

66. Mary Elliott Johnstone to Mrs. William Elliott, January 10, 1866, Ser. 1.7, Elliott-Gonzales Papers, SHC; and E. C. P. to Hattie, [1866] and 24 May 1868, both in Palmer Family Papers, SCL.

67. Alice Palmer to [My Dear Hattie], 19 Sept. 1866, and E. C. P. to Hattie, 25 Sept., [1866], and 28 Nov. 1867, all in Palmer Family Papers, SCL.

68. Mary Elliott Johnstone to Mrs. William Elliott, Jan. 10, 1866, and Mary Elliott

Johnstone to Ralph E. Elliott, July 9, 1865, both in Ser. 1.7, Elliot and Gonzales Papers, SHC.

69. Elizabeth Fox-Genovese has explored white women's identities as household mistresses in *Within the Plantation Household: Black and White Women of the Old South* (Chapel Hill: University of North Carolina Press, 1988); see also Emily Elliott to Mary Elliott Johnstone, Sept. 21 1866, Elliott-Gonzales Papers, SHC.

2   The Quicksands of Economic Insecurity: African Americans, Strikebreaking, and Labor Activism in the Industrial Era

In the last decade of the nineteenth century, the outcome of the clash between the miners and the Black Diamond Coal Company in the western mountain community of Mansfield appeared preordained. A labor force that had once numbered about 2,500, composed of white men, mostly American, Welsh, Irish, and Canadian, had seen its ranks reduced by unemployment; those still employed endured repeated wage cuts (wages had been reduced by 25 percent in just over a year), which made it a struggle for "many a miner's family to exist." In an earlier bout of labor conflict, employers' reliance on Italian strikebreakers and militiamen led to a decisive defeat for the miners' unions. Now, once again on strike, miners found themselves evicted from their company-owned homes and threatened by "Actual starvation." With strikers reportedly in an "ugly mood," an outbreak of violence was only a matter of time.[1]

Then the company delivered the coup de grâce by importing large numbers of African Americans to replace the white union men. Labor agents scoured the Tennessee and Alabama mining districts for experienced black miners. Upon hearing of the imminent arrival of "ignorant negroes from the South," strikers recognized that the "end was near" and assembled in large numbers; their "excitement became intense." When strikers failed to obey an order to disperse, militiamen fired "volley after volley" into the "ranks of an emaciated, half-starved, half-clad humanity," resulting in numerous casualties. To "avoid future riots and to bring peace and contentment to Mansfield," the local *Mining Review* reported, "only colored labor would be employed by the Black Diamond Company in the future." With the importation of southern blacks, the *Review* predicted, "Mansfield had seen an end of the disgraceful scenes that had been reenacted every time the Black Diamond Coal Company had attempted to manage its own business in its own way." Those "who had tired of rioting and strife," it advised, owed the "colored men" a "warm welcome." Black workers, who were housed in newly erected stockades around the mines, found significant employment opportunities awaiting them.[2]

The conflict engulfing the Black Diamond Company in the 1890s was unique in industrial America in only one regard: it was fictional. The author, W. S. Carter, was the president of the all-white and virulently exclusionary Brotherhood of Locomotive Firemen and Enginemen. In "The Mills of God," a serialized parable printed in his conservative union's monthly journal, he offered a melodramatic tale of exploited if virtuous white workers, haughty employers and plutocrats, and impoverished, manipulated blacks. This story, Carter suggested, was an all-too-familiar one: "All have read of similar incidents—occurring year by year, and all terminating in like manner."[3] Indeed, "The Mills of God" derived its inspiration and narrative structure from the annals of industrial warfare in coal-mining communities. In the 1880s and 1890s, mining companies procured African Americans to break strikes by white coal miners in Washington, Illinois, Indiana, Iowa, West Virginia, and other states.

Not all labor conflicts ended as did the one recounted by Carter. Concurrent with the publication of "The Mills of God" was a bloody confrontation between white miners and mine owners in the Illinois towns of Virden and Pana that bore a conspicuous resemblance to Carter's fictionalized account. When mine owners imported Alabama blacks to break a United Mine Workers' strike, white workers determined to "have living wages and that negro labor shall not supplant them in the mines and thus deprive them of their means of livelihood." A virtual race war erupted. In what some white unionists described as "one of the bitterest fights in the industrial history of this country," white miners won the battle. The lessons drawn merely reconfirmed a longer-held fear: that the "entire social fabric of the Northern states may crumble before the invasion of hordes of cheap negro laborers from the South" and that an "industrial race war" was only just beginning.[4]

The image of the black male strikebreaker in the late nineteenth and early twentieth centuries was a powerful and broadly provocative one,[5] arousing the concern, albeit in opposing ways, of white trade unionists and black elites alike. That image haunted organized white labor. The black strikebreaker appeared both ignorant and aggressive, manipulated and defiant, docile and violent. In their reflections and their policies, white trade unionists exaggerated black strikebreakers' role and deemed them a greater threat to white labor's interests than other groups of nonblack strikebreakers. But over the closing decades of the nineteenth century, many, perhaps most, whites would scarcely have questioned the characterization of African Americans as a scab race. After all, too many strikes in too many trades and industries—including mining, meatpacking, longshoring, team driving, and even textiles and iron and steel—had been weakened, at times decisively, by employers' deployment of black labor. Although in reality blacks constituted only a small, if ultimately undeterminable, percentage of strikebreakers in the history of American industrial relations—native-born white and especially immigrant workers constituted a clear majority—white trade unionists and, indeed, much of American society would express little hesitation in hanging the charge, like a proverbial lynching rope, around the neck of the race.[6]

If white workers perceived African Americans as a threat to their economic well-being, they made little attempt, by and large, to understand the motivations and goals of the black workers they confronted on the industrial battlefield. Instead, they depicted black strikebreakers as depraved and dangerous threats to their livelihoods and collective power. Viewing black workers as ignorant, largely inassimilable, and the dupes of capital, they drew the line at admitting blacks into membership in the labor movement, with little apology. Black strikebreakers, American Federation of Labor (AFL) official John Roach insisted in 1904, were "huge strapping fellows, ignorant and vicious, whose predominating trait was animalism"; a white socialist described those same strikebreakers as a "horde of debased, beastialized blacks" and as "disgusting products of capitalism."[7] In response to the arrival of southern black strikebreakers during the 1894 Chicago packinghouse strike, white stockyard workers even hung the effigy of a black roustabout from a telegraph pole. "A black false face of hideous expression had been fixed upon the head of straw," a Chicago white daily paper reported, "and a placard pinned upon the breast of the figure bore the skull and cross-bones with the word 'nigger scab' above and below in bold letters."[8] A decade later, another influx of southern black laborers—perhaps as many as 5,800—was met by outrage and widespread racial violence on the part of white workers and their sympathizers in the teamsters' conflict. "It was the niggers that whipped you in line," the rabidly antiblack southern politician Ben Tillman informed white Chicago stockyard workers after the collapse of their strike. "They were the club with which your brains were beaten out."[9] The number of examples could easily be expanded; again and again, white workers drew similar connections between black strikebreakers and the failure of their strikes.

At their most charitable, white workers tended to dismiss black strikebreakers as misguided, ill-informed pawns of capital. Had they inquired further into their opponents' motives, many of their fears would have undoubtedly been confirmed. Certainly some black strikebreakers were recruited under false pretenses or were honestly unaware that they were being used as weapons against white labor, as whites occasionally claimed. "The reason I left the camp," explained black strikebreaker Daniel Webster during the 1891 Washington state mining strike, "was that matters had been misrepresented to us. We were told there was no strike, but that we were going to a new mine."[10] But others knew exactly what they were doing: the Negro "fairly aches for the opportunity" to scab against whites," one white union journal insisted.[11] Indeed, Daniel Webster was only one of a small handful of defectors from the ranks of black strikebreakers taken to the mines of Franklin, Washington; the vast majority, numbering as many as 600, clung to their new jobs despite white harassment and racial violence. Given the racially exclusionary barriers erected by many white unions and the racial division of labor that confined blacks to inferior positions, strike-breaking by African Americans could naturally serve as the threat white unionists perceived it to be.

It also represented something that most white workers, as well as black leaders, were scarcely prepared to comprehend: black strikebreaking was nothing less than a form of working-class activism designed to advance the interests of black workers and their families. In many instances a collective strategy as much as trade unionism, strikebreaking afforded black workers the means to enter realms of employment previously closed to them and to begin a long, slow climb up the economic ladder. As a strategy, of course, strikebreaking was not without its drawbacks, as many contemporaries, white and black, pointed out. The strikebreaking option was always a calculated risk. Black workers' value to white employers rested largely on their ability to check the power of white workers; they remained highly vulnerable in the labor market, often subject to the harsh—or even harsher—conditions that had prompted whites to organize in the first place. They also exposed themselves to potential or real violence at the hands of strikers and their sympathizers, who bitterly resented their intrusion into local industrial conflicts. Many white workers rejected outright the legitimacy of black workers' grievances about racial exclusion from unions and employment. Choosing instead to blame the victim, they not only refused to see strikebreaking as a form of working-class activism, but often proved resistant to recognizing or appreciating more familiar forms of activism—namely labor organizing—in which black workers might engage.

Black elites—conservative clergymen, businessmen, and politicians, as well as newspaper editors and educators—also devoted considerable attention to the black male strikebreaker. Unlike white unionists, they did not object to his actions but rather encouraged him as a way of demonstrating loyalty and obedience to white employers and attaining economic advancement.[12] As for trade unions, elites admonished black workers simply to steer clear of them. This vision of black advancement rested on a clear bargain: blacks would faithfully perform the South's labor and, in exchange, white employers would protect them and supply them with jobs and economic security. Just as their adherence to racial stereotypes prevented white labor activists from appreciating the rationale for black workers' actions, so, too, did an obsession with race blind black elites to the limitations of their own advancement strategies. Few understood the genuine workplace concerns of black labor beyond access to employment; few recognized, valued, or acted on a central fact of industrial life—the existence of black working-class activists committed to challenging their employers' workplace practices through the trade union movement. From the 1880s through World War I, a relatively small but significant number of African Americans ignored elites' exhortations to faithful and loyal service and embraced workplace labor activism in general, and trade unionism in particular, as vehicles for combating economic and racial inequality.[13] Whites' belief in blacks' inferiority and fear of black strikebreaking, on the one hand, and black elites' sole interest in opposing racial discrimination in access to employment through alliances with powerful whites, on the other, obscured the degree to which black workers adopted a variety of strategies, from strikebreaking to labor organizing, that reflected both racial and class concerns.

It took no particular perceptiveness for students of late nineteenth-century and early twentieth-century labor markets to observe the obvious: a sharp color line ran through most jobs in industrial America, a line that worked to blacks' distinct disadvantage. As a rule, the more skilled, technical, or supervisory a position, the less likely it was that an African American could gain access to it. In the postbellum North, a relatively small number of urban black workers found skilled and remunerative employment. "What is the present condition of the colored people of this City?" asked a *New York Times* correspondent in 1869. "The men are principally occupied as coachmen in private families, waiters in hotels and dining saloons, barbers, whitewashers, [and] bricklayers . . . ; while many of them are teamsters and 'longshoremen, and a few work privately as artisans in different trades." Black women were concentrated in washing and ironing, dressmaking, and hairdressing jobs. To a degree, the relegation of black workers to unskilled and service positions reflected their skill and education levels. Far more important, however, was naked prejudice. Employers refused to hire blacks into skilled jobs, and skilled white workers refused to work with them and rejected black membership in their unions. The trade unions of skilled workers affiliated with the AFL typically implemented explicit or implicit bans on black membership, many of them persisting well into the twentieth century. If a northern black worker succeeded in obtaining a better job, the *Times* reported, success could be expected to come at a high cost: "he has to accept lower wages, and is always expected to work harder than a white man, while his fellow-workmen 'put upon' him whenever they get the opportunity, and ceaselessly jeer at him and make him the butt of their jokes."[14]

More than half a century later, some things had changed, but black workers' subordinate labor market position had not. During World War I, the conscription of whites into the military and the sharp reduction of European immigration to the United States had generated severe labor shortages across the industrialized North and Midwest. Roughly half a million southern blacks departed a region marked by poverty, racial violence, segregation, and political disfranchisement to take up positions in basic industry in the North. The 1920s witnessed an even greater migration to northern urban centers. In many instances, industrial employment was a vast improvement over southern sharecropping and black migrants appreciated the cultural, social, and political advantages—however imperfect—the North had to offer over the South.[15] Yet their economic breakthroughs were limited at best. Black New Yorkers, for instance, ran up against a "barrier erected especially for them, a barrier which pens them off on the morass—no, the quicksands—of economic insecurity," civil-rights activist and writer James Weldon Johnson concluded in 1930. "Fewer jobs are open to them than to any other group; and in such jobs as they get, they are subject to the old rule, which still obtains, 'the last to be hired and the first to be fired.'"[16] As the United States engaged in battle with the Axis powers during World War II, poet Langston Hughes concurred. "[T]here has been an economic color line of such severity that since the Civil War we have been kept most effectively, as a racial group, in the lowest economic brackets," he noted in his contribution to Rayford Logan's book *What the Negro Wants*.[17]

The vastly larger numbers of blacks and employers' virtual dependence on them created a different set of dynamics in the South. As in the North, newer industries (such as cotton textiles) and the skilled trades remained largely off-limits to blacks.[18] "We are the unskilled labor of the country," one black writer remarked in 1886. "It has been the unwritten law of the land that color disqualifies a man for positions that involve master minds and trained hands."[19] Although black artisans and skilled workers could be found in a number of southern trades, their position was a precarious one by the end of the nineteenth century. The "universal feeling" among one group of white southerners queried by Charles B. Spahr in 1900 was that "'People don't think it right to employ negro labour when there is white to be had.'... The South believes in giving the preference to white men."[20] Preference was given to whites in some economic arenas, but not all. In the postbellum years, former slaves remained overwhelmingly on the land, locked into a cycle of debt peonage as sharecroppers, tenants, and agricultural wage laborers producing cotton, sugar, and rice. In the expanding extractive industries of the New South, they constituted a significant proportion of the ranks of timber workers and coal, iron ore, and phosphate miners, as they did in the transportation sector as longshoremen and teamsters on the docks of the Gulf and South Atlantic coasts and as track layers and maintenance-of-way laborers in the railroad industry. "The Negroes are the workers. They are today the bone and sinew of the South," one white writer noted in 1887.[21] "I doubt whether, on the whole, a better labouring population, more suited to the climate and country in which they find themselves, is anywhere to be found," concluded a British member of Parliament investigating the South in 1879. "The whites certainly cannot do without them."[22] That dependence aside, white employers in slavery's aftermath never reconciled themselves fully to the tenets of a free labor system that held that labor and capital each possessed rights, which for labor included voluntary contractual agreements, geographical mobility, and the right to quit. Convinced that freedmen and -women would not work without compulsion, white employers applied force; determined to prevent black economic advancement, they used harsh discipline to enforce often rock-bottom wages, poor working conditions, and relentless, unrelieved labor. Although black workers sought individually and collectively to check such practices, the greater power usually rested with the employers. Black resistance to employers' abusiveness only reinforced white attitudes toward black labor. For decades following the demise of Reconstruction, southern white managers would complain ceaselessly about what they saw as African Americans' shiftlessness, laziness, propensity toward absenteeism, and inability to perform skilled and complex tasks, characteristics that conveniently confirmed the need to supervise black workers strictly.[23]

Whatever qualms whites might have had about the character of southern black labor, African Americans had two things going for them that appealed greatly to white employers: their reputed aloofness from organized labor and their reluctance to engage in disruptive workplace conflicts. In an age in which industrial unrest and violence captured headlines and inspired widespread fear among men of property, these were attractive qualities indeed. Southern proprietors exhibited a marked "disposition . . . to rely on black labor as a conservative element," concluded George Campbell, an

Englishman who studied the South at the end of Reconstruction, "securing them against the dangers and difficulties which were arising from the combinations of the white labourers [that is, unions] in some of the Northern States." On "this ground," he found, "the blacks are cherished."[24] Decades later, blacks' reputation for industrial peace continued to endear them to southern industrialists. "One quality of the negro held to be valuable is that he shows no disposition to unionize or to strike in the aggregate," the *Manufacturers' Record* declared in 1905.[25] "[N]ever has a bomb been found in his hand nor has he ever been branded as an anarchist," insisted Frank D. Rash, the vice president of the Kentucky Manufacturers Association, in 1916. The "Southern Negro" is "one of the South's greatest industrial assets."[26]

These were assessments that many black spokespeople enthusiastically endorsed. The Negro "is the most faithful laborer and the very best friend this section has ever had," one southern black newspaper insisted in 1903.[27] Black conservatives in particular ceaselessly reminded elite whites of the region's dependence on the labor of black workers, who, in exchange for white protection and employment, could be counted on to render loyal and dedicated service in times of labor unrest. The bargain they promoted was a straightforward one. If "you of the dominant race will be generous in your dealings with us," one group of conservative black ministers and educators petitioned the constitutional convention of Alabama in 1901, "you will ever have at your door a people who *will not trouble your sleep with dynamite nor your waking hours with strikes.*"[28] These were neither idle promises nor minority views. For decades, black workers' supposed coolness to organized labor and strikes became a major selling point, one that black elites hammered away at year in and year out, in an effort to demonstrate the indispensability of black labor to white employers. During organized labor's Great Upheaval in 1886, one black newspaper observed, the black worker was "for the most part . . . a disinterested spectator," a "passive" observer "of this far-reaching revolution."[29] A few years later, during the nationwide Pullman strike/boycott, a midwestern black weekly boasted that "Negro labor is the most reliable and contented in the world. . . . Throughout the south land no alarm is heard. . . . The colored man labors on."[30] "Already the country has had reason to be thankful that the black man is not usually willing to join with the laborers from foreign countries in the great strikes," Hampton University's *Southern Workman* declared in 1908.[31]

Over time, these selling points proved persuasive, at least among some white employers. Prior to World War I, however, most northern industrialists preferred immigrant labor from southern and eastern Europe, maintaining an informal hiring bar against the relatively small number of blacks in the North or the small stream of migrants from the South. Only in the longshore and mining sectors, and to a lesser extent in the building trades and teamstering, did African Americans prove attractive as an alternative labor supply during periods of labor unrest. Yet the migration of as many as half a million southern blacks to the North during World War I, inspired by both oppressive conditions in the South and a desire for a better life in the North and facilitated by severe labor shortages caused by the cutoff of European immigration, gave northern employers considerable firsthand experience with a group of workers they had previously ignored or scorned. Black workers' value in employers' eyes only grew when the latter witnessed black workers' reluctance to join new unions or their willingness to cross picket lines during and after the war. "Niggers did it" was a common remark heard among company officers seeking to explain their crushing of the 1919 steel strike. Evidence from individual communities bore out the claim. In the steel mills in Duquesne, Pennsylvania, for instance, only one black worker walked off the job.[32] By the mid-1920s, as historian Peter Gottlieb has observed, "testimonies to blacks' value as essentially conservative, nonunion workers poured from company offices in Pittsburgh and in other industrial centers," as steel executives applauded blacks' supposed immunity to "radical doctrines" and "Bolshevistic attitudes," their amenability to "discipline," and the "admirable fortitude" with which they accepted their "lot."[33]

As dominant as the image of the black strikebreaker was, strikebreaking was only one option open to black workers, and only a comparatively small number actively pursued it. Another minority among African Americans rejected that path, instead embracing trade unionism and the labor movement as their own. Despite the opposition of most union internationals, from the Reconstruction era onward, some blacks formed workplace associations to press for higher wages, better working conditions, and dignity and fair treatment on the job, particularly in trades in which they were concentrated in the South. By the 1880s, literally tens of thousands of African Americans were members of all-black trade unions. Their membership in such associations did not always depend on the approval of white workers, who often responded to black initiatives with indifference or hostility and only occasionally with enthusiasm. But when whites did make common cause with blacks, the results could be impressive. On southern docks and in coal mines, vibrant biracial labor movements emerged beginning in the 1880s. In New Orleans, to take but one example, white dock workers allied with blacks after the turn of the twentieth century not because of an ideological or humanitarian conversion experience, but because blacks themselves were organized, numerous, and strong, threatening to stand in the way of whites' advance if it promised to come at blacks' expense.

Although often organized into racially distinct locals, these organizations defied significant aspects of the southern racial order in their promotion of a common front across racial lines.[34]

Yet Gilded Age and Progressive Era efforts by longshoremen in New Orleans, Louisiana, and Galveston, Texas, or miners in Alabama's Birmingham district were exceptional, and even these were vulnerable to the vagaries of economic cycles, the determination of southern employers to live without unions, and the willingness of local and state officials to use force to back up employers' wishes. These local movements garnered occasional and provisional praise from black leaders, but more often than not such figures ignored them or criticized them as too risky. Organized labor's larger reputation for antiblack animus, black workers' precarious economic status, and leaders' class perspectives and ideological preferences ensured that that black elites would advise black workers to play it safe and stand clear of entangling alliances with their white counterparts. Given their commanding position in the pulpit and the black press, elites' preaching of the gospel of anti-unionism drowned out the quieter alternative voices of the black trade union.

Negroes, Booker T. Washington bluntly noted in 1913, were "very willing strike-breakers."[35] But how and why did black men, individually or collectively, arrive at their decision to cross white union picket lines and subject themselves to the scorn of the white community and often its violence? One explanation rests with the role of black elites: The actions that invariably provoked objections from white workers in the late nineteenth and early twentieth centuries usually evoked approval from black leaders.[36] Viewing white unions as a disruptive, hostile, discriminatory, and even un-American force, black elites (and, presumably, many black workers who broke strikes) had few ethical qualms about black strikebreaking. To the contrary, strikebreaking afforded advantages, not the least of which was jobs. "Those who have watched the strikes in this country for a decade or more," concluded the New Orleans *Southwestern Christian Advocate,* "have noted that the result of nearly every one has been the opening of some new door for the black laborer." By replacing white striking coal miners in Pana, Illinois, in 1898, black men from Alabama won, in the *Advocate's* eyes, "a fair chance to prove their worth as laborers to the Northern capitalist."[37] On the eve of the U.S. entry into World War I, the black weekly the *Chicago Defender* attributed black strikebreaking to the "prejudiced clannishness" of white trade unionists. "STRIKE-BREAKING is not the fort[e] of the Afro American," the paper explained, "yet he is perfectly justified under existing conditions. It is a matter of earning a livelihood."[38] To the *St. Louis Argus,* another black weekly, organized labor's racial policies rendered the very term *strikebreaker* a misnomer. "We do not relish the expression 'strike breaker' when referred to the Negro, because we want to be men as other men," it asserted during the 1919 steel strike. But the denial of the "privilege of joining most of the labor organizations," particularly the AFL, meant that blacks' opportunity to work in many industries has only "come when the wheels of these plants have been stopped or threatened with stoppage by reason of strikes." Should this earn black workers the harsh sobriquet of strikebreaker? The *Argus* claimed no—the charge of strikebreaker was "unjust." "We are not strike breakers . . . but we are workers, seeking to earn an honest living by the sweat of our brow." Blacks simply had "no alternat[iv]e," for they "must work when given the opportunity"; if that opportunity came only when white workers struck, so be it, for "necessity forces us to accept work when and where we can get it." All white unions had to do was "remove their ban on admitting colored men to their councils" and they would find the black worker "true and loyal" to the union cause.[39]

But even the rise of the more inclusive Congress of Industrial Organizations did not convince all black leaders that the time had come to adjust their thinking. As late as 1944, black educator Gordon B. Hancock would conclude that it was a "highly debatable question whether the Negro by reason of his desperate economic condition is morally bound to support the unions that deny him membership. . . . To expect impecunious Negroes to turn suddenly in their hunger and wretchedness and play the role of philanthropists is expecting too much of a group living on the ragged edge of existence." Strikebreaking might make unorganized black workers a "menace to organized labor." But, Hancock insisted, it was "better to be a menace than to be disregarded."[40]

Black elites' advocacy of faithful service, anti-unionism, and even strikebreaking stemmed from more than disapproval of white trade unions' racial values and practices. Beliefs about political economy and strategic necessity, as well as a paternalistic desire to advance black workers' interests in a discriminatory labor market, provided additional motivation. Racial dynamics aside, black conservatives often sounded a lot like white conservatives on the subject of labor unrest. Strikes caused "great annoyance and frequent discomfort to a large number of citizens" not involved in labor conflicts, went the argument advanced by black elites, and unions overleap their bounds when they try "to dictate to any man the kind of labor he must or must not employ." Trade unionists simply had no right to "dictate to another terms upon which they shall enter into a contract," no right to "interfere with the prosperity of individuals or corporations . . . or to prevent free and untrominelled [*sic*] use by its owners."[41]

Rights aside, black elites also appreciated the greater power often wielded by employers. "Strikes are dangerous; capital is powerful and the hard times are upon us," declared the Des Moines *Avalanche* during a miners' strike in Muchakinock, Iowa, in 1894. Applauding black miners' refusal to join their white counterparts, it simply advised: "Work while it can be had, arbitrate all matters and settle all difficulties."[42] When it came to providing jobs, black conservatives reminded anyone who would listen, it was capitalists—not white workers—who possessed what black labor desired. The "great industries" want to "foster and favor the Negro workman," Howard University's Kelly Miller explained in 1925. "For the Negro wantonly to flout their generous advances by joining the restless ranks which threaten industrial ruin would be fatuous suicide." Capitalists, not white workers, had extended the hand of friendship; it was the capitalist class, not white workers, that possessed the "culture and consciousness which hold even the malignity of race passion in restraint," Miller argued in a widely held assessment. "There is nothing in the white working class to which the Negro can appeal. They are the ones who lynch and burn and torture him. He must look to the upper element for law and order."[43]

However pragmatic such advice might sound, black elites further insisted that the struggle for employment was a matter of race workers' rights and dignity and worth whatever risks strikebreaking entailed. And there was little doubt that strikebreaking indeed involved risks. When white miners' violence resulted in blacks' deaths in Cartersville, Illinois, in 1899, one southern black editor expressed no regrets that blacks were opposed to white strikers. "[W]e prefer by great odds that seven Negroes should lose their lives in an attempt to make an honest living for their families than that one should be lynched on an accusation of rape," the *Advocate* solemnly but righteously insisted. "There is a great deal more in it for the race."[44] Six years later, black Chicagoans amplified the point. Following brutal white attacks on black strikebreakers during the 1905 teamsters' strike, clubwoman and antilynching activist Ida B. Wells-Barnett introduced a resolution praising the strikebreakers as "men who proved their value by risking their lives to obtain work" and endorsing the "constitutional right of all men to earn a living and protect themselves in the exercise of that right." At a mass protest meeting, black Chicagoans readily agreed, endorsing her resolution.[45]

As important as black leaders' advice and counsel might have been, other factors undoubtedly contributed to black men's decision to cross a white union picket line. Contemporaries, novelists, and historians have provided

numerous explanations for strikebreakers' behavior, including an unaware-
ness of strike conditions when recruited by labor agents, an unfamiliarity
with trade union principles, prior negative experience with white unions,
philosophical or practical objections to white union practices, and a desperate need for jobs.[46] Those who had recently migrated from the South to
the North, for instance, carefully measured their current situation against
the recent past, encouraging their course of action. Whatever problems
they faced in the North paled in comparison to those in the South. The
character of Big Mat, a southern migrant working in a northern steel mill
after World War I in William Attaway's 1941 novel *Blood on the Forge,* was
undoubtedly representative of a significant number of black newcomers
to the industrial North. As a union drive built up momentum in his community, "he knew that he would not join the union," Attaway explained.
"For a man who had so lately worked from dawn to dark in the fields twelve
hours and the long shift were not killing. For a man who had known no
personal liberties even the iron hand of the mills was an advancement."[47]
For other migrants, unfamiliarity with trade unionism likely was involved.
The white Chicago social reformer Mary McDowell recounted to black
social scientists Sterling Spero and Abram Harris an encounter between
a newly employed black stockyard worker and a union organizer during
the union drive of World War I. "'It all sounds pretty good to me,' said the
Negro" when the advantages of union membership were explained, "'but
what does Mr. Armour think about it?'"[48] The Interchurch World Movement's Commission of Inquiry into the 1919 steel strike also invoked the
novelty of northern jobs and the character of black workers' relationship
to management. "Unaccustomed to the complexities of modern large-scale
industry," it concluded, "the colored worker still regards his relationship to
his employer as a personal one. His grievances are his own affair."[49]

The behavior of many black strikebreakers, at least in Chicago and
Pittsburgh, could not be attributed solely to industrial inexperience, for
the commission also discovered that "the great numbers of negroes who
flowed into the . . . plants were conscious of strike breaking. . . . Through
many experiences negroes came to believe that the only way they could
break into a unionized industry was through strikebreaking." The Chicago Commission on Race Relations, established after the 1919 race riot,
arrived at a similar conclusion. The African Americans interviewed by its
members "often expressed themselves as distrustful of the unions because
prejudice in the unions has denied them equal benefits of membership."
Their first opportunity to break into a new industry often came only
through strikebreaking, and even if they earned less than the union scale,
their new wages were often higher than they had earned before. This, the

commission concluded, "tends to make them feel that they have more to gain through affiliation with such employers than by taking chances on what the unions offer them."[50] In such infertile soil, the seeds of trade unionism failed to take root among many black migrants.

Reconstructing the motivations and aspirations of black strikebreakers remains frustratingly difficult.[51] Largely if not entirely missing from discussions by contemporaries and historians are the voices and perspectives of black strikebreakers themselves. This should not be too surprising, for, after all, strikebreakers formed no lasting organizations that might have left a paper trail and published no newspapers or journals in which they explained their position. The black strikebreaker remains, to a large extent, a shadowy, silent figure glimpsed only through his actions or through the eyes of others. His portrait, painted by black elites, white trade unionists, and employers, is necessarily sketchy and impressionistic; it likely reflects the perspective of the observer more than that of the observed. Although the distortions produced by white employers, unionists, and journalists reflected their racial views or antipathies, those produced by the black elite reflected to a large extent its class bias. Black commentators frequently framed strikebreaking as a racial issue—as a legitimate response by African Americans to labor market discrimination and trade union exclusion. Strikebreaking was a racial issue, to be sure. But it was also a particular kind of class or labor issue. As much as black elites thought they spoke for black workers, their interests and perspectives could differ, sometimes subtly, sometimes sharply. Those elites' static and often caricatured portrayals of black workers and strikebreakers are undermined by explorations of the more complex world inhabited by black workers in the late nineteenth and early twentieth centuries. Two examples of black strikebreaking on the West Coast—on the Seattle docks in the World War I era and in western Washington state coal mines in the early 1890s—offer a lens into black working-class perspectives and are worth examining in detail.

In the 1960s, social scientist Horace Cayton recalled a revealing encounter he had during his youth in the World War I years near Yakima, Washington, with a white member of the Industrial Workers of the World. "I got nothing against the colored," his new friend "Red" lectured him. "But on the whole the colored don't make good union men. The white bosses have held them down so long they can't believe in anything except the rich." Red had "no use" for "race prejudice," which "just divides and confuses the working class, like religion." "The bosses make scabs out of Negroes to divide the workers," he continued. "Negroes shouldn't let themselves be used but they do. I remember one Negro we took care of during the strike on the waterfront. Caught him walking through the picket line and when we got through with him he'd learned about the class struggle. Bet he never broke a strike again!" Cayton was unimpressed. "I'd break a strike to get a decent job, beating or no beating," he replied. "Son, you got to realize that your people, and my people, too, have been the victims of a hundred and fifty years of slavery," Red retorted. "Right here in America. Human slavery. But there's wage slavery, too. . . . Negroes will have to learn to endure the present temporary state of things in order to bring about the new world of the workers. You got to have faith in the future, in the real leaders of labor."[52]

That, to young Cayton, proved to be pie in the sky. Just as Christianity was a myth to Red, the "new world of the workers" in the future was a myth to Cayton. The Wobbly's arguments made no convert of Cayton, and his subsequent experiences would only underscore its utopian fallacy. Upon receiving a letter from his father that a longshore strike in Seattle meant that waterfront jobs were numerous, he abandoned his position with the Great Northern and journeyed east to try his hand at dock work. With a newly purchased cargo hook and work gloves, Cayton finally felt himself "a man" ready to "earn big money." Dispatched to the piers at Smith's Cove, he and two other black strikebreakers were accosted by white strikers who pulled their trolley off the tracks. "Get up, you black son of a bitch!" angry whites howled at one of the men. "We'll teach you to break a strike and take the food out of our kids' mouths." When the man didn't move, his attacker swung a cargo hook into his neck, hauled him to his feet, and shouted, "We should burn you alive like they do down south!" The wounded man was taken from the car, accompanied by the second black strikebreaker. Stunned into absolute silence, Cayton was saved only by the timely intervention of an "apple-cheeked" white woman who angrily declared that Cayton was with her. White strikers demurred. "He looks too young, anyway," one replied. "No one is going to get hurt who isn't scabbing." Despite his brush with death, Cayton became a longshoreman, and the strike, with the assistance of numerous black strikebreakers, was eventually broken.[53]

Decades earlier, black pioneers in Cayton's Washington acted their part in a comparable drama involving the region's developing mining industry. Labor unrest was nothing new in King County, Washington, when the latest bout of union-management conflict erupted in the spring of 1891. In many respects the unfolding drama was a familiar one, resembling in broad strokes, if not in all its particulars, those taking place in coal-mining communities in Indiana, Illinois, Missouri, and Iowa.[54] In the early 1880s, white miners in the Washington mining towns of Newcastle, Roslyn, and Franklin had affiliated with the Knights of Labor. Although they had successfully driven Chinese workers out of the mines, the introduction of

400 black strikebreakers from the Midwest in 1888 enabled the Northern Pacific Coal Company to keep its union at bay in Roslyn for over a decade. Local managers of the financially strapped Oregon Improvement Company (OIC) drew inspiration from the Northern Pacific's example. In 1891, they brought matters to a head by demanding that the Knights accept a contract providing lower wages, barring any work stoppages, and imposing other onerous work rules. To the miners, this was nothing less than a "virtual surrendering by the employees of their individuality to the company," something the miners rejected as creating "a system of bondage equal [to] if not worse than chattel slavery." Predictably, they vowed to refuse to "submit to a surrender of their rights as American citizens." The stage was set for confrontation.[55]

According to the company's plan, OIC mine superintendent T. B. Corey then traveled east to Missouri, Iowa, Indiana, and Illinois, where he distributed handbills advertising for 500 black miners and laborers, promising "Good wages," "Steady work," and, apparently, "No strikes or trouble of any kind." Corey was familiar with the region and with black strikebreakers, having earlier worked as a mining superintendent in Braidwood, Illinois, where he had successfully recruited hundreds of blacks to break a white union strike. On May 13, his "Black Train" departed Saint Paul, Minnesota, with hundreds of experienced miners and at least 50 family members; they numbered as many as 675. Arriving in Washington on May 17, they began working the following day under the protection of 150 armed guards. To local whites, Franklin resembled "a place occupied by a hostile invading army," with whites playing the part of "natives of a captured city, the guards and their black cohorts answering to the captors."[56] Sympathy strikes by nearby white workers ensued, as did violence in late June; the Washington National Guard patrolled the mines for almost a month. Finally, in late July, white miners surrendered, agreeing to the wage cuts and conditions they had previously rejected. The Knights of Labor was effectively dead in King County, and black miners, once reviled as outsiders, found a permanent place in the region's mines.[57]

From the moment of their arrival, blacks were the targets of white workers' contempt. "'Well, boys, the niggers are coming!'" white strikers declared when they first heard word of the strikebreakers' impending arrival. "Look at Corey's black slaves," their wives declared as the train carrying hundreds of blacks pulled into Franklin.[58] Strikers invoked a common litany of charges against the newcomers: they were "ignorant blacks" who were part of a "systematic attempt to force the condition of Washington coal miners lower and lower until they should become absolutely passive instruments in the hands of the corporation"; they were "more submissive than white men," were poor miners, and were "only a little removed from slavery and barbarism." The 600 or so African American newcomers were "worthless individuals" taking the place of "honest laboring men," insisted a strike supporter. "These negroes, as serfs of a greedy corporation, have been brought here and protected in slavery by armed men for blood money." "Shame to the colored man who would advise the slavery of his race," he concluded; "shame to those who would perpetuate this slavery."[59]

The objects of relentless physical and verbal attacks, black strikebreakers and their supporters defended themselves, refuting accusations of inferiority, violence, and ignorance leveled at them by their white working-class opponents. In many cases experienced miners themselves, they had had ample opportunity to observe white unions in action and found them wanting. Far from the ignorant dupes of capital that whites found them to be, black miners knew what they were doing, and many, in fact, justified what they did on the grounds of American citizenship, which they asserted against a backdrop of deep discrimination and white hostility as a matter of economic necessity and as a matter of pride.

To black miner Charles H. Johnson, America's long and enduring history of oppressing its black population gave African Americans little choice if they hoped to survive economically. "We know that we are scoffed at and looked upon as the dregs of all races because we have been oppressed by the cursed yoke of bondage," he informed readers of the *Seattle Post-Intelligencer*. "If there is one race on the globe which has a grievance, it is the poor colored folk," a people abused and excluded by other groups. "Now, the labor unions will condemn us and make us believe that we are everything but a people. They say we are insulting, presumptuous and without character. We take all that without a murmur." Aware that "prejudice is against us" in Franklin, he insisted that it "is against us everywhere," with whites expecting blacks to "stand back and suffer while others live." This Johnson and his cohort refused to do. "Let them call us scabs if they want to," he noted of the white strikers. "We have concluded that half a loaf is better than none." Disavowing any malice, Johnson wanted "the world to know that we are not the fools that some think we are. We want to live and to let others live."[60]

Citizenship rights and resistance to racial subordination were the themes emphasized by black miner G. S. Bailey: "[W]hen a black man begins to assert his rights of American citizenship it very often creates a commotion in the public mind," for "[e]vil and designing men hold him up to the public gaze with scorn and derision, falsifying almost every statement made in regard to him." Any man with "courage to champion his cause" is "branded as a villain and unfit for public confidence." But the time had finally come for African Americans to show that "the cry, 'This is a white man's country,' does not hold water." Yet doing so would come at a cost: for exercising the rights of citizenship guaranteed under the law, "we are misrepresented and all manner of bad things said about us"; whites "seek to assassinate and murder us." The "white man has had our sweat, our blood, our strength, and our lives for nearly 300 years," he continued, robbing blacks and depriving them "of the chance to accumulate wealth and accomplishments of learning and are seeking to do the same things today. They deny us the right to make a contract to suit ourselves, and when we have done this they call us savages," boycotting blacks' employers and threatening their lives, "simply because they give us the work that the white men refused to do." But blacks would no longer be deterred; "we do not care who it pleases or who it does not. We will make just such contacts as we want to make, and live up to them when they are made. . . . All we ask is to be let alone." This was not an isolated struggle, confined to the ranks of Washington's newest black arrivals. Bailey predicted that blacks would "continue to use all our energy and influence to infuse into the minds of the people of color of the United States that spirit of manhood and independence that so fitly characterizes true American citizens, for which our color sacrificed their lives in the late civil war. . . . We shall endeavor to attend to our own business, make our own contracts, work for whom we please[,] get as much wages as we can, save our earnings and claim a respectable place among the people in the community in which we live."[61]

These views were amplified in the joint statement of three other black miners—John Bedell, Phil Taylor, and Prest Loving—who also invoked notions of patriotism and nativism. "This is a free country to all law-abiding American citizens," they insisted in an attempt to contrast African Americans' behavior with that of immigrant radicals. The "colored men's record stands upon the pages of history." That history included not just a long-term residence in America, but consistent loyalty and patriotic service to the nation through the taking up of arms on behalf of "liberty and freedom" during the war for American independence, the War of 1812, the Mexican war, and, of course, the "war of the late rebellion" to defend "our flag of liberty." "Hence we feel a right to work in any part of our native country," they continued, to which "no true born American citizen would raise any objection." Only "European paupers"—men "who come to this country for their liberty and freedom" and who even before they are "naturalized . . . are ready to agitate strikes and lead riots"—questioned blacks' right to work. "[T]rue born Americans—like African Americans—were too proud "to engage in anything to disgrace" their country; in contrast, labor unions were "largely composed of the foreigners to rule or ruin" who daily harassed the black miners in Washington. Then came the challenge: If white miners were "so aggrieved by the colored man mining in King county," they concluded, "we would advise them to leave and make room for a more peaceable class of citizens."[62]

Denied equal rights and respect in the nation's political, social, and economic arenas, the black strikebreakers in western Washington expressed bitter resentment at the history of racial inequities and their treatment at the hands of white society. They also unapologetically justified their taking of jobs from striking white miners as an economic necessity, as an exercise of their right to employment and contract in a market economy, and as a matter of right based on decades of patriotic service and citizenship. For many, the journey west was a permanent move in search of opportunity. Some were accompanied by their families—an indication of their desire to settle in Washington—whereas many others sent for relatives once they firmly established themselves in the mining communities. In subsequent generations, these men and women would be remembered by their descendants as "black pioneers," family firsts who established an enduring black presence in Washington state. Long after African Americans, both workers and elites, warmed to the labor movement, black Washingtonians would recall with pride, and without apology, the courageous accomplishment of this pioneering generation. There is no question that in breaking racial employment barriers, Washington's black pioneers had demonstrated the capacity of black workers to compete with whites and, in so doing, furthered the economic advancement of the race. That much black elites would have approved of and white workers would have objected to. But in their own way—a way that neither black elites nor white unionists could appreciate—they were engaged in a distinctive form of black working-class activism, one that entailed physical risks, required group solidarity, and demonstrated collective bravery, forethought, and determination.

———————

Across the country in Rendville, Ohio, the Washington state coal miners' strike caught the eye of Richard L. Davis, an African American organizer for the United Mine Workers of America (UMWA). Born in Roanoke, Virginia, in 1865, Davis had lived in Rendville, a Hocking Valley mining community, since 1882. He gravitated toward the orbit of organized labor by 1890, when he was elected to the young UMWA's District 6 executive board in Ohio; in 1896, he was elected to the union's national executive board. In addition to his organizing efforts, Davis devoted considerable energy to writing about organized labor and the relationship between black and white workers, penning a steady flow of letters to labor periodicals such as the *United Mine Workers Journal* and the *National Labor Tribune* that revealed him to be a tireless advocate of black trade union affiliation, a proponent of interracial unionism, and a critic of white labor's racism. In late July 1891, Davis received a clipping from a friend, containing the letter to the *Seattle Post-Intelligencer* written by strikebreaker G. S. Bailey and recounted above. Davis, who rarely missed an opportunity to preach organized labor's cause, again took up the pen to refute the Franklin miner's arguments, which, in Davis's eyes, needed "severe criticism." In so doing, he articulated a moral and political vision that ran counter to the advice of most black elites and charted a far different path for black workers' advancement.[63]

At the heart of his critique, Davis damned those who would break strikes like Bailey. The "blackleg," he charged, "should not be allowed to live among decent people." To Bailey's depiction of white strikers' efforts to "murder and assassinate" African Americans, Davis firmly responded by justifying white trade unionists' violent response: "I would like to ask the gentlemen this question, suppose that you were working in a place and the company brought in three or four hundred white men to take your places." What would be the result? "I fancy you would not speak as you do now," Davis continued. "No, sir, you would pick [up] your gun if you had one, and you would try to kill every white man that you saw, whether he was your enemy or not." The defense of community and union standards rendered understandable, even sympathetic, white attempts to repulse the strikebreakers' advance, in Davis's opinion.

Fundamentally, Davis charged Bailey with misrepresenting the status of African Americans at the end of the nineteenth century. "How utterly false!" was Bailey's claim that the Negro had been a chattel slave a quarter century earlier but was now a "free American citizen." Drawing on a broader white labor discourse of wage slavery, Davis contrasted the antebellum and postbellum eras. "None of us who toil for our daily bread are free. At one time, as he has said, we were chattel slaves; to day [*sic*] we are, one and all, white and black slaves." The "chains of bondage" were firmly forged around workers by "just such actions as have been taken in the state of Washington." And, for Davis, black strikebreakers merely played into employers' hands. The time had finally come "that the negro should know better than to run from place to place to break down wages. . . . He can plainly see that the money kings of this country are only using him as a tool to fill his own coffers with gold." Black gains at whites' expense involved undercutting white labor and an acceptance of an inequality of condition. If and when black strikebreakers came around to asking for the same conditions as unionized whites, employers would "have no further need for you." The answer was not for blacks to stoop beneath whites' level, but to organize themselves:

> I would say to the negro, of which race I am proud to be connected, let us be men; let us demand as much for our labor as any other nationality; let us not suffer ourselves to be trampled upon any more than any other people. We are a people; we are men; we constitute one-sixth of this great country so far as numbers are concerned, consequently it is not a white man's country; it is partly ours as well, so let us prove ourselves men and the equal of any others.

Where black elites counseled reliance on employers, regardless of the conditions of work or rates of pay, Davis insisted on another path: "the labor organizations will do more for the negro than any political party can or ever will do. So let us get into them and try to make this country what it should be."[64]

Davis's jeremiad was, in this instance, directed at blacks who not only engaged in strikebreaking activity, but did so proudly and aggressively. Answering G. S. Bailey required Davis to ignore the strikebreaker's complaints against white violence and the long history of white opposition to black economic advancement. But Davis was hardly unmindful of the realities Bailey addressed and, on other occasions, would direct his tirades against whites who refused to deal fairly with blacks. "I assure anyone that I have more respect for a scab than I have for a person who refers to the negro" as "big black buck niggers," as one white did in the pages of his union journal, Davis declared in 1898, "and God knows the scab I utterly despise." Strikebreaking (as Bailey implied) stemmed from white hostility to blacks. "[Y]ou seldom hear of negroes being brought in . . . to break a strike" where blacks and whites worked together. "I say treat the negro right and he will treat you right."[65]

In this last piece of advice, Davis was not entirely wrong. During the 1880s, some 60,000 African Americans (other estimates put the number at 90,000 in 1887), organized into 400 union locals, affiliated with the Knights of Labor, an association open to workers regardless of race (with the exception of the Chinese). In defiance of black elites' standard advice, black Knights and other trade unionists engaged in extensive strike activity in Virginia, Florida, Alabama, Texas, and Louisiana, among other places. As Sidney Kessler concluded more than a half century ago, from the end of Reconstruction through the Populist upsurge of the 1890s, black workers did "not resign themselves to passivity," as elites recommended, but "pressed for their demands, not only as Negroes, but also as working men and women."[66] Even when the inclusionary Knights collapsed and the restrictive American Federation of Labor became the nation's dominant labor organization in the 1890s, black workers in specific industries formed numerous all-black unions, whose successes or failures reflected those of the larger labor movement, as well as the racial dynamics in their trades and communities. By the opening of the twentieth century, as many as 5,000 black dock workers were union members in New Orleans alone, and thousands more organized in Galveston and Houston, Texas; Mobile, Alabama; Key West, Florida; Savannah, Georgia; Newport News, Virginia; and Baltimore, Maryland. African American unionists in the Birmingham coal district numbered just over 5,000, and in the piney woods of Louisiana and east Texas they also numbered in the thousands. Black domestic workers and washerwomen formed small union locals in St. Petersburg, Florida; Norfolk, Virginia; Little Rock, Arkansas; Houston, Texas; Mobile, Alabama; and New Orleans, Louisiana, during the 1910s, as did Virginia tobacco stemmers and oyster shuckers, Florida phosphate miners, and Chicago and New York Pullman porters. Where white workers erected few organizational barriers or treated "the negro right," in Davis's words, black workers often proved ready converts to the union cause. And even where whites did erect barriers, blacks often found self-organization to be a necessary tool of self-defense. Although the genuine breakthrough of black workers into the labor movement would await the rise of the industrial union movement of the 1930s, a tradition of black unionism embracing literally tens of thousands of African American workers—albeit a small if nonetheless significant minority of all such workers—emerged in the years between the 1880s and 1920s.

What black elite proponents of industrial accommodationism consistently failed to understand was that for many black workers, not all workplace issues were primarily racial; that is, everything experienced in the labor market could not be reduced to a matter of race. Like whites, black workers objected to low wages, intolerable working conditions, abusive managers, and workplace humiliation, some of it racial, much of it not. Nothing in the black elites' program spoke to these on-the-job realities. To the contrary, their advice suggested that blacks should work harder, accept lower wages, and endure harsher conditions than whites, in an attempt to curry employers' favor. All that seemed to matter was access to jobs, not the quality of life on the job. For all their talk about manhood, economic citizenship, and dignity, the elites' strategy in effect counseled black labor loyalty, passivity, and subordination to employers. Some black workers were willing to take the bargain, but many were not, and they turned to collective action in an attempt to address the exploitative and often brutal conditions under which they labored. By the late nineteenth and early twentieth centuries, the gospel of trade unionism appealed not merely to whites, but to a significant minority of African Americans, as well.[67]

If trade unionism and strikebreaking were both forms of black working-class activism, the factors pushing black workers in one direction or the other were grounded in their concrete experiences and evolved over time. To World War I–era migrants from the southern countryside where unions were nonexistent, or from urban centers where they were discriminatory, a policy of skepticism or caution toward the northern union movement appeared prudent. But with industrial experience came a frustration that black elite wisdom proved incapable of addressing. Following the collapse of the Seattle waterfront strike, even young Horace Cayton, who had witnessed brutal physical attacks on his fellow black strikebreakers, eventually joined a revived union in an effort to improve working conditions, encouraging other blacks to join, as well. In this instance, however, their effort was to little avail. Although they succeeded in establishing a black and white local and winning a closed shop and union dispatching office, persistent discrimination against blacks soured Cayton on the experience, leading him to conclude, "you just couldn't trust any white man."[68]

But others arrived at a different conclusion. Many black miners in western Washington slowly migrated to larger towns and to Seattle, where work opportunities were greater. By the time the United Mine Workers revived after 1900, former strikebreakers joined with their white counterparts to tackle their common workplace grievances. Black migrants in northern packinghouses also made the transition from union skeptics, opponents, and strikebreakers during and after World War I to union stalwarts in the 1930s; as shop-floor veterans during the Great Depression, many spearheaded organizing efforts in the 1930s and contributed to the formation of one of the nation's most racially progressive unions, the Packinghouse Workers Organizing Committee. Together with whites, they tackled not only workplace racial discrimination, but issues ignored by black elites— "slim pay envelopes," the "lean months of poverty," the "prolonged agony of layoffs," and the "mutual fear and distrust" that blacks and whites "slaved side by side in." Similarly, the Brotherhood of Sleeping Car Porters campaigned tirelessly, and successfully, in the late 1920s through the mid-1930s to win over not just black workers but the black elite to a pro-union stance.[69]

Black elites were slower to abandon their conventional economic nostrums and traditional accommodationist advice, but many came around slowly to supporting black workers' collective initiatives by the Great Depression and World War II. So did an important wing of the American labor movement, particularly the industrial unions affiliated with the new Congress of Industrial Organizations (CIO). The "colored workers should lose no time in getting in on the ground floor of this new labor movement," the

Washington *Afro-American* implored in 1937. With the CIO's "doors wide open" to blacks, there was "absolutely no future in scabbing." In contrast to the sorry record of the AFL, concluded black scholar Rayford Logan in 1944, the CIO "has been the most aggressive organization in recent years in promoting not only economic equality for the Negro but also political and even social equality." That same year, the *Northwest Herald,* a weekly black paper from Seattle, similarly observed that "in less than 10 years, the Labor Movement has become the most powerful force for progress in the Negro community. . . . Where the Negroes feared unions yesterday, today Negroes look to the labor unions with hope for a New Day." Shortly after the end of World War II, Julius A. Thomas informed readers of the National Urban League's *Opportunity* that "[N]o observer of the current scene can overlook the fact that a change has taken place in the Negro's economic thinking." In contrast to their experiences during and after World War I, "there are no Negro strikebreakers in 1946. Instead, thousands of black workers have merged their strength and voices with those of millions of white workers in one nation-wide demand for a better place in the sun."[70] There was an element of exaggeration in these claims, to be sure, but such assessments would have been unthinkable only a decade or two earlier. As contemporaries recognized, the emergence of a new generation of black workplace activists, coupled with the rise of a hopeful new industrial union movement during the 1930s and 1940s, irrevocably altered the relationship of African Americans to the organized labor movement for the better.

The historic 1941 face-off between the United Automobile Workers of America (UAW) and the Ford Motor Company in Detroit wrote something of an obituary for the classic strikebreaker saga. Although not all of black Detroit's leaders endorsed the UAW, many did; although not all black workers left the Ford plant when the strike was declared, many responded to the strikers' plea for support. And although Ford "had deliberately injected the race issue by utilizing blacks as strikebreakers," in August Meier and Elliott Rudwick's words, the UAW and pro-union black leaders closely collaborated to defuse racial tensions, appealing to strikebreakers to join the walkout and holding "the Ford Motor Company, not the blacks, responsible for the 'crime' of strikebreaking." Their efforts proved successful.[71] The growing number of black trade unionists did not mean that labor movement discrimination had vanished. Rather, black activists would campaign to eliminate barriers to participation and advancement by working within unions or through institutions such as the state and federal courts and the World War II–era Fair Employment Practice Committee. The figure of the black strikebreaker—long a fearful specter looming in the collective white working-class imagination, as well as a conservative, even valiant, force in the eyes of black elites—lost much of its emotional, psychological, and political force. Strikebreaking, by both blacks and whites, never vanished, of course. But the once-powerful concept of the black strikebreaker was largely laid to rest.

Notes

1. W. S. Carter, "The Mills of God," serialized in *Locomotive Firemen's Magazine* (February 1898), 146; (May 1898), 488; (June 1898), 632; (November 1898), 498; 25, no. 6 (December 1898), 606–8.

2. Carter, "The Mills of God," *Locomotive Firemen's Magazine* 25, no. 6 (December 1898), 606–7.

3. Carter, "The Mills of God" (December 1898), 606.

4. "The Labor Movement: A Race War in Illinois," *Locomotive Firemen's Magazine* 25, no. 4 (October 1898), 378–79; Letter from W. L. F., *Locomotive Firemen's Magazine* 25, no. 5 (November 1898), 541–42; "Illinois Miners Win," *Railway Trainmen's Journal* 15, no. 12 (December 1898), 1005–96; Victor Hicken, "The Virden and Pana Mine Wars of 1898," *Journal of the Illinois State Historical Society* 12, no. 2 (Summer 1959), 263–78; "The Labor Factor in Race Troubles," *The Literary Digest* 27, no. 26 (December 24, 1898), 740–41; Ray Ginger, "Were Negroes Strikebreakers?" *Negro History Bulletin* 15, no. 4 (January 1952), 73–74. Also see Ronald L. Lewis, *Black Coal Miners in America: Race, Class, and Community Conflict, 1780–1980* (Lexington: University Press of Kentucky, 1987).

5. This essay addresses the image of black male strikebreakers only. Although black women (like white women) also served as strikebreakers, they were far fewer in number and never commanded the attention nor generated the hostility from whites that black men did. Similarly, black elites addressed themselves primarily to the issue of black men's anti-unionism and strikebreaking, not that of black women.

6. As economist Warren Whatley has demonstrated, immigrant strikebreakers outnumbered African American ones, and employers were most likely to turn to blacks as a source of strikebreakers when immigration rates were low. Warren Whatley, "African-American Strikebreaking from the Civil War to the New Deal," *Social Science History* 17 (1993), 555–58; Joshua L. Rosenbloom, *Looking for Work, Searching for Workers: American Labor Markets during Industrialization* (New York: Cambridge University Press, 2002), 42, 54. On the extent and character of black strikebreaking, see Ginger, "Were Negroes Strikebreakers?" 73–74; Sterling D. Spero and Abram L. Harris, *The Black Worker: The Negro and the Labor Movement* (1931; rpt. New York: Atheneum, 1969), 128–46.

7. Roach quoted in Rick Halpern, *Down on the Killing Floor: Black and White Workers in Chicago's Packinghouses, 1904–54* (Urbana: University of Illinois Press, 1997), 39; "Race Hatred Cannot Displace Class Struggle," *Chicago Socialist,* October 8, 1904.

8. Quoted in William M. Tuttle, *Race Riot: Chicago in the Red Summer of 1919* (1970; rpt. New York: Atheneum, 1985), 112. White packinghouse strikers would again hang a black effigy marked "nigger scab" a decade later during the 1904 strike. See James R. Barrett, *Work and Community in the Jungle: Chicago's Packinghouse Workers, 1894–1922* (Urbana: University of Illinois Press, 1987), 172.

9. *Broad Ax,* October 15, 1904, quoted in Allan H. Spear, *Black Chicago: The Making of a Negro Ghetto, 1890–1920* (Chicago: University of Chicago Press, 1967), 39. Whites did not monopolize this metaphor. During the Chicago teamsters' strike the following year, the black weekly *Broad Ax* questioned employers' use of blacks merely as "brutish clubs to beat their white help over the head." *Broad Ax,* May 6, 1905, quoted in Spear, *Black Chicago,* 39. On blacks and the 1904 packinghouse strike, also see Daniel Murray, "The Industrial Problem of the United States and the Negro's Relation to It," *Voice of the Negro* 6, no. 9 (September 1904), 403–4; William M. Tuttle Jr., "Some Strikebreakers' Observations of Industrial Warfare," *Labor History* 7, no. 2 (Spring 1966), 193–96; "Labor Notes," *Chicago Socialist,* August 13, 1904; A. M. Simons, "The Packingtown Strike," *Chicago Socialist,* August 6, 1904; A. M. Simons, "The Battle of the Meat Makers," *Chicago Socialist,* August 27, 1904. On the 1905 Chicago teamsters' strike, also see R. R. Wright Jr., "The Negro in Times of Industrial Unrest," *Charities* 15, no. 1 (October 7, 1905), 69–73; David Witwer, "Unionized Teamsters and the Struggle over the Streets of the Early-Twentieth-Century City," *Social Science History* 24, no. 1 (2000), 183–222. A black socialist writer, D. E. Tobias, offered his interpretation in "Black Strike-Breakers," *Chicago Socialist,* May 27, 1905, and "Black Strike-Breakers," *Chicago Socialist,* May 13, 1905.

10. *Seattle Post-Intelligencer,* May 19, 1891. On strikebreakers being held as virtual prisoners at their new work sites, see Linda Nyden, "Black Miners in Western Pennsylvania, 1925–1931: The National Miners Union and the United Mine Workers of America," *Science and Society* 41, no. 1 (Spring 1977), 82–83.

11. "The Labor Movement: A Race War in Illinois," *Locomotive Firemen's Magazine* 25, no. 4 (October 1898), 379.

12. A small number of black leaders, including T. Thomas Fortune, rejected strike-breaking as a viable or desirable option for black workers. "We lay it down dogmatically that the colored laborers cannot afford to antagonize the interests of white laborers, for the interests of the one and the other are identical in every particular." "Pernicious Labor Teachings," *New York Freeman,* May 1, 1886; see also "White and Colored Laborers Detrimental," *New York Freeman,* December 4, 1886.

13. The scholarly literature on black labor activists in the late nineteenth and early twentieth centuries is large. See Herbert Gutman, "The Negro and the United Mine Workers of America: The Career and Letters of Richard L. Davis and Something of Their Meaning, 1890–1900," in *The Negro and the American Labor Movement* (New York: Anchor Books, 1968), 49–127; Peter J. Rachleff, *Black Labor in Richmond, 1865–1890* (1984; rpt. Urbana: University of Illinois Press, 1988); Dolores E. Janiewski, *Sisterhood Denied: Race, Gender, and Class in a New South Community* (Philadelphia: Temple University Press, 1985); Robin D. G. Kelley, "'We Are Not What We Seem': Rethinking Black Working-Class Opposition in the Jim Crow South," *Journal of American History* 80 (June 1993), 73–112; Ronald Lewis, *Black Coal Miners in America: Race, Class, and Community Conflict, 1780–1980* (Lexington: University of Kentucky Press, 1987); Daniel Letwin, *The Challenge of Interracial Unionism: Alabama Coal Miners, 1878–1921* (Chapel Hill: University of North Carolina Press, 1997); Brian Kelly, *Race, Class, and Power in the Alabama Coalfields, 1908–21* (Urbana: University of Illinois Press, 2001); Daniel Rosenberg, *New Orleans Dockworkers: Race, Labor, and Unionism, 1892–1923* (Albany: State University of New York Press, 1988); Eric Arnesen, "Biracial Waterfront

Unionism in the Age of Segregation," in Cal Winslow, ed., *Waterfront Workers: New Essays on Race and Class* (Urbana: University of Illinois Press, 1998); Stephen H. Norwood, "Bogalusa Burning: The War against Biracial Unionism in the Deep South, 1919," *Journal of Southern History* 63 (August 1997), 591–628; Earl Lewis, *In Their Own Interests: Race, Class, and Power in Twentieth-Century Norfolk, Virginia* (Berkeley: University of California Press, 1991); Eric Arnesen, "Following the Color Line of Labor: Black Workers and the Labor Movement before 1930," *Radical History Review* no. 55 (Winter 1993), 53–87; Tera W. Hunter, *To 'Joy My Freedom: Southern Black Women's Lives and Labors after the Civil War* (Cambridge, Mass.: Harvard University Press, 1997).

14. "The Dusky Race," *New York Times,* March 2, 1869. Also see Henry Gannett, "Occupation of the Negroes," the Trustees of the John F. Slater Fund Occasional Papers, no. 6 (Baltimore: Trustees of the John F. Slater Fund, 1895).

15. On black workers and the World War I–era "Great Migration," see Eric Arnesen, "The Great American Protest," in Arnesen, *Black Protest and the Great Migration: A Brief History with Documents* (Boston: Bedford Books, 2002).

16. James Weldon Johnson, *Black Manhattan* (New York: Knopf, 1930), 61.

17. Langston Hughes, "My America," in Rayford Logan, ed., *What the Negro Wants* (Chapel Hill: University of North Carolina Press, 1944), 300.

18. William Garrott Brown, *The New Politics and Other Papers* (Boston: Houghton Mifflin, 1914), 111.

19. C. Fabe Martin, Washington, D.C., in "Land and Labor Problems," *New York Freeman,* March 13, 1886.

20. Charles B. Spahr, *America's Working People* (New York: Longmans, Green, 1900), 78–79.

21. Will M. Clemens, "The Workers of the South," *New York Freeman,* January 22, 1887 (from *New York Standard*).

22. Sir George Campbell, M.P., *White and Black: The Outcome of a Visit to the United States* (1879; rpt. New York: Negro Universities Press, 1969).

23. "Negro Shiftlessness," *Manufacturers' Record* 48, no. 23 (December 21, 1905); "Some Casual Observations on the Condition of the Southern Laborer," *New York Age,* July 7, 1888.

24. Campbell, *White and Black,* 143.

25. "Difficulties of the Labor Problem in Southern Industries," *Manufacturers' Record* 48, no. 1 (July 20, 1905), 5.

26. "Industrial Asset," *New York Age,* May 25, 1916.

27. "Importance of the Labor Question," New Orleans *Southwestern Christian Advocate,* October 15, 1903; "The Labor Question in the South," New Orleans *Southwestern Christian Advocate,* September 20, 1906. Also see "The Negro Laborer," *Southern Workman* 37, no. 1 (January 1908), 4–5.

28. Quoted in Horace Mann Bond, *Negro Education in Alabama: A Study in Cotton and Steel* (1939; rpt. New York: Atheneum, 1969), 170. Also see Kelly, *Race, Class, and Power in the Alabama Coalfields,* 98–101.

29. "Editorial Perambulations," New Orleans *Southwestern Christian Advocate,* May 20, 1886.

30. "The Reliable Laborer," *Weekly Call,* July 21, 1894.

31. "The Negro Laborer," *Southern Workman,* 4.

32. The Commission of Inquiry, the Interchurch World Movement, *Report on the Steel Strike of 1919* (New York: Harcourt, Brace and Hoe, 1920), 177–78; James D. Rose, *Duquesne and the Rise of Steel Unionism* (Urbana: University of Illinois Press, 2001), 31. A National Urban League official concluded that although blacks in Pittsburgh "did not know what the issues were between the white steel worker and the employer"—whites had made no effort to "acquaint" blacks with the issues—he believed that "the results would have been the same if they had made such an effort," for the "experiences of the Negro seeking work in steel had forced him to believe that there was as much sacredness about the principles involved in the right to earn a living as were involved in the principles for which white steel workers were striking." John T. Clark, "The Negro in Steel," *Opportunity* 2, no. 22 (October 1924), 300.

33. Arnesen, "The Great American Protest"; Peter Gottlieb, *Making Their Own Way: Southern Blacks' Migration to Pittsburgh, 1916–30* (Urbana: University of Illinois Press, 1987), 161–62. Black leaders, too, employed the argument that black workers eschewed radicalism. See Emmet J. Scott's letter to US Steel Corporation president Elbert H. Gary in "Negro Labor for the Steel Mills," *World's Work* 46, no. 3 (July 1923), 243.

34. Daniel Letwin, *The Challenge of Interracial Unionism: Alabama Coal Miners, 1878–1921* (Chapel Hill: University of North Carolina Press, 1998); Eric Arnesen, "Biracial Waterfront Unionism in the Age of Segregation," in Calvin Winslow, ed., *Waterfront Workers: New Perspectives on Race and Class* (Urbana: University of Illinois Press, 1998), 19–61.

35. Booker T. Washington, "The Negro and the Labor Unions," *Atlantic Monthly* 111 (June 1913), 757.

36. On the influence of black elites among black workers, see Horace R. Cayton and George S. Mitchell, *Black Workers and the New Unions* (Chapel Hill: University of North Carolina Press, 1939), 375–80, 393–96.

37. "Prepare for the Industrial Warfare," New Orleans *Southwestern Christian Advocate,* September 4, 1902.

38. "Labor Troubles," *Chicago Defender,* July 3, 1915.

39. "The Steel Strike," *St. Louis Argus,* October 24, 1919.

40. Gordon B. Hancock, "Race Relations in the United States: A Summary," in Rayford Logan, ed., *What the Negro Wants* (1944; rpt. Notre Dame, Ind.: University of Notre Dame Press, 2001), 231, 243.

41. New Orleans *Southwestern Christian Advocate,* July 21, 1904; Editorial, Kansas City, Missouri *American Citizen,* July 6, 1894. On opposition to sympathy strikes, see *Southwestern Christian Advocate,* July 28, 1904.

42. Des Moines, Iowa, *Avalanche,* quoted in *Huntsville Gazette,* May 26, 1894. Also see *McDowell Times,* December 5, 1913.

43. Kelly Miller, "The Negro as a Workingman," *American Mercury* (November 1925), 313, quoted in Spero and Harris, *The Black Worker,* 134.

44. New Orleans *Southwestern Christian Advocate,* September 1, 1898.

45. Stephen H. Norwood, *Strikebreaking and Intimidation: Mercenaries and Masculinity in Twentieth-Century America* (Chapel Hill: University of North Carolina Press, 2002), 103.

46. James R. Grossman, *Land of Hope: Chicago, Black Southerners, and the Great Migration* (Chicago: University of Chicago Press, 1989), 210, 214–17; Spear, *Black Chicago,*

37; Arna Bontemps and Jack Conroy, *Anyplace but Here* (New York: Hill and Wang, 1966), 136–44; Eric West Hard, "The Relation of the Negro to Trade Unionism" (M.A. thesis, University of Chicago, 1901), 34–36.

47. William Attaway, *Blood on the Forge* (1941; rpt. New York: Monthly Review Press, 1987), 222.

48. Spero and Harris, *The Black Worker*, 130.

49. Commission of Inquiry, Interchurch World Movement, *Report on the Steel Strike of 1919* (New York: Harcourt, Brace and Hoe, 1920), 138, 178. On the 1919 steel strike, also see Cliff Brown and Terry Boswell, "Strikebreaking or Solidarity in the Great Steel Strike of 1919: A Split Labor Market, Game-Theoretic, and QCA Analysis," *American Journal of Sociology* 100, no. 6 (May 1995), 1479–1519.

50. Commission of Inquiry, Interchurch World Movement, *Report on the Steel Strike of 1919*, 138, 178; Chicago Commission on Race Relations, *The Negro in Chicago: A Study of Race Relations and a Race Riot* (Chicago: University of Chicago Press, 1922), 404. Also see Wright Jr., "The Negro in Times of Industrial Unrest," 69–73; Joe William Trotter Jr., *Black Milwaukee: The Making of an Industrial Proletariat, 1915–45* (Urbana: University of Illinois Press, 1988), 39–40, 276–77.

51. "[L]ittle is known about strikebreakers: who they were; their motives in signing on for such employment; working conditions they encountered. . . . Strikebreakers are anonymities," William Tuttle argued in 1966. Tuttle, "Some Strikebreakers' Observations of Industrial Warfare," *Labor History* 7, no. 2 (Spring 1966), 193. Recently, Stephen H. Norwood provocatively argued that strikebreaking "appealed to many African Americans because it provided the black man his best opportunity to assume a tough, combative posture in public and to display courage while risking serious physical injury or even death. Strikebreaking thus allowed African American men to challenge openly white society's image of them as obsequious, cowardly, and lacking the ability to perform well under pressure." This may have been the case, but in discussing his two principal examples—the national 1904 packinghouse strike and the 1905 Chicago teamsters' strike—Norwood featured few voices of strikebreakers and instead relied heavily on the views of the white press, labor leaders, and the black middle class. His emphasis on the centrality of black masculinity is not based on black workers' own interpretations of their motivations. Norwood, *Strikebreaking and Intimidation*, 80. For a similar critique, see Brian Kelly's review, "Bad Ol' Boys: Scabs, Labor Spies, and Gun-Slinging Entrepreneurs," *Reviews in American History* 31, no. 1 (March 2003), 101–9.

52. Horace R. Cayton, *Long Old Road: An Autobiography* (1963; rpt. Seattle: University of Washington Press, 1970), 101, 107, 109.

53. Ibid., 110–14. On Seattle longshoremen in this era, see Dana Frank, *Purchasing Power: Consumer Organizing, Gender, and the Seattle Labor Movement, 1919–1929* (New York: Cambridge University Press, 1994), 27–28, 165–66. On race and Seattle's dock workers, also see *Seattle Union Record,* July 22, 1916; "Water Front Strike," *Cayton's Weekly,* April 19, 1919.

54. Herbert Gutman, "Labor in the Land of Lincoln: Coal Miners on the Prairie," in Gutman, *Power and Culture: Essays on the American Working Class* (New York: Pantheon Books, 1987), 117–212; Ronald Lewis, *Black Coal Miners in America.*

55. "300 Miners Strike," *Tacoma Daily News,* April 2, 1891; "Out in Washington,"

United Mine Workers Journal, June 4, 1891; Mark Stern, "Black Strikebreaking in the Coal Fields: King County, Washington—1891," *Journal of Ethnic Studies* 5, no. 3 (Fall 1977), 60–70; Robert A. Campbell, "Blacks and the Coal Mines of Western Washington, 1888–1896," *Pacific Northwest Quarterly* 73, no. 4 (October 1982), 146–55; Alan A. Hynding, "The Coal Miners of Washington Territory: Labor Troubles in 1888–89," *Arizona and the West* 12, no. 3 (Autumn 1970), 221–36; Norwood, *Strikebreaking and Intimidation;* Hobart W. McNeill, "Trouble in the Coal Mines, 1889," *Pacific Northwest Quarterly* 37, no. 3 (July 1946), 231–57.

56. *Seattle Post-Intelligencer,* May 18, 1891.

57. "Washington State: The Deplorable Changes of a Year," *United Mine Workers Journal,* November 12, 1891; "From Far West: Deplorable Conditions Result from Bad Management," *United Mine Workers Journal,* February 25, 1892.

58. "Breaking a Strike," *Mobile Register,* May 19, 1891; *Seattle Post-Intelligencer,* May 17, 1891.

59. *Tacoma Daily News,* May 25, 1891; *Seattle Post-Intelligencer,* May 17, 25, 1891.

60. *Seattle Post-Intelligencer,* July 5, 1891.

61. Ibid., July 7, 1891.

62. Ibid., July 4, 1891.

63. Herbert G. Gutman, "The Negro and the United Mine Workers of America: The Career and Letters of Richard L. Davis and Something of Their Meaning," in Julius Jacobson, ed., *The Negro and the American Labor Movement* (New York: Anchor Books, 1968), 52–57; R. L. Davis, "From Rendville," *National Labor Tribune,* July 25, 1891. On Richard Davis's black contemporaries in the UMWA, see Karin A. Shapiro, "William R. Riley: Limits of Interracial Unionism in the Late-Nineteenth-Century South," in Eric Arnesen, ed., *The Human Tradition in American Labor History* (Wilmington, Del.: Scholarly Resources, 2004), 69–87; Ronald L. Lewis, "Race and the United Mine Workers' Union in Tennessee: Selected Letters of William R. Riley, 1892–1895," *Tennessee Historical Quarterly* 36, no. 4 (Winter 1977), 524–36.

64. Davis, "From Rendville," *National Labor Tribune,* July 25, 1891.

65. Gutman, "The Negro and the United Mine Workers of America," 103.

66. Sidney H. Kessler, "The Negro in Labor Strikes," *The Midwest Journal* 6, no. 2 (Summer 1954), 17; Kessler, "The Organization of Negroes in the Knights of Labor," *Journal of Negro History* 37 (1952), 248–76; Leon Fink, "'Irrespective of Party, Color or Social Standing': The Knights of Labor and Opposition Politics in Richmond, Virginia," *Labor History* 19 (Summer 1978), 325–49.

67. On African Americans and the gospel of unionism in this era, see note 12. Also see Arnesen, "The Great American Protest," 26–29.

68. Cayton, *Long Old Road,* 118.

69. Federal Writers Project, *Washington: A Guide to the Evergreen State* (Portland, Or., Binfords and Mort, 1941), 317; "General History—Mr. Powell Barnett," in Powell Barnett Papers, Manuscripts and University Archives Division, University of Washington Libraries, Box 1, Folder 1; "Through Open Eyes: Ninety-Five Years of Black History in Roslyn, Washington" (pamphlet sponsored by the Ellensburg Public Library, n.d.); quote from Harold Preece, "What Goes On in Packingtown? Black Workers Have Learned to Raise Their Heads and to Act Unitedly for Their Full Rights in Industry," *Chicago Defender,* September 23, 1939. On packinghouse work-

ers, see Roger Horowitz, *"Negro and White, Unite and Fight!": A Social History of Industrial Unionism in Meatpacking, 1930–90* (Urbana: University of Illinois Press, 1997); on Pullman porters, see Eric Arnesen, *Brotherhoods of Color: Black Railroad Workers and the Struggle for Equality* (Cambridge, Mass.: Harvard University Press, 2001), 84–96; Beth Tompkins Bates, *Pullman Porters and the Rise of Protest Politics in Black America, 1925–1945* (Chapel Hill: University of North Carolina Press, 2001). On the broader shift in black politics in the 1930s, see Beth Tompkins Bates, "A New Crowd Challenges the Agenda of the Old Guard in the NAACP, 1933–1941," *American Historical Review* 102 (April 1997), 340–77.

70. "No Future in Scabbing," Washington *Afro-American,* June 26, 1937; Rayford W. Logan, "The Negro Wants First-Class Citizenship," in Logan, ed., *What the Negro Wants,* 12–13; "Labor Unions Most Powerful Force in Negro Community," Seattle *Northwest Herald,* October 18, 1944; Julius A. Thomas, "The Negro Worker Lifts His Sights," *Opportunity* 24 (April–June 1946), 54.

71. The classic and unsurpassed account of the 1941 Ford strike is August Meier and Elliott Rudwick, *Black Detroit and the Rise of the UAW* (New York: Oxford University Press, 1979), 82–107. Also see Herbert R. Northrup, *Organized Labor and the Negro* (New York: Harper and Brothers, 1944), 192–97.

3   "Work That Body":
    African American Women, Work, and
    Leisure in Atlanta and the New South

The expansion of capitalism at the turn of the twentieth century substantially transformed work and leisure everywhere in America. Increasing numbers of industrial workers enjoyed higher wages and more leisure time; many nonindustrial workers, however, did not reap such benefits. Domestic workers continued to work seven days a week and had little time off for themselves. Alice Adams, a domestic worker in Atlanta in the 1910s, recalled the difficulties of going out in the evenings after working long hours every day. "I wanted time off," she stated. "Time off to visit my friends and my friends to visit me, just like I was entertaining [my employer's] friends, I wanted to entertain my friends, and I wasn't satisfied until I did." Although her husband reminded her that she was fortunate to have nice employers, Adams persisted: "I say, that's not the thing, I wants time off. And I got it."[1]

The study of working-class history has widened considerably in recent decades, since the pioneering work of John R. Commons and his protégés, to include considerations of the issues raised by Alice Adams. David Montgomery, Herbert Gutman, and other scholars in the 1960s began to broaden the field beyond earlier preoccupations with labor unions, to include additional dimensions of working-class experiences both within and beyond the workplace. Labor history remains focused primarily on work; leisure has devolved to cultural historians. The limitations of such a bifurcation become readily apparent when one considers seminal scholarship such as Lawrence Levine's *Black Culture and Black Consciousness: Afro-American Folk Thought from Slavery to Freedom* (1977). Levine shows us that racial and class consciousness were formulated in cultural practices outside workplaces as well as those within them. Following in the wake of books such as Levine's, labor historians since the 1980s have increasingly devoted attention to recreation and leisure to reconstruct fuller pictures of working-class experiences.[2]

This essay contributes to this growing body of literature through an examination of the everyday lives of women like Alice Adams at work, at home, and in their leisure from the 1870s through the 1910s. In the urban South, African Americans and white southerners developed distinctive and competing ideas about work and leisure within a context marked by the vestiges of slavery and the codification of segregation. African American women were at the heart of the contests that ensued as a result of these differences. While their work as domestics was considered marginal to the New South economy, it was in fact ubiquitous in southern cities and indispensable to the sustenance of white family livelihood and the perpetuation of racial inequalities. As African American women struggled to balance the demands of wage work with the imperatives of nonwage work required for maintaining homes of their own, and the desire for personal growth and enrichment, they placed a high priority on autonomy and collective life and the creation of social spaces for respite and recreation. In the process, they helped to create a distinctive culture in their neighborhoods and communities. This essay analyzes controversies over the relationship between work and play that were particularly pronounced with regard to public dancing. Black vernacular dancing drew sharp criticism from middle-class Atlantans—black and white—reflecting broader anxieties about race, class, and sexuality in the Jim Crow South. Conflicts over the rules and expectations of public etiquette and social decorum attending the changes in the modernization of popular culture were especially conspicuous in Atlanta, the self-proclaimed model of the New South.

By the turn of the century, Atlanta was en route to becoming the metropolis that its urban boosters had imagined. The city had traveled far from the antebellum period, when it was a mere hamlet in the foothills of north Georgia, to its soaring growth as a strategic transportation point for the Confederate Army during the Civil War, and to its continued rise as a regional center of commerce and industry over the next several decades. Ambitious young businessmen, journalists, and politicians had colluded since the 1880s to make Atlanta the model of the New South. They promised to rescue the region from plantation slavery and one-crop agriculture, by diversifying economic development and harmonizing race relations. They accomplished the former by building cotton mills, rolling mills, and foundries, as well as manufacturing plants that produced a multitude of such consumer products as the world-renowned Coca-Cola, clothing, pianos, and furniture. They accomplished the latter by codifying a modern system of segregation to control interracial commerce, residency, and mobility in the interests of whites.[3]

The fortunes of African Americans in the city dovetailed with its overall development. The black population soared after the Civil War as slaves and ex-slaves migrated to find work and respite from the debilitating economic and social conditions of plantation life. As agriculture was reorganized, women who were single, divorced, or otherwise unattached to men proved particularly disposable to landowners. As a result, women far outnumbered men in the migration stream, and black women moved to cities like Atlanta in disproportionate numbers to find work to support themselves and to feed their families. By 1880, black women constituted 50 percent of the city's entire black workforce.[4]

Black women migrants encountered something less than the freedom they had hoped to find in Atlanta. Despite a diverse and burgeoning economy, they were relegated to the bottom of the labor market in the worst-paid and least-desirable manual jobs. Barred from industries reserved for white or male workers, black women were primarily confined to domestic work from adolescence until disability or death. They labored as cooks, maids, and child-nurses in the homes of white employers, and as laundresses in their own homes on behalf of white clients. Yet their paltry wages did not meet their most fundamental needs for food, shelter, and clothing. Black men were only slightly better off in some ways, and worse off in others. They found more diverse jobs open to them on the railroads, in city government, hotels, restaurants, and in a variety of businesses that hired common labor. Although their wages were higher than women's, on average, they faced more frequent layoffs and firings in a capricious labor market.[5]

Black women found ways to reconcile the hardships of their occupational confinement in domestic labor. Married women and women with children often chose to do laundry work, because it allowed them to juggle wage work with the responsibilities of household maintenance. Washerwomen picked up loads of dirty clothes from their patrons on Monday; washed, dried, and ironed throughout the week; and returned the finished garments on Saturday. This work yielded a day off and exempted workers from employer supervision. It also allowed them to care for children, perform other duties intermittently, and incorporate other family members into the work routine.[6] Laundry workers represented the largest single category of women in waged housework in Atlanta. According to the U.S. Census, by 1900 there were 4,817 laundresses, as compared to 4,261 women in all other domestic jobs combined.[7]

Laundry work also provided the benefits of community, since it allowed women to work together within their neighborhoods. Women who washed in nearby streams or at common wells commiserated over shared struggles, swapped news and information, and ultimately created the networks of reciprocity that sustained them.[8] The value of this support system rose appreciably in crises caused by sickness, unemployment, disability, or death.

African American domestic workers, such as cooks, maids, and child-nurses, who spent most of their time in white households sought to establish autonomy by insisting on living in their own homes. "They seem to think that it is something against their freedom if they sleep where they are employed," one employer explained. "Married or unmarried. They will rent a little house, perhaps a mile off, and pay $10 a month for it, and go there to sleep, when perhaps you would be willing to pay them just as much and give them a comfortable bed or cottage on your own place," he continued.[9] Black women recognized that the benefits of live-in service accrued mostly to employers. "Free" accommodations and food were usually meager and paled in comparison to the benefits of a separate life. Independent living arrangements distinguished domestic work in the South from the North, where live-in service predominated until blacks began migrating there in large numbers between the 1910s and 1940s.[10]

Household workers pursued autonomy in other ways. They fought against the long hours and low wages that deprived them of a just standard of living. When employers refused to compromise or relent, the workers seized the initiative by quitting and seeking other employers. Although long hours and low wages were fairly uniform and changing jobs did not guarantee improvement, quitting gave workers some control over their labor. It also kept employers frustrated on their inability to keep the same workers permanently. Domestic workers also moved in and out of the labor force for temporary periods—frequently returning to the same employer after meeting whatever "emergency" prompted departure.[11] Movement from job to job was relatively easy, because the demand for domestics was high and labor markets tight. Moreover, quitting did not require direct confrontation, for workers could imply not show up for work. This allowed household workers to maneuver creatively within the strictures of wage work, to balance competing demands on their time as mothers and wives.

Household laborers resorted to a number of age-old working-class survival strategies to increase resources and stretch their meager budgets. Women and children rummaged through the streets in search of recyclable goods in garbage pails of grocery stores, restaurants, fruit stands, and other merchants. Desperate washerwomen even gathered discarded cinders for fuel to heat water for the laundry. Women also recycled goods from the public domain for use, trade, or resale in the neighborhood or took them to local pawn shops in exchange for cash. Unable to take advantage of buying large quantities at volume discounts, they stretched their dollars by buying fresh foods and pantry items in small amounts, which at least had the benefit of preventing spoilage.[12]

Women's nonwage work at home was encumbered by the challenges of living in a city, which was still primitive. By the 1870s, such city services as water, gas lines, street paving, sewer connections, and fire protection were reserved largely for industries and wealthy white neighborhoods, reflecting the larger pattern of nascent segregation in the South. African Americans lived in the worst areas of the city on low-lying areas subject to floods and sewerage spills. Their one- to three-room shanties were constructed of cheap materials, badly ventilated, built on wood or brick piles for foundations, and lined alleys or unpaved and muddy streets with stagnant cesspools that met occupants at the front door. Common outdoor privies, wells, and street hydrants provided the only options for water and sanitation.[13]

Women negotiated the rugged conditions of urban life by pooling resources, mobilizing informal relationships in their neighborhoods. Their dense networks underpinned such formal institutions as mutual aid and benevolent associations, also called secret societies, extensive throughout the South after the Civil War, especially in cities. These associations paid benefits for sickness, death, and unemployment and offered outlets for education, socializing, trade association, and political organizing. They were at the center of institutions designed for urban survival, race advancement, and personal enrichment. Domestic laborers participated actively and visibly as leaders and members in the Daughters of Bethel, Daughters of Zion, Sisters of Friendship, and Sisters of Love. Elizabeth Russell and Mildred Fane, president and vice president of the Daughters of Bethlehem, were both washerwomen. The True Sisters of Honor elected Harriet Tolliver, a washerwoman, as vice president, and her daughter Keziah Wood as a member of the finance committee.[14]

Domestic workers demonstrated their commitment to these groups by taking leave from work to carry out organizational duties and obligations. The benefits of community occasionally outweighed the wages earned by cooking, cleaning, or washing for white employers. Organized mutuality also strengthened the workers' hand against employers, as one employer regretfully acknowledged: secret society membership "makes them perfectly independent and relieves them from all fear of being discharged, because when they are discharged they go right straight to some of these 'sisters.'"[15] Although the number of associations designated as labor groups were few, organizations that brought workers together for other purposes sometimes assumed trade union functions.[16] The domestic workers who shared their work experiences and frustrations with fellow members also drew up blacklists or boycotted recalcitrant employers. Such organizations transformed seemingly individual tactics, such as quitting or refusing to work for a particular employer, into collective power. Local and state candidates for political office such as George Brown, who ran for mayor in Atlanta in 1912, and Joseph M. Brown, of no relation, who ran for governor of Georgia in 1914, promised that if elected they would regulate or outlaw black secret societies for these reasons.[17]

By the turn of the century, then, African Americans were linked to one another through kinship, friendship, and organizational affiliations across the city. As African American women negotiated their livelihoods as wives, mothers, wage earners, fraternal members, and neighbors at work and at home, they sought to balance wage work with other ways of fulfilling social, material, and emotional needs. Their capacity to fulfill needs and desires faced constant challenges from bosses bent on keeping them subordinate and oppressed. White households were sites of conflict between workers and employers, not unlike more conventional workplaces. Relief or concessions could not be sustained without continuous struggle.[18]

Employers developed their own tactics to counter workers' resistance and maintain the upper hand. They implemented "insurance fees," or monetary advances against the future wages of newly hired domestics, to discourage quitting. They imposed severe penalties and fines for petty lapses and infractions. Some employers coerced workers to buy discarded items, such as old clothing, deducting the prices from wages to keep workers in debt and minimize cash wages. Or they simply refused to pay wages at all. Some organized "Housewives' Unions" to unite employers against workers. And when all else failed, employers resorted to the law, to extralegal vigilante violence exercised by the Ku Klux Klan, or to officially sanctioned brutality perpetrated by the police.[19]

The daily grind of the physical labor of wage housework and the constant battles with employers prompted black women to find other means of earning a living wherever opportunities arose. The first sign of any measurable change in black women's occupational distribution occurred between 1900 and 1910, when the proportion of black women in domestic work dropped from 92 to 84 percent. Black women were beginning to enter the sewing trades, commercial laundries, and small manufacturing jobs.[20] As an entertainment industry grew after the turn of the century, black women also found jobs in the "underworld" economy of gambling, bootlegging, and prostitution.[21] The boundary between work and play blurred for these women workers whose jobs involved excitement and danger. Still, few black women could escape domestic work, no matter how hard they tried; they sought instead to balance their pecuniary interests with other needs, off-setting the rigors of wage labor in their own world of popular amusements. But when they left behind the mops, brooms, washtubs, kitchen stoves, and sinks at the end of the day, the women encountered other challenges. In the dynamic world of commercial entertainment lurked many of the same racial, class, and gender conflicts that permeated their work lives. The interconnections between their struggles at work and at play are revealing, especially in the pursuit of leisure in the dance halls on Atlanta's Decatur Street.

———————

By the 1910s, African Americans enjoyed greater opportunities for night-life in saloons, billiard rooms, restaurants, gambling dens, vaudeville, and motion picture houses. Most of these outlets were clustered on the infamous Decatur Street, the epicenter of the urban leisure milieu. Its resemblance to other seamy metropolitan districts sometimes conjured comparisons with Canal Street in New Orleans, the Bowery of New York City, the Champs-Élysées of Paris, and Chinatown of San Francisco. On weekends, local residents and country transients flocked to Decatur Street in large numbers to dicker with street vendors or auctioneers amid the commingled smells of peanuts, tobacco, near beer, hot dogs, fried fish, horse manure, and cheap perfume. Secondhand clothing stores and a multitude of shoe stores attracted scores of astute consumers looking for snazzy outfits at bargain prices. Others brought items to exchange for cash in the pawnshops—the places where victims of larceny headed hot on the heels of thieves in hopes of reclaiming stolen property.[22]

The conspicuous presence of Chinese laundrymen, Jewish and Greek shop owners, Yankee spielers, Italian chorus men, and moonshine moun-taineers rubbing shoulders with one another reinforced the street's repu-tation as the "melting pot of Dixie." Petty entrepreneurship among black women was also visible along Decatur Street—another avenue of escape for black women seeking nondomestic work. Ella Jackson and Nettie Penn, two black women who owned lunchrooms, shared the same block with Fred Ketchum's jewelry store and Nathan Weitzman's barbershop. Similarly, Lina Richardson's lodging house sat a few doors away from Isaac Sinkovitz's pawnshop, Evan Williams's grocery store, and Lula Edwards's brothel. Decatur Street's melting pot meant more than the coexistence of ethnic businesses, however. It was one of the few places where different racial and ethnic groups mingled freely. Nonetheless, Decatur Street was best known as a "negro playground."[23]

African American workers were especially devoted to the dance halls that were concentrated on Decatur Street. Dancing was becoming popular throughout urban America in the 1910s as prejudices about the propriety of heterosexual socializing began to change. Previously, social dancing, as defined by polite society, required strict boundaries of patterned movements, disciplined gestures, and formal distance between acquaintances to minimize intimacy. In the pre–World War I era, however, dancing between strangers became more acceptable, and dance itself became more inventive and less rigid in style and bodily movement, encouraging lingering physical contact.[24] Black culture heavily influenced these changes; the syncretism of African and European inflections in their music and their movements traveled back and forth through migrants and itinerant entertainers moving from country to town to city and from South to North, forming common ties with people of African descent across the nation. White Americans adopted some black dance styles witnessed in the cabarets where blacks performed for them and in black dance halls where they went "slumming."[25] Still, neither public dancing in general nor black vernacular dance in particular enjoyed universal acceptance.

As early as the 1870s and 1880s, the emergent black bourgeoisie and the white elite in Atlanta and other southern cities voiced strong objections to black dance and the social institutions that sustained it.[26] The drive to get rid of dance halls and other "dives" intensified at the peak of the Progressive Era. Black and white ministers, politicians, and social purity reformers were prominent critics of such black dance halls. The opposition heated up in 1903 when the Atlanta City Council imposed an exorbitant tax on black dance halls in an effort to force them out of business. This effort failed, as proprietors and patrons reconfigured makeshift spaces out of sight if necessary to circumvent regulation. The council moved to abolish these establishments altogether, blaming them for producing a "carnival of crime," but again failed to control devoted dancers who averted these and other attempts to regulate or prohibit dance halls.[27]

Black and white critics of dance halls articulated several arguments against them. The seamy reputation of Decatur Street in general and the close proximity of legal and illegal merriment tainted the reputation of dance halls in the minds of critics who associated them with crime and vice. Some dance halls continued earlier traditions of sharing quarters with saloons, although most were makeshift rooms, usually located in basements—ergo the moniker *dives*. The combination of gambling, alcoholic drinks, and excited bodies moving in time to the music intoxicated some, leading to misunderstandings that could occur in festive crowds on any occasion, as petty skirmishes sometimes ended in melees. Police records in Atlanta are replete with examples of lively partying gone awry, and fights that included women domestic workers were commonplace. Pinkie Chandler, for example, was injured by a beer glass thrown in her face by Helen Henry when she accidentally brushed up against Henry's partner while dancing. Delia Mitchell created trouble when she tried to squeeze onto an already crowded dance floor, only to be pushed aside by another woman. The action outside the dance halls could generate a theater of its own, as couples necked or said their farewells and youths gathered for the last brouhaha. Lighthearted fraternizing on the way home could turn sour, as well, embroiling women in fights with each other or with men.[28]

Opponents also disapproved of the distinctive physicality of black vernacular dance, which challenged Euro-American conceptions of proper bodily carriage and etiquette. African American dance emphasized the movement of body parts, often asymmetrically and independent of one another, whereas Euro-American dance demanded rigidity to mitigate sensuality. Black vernacular dance generally exploded outward from the hips; it was performed from a crouching position with the knees flexed and the body bent at the waist, which allowed a fluidity of movement in a propulsive rhythmic fashion. Facial gestures, clapping, shouting, and yelling of provocative phrases reinforced the kineticism.[29]

Middle-class observers discerned cultural differences that they interpreted to fit ideas about black inferiority. Even some middle-class blacks saw black vernacular dance through the lens of dominant pejorative assumptions. As Henry Hugh Proctor, the pastor of the First Congregational church and a leading dance hall opponent, stated bluntly: "In the name of Anglo-Saxon civilization, remove these things that are ruining the character of our young men and stealing away the virtue of our young women."[30] Proctor, a product of the black elite, used choice words—*Anglo-Saxon civilization, character,* and *virtue*—that were loaded racial constructions frequently invoked in the ideology of white supremacy.[31] Proctor reinforced what many whites believed, that "primitive" black expressive culture threatened Victorian notions of self-restraint.

While Proctor drew on narrow cultural standards, he recognized the sexual connotations evident in black working-class dance. The sultry settings, dimmed lights, and prolonged musical renditions did invite intimacy. The "slow drag," one of the most popular dances, was described by one observer this way: "couples would hang onto each other and just grind back and forth in one spot all night." The Itch was described as "a spasmodic placing of the hands all over the body in an agony of perfect rhythm." The Fish Tail put the emphasis on the rear end, as the name suggested; the "buttocks weave out, back, and up in a variety of figure eights." The names of other dances had erotic overtones, also: the Grind, the Mooche, the Shimmy, the Fanny Bump, Ballin' the Jack, and the Funky Butt. Skirt lifting, body caressing, and thrusting pelvic movements were indecent in the eyes of moral reformers.[32]

Vernacular dance assumed these characteristics in large part from the inspiration of the music, reflecting the inseparability of music and dance in black culture. African American music of the era was an engaging social practice in which audiences and performers were expected to respond to one another orally and physically. Complex rhythmic patterns of voice and instruments inspired mimicry of the emotions they evoked, using bodily movement such as foot stomping, hand clapping, and leaping around.[33]

The music enjoyed in the dance halls was varied and fluid, typically characterized as ragtime or "lowdown" blues, usually performed live. The blues, with its roots in the field hollers, work songs, and spirituals of the South, emerged toward the end of the nineteenth century and matured in the dance halls, rent parties, and vaudeville theaters, becoming more formalized in the 1910s and 1920s. In some venues, the blues were played by a pianist, by a fiddler, or by one or more individuals "patting Juba"—a practice dating back to slavery that involved clapping hands, snapping fingers, and patting limbs and armpits rhythmically, shouting and yelling as they moved.[34]

While the sight and sound of black music and dance suggested certain ideas to middle-class critics, black workers invested them with different kinds of meanings.[35] The blues and popular dance evoked positive affirmations of cultural memories and revisionings of postemancipation life. Like its ancestors, the blues inspired active movement rather than passive reception, and dance provided the mechanism for the audience to engage the performer in a ritual communal ceremony. Despite the connotations of its name, the blues was good-time music that diverted and drove away depression among a people whose everyday lives were filled with adversity. The blues served as the call and dance as the response in a symbiotic performance in which ecstatic bodily movements mocked the lyrics and instrumentation that signified pain and lamentation.[36]

This close link between the blues and dance troubled middle-class and religious people as African Americans renegotiated the relationship between sacred and secular culture. Secular culture assumed a larger significance to blacks facing the exigencies of a new urban, industrializing world. The tensions that resulted were most pronounced in the evolution of music and dance and their relationship to religion and the church. The shared pedigree of sacred and secular music and dance complicated matters for the pious, who drew a sharper line between shouting for the Lord and shouting for the Devil. The similarities in the ritual, cathartic, communal, and expressive purposes of secular and sacred music and dance threatened the province once occupied primarily by religion in African American life. For middle-class Christians like Proctor, the close resemblance between raucous secular dancing and ecstatic religious worship made the former doubly objectionable. Small wonder that elite black religious denominations and individual churches consciously sought to divorce themselves from traditional styles of worship, preaching, and singing that were considered heathen or reminiscent of Africa and the plantation South.[37]

The masses of black worshipers continued to practice ecstatic religious expressions despite middle-class criticism. The sacred shout, as musical sound and bodily movement, was a variant of the lowdown blues that filled the airwaves of the nightclubs and dance halls.[38] Such black worshipers, however, objected less to vernacular dance and more to the fact that secular performances paid homage to the Devil rather than to the Holy Ghost. In other words, the social context and intentions of dance mattered more than the physical movements per se. In fact, members of the Sanctified Church movement, the most fervent practitioners of the ring shout, eagerly embraced corporeality, which they validated as ultimate expression of salvation.[39]

Reconciling worldly pleasure and spiritual reverence was not always as simple as choosing right over wrong, or God over the Devil, even for devout churchgoers. In 1916, delegates at the annual Georgia Conference of the African Methodist Episcopal (AME) Church railed against the evils of the card table, the theater, and the modern dance.[40] Yet those individuals who engaged in popular amusements on Saturday night were often among those who attended church on Sunday morning. Even as the gap between the sacred and the secular widened, the boundaries between these domains remained permeable and fluid. How else could one explain the pronouncements by the AME church and the simultaneous practices of its congregates in Atlanta openly embracing popular amusements even in their own sanctuaries? Henry McNeal Turner, himself an AME bishop, hosted vaudeville and minstrel shows in his well-regarded tabernacle. Allen Temple AME sponsored Leon the Boy Magician, Ebenezer Baptist Church entertained Ulysses the Magician, and, along with Olive Baptist Church and Phillips ME Church, they also showed nightly motion pictures. Even Proctor's church sponsored an annual secular music festival, although he clearly intended Negro jubilee and European classical music to provide a moral alternative to those "places in this city that tend to drag down the colored servant."[41]

Critics of public dance halls were especially harsh on black women domestic workers. The ubiquity of black female servants on the urban land-scape, in the minds of most whites, made them metonyms for the black race. The black bourgeoisie fully understood and resented this guilt by association. It dealt with this tendency by lamenting the shame that befell the entire race when workers failed to live up to the expectations of dutiful service. Dance halls were a menace, declared Proctor, because "the servant class tried to work all day and dance all night."[42] He warned employers that household laborers would perform poorly if they used their leisure unproductively—dancing instead of resting in preparation for the next day of work. The white newspaper agreed and called for a reform: "Let the dance halls and places of low resort for the negro give way to schools for the domestic training of the race—schools for cooking and housework." It continued, "instead of dancing and carousing the night away, he (and especially she) will learn to become proficient in the task [for which] he is employed."[43]

For their part, white employers echoed Proctor's sentiment; they op-posed the violation of what they considered their rightful claim to restrict black women's exertions to manual work. They also objected to black do-mestic workers' dancing because they feared that the dance halls bred social contagions that would infect their homes. Some child-nurses were accused of sneaking into the dives with white children during the day, ex-posing the little ones to immorality and vice. The discourse of scientific racism bolstered fears of racial and sexual pollution. According to one clergyman: "The servants of the white people of the city were enticed into [dance halls] and corrupted by them. So the white people of the city were also affected by their presence."[44] Here again, the close affiliation between music and dance implicated both cultural expressions. The se-ductions of black music proved difficult to contain, even in this era of racial segregation. Dancing embodied the music and became the means by which abstract, fleeting sounds were extended and articulated kines-thetically. The sexual connotations of black dance exacerbated anxieties about women's behavior. The black and white middle classes believed that dancing encouraged sexual promiscuity among black women, who would then pollute white households. The combination of the racial threat and the sexual fears of black bodies contaminating white bodies heightened the anxieties of late Victorian middle classes, all the more so given the interracial conviviality on Decatur Street.

Ironically, aspects of middle-class criticism had something in common with the meaning conferred by the working class itself. Although working-class people did not have a voice in public discourse, as it was circulated through the media and civic proceedings, they made their views known through their actions. Both sides understood that dancing interfered with wage work, although they viewed it from antithetical perspectives. The elite saw dancing as a hindrance to a chaste, disciplined, and submissive labor force. Workers saw it as a respite from the drudgery of toil and an important aspect of personal independence. Blacks could reclaim their bodies from appropriation as instruments of physical toil and redirect their energies toward other diversions.[45]

More than this, black dance embodied a resistance to the confinement of the body in wage work. The transformation of physical gestures in black dance from slavery to freedom constituted rejection of wage work as the only outlet for physical exertion. Ex-slaves thus abandoned references and gestures mimicking labor routines in their dances that they had practiced during slavery (such as "pitchin' hay" or "shuckin' corn") as urban freedom enabled a living standard beyond the needs of subsistence.[46] Increased levels of consumption, new forms of entertainment, and greater personal gratification were vital to working-class livelihoods and an essential component of an emergent modern ethos. In the world of urban poverty and segregation, where enjoyments were limited, the affirmation of life embodied in dancing captivated working-class women and men and offered moments of symbolic and physical restoration of their subjugated bodies for joy, pleasure, and self-delight.

Further evidence of black women workers' pursuit of alternatives to wage work can be detected in their dress. Domestic workers wore uniforms to work or other plain outfits that signified poverty and social subordinance. But when they left work behind, they shed the sartorial symbols of servility for clothes that reflected respectability and self-worth. As Alice Adams remarked: "I would always go to work neat and clean. But my dress up clothes, I didn't wear 'em to work. Because when I went out I wanted to change and I wanted to look different."[47] For Adams, demarcating the line between work and play was an important part of claiming personal dignity. Changing clothes was a clear way to draw that line.

The emphasis on dress provided another line of assault for critics of women in dance halls. The proclivities African Americans were presumed to have for stylish dress, conspicuous consumption, and personal adornment were seen as immoral. As Anthony Binga, a black minister from Virginia and critic of dancing and other urban "vices," complained: "The fashionable dress, which is too thin and scantily cut to sleep in—even in a tropical clime—is worn through the cold night air to and from this [dance] room, where the temperature is sometimes in the nineties." He concluded: "the child of vanity will scarcely allow wrapping to touch her body for fear of disarranging her toilette."[48]

Women's fashion was increasingly less modest and restrictive, but Binga overstated the case. Some extant photographs of dance-hall dress indicate appropriation of middle-class taste, although African American workers had their own aesthetic standards and put their own twist on fashion instead of blindly adopting mainstream forms. The men donned hats, vests, jackets, and trousers held up by suspenders. The women wore flat-top or wide-brimmed hats, full-length skirts that hugged the hips and flared out at the bottom, and blouses with pouter pigeon bodices and sleeves that were puffed near the shoulders and fitted around the forearms.[49] The women gave careful attention to their dress style, from their hairdos down to their underwear. The disclosure of pretty petticoats made of fine linen and crocheted edges became a part of such dances as the Funky Butt. Moreover, the emphasis and glorification of body parts, such as the buttocks, subverted dominant standards of beauty. Black women were caricatured as grotesque and ugly in popular representations in the dominant culture. But in dance halls, black beauty could be highlighted and celebrated. Anthropologist Zora Neale Hurston summed up one alternative criterion of good looks in a colorphobic society: "even if she were as black as the hinges of hell the question was 'Can she jook?'"[50]

The literal stripping of the outward symbols of servility helped to reinforce the importance of dance as an activity used to recover from the exploitation of wage labor. It is also important to note that the connotation of *work* in black culture was complex. The title of this article, "'Work That Body,'" is a play on these multiple meanings. Work not only meant physical labor, it also meant dancing. The phrase "work that body" is a variation of a common refrain shouted on the dance floor to praise and encourage the talents of dancers and musicians. In addition, it meant engaging in sex.[51] Dancing enabled an escape from wage work, even as dance itself was considered work—of a different order. The ethics of drive, achievement, and perseverance took on a different meaning when removed from the context of wage relations. Dancers put a high value on mastery of technique and style and competed with one another in jest and formal contests in which "working hard" became the criterion of a good performance. The proof was found in the zeal and agility of body movements or in the perspiration that seeped through one's clothes. James P. Johnson, a pianist, suggested another way: "I saw many actually wear right through a pair of shoes in one night. They danced hard."[52]

The value placed on dancing as hard work resonated in particular with African American women workers in a society in which the highest valorization of womanhood was largely defined by abstinence from work. The ideal woman avoided wage work for the obligations of motherhood and comforts of home. Leola B. Wilson (aka Coot Grant) remembered her childhood in Birmingham, Alabama, at the turn of the century. Her aspirations to become an entertainer were nourished by her furtive glimpses through a peephole she drilled in a wall of her father's honky-tonk to observe adult entertainment. Wilson's recollections years later demonstrate how black women could reconstruct notions of womanhood through dance. "I remember a tall, powerful woman who worked in the mills pulling coke from a furnace—a man's job," she added. "It was Sue, and she loved men. When Sue arrived at my father's honky tonk, people would yell: 'Here come Big Sue! Do the Funky Butt, Baby!' As soon as she got high and happy, that's what she'd do, pulling up her skirts and grinding her rear end like an alligator crawling up a bank."[53] Sue worked hard, like a man, during the day, but at night she shed her industrial pants and worked hard as a woman in a setting in which femininity was appreciated for its compatibility with work—of several different orders.

Working-class women found respite in commercialized establishments on Decatur Street, especially in dance halls where they could make their bodies their own. They danced for fun and recreation, above all. They used dance to heal, commune, and transcend, momentarily, their daily travails. Dance was an affirmation of their racial heritage, a reinforcement of shared cultural values, and a means of reenacting community. It also enabled the construction of positive self-identities in a society that measured them against standards of womanhood that they could not or would not meet.

Dancing became transgressive in light of the criticisms and actions of middle-class reformers intent on exorcizing it from the public realm. The mere sight of African Americans, especially domestic workers, deriving pleasure and expressing symbolic liberation in dance halls by posing alternative meanings of bodily exertion was unsettling.[54] The distinctive features of black dance seemed threatening to whites who expected deference from African Americans and who were increasingly wary of signs and symbols of their independence. Unlike other commercialized recreation, such as the new amusement parks, where one encountered replicas of industrial life in the mechanized, standardized forms of play, dance halls still allowed for a great deal of creativity, imagination, improvisation, and, thereby, change.[55] Dance halls contained a strong element of impulsiveness and unpredictability, as dancers and musicians inspired one another to enact infinite permutations of gestures and utterances. Some social purity reformers tried to mitigate these tendencies by introducing tame, patterned movements to counteract the forms of free expression that were difficult to suppress when dancers were left to their own devices.[56]

Yet despite the tirades of incensed critics, dancing probably did have the effect of renewal and recovery, even if on the workers' own terms. It reinvigorated them for the next day of work and enabled them to persevere. It was one among many elements that helped to maintain social stability by providing an outlet for workers to release their tensions, to purge their bodies of their travails on the dance floor. Dancing hard, like laboring hard, was consistent with the work ethic of capitalism. African Americans' assertion of this expressive practice replicated dimensions of the social order around them.

Much was at stake for the black middle class in this struggle over vernacular dance. The controversy occurred as a modern black bourgeoisie asserted its claim to define progress and lead the race. The black elite sought to impose its own values and standards on the masses, to obliterate plebeian cultural expressions that, in its view, reinforced racial degradation. While the black elite asserted its paternalism through the language of morality, "civilization," law and order, and the Protestant work ethic, the white elite exercised rhetorical and repressive authority through state power. White southerners had even more at stake in controlling black leisure and dancing as they sought greater control over black labor power. White fears of the bodily excesses perceived in dance were rooted in racial and class-coded constructions of bodily carriage, in their own obsessions with sex, and in their anxieties about interracial coupling. The racial paranoia was further nurtured by the context in which much of the dancing occurred, in the subterranean world of the red-light district on Decatur Street, "the melting pot of Dixie," where urban dwellers crossed over the color line more freely than elsewhere in the city. White fears were contradictory, however; the very Anglo-Saxon values used to measure racial fitness were themselves undergoing change. Victorianism was losing its luster; white middle-class people felt shackled by their own inhibitions and began adopting the very same behaviors (such as passion, rough sport, and visceral amusements) that they so derisively associated with the "lower orders."[57]

African American women demonstrated through their resilient public dancing, as they had in their work and community activities, that they valued autonomy and collectivity. They made efforts to carve out space for self, family, and community within the constraints of their confinement to poorly paid jobs at the bottom of the wage labor hierarchy. For laundry workers, the realms of wage labor, family, and community overlapped; they could find pleasure in the social dimensions of their labor. For domestics like Alice Adams, who worked full time in white workplaces, however, it became even more important to find avenues of escape totally removed from the workplace. Yet no matter what their occupation, black women could not escape the inevitable tensions produced by race, class, and sexuality in the Jim Crow South—on or off the job.

Notes

This essay first appeared as "'Work That Body': African-American Women, Work, and Leisure in Atlanta and the New South," in Eric Arnesen, Julie Greene, and Bruce Laurie, eds. *Labor Histories: Class, Politics, and the Working-Class Experience* (Urbana: University of Illinois Press, 1998), 153–74.

1. Alice Adams, interview by Bernard E. West, 20 Nov. 1979, tape recording, Living Atlanta Collection, Atlanta History Center, Atlanta, Ga. (hereafter cited as AHC).

2. Roy Rosenzweig, *Eight Hours for What We Will: Workers and Leisure in an Industrial City, 1870–1920* (Cambridge, England: Cambridge University Press, 1983); Kathy Peiss, *Cheap Amusements: Working Women and Leisure in Turn-of-the-Century New York* (Philadelphia: Temple University Press, 1986); Robin D. G. Kelley, *Race Rebels: Culture, Politics, and the Black Working Class* (New York: Free Press, 1994); Earl Lewis, *In Their Own Interests: Race, Class, and Power in Twentieth-Century Norfolk, Virginia* (Berkeley: University of California Press, 1991); Joe William Trotter Jr., *Coal, Class, and Color: Blacks in Southern West Virginia, 1915–32* (Urbana: University of Illinois Press, 1990); Lizabeth Cohen, *Making a New Deal: Industrial Workers in Chicago, 1919–1939* (Cambridge, England: Cambridge University Press, 1990); Jacquelyn Dowd Hall et al., *Like a Family: The Making of a Southern Cotton Mill World* (Chapel Hill: University of North Carolina Press, 1987); Gary R. Mormino and George E. Pozzetta, *The Immigrant World of Ybor City: Italians and Their Latin Neighbors in Tampa, 1885–1985* (Urbana: University of Illinois Press, 1988); Alexander Saxton, *The Rise and Fall of the White Republic: Class Politics and Mass Culture in Nineteenth-Century America* (London: Verso, 1990); David R. Roediger, *The Wages of Whiteness: Race and the Making of the American Working Class* (London: Verso, 1991); Christine Stansell, *City of Women: Sex and Class in New York, 1789–1860* (1986; reprint, Urbana: University of Illinois Press, 1987).

3. Howard N. Rabinowitz, *Race Relations in the Urban South, 1865–1890* (New York: Oxford University Press, 1978); John Dittmer, *Black Georgia in the Progressive Era, 1900–1920* (Urbana: University of Illinois Press, 1977); James Michael Russell, *Atlanta, 1847–1890: City Building in the Old South and the New* (Baton Rouge: Louisiana University Press, 1988).

4. Jacqueline Jones, *Labor of Love, Labor of Sorrow: Black Women, Work, and the Family from Slavery to the Present* (New York: Basic Books, 1985); Tera W. Hunter, *To 'Joy My Freedom: Southern Black Women's Lives and Labors after the Civil War* (Cambridge, Mass.: Harvard University Press, 1997); Jerry Thornberry, "The Development of Black Atlanta, 1865–1885" (Ph.D. dissertation, University of Maryland, 1977); Rabinowitz, *Race Relations in the Urban South;* U.S. Department of the Interior, *Statistics of the Population of the U.S. at the Tenth Census* (Washington, D.C.: Government Printing Office, 1883), 1:862.

5. Jacqueline Jones, *Labor of Love;* Hunter, *To 'Joy My Freedom;* David M. Katzman, *Seven Days a Week: Women and Domestic Service in Industrializing America* (1978; reprint, Urbana: University of Illinois Press, 1981); Rabinowitz, *Race Relations in the Urban South.*

6. On laundry work see Sarah Hill, "Bea, the Washerwoman," Federal Writer's Project Papers, Southern Historical Collection, University of North Carolina, Chapel Hill (hereafter cited as SHC); Jasper Battle, "Wash Day in Slavery," in George P. Rawick, ed., *The American Slave: A Composite Autobiography* (Westport, Conn.: Greenwood Press, 1972–78), vol. 2, pt. 1, 70; Katzman, *Seven Days a Week,* 72, 82, 124; Daniel Sutherland, *Americans and Their Servants: Domestic Service in the United States from 1800 to 1920* (Baton Rouge: Louisiana State University Press, 1981), 92; Faye E. Dudden, *Serving Women: Household Service in Nineteenth-Century America* (Middletown, Conn.: Wesleyan University Press, 1983), 224–25; and Patricia E. Malcolmson, *English Laundresses: A Social History, 1850–1930* (Urbana: University of Illinois Press, 1986), 11–43.

7. U.S. Department of Commerce and Labor, Bureau of the Census, *Special Reports: Occupations at the Twelfth Census* (Washington, D.C.: Government Printing Office, 1904), 486–89.

8. For an example of a communal laundry location see *Atlanta Constitution,* 20 July 1881.

9. Testimony of Albert C. Danner, U.S. Senate Committee on Education and Labor, *Report upon the Relations between Labor and Capital* (Washington, D.C.: Government Printing Office, 1885), 105 (hereafter cited as *Labor and Capital*).

10. See Katzman, *Seven Days a Week;* Elizabeth Clark-Lewis, *Living In, Living Out: African American Domestics in Washington, D.C.* (Washington, D.C.: Smithsonian Institution, 1994); Hunter, *To 'Joy My Freedom.*

11. For examples of the role and impact of quitting see *Atlanta Daily Intelligencer,* 25 Oct. 1865; Myrta Lockett Avary, *Dixie after the War: An Exposition of Social Conditions Existing in the South during the Twelve Years Succeeding the Fall of Richmond* (Boston: Doubleday, 1906; reprint, 1937), 192; entries for 17 June through 2 Dec. 1866, Samuel P. Richards Diary, AHC; entries for May 1865, Ella Gertrude Clanton Thomas Journal, Duke University Archives, Durham, N.C. (hereafter cited as DU); Emma J. S. Prescott, "Reminiscences of the War," 49–55, AHC.

12. See, for example, *Atlanta Journal of Labor,* 14 May 1915; and *American Missionary* 13 (Apr. 1869): 75; Ruth Reed, *The Negro Women of Gainesville, Georgia* (Athens: University of Georgia, 1921), 31.

13. James M. Russell, "Politics, Municipal Services, and the Working Class in Atlanta, 1865 to 1890," *Georgia Historical Quarterly* 66 (Winter 1982): 467–91; Thornberry, "Development of Black Atlanta"; Dana F. White, "The Black Sides of Atlanta: A Geography of Expansion and Containment, 1970–1870," *Atlanta Historical Journal* 26 (Summer–Fall 1982–83): 199–225; W. E. B. Du Bois, "The Problem of Housing the Negro: V. The Southern City Negro of the Lower Class," *Southern Workman* 20 (Dec. 1901): 688–93; Rabinowitz, *Race Relations in the Urban South;* and C. Vann Woodward, *Origins of the New South, 1877–1913* (Baton Rouge: Louisiana State University Press, 1951), 355.

14. U.S. Department of Treasury, Register of Signatures of Depositors in the Branch-

es of the Freedmen's Savings and Trust Company, Atlanta Branch, 1870–74. The Freedmen's bank records provide information on individual mutual aid groups and listings of officers. For more information on these organizations, see W. E. B. Du Bois, ed., *Efforts for Social Betterment among Negro Americans* (Atlanta: Atlanta University, 1909); Evelyn Brooks Higginbotham, *Righteous Discontent: The Women's Movement in the Black Baptist Church, 1880–1920* (Cambridge, Mass.: Harvard University Press, 1992); Armstead Robinson, "'Plans Dat Come from God': Institution Building and the Emergence of Black Leadership in Reconstruction Memphis," in Orville Vernon Burton and Robert C. McMath Jr., eds., *Toward a New South? Studies in Post–Civil War Southern Communities* (Westport, Conn.: Greenwood Press, 1979); Elsa Barkley Brown, "Womanist Consciousness: Maggie Lena Walker and the Independent Order of Saint Luke," *Signs* 14 (Spring 1989): 610–33; Peter J. Rachleff, *Black Labor in the South: Richmond, Virginia, 1865–1890* (Philadelphia: Temple University Press, 1984); Kathleen C. Berkeley, "'Colored Ladies Also Contributed': Black Women's Activities from Benevolence to Social Welfare, 1866–1896," in Walter J. Fraser Jr., R. Frank Saunders Jr., and Jon L. Wakelyn, eds., *The Web of Southern Social Relations: Women, Family, and Education* (Athens: University of Georgia Press, 1985); Anne Firor Scott, "Most Invisible of All: Black Women's Voluntary Associations," *Journal of Southern History* 56 (Feb. 1990): 3–22.

15. Testimony of Mrs. Ward, in *Labor and Capital*, 344. See also Ma [Margaret Cronly] to darling Rob [Cronly], 29 June 1881, Cronly Family Papers, DU.

16. *Atlanta Constitution*, 31 Mar. 1910; Reed, *Negro Women of Gainesville*, 46. Canadian and other working-class mutual aid organizations carried out similar functions. See Varpu Lindström-Best, *Defiant Sisters: A Social History of Finnish Immigrant Women in Canada* (Toronto: Multicultural History Society of Ontario, 1988), 56–60; and E. P. Thompson, *The Making of the English Working Class* (New York: Pantheon, 1966), 418–29.

17. See 1914 campaign literature, Joseph M. Brown Papers, Atlanta History Center. On George Brown see *Atlanta Constitution*, 8–29 Sept. 1912. For a fuller discussion of these events see Hunter, *To 'Joy My Freedom*.

18. See David Montgomery, *Workers' Control: Studies in the History of Work, Technology, and Labor Struggles* (Cambridge, England: Cambridge University Press, 1980).

19. See, for example, Elizabeth Kytle, *Willie Mae* (New York: Knopf, 1958), 116; Meta Morris Grimball to J. Berkeley Grimball, 18 Dec. 1865, Grimball Family Papers, SHC; "Account of Ann Crawle," 1884, Edwin Edmunds Papers, SHC; Valeria Burroughs Commonplace Book, 1865, SHC; *Atlanta Constitution*, 8 Oct. 1914. On Ku Klux Klan violence see, for example, testimony of Alfred Richardson, in *Testimony Taken by the Joint Select Committee to Inquire into the Condition of Affairs in the Late Insurrectionary States*, 42d Cong., 2d sess., House Report 22, pt. 6 (Washington, D.C.: Government Printing Office, 1872), 1:12, 18.

20. W. E. B. Du Bois, ed., *The Negro American Artisan* (Atlanta: Atlanta University Press, 1912), 46; U.S. Department of Commerce and Labor, Bureau of the Census, *Special Reports: Occupations Twelfth Census* (Washington, D.C.: Government Printing Office, 1904), 486–89; U.S. Department of Commerce and Labor, Bureau of the Census, *Thirteenth Census: Population, Occupations* (Washington, D.C.: Government Printing Office, 1914), 536–37.

21. For black prostitutes and bootleg operators see *Atlanta Constitution*, 15 May and

18 June 1900, 30 Nov. 1902; *Atlanta Journal,* 12 Apr. and 12 Aug. 1901; *Atlanta Independent,* 22 Sept. 1906; "Condition of the Negro in Various Cities," *Bulletin of the Department of Labor* 2 (May 1897): 257–359; Gretchen Maclachlan, "Women's Work: Atlanta's Industrialization and Urbanization, 1879–1929" (Ph.D. dissertation, Emory University, 1992), 203–25; "Reports of the Martha Home," 1913–15, in Christian Council Papers, Men and Religion Forward Movement, AHC; Minute Book, 1908–18, Neighborhood Union Papers, Robert W. Woodruff Library, Clark Atlanta University, Atlanta, Ga.

22. *Journal Magazine,* 18 May 1913, in Franklin Garrett, *Atlanta and Environs: A Chronicle of Its People and Events,* 3 vols. (Athens: University of Georgia, 1969), 2:607–9.

23. Ibid.; and Atlanta City Directory, 1910.

24. Lewis A. Erenberg, *Steppin' Out: New York Nightlife and the Transformation of American Culture, 1890–1930* (Westport, Conn.: Greenwood Press, 1981), 20, 150–55.

25. Katrina Hazzard-Gordon, *Jookin': The Rise of Social Dance Formations in African American Culture* (Philadelphia: Temple University Press, 1990), 63–94; Zora Neale Hurston, "Characteristics of the Negro," in Nancy Cunard, ed., *Negro Anthology* (1934; New York: Negro Universities Press, 1969), 29–30.

26. Rabinowitz, *Race Relations in the Urban South,* 243–46.

27. Atlanta City Council Minutes, 6 Apr. 1903, 20:19, AHC; *Atlanta Constitution,* 13 July 1903; and *Atlanta Journal,* 28 May 1903.

28. For stories of police arrests of women and men for crime related to dance halls see *Atlanta Constitution,* 23 June 1900, 7 May 1904, 9 Mar. 1905; *Atlanta Journal,* 19 and 23 June, 12 Sept. 1900. See comments by Henry Hugh Proctor and Monroe N. Work in W. E. B. Du Bois, ed., *Some Notes on Negro Crime* (Atlanta: Atlanta University, 1904), 50–51.

29. Hazzard-Gordon, *Jookin',* 15–20, 83–84; Marshall Stearns and Jean Stearns, *Jazz Dance: The Story of American Vernacular Dance* (New York: Macmillan, 1968).

30. *Atlanta Constitution,* 7 July 1903.

31. For a cogent analysis of the racial implications of the discourse of "civilization" at the turn of the century see Gail Bederman, *Manliness and Civilization: A Cultural History of Gender and Race in the United States, 1880–1917* (Chicago: University of Chicago Press, 1995).

32. Stearns and Stearns, *Jazz Dance,* 1–12, 21, 24, 27; William H. Jones, *Recreation and Amusement among Negroes in Washington, D.C.: A Sociological Analysis of the Negro in an Urban Environment* (Westport, Conn.: Negro Universities Press, 1970), 121–23.

33. Sterling Stuckey, *Slave Culture: Nationalist Thought and the Foundations of Black America* (New York: Oxford University Press, 1987), 57–59; Lawrence Levine, *Black Culture and Black Consciousness: Afro-American Folk Thought from Slavery to Freedom* (New York: Oxford University Press, 1977), 16, 203; Susan McClary, *Feminine Endings: Music, Gender, and Sexuality* (Minneapolis: University of Minnesota Press, 1991), 8–25, 54–57, 153.

34. *Atlanta Constitution,* 6 Aug. 1900, 13 July 1902; Paul Oliver, *Blues Fell This Morning: Meaning in the Blues* (Cambridge, England: Cambridge University Press, 1960), 1–11; Levine, *Black Culture and Black Consciousness,* 221–39; Leroi Jones, *The Blues People: Negro Music in White America* (New York: William Morrow, 1963), 50–94; Roger D. Abrahams, *Singing the Master: The Emergence of African American Culture in the Plantation South* (New York: Pantheon Books, 1992), 94–95.

35. On the importance of the sight of music and dance performed see Richard Leppert, *Music and Image: Domesticity, Ideology, and Socio-Cultural Formation in Eighteenth-Century England* (Cambridge, England: Cambridge University Press, 1988), chap. 5; and Leppert, *The Sight of Sound: Music, Representations, and the History of the Body* (Berkeley: University of California Press, 1993).

36. Albert Murray, *Stomping the Blues* (New York: McGraw-Hill, 1976); Larry Neal, "The Ethos of the Blues," *Black Scholar* 3 (1972), reprinted in Michael Spencer, ed., *Sacred Music of the Secular City* (Durham, N.C.: Duke University Press, 1992); Paul Oliver, *Songsters and Saints: Vocal Traditions on Race Records* (Cambridge: Cambridge University Press, 1984), 18–46; Levine, *Black Culture and Black Consciousness.*

37. Levine, *Black Culture and Black Consciousness,* 136–297; Murray, *Stomping the Blues,* 21–42; William H. Jones, *Recreation and Amusement,* 65–66; Higginbotham, *Righteous Discontent,* 44, 199–200.

38. See *Atlanta Constitution,* 10 Nov. 1908, 13 and 14 Aug. 1910. A group of white Holy Rollers were arrested on similar charges. See *Atlanta Constitution,* 13 Oct. 1910.

39. Jerma Jackson, "Testifying at the Cross: Thomas Andrew Dorsey, Sister Rosetta Tharpe, and the Politics of African-American Sacred and Secular Music" (Ph.D. dissertation, Rutgers University, 1995), 60–61.

40. Dittmer, *Black Georgia,* 53.

41. *Atlanta Constitution,* 15 and 29 June 1913, 4 July 1914. For advertisements and news stories of church events see *Atlanta Independent,* 1903–10.

42. *Atlanta Constitution,* 3 July 1903. Employers of domestics and other workers in the North also complained about "Blue Monday," the trouble getting workers to perform their duties after a weekend of festivities. See Peiss, *Cheap Amusements,* 34.

43. *Atlanta Constitution,* 19 and 21 Feb. 1905.

44. *Atlanta Constitution,* 20 Feb. 1905; and *Atlanta Journal,* 10 Jan. 1900.

45. See Paul Gilroy, "One Nation under a Groove: The Cultural Politics of 'Race' and Racism in Britain," in David Theo Goldberg, ed., *Anatomy of Race* (Minneapolis: University of Minnesota Press, 1990), 74.

46. Hazzard-Gordon, *Jookin',* 87.

47. Alice Adams interview, AHC.

48. Anthony Binga, *Binga's Address on Several Occasions: Should Church Members Be Disciplined for Attending Balls or Theaters* (Printed by Vote of the General Association of Virginia, ca. 1900), 9, Schomburg Center for Black Culture, New York Public Library, New York.

49. *Atlanta Constitution,* 6 Aug. 1900, 5; 13 July 1902, sect. iv, 1. For a range of dress during the period see Patricia K. Hunt, "Clothing as an Expression of African-American Women in Georgia, 1880–1915," *Georgia Historical Quarterly* 76 (Summer 1992): 459–71. Also see Peiss, *Cheap Amusements,* 57–65.

50. Hurston, "Characteristics of the Negro," 30. This is not to romanticize notions of beauty among African Americans. By this time, ads for skin whiteners and hair straighteners were appearing regularly in black newspapers. Hurston makes the point that black women were disparaged in some black folklore and songs, some of which were probably sung in jook joints.

51. See Oliver, *Blues Fell This Morning,* 108–11; Levine, *Black Culture and Black Con-*

sciousness, 243; Paul Gilroy, *"There Ain't No Black in the Union Jack": The Cultural Politics of Race and Nation* (1987; reprint, Chicago: University of Chicago Press, 1991), 203.

52. Stearns and Stearns, *Jazz Dance,* 24.

53. Ibid.

54. See John Fiske, *Understanding Popular Culture* (Boston: Unwin Hyman, 1989), 49–95.

55. See John Kasson, *Amusing the Million: Coney Island at the Turn of the Century* (New York: Hill and Wang, 1972).

56. Irene and Vernon Castle were among the most famous dance instructors who tried to introduce tamed versions of vernacular dance. See Vernon Castle and Irene Castle, *Modern Dancing* (New York: Harper and Bros., 1914); Peiss, *Cheap Amusements,* 103, 187.

57. Bederman, *Manliness and Civilization,* 10–15.

4 Industrial Sentinels Confront the "Rabid Faction": Black Elites, Black Workers, and the Labor Question in the Jim Crow South

American southerners on both sides of the color line watched with increasing trepidation as racial tensions in early twentieth-century Cuba drifted toward open insurrection. Shaped in fundamental ways by its shared experience with African slavery, the Caribbean island nation had long mesmerized an expansion-driven white southern planter class that had, for much of the nineteenth century, coveted the wealth and resources of the "Pearl of the Caribbean." Later, after dreams of a slaveholding empire had expired, the island continued to serve as a point of reference for white southerners attempting to gauge their own success in re-anchoring class and racial hierarchy in the postemancipation social order, and the rise of the race-based Partido Independiente de Color out of the cauldron of disaffection in Cuba seemed to offer vital lessons to those watching from a distance.[1]

The advent of armed revolt in 1912, led by outraged Afro-Cuban war veterans demanding their "rightful share" in the newly independent nation, seemed to confirm the white South's prescience in adopting aggressive measures aimed at keeping freed blacks in their place. When the revolt was finally suppressed by the U.S.-backed government, at a cost of some 3,000 lives, a clear consensus became evident among white southerners about the implications of the upheaval for their own society. Startled at what seemed to them a costly failure in racial control, whites congratulated themselves on having eliminated the volatility intrinsic in biracial coexistence by anchoring racial difference in an elaborate system of formal segregation: its absence in Cuba seemed a perilous defect.

A more remarkable evaluation of the Cuban events came from Booker T. Washington, who had emerged as the dominant figure in African American politics nearly two decades earlier when, during the 1895 Atlanta Exposition, he issued a public call for reconciliation based on black accommodation to the southern status quo. In an article addressed to the northern white readership of *The Continent* and titled "Negro Leaders Have Kept Racial Peace," Washington expounded on why African Americans, with "much more reason for a resort to physical violence" than their Cuban counterparts, had held back from "rebellion or insurrection." "The answer is simple," he explained. After emancipation, "wise . . . self-sacrificing" whites had undertaken the "training of negro leaders ["teachers and ministers . . . doctors, pharmacists, lawyers, farmers, businessmen or politicians"] who were placed . . . as sentinels in every negro community in the South" and who "kept a steady hand on the masses of the colored people." Exalted by a relieved white America as the authentic embodiment of diminished black aspirations, Washington had often pointed out to whites the utility of conservative leadership in sustaining racial détente, but seldom had he offered such an unguarded appraisal of its role in containing black insurgency.[2]

Historians have been reluctant to accept Washington's word that one essential function of post-Reconstruction race leadership had been to reconcile the black "masses" to their place in the segregated South. One prominent recent study has credited him instead with "la[ying] the groundwork for the militant confrontation of the Civil Rights Movement," and a second describes Washington as a "radical and effective [advocate] of African-American power."[3] Others understate the tensions that developed between race leaders and black workers, stressing the contribution of elite-led "uplift" to institution building in the black community, locating within such work an important sphere of agency, and asserting its ostensible cross-class appeal. But this mildly exuberant tone is difficult to square with the meager gains secured for ordinary black southerners in the Age of Washington, and it obscures the regressive thrust at the heart of the accommodationist project. The considerable gains made during the past generation in reconstructing black southerners' experience under Jim Crow, evident in a vibrant and expanding historical literature,[4] are undermined by a continuing reluctance to examine tensions within the black community. A historiographical lineage that began, appropriately, with recognition of the need for nuanced scholarship has delivered, over time, a mostly laudatory evaluation that emphasizes accommodationism's subversive capacity[5] but prevaricates in delineating its relationship with southern white elites or its complicity in shoring up the system under which black workers languished.

This essay attempts to lay the groundwork for a reevaluation of elite-led racial uplift by excavating the relationship between Washington-style accommodation and white elite designs for the industrializing South. It aims to demonstrate that the "race problem" extant at the New South during the traumatic years of its early industrial development was, to a far greater extent than most historians have acknowledged, rooted in the antagonism between propertied white elites committed to industrial transformation and a mostly propertyless black working class that would provide the fodder for the remaking of the South. Jacquelyn Dowd Hall's compelling proposition that Jim Crow can best be understood as "racial capitalism"—"a system that combined de jure segregation with hyperexploitation of black and white labor"—suggests that black workers belong at the very center of any meaningful understanding of the period, and not relegated to the margins or written off as an inert mass carried along under the protective wing of black petit bourgeois leadership, well-intentioned or otherwise.[6]

A wide range of sources confirm that black labor was the lever with which New South modernizers hoped to lift their region out of the lethargy to which plantation slavery had condemned it. Industrial promoters agreed that "cheap, docile, black labor"[7] was the key to the region's future, an axiom they articulated frequently and in remarkably explicit terms. Booker T. Washington's significance—and the function of accommodation more generally—can best be understood in terms of the compatibility of his formula for race progress with elite requirements for a tractable workforce. Historians working from a race-relations framework continue to gauge the efficacy of Washington's strategy by drawing up a balance sheet of losses and gains for the race as a whole, and then speculating about whether the protest strategies advocated by rivals W. E. B. Du Bois or William Monroe Trotter might have delivered more. But like Washington's admirers, they assume a "unitary racial experience" under Jim Crow that, as Judith Stein has suggested, "denies the historical existence of those blacks who lost both to Booker T. Washington and the dominant [white] classes in the age of segregation."[8]

The "new men" brought to power in the South after the overthrow of Reconstruction—industry-oriented individuals such as *Atlanta Constitution* editor Henry W. Grady, his cothinker at the *Manufacturers' Record,* Richard H. Edmonds, lumber baron John Henry Kirby and his counterparts in coal and iron, Alabama's Henry DeBardeleben, and Tennessee's A. S. C. Colyar—exhibited a contradictory attitude toward the mass of black laborers in their midst. None of them entertained the notion that freedmen or -women should enjoy the same rights of citizenship as their white neighbors, and few showed any restraint in cataloguing the Negro's deficiencies, invariably ascribed to innate racial characteristics. Although they refrained, on most occasions, from publicly indulging in the crass style of race-baiting associated with the demagogues of the age, New South industrial elites were hardly paragons of racial egalitarianism. At best they exhibited a paternalistic attitude toward the supposedly inferior race; confronted with a challenge to their ascendancy, they proved themselves as adept at playing the race card as the most extreme white "demagogues."

Simultaneously, however, modernizers recognized black labor as a vital asset in the New South's industrial renovation. Frustrated at times by what they regarded as its undependability, industrialists were nevertheless unanimous in acknowledging that black labor constituted one of the cornerstones in constructing a prosperous future. "The greatest resource of the South," a typical editorial in the *Manufacturers' Record* asserted in 1893, "is the enormous supply of cheap colored labor." Opportunity "for the masses of negroes" lay in transforming the region's untapped natural endowment into profits. "Its vast mineral wealth is to be uncovered, millions of feet of timber are to be cut, thousands of miles of railroad are to be constructed[, and] great drainage projects are to be carried through . . . with all the incubuses placed upon them, the negroes are a vital factor in Southern advancement," they insisted. "Today the South could not do without them for a week."[9]

Although it may be true, as some have argued, that black workers provided the most fertile ground in which southern trade unionism could sink its roots in the 1950s,[10] the opposite seems to have been the case for much of the period between the overthrow of Reconstruction and the outbreak of World War I. If we take white employers at their word, the most attractive qualities manifested by black labor after Redemption were vulnerability and lack of a disposition for collective organization. "As a laborer [the black worker] has no equal for patient industry and mule-like endurance," a South Carolinian wrote in 1890, articulating a nearly universal theme. The ex-slave, "by the blessings of freedom, is now willing to toil from year's end to year's end for about one-half of the [former costs] which [we] once paid for the fruits of his labor. This same man is the iron mine laborer, the furnaceman and the mill man of the future that will yet aid his white friends of the South to take the lead in the cheapest production on the continent."[11]

With all its limitations, the Populist revolt provided the last large-scale opportunity for black plebeian self-assertion before World War I. Although the years following its decline in the mid-1890s would be punctuated by intermittent, localized confrontation between organized black workers and their employers,[12] the possibility that these could feed into a wider challenge to the status quo—as they had during the upheaval accompanying Reconstruction and the various insurgencies of the late 1880s and 1890s—had been dramatically weakened. Populism's defeat and the wave of reaction accompanying it hastened the disintegration of the collectivist impulse that had infused black politics since emancipation, and disfranchisement eviscerated the political terrain on which that impulse could be expressed. Among the mass of black agricultural workers and the growing numbers abandoning the Cotton Belt for the mines, mills, and timber camps of the New South, the deteriorating racial climate taxed remaining reserves of optimism and cohesion. From the perspective of southern employers, Jim Crow's utility in anchoring the vulnerability of black workers and sustaining the low-wage regime they deemed essential to regional development was among its most attractive features.

In the new era commencing with the elites' triumph over the agrarian challenge in the mid-1890s, leading proponents of southern industrialization labored systematically to revive the paternalist rapport their agrarian forebears had formerly enjoyed with the black masses. Black workers anxious to leave behind the stifling despotism of plantation life represented to men of the New South a ready-made army of cheap menial laborers who could not only be profitably deployed in the extractive industries emerging throughout the region, but, it was assumed, might potentially operate as a massive labor reserve indispensable for restraining the inflated expectations of working-class whites. By 1910, some 1.2 million African Americans labored on the nation's railroads and in its factories and mines, an overwhelming majority of them in the South.

The revival of this elite-led racial paternalism at the nadir shaped, in profound ways, the new orientation of black politics articulated by Washington in his speech before the 1895 Atlanta Exposition. The pact announced by Washington at Atlanta has been evaluated almost exclusively in racial terms—as a declaration of the surrender of black political aspirations and the postponement of the struggle for civil equality. But an exclusive focus on its implications for the color line obscures the degree to which compromise reflected a class-based rapprochement between elites on both sides of the color line—one that had been germinating for nearly twenty years. Washington's intervention might be more meaningfully understood as the public inauguration of a partnership between New South white elites and their counterparts in an increasingly conservative black middle class, now convinced of the futility of political agitation and increasingly enamored with the gospel of wealth. The real losers in this pact were not black southerners generally, but more specifically the black working classes.

In articulating the basis for elite collaboration, Washington gave voice to a tendency that had been coalescing among black conservatives since the overthrow of Reconstruction. African Americans who, following emancipation, had linked their fortunes to the Democratic Party had evolved from being an exotic, inconsequential, and widely detested fringe on the margins of the black community to one that, aided by the patronage of white elites, grew in numbers and self-confidence in the 1880s and 1890s.[13] Almost from the moment that freedmen had been granted the ballot, white conservatives had attempted, through a combination of paternalism and terror, to win sections of the freed community to the Democratic fold, but their early efforts had met with resounding failure. It was only after the tide had begun to turn against black and white Radicals that the Democrats started to cobble together a constituency from among an increasingly demoralized black community.

Some of this support appears to have been drawn from rural laborers especially vulnerable to victimization at the hands of their employers,[14] but more significant for the transformation of black politics was the growing collaboration between white elites and an emerging black middle class anxious to purge itself of the odium of Radical Reconstruction. The egalitarian élan that accompanied the downfall of slavery had militated against factionalism based on skin color or social standing, and near-universal white hostility promoted a powerful sense of solidarity among southern blacks, but as the terror unleashed on black laboring men and women loosened their grip on an increasingly defensive black politics, fracture lines that had been submerged became increasingly apparent, and the restoration of white supremacy tilted formal politics in favor of "representative men" of the race. Some indication of the new direction was discernible in the confrontation between the prominent Texas Republican Norris Wright Cuney and a group of striking black workers in Galveston in 1877. Cuney, the northern-educated son of a prominent white planter and his slave, intervened at the height of a strike over wages to "[deprecate] in the severest terms the follies into which . . . colored men had fallen," accusing them of being "guilty in a vain attempt to revolutionize industrial interests" and warning them to "disperse and to go to their homes," advice that earned him "contempt [from] the rabid faction" of the strikers and undying gratitude from leading white men of the city, who considered him a "friend of law and public tranquility."[15]

The Galveston episode illustrated in stark terms a fragmenting of black politics that was under way across much of the South. Within the Republican Party, the radicalized freedmen and -women who had constituted the phalanx of the Union Leagues during Reconstruction had experienced a string of stinging defeats—initially at the hands of the Klan and white paramilitaries, but later from their own "lily-white" Republican leadership. Redemption did not completely extinguish the spark of radicalism that had infused the black South, but the restoration of white power did mean that "the larger context in which black political power existed had been fundamentally transformed." Many who remained prominent in the party at the end of the 1880s had long since jettisoned the plebeian radicalism manifest at the high tide of Radical Reconstruction; their numbers consisted increasingly of place-seekers and rising elites,[16] who "found themselves tied inextricably to the lot of the black masses even when they no longer articulated their interests." The scale of the political shift is evident in the recollections of prominent North Carolina accommodationist Charles N. Hunter, who recalled in 1902 that when, more than a quarter century earlier, he had traveled to South Carolina to convince black Radicals of the error of their ways, they refused "even [to accord him] a decent hearing." In the very different context of the turn-of-the-century South, Hunter felt "vindicated," noting with satisfaction that "the mass of my people are now willing to hear me."[17]

Paradoxically, the formalization of the color line punished black workers even as it promoted the ascendancy of a black entrepreneurial elite within the confines of the ghetto,[18] widening the gulf between rising elites and the mass of black laborers even further. The Populist insurgency had divided the black middle class, rekindling for a minority the vision they had entertained before Redemption, but its main effect was to inject a sense of urgency into the attempts by white planters and rising industrial elites to solidify their alliance with black conservatives. And this emerging milieu did not leave them wanting.

It was their evolving collaboration with emerging race leaders that permitted New South propagandist Henry Grady to state with confidence, amid the early rumblings of the agrarian revolt in 1887, that he and his counterparts across the region had "no fear" of black "domination." "Already we are attaching to us the best elements of the [black] race," he told an audience at Texas, "and as we proceed our alliance will broaden."[19] Washington and others did not merely resign themselves, reluctantly, to weathering hard times in partnership with white elites; they shared the logic underpinning Grady's program. Louis Harlan, who can hardly be accused of projecting a hypercritical image of Washington, described him candidly as "a black counterpart of Grady," insisting that "it was not merely that Washington was circumspect, that the mask he turned to Southern whites was a mirror. Washington not only *seemed* to agree with whites who were racially moderate and economically conservative; he actually *did* agree with them" [emphasis in original].[20] No surprise, then, that *Atlanta Constitution* editor Clark Howell, after noting that there had been some "initial opposition" among white directors of the 1895 Exposition to permitting a Negro to share the podium, insisted that Washington's speech amounted to a "full vindication" of Grady's views and that "there was not a line in the address which would have been changed even by the most sensitive of those who thought the invitation to be imprudent."[21]

In the context of this developing affinity between elites on either side of the color line, it was unremarkable that, in his appeal to white southern employers to "cast down your buckets where you are," Washington stressed the tractability of black labor in terms aimed at alleviating concerns being expressed in the industrial press. "Cast your buckets among those people who have, *without strikes and labor wars,* tilled your fields, cleared your forests, [built] your railroads and cities, and brought forth treasures from the earth" [emphasis added]. Confronted several years later with a growing clamor for immigrant labor to remove solve the problem of black "inefficiency," he stressed the same qualities: "We have never disturbed the country by riots, strikes, or lockouts," he reminded whites. "Ours has been a peaceful, faithful service." Or again, in an article that appeared in the *Southern States Farm Magazine* in 1898: "The negro is not given to strikes and lockouts. He believes in letting each individual be free to work where and for whom he pleases," a declaration that complemented perfectly the open-shop policy upheld by southern industry. "He has the physical strength to endure hard labor, and he is not ashamed or afraid to work."[22]

Washington's affirmation of black working class passivity should be understood not merely as a rhetorical mask with which he sought to cultivate the support of influential whites. Nor was his an idiosyncratic position out of step with the thinking of black elites elsewhere in the South. Although some in that milieu resented the obsequiousness that pervaded so much of Washington's public posturing, in general they were united in acquiescing to white elite prerogatives, and the subordination of labor to capital formed an essential element of that outlook in Gilded Age America. The outlook popularized by Washington resonated in the statements of numerous black ministers, educators, and newspaper editors. There remained, to be sure, small corners of community life outside the control of the accommodationists, but few advocates of racial uplift contemplated a fundamental challenge to the existing social order.

If Populism at its zenith had broached the possibility of a coalition of lower-class blacks and whites, the accommodationists' prescription for race progress was founded on the opposite proposition: an alliance with the "better class of white men." Washington explicitly held up the example of black support for Populism, and Radical Republicanism before it, to support the accommodationist view that freedmen had been given the franchise prematurely.[23] In a speech that reconstructed in its entirety the white elite rationale for the color bar and positively welcomed southern restriction of the ballot by property and educational qualifications, a speaker at the first annual meeting of Washington's National Negro Business League (NNBL) in Boston (1900) recalled freedmen's susceptibility to "all sorts of wild doctrines" that had aimed at "break[ing] down the political power of his former masters" and elevating former slaves to "places of trust and responsibility."[24]

The accommodationist doctrine in fact reproduced all the main elements of the vulgar white supremacist interpretation of the recent past: that the "fidelity and love" of black southerners for their ex-masters had been corrupted by unscrupulous carpetbaggers and scalawags taking advantage of black ignorance (a theme regularly deployed by Grady); that federal intervention under Reconstruction had "artificially forced" racial equality on the region, upsetting its natural hierarchy; even the notion that slavery had provided blacks with a "school of civilization," the benefits of which had been allowed to slip away during the rupture in paternalist relations. The ideological foundations for a growing convergence between accommodation and an increasingly innocuous racial uplift borrowed heavily from the consensus among white elites that the black "race"—deprived after emancipation of white moral guardianship—was in free fall, deteriorating rapidly and perhaps even on the road to extinction.[25]

Even where they took exception to the malevolence underlying this new consensus, race leaders committed to uplift acquiesced in the assertion that reform of the black masses was an essential element in, and a precondition for, defusing racial tensions. Having abandoned any possibility of a frontal challenge to white supremacy, race leaders resigned themselves to helping black workers adapt to a sharply circumscribed existence within the boundaries set by Jim Crow. One prominent black Alabama educator identified "two distinct problems" facing graduates of Washington's Tuskegee Institute: "the problem of extending education to the masses of our people and the problem of so adjusting the people to their actual conditions that the two races [can] live and work together in harmony." "We must admit," he continued, "that there are entirely too many [African Americans] who are ignorant and superstitious, too many who are gamblers and drunkards.... Tuskegeeans operate under the motto: 'Go ye into all parts of the South and change these conditions.'"[26]

Leavened with an uncritical faith in the ameliorative powers of the market, uplift relieved southern white elites of their own culpability in black laborers' plight, placing the burden for advance squarely on the black working class itself. Shaped by the twin imperatives of "Jim Crow terror and New South economic development," Kevin Gaines has written, black elites adopted a strategy of moral guardianship that "transformed the race's collective historical struggles against the . . . planter class into a self-appointed duty to reform the character and manage the behavior of black workers themselves." As a solution to the problem s of black poverty and powerlessness, uplifters attempted to instill faith in the bourgeois imperatives of individual thrift, faithful service to one's employer, sobriety, and self-discipline. But, as Leon Litwack has observed, the "rhetoric of uplift proliferated almost in direct proportion to its irrelevance to the working lives of most black Southerners."[27]

Some race leaders won to uplift were hopeful that a protracted demonstration of service and submission would gradually clear the way to meaningful reform; others seemed driven by a palpable contempt for the masses that mirrored white hostility. Either way, their embrace of uplift affected powerfully the black middle class's outlook on the labor question, with consequences that can be gleaned in elite attempts to "reform" black domestic workers at the turn of the century. Evidence of white impatience with the impertinence of black female domestics littered the southern press intermittently at the close of the nineteenth century. The protest by one employer in 1883 that the domestics' penchant for "leaving without any particular reason at all . . . from some foolish desire for change" was making it "dangerous to invite company three days ahead" bears witness to the exasperation that the 'servant problem' gave rise to and the paternalistic demeanor of those on the receiving end of black disaffection.[28] In the early years of the new century, a general perception seems to have emerged among employers of female domestics that the situation had become intolerable, and a corrective campaign ensued, enthusiastically supported by prominent accommodationists.

In introducing *New York Post* editor Oswald Garrison Villard to the Sixth Convention of the NNBL in 1905, Booker T. Washington announced to delegates that the grandson of famed abolitionist William Lloyd Garrison would lecture on a subject that race leaders "have been too timid" in discussing, but one that "vitally concerns the interest of [the] race." The guest speaker proceeded to dissect the South's labor problem in terms entirely compatible with Grady's vision and in language laced with the most denigrating racial stereotypes. Expressing astonishment at the "intense feeling with which the servant problem is discussed" in southern homes he had visited, Villard identified the "available but unwilling supply of household servants" as a "genuine menace to the welfare of the colored race" and a state of affairs that "gives the white mistresses a feeling of personal injury as one shamefully wronged."

"The work is there, and the pay is ready," Villard asserted, "but many colored people simply will not avail themselves of their opportunities. They prefer to live in their dilapidated Negro quarters until driven to work by necessity. And then—so runs the all-too familiar tale—they come only to be wished away. They are dirty, slovenly, often impudent, habitually lazy and dishonest and unwilling to work steadily." Citing a recent article by the Dunning school Reconstruction historian Walter L. Fleming on "The Servant Problem in a Black Belt Village," Villard acknowledged that there were "some good colored washer-women, as there are a few good capable servants," but held that the majority were "shiftless, work irregularly, and do not always know the difference between mine and thine." In concluding, he recalled an encounter with a "millionaeir [*sic*] southern banker" who had been brought to tears when recounting "the wonderful tact and ability and skill of his old Negro mammy who had . . . served five generations of his family." "Is not the colored race recreant to its duty if it fails to produce thousands of mammies like this?" he prodded delegates, attempting to impress on them the "supreme need of household training for the mass of colored women of this country."[29]

No evidence survives of delegates' reaction to Villard's scathing speech, but Washington's laudatory, anticipatory remarks at the outset, along with the fact that the NNBL chose to reprint the talk in its entirety, suggests that although those present may have cringed at its most derogatory elements, they accepted its main premise. Washington and others were on record several years earlier calling for action along the same lines. Extolling the "love and attachment between the races at the South," the Tuskegeean's cothinker and sometime rival William H. Councill wrote in the *Colored American* of the "wonderful chance" for "honorable" domestic work, urging black domestics to make themselves "the choicest jewel of every Southern home." The first Hampton Negro Conference at Washington's alma mater in 1897 stressed the importance of domestic training for relaxing racial tensions: "One way to establish better relations with the white people will be to give them better cooks, better laundresses, better chambermaids, better housekeepers," the gathering's most influential speaker suggested. Both Hampton and Tuskegee rejected education for women in "belles letters, art and music" in favor of courses that emphasized domestic skills, and one of Washington's trusted confidants, Melvin H. Chisum, served in his early years as the "proprietor of a 'Training School for Colored Servants.'" Washington himself would later assert, in the *Colored Alabamian,* that because "[t]he white child spends a large proportion of its time in the arms of the Negro woman or Negro girl," black domestics "should be clean . . . intelligent, and . . . above all, moral."[30]

The cadre of race leaders influenced by Washington accepted without serious objection white employers' allegations about black workers' thriftlessness and lack of discipline. Like their counterparts elsewhere in the South, Birmingham's iron and steel bosses grumbled about black workers' "shiftlessness" and their proclivity for "wandering and moving about." "Generally speaking," a reporter for the *Birmingham Age-Herald* asserted in 1903, "the colored worker of Alabama is not a success when he is taken from the cotton field and harnessed to the chariot of coal and iron." A steel executive's complaint that blacks exhibited a tendency to walk off the job "whenever the notion strikes them" typified the tone of the Southern industrial press generally. "If there is a show in town, or an excursion on the Fourth of July, or a burial, it makes no difference what the excitement may be," he protested. "[T]hey will just drop their work and go off."[31]

Washington expressed similar consternation: "One of the weak points in connection with our people being employed in [manufacturing]," he wrote, "is that too many of them yield to the temptation to go off on excursions, picnics, etc., when their work demands their time and attention." In her important North Carolina study, Jeannette Thomas Greenwood notes that the "better class" of blacks "expressly targeted camp meetings, public baptisms, and excursions," identified by one local editor as "three of the strongest agents in the demoralization and breaking down of our people." The *Manufacturers' Record* published in October 1897 a flattering review of a sycophantic "study" by Georgia accommodationist Dr. R. H. Johnson that, in its view, delivered "gratifying relief from the insane optimism which has characterized much of the treatment of the negro question in certain quarters." Crediting Washington's leadership with "opening the way to such a study," the review quoted at length a passage urging Negroes "all over the country" to "organize against laziness, immorality, drunkenness, immoral ministers, teachers, physicians and reformers of all kinds, organize against excursions, hot suppers as now conducted, and let us as a race respect the laurels of virtue of all women."[32]

In many areas, Washington's National Negro Business League, described by one historian as "the organizational center of black conservatism,"[33] served as a supplier of unskilled black labor to employers, and here the potential for a clash between uplifters anxious to demonstrate black workers' employability and workers unimpressed with the wages and conditions on offer was evident. Birmingham *Hot Shots* editor Rev. William T. McGill exhorted black miners during a strike in 1908 to stop their "[constant] grumbling about the white people not paying us for what we do," insisting on another occasion that "at none of the [steel and iron] plants is the colored man discriminated against in any way or manner." His more prominent successor, W. H. Councill protégé Oscar Adams, used his weekly *Birmingham Reporter* to harangue black workers on the importance of steady work habits and loyalty to one's employer. After an unsuccessful attempt to recruit workers for openings at a plant employing black labor exclusively, Adams conveyed his bitterness that after sending "twenty-five or thirty men to the factory . . . not a third of them remained, not half of them began to work." Unable to fathom any other explanation why workers might walk away from such a generous "opportunity," Adams attributed the embarrassing outcome to their failure to "see the need for so much money at the loss of their usual frolic."[34]

Race leaders discouraged by pervasive working-class ambivalence were led to denounce the black poor in terms that matched the invective peddled by hostile whites. They worried openly that the irredeemable element would "drag the race down" and attempted to proscribe elements of working-class life that seemed to breach proper race decorum. Adams used the pages of the *Reporter* to warn his readership regularly against association with the "unworthy Negro," the "Negro swell," the "Negro gambler . . . of the crap game gentry," and the "dishonest Negro," all of whom seemed to be "conspiring to pull down what the 'worthy' of the race had built up." In Charlotte, Greenwood argues, race leaders "attempted to distance themselves from the rest of the African-American community, articulating disgust and occasionally revulsion for 'the masses' even as they stressed race pride, solidarity, and uplift." The temperance question, especially, exposed the chasm dividing the city's black workers and elites: defeat of a prohibition ordinance revealed that race leaders "had little political clout in their own community—despite their alliance with powerful whites and their contention that they were the new race leaders." Tera Hunter's rich depiction of dance hall culture in early twentieth-century black Atlanta reveals a comparable rift: elites added their influence to white attempts to shut down the halls, arguing that "the better class doesn't want them, and the worst element should not be permitted to have them."[35]

Their conspicuous targeting of secular black working-class leisure activity, and in particular the unregulated, sexually charged atmosphere of the dance halls, "blind tigers," and jook joints suggests that uplifters were particularly embarrassed by their inability to win the masses to prevailing middle-class standards of sexual morality. In this effort black clergy, female church auxiliaries, and women's sections of the fraternal orders fought a rearguard action against what they perceived as rampant promiscuity, trying to win skeptical black working-class women to a "higher and nobler womanhood"[36] that stressed the importance of legal unions—and of chastity before marriage and monogamy within it. But, as Deborah Gray

White has argued, the reformers' designation of chastity as the "litmus test of middle-class respectability . . . established an orthodoxy bound to drive a wedge between themselves and the masses of black women."[37]

The declining authority of mainstream churches among black workers, expanded possibilities for secular leisure activity, and the growing social distance between black elites and newly urbanized African Americans were all likely contributors to this failure. In some parts of the urban South, black elite congregations had by the turn of the century established themselves in buildings physically and socially removed from the black masses,[38] and their disdain for the emotional style of worship prevalent in working-class congregations is heavily documented. In the feudal company towns taking form around the extractive industries and home to a large percentage of the industrial working class, believing workers of both races manifested a preference to worship away from the surveillance of company officials and employer-subsidized ministers.[39] Often they were attracted to independent preachers or to the Holiness and Pentecostal sects that proliferated in such settings.[40]

Substantial numbers of black workers seem to have exhibited scant enthusiasm for formal worship of any kind. A Birmingham camp physician noted in 1907 that the "churches wield only a limited influence" over the lives of black miners, who "make no pretense toward being religious, even tho [sic] moral," and maintained that the "lodges seem to draw many that are uninfluenced by the church." More suggestive was the report of a perplexed Texas sawmill manager who informed superiors that although "we have got a good bunch of people in this [racially mixed] camp . . . they care nothing about Church work and will not donate anything" to maintaining a minister, even though workers found it "no trouble to make up three or four hundred dollars when one of their co-workers get burnt out, sick or something." Anxious to promote religious work, the official nevertheless warned management against solving the problem by sending an occasional preacher, because "they will not go to hear him preach unless they just want to have some place to go."[41]

The unwillingness or inability of black workers to voluntarily abide race leaders' moral injunctions occasionally led uplifters to resort to more authoritarian means. Mississippi's leading exponent of black self-help and racial accommodation, Isaiah Montgomery, recounted in a 1907 interview the methods by which his all-black colony at Mound Bayou had purged itself of indecency. When the "moral condition" of the community had become an "issue" some years previously, "a committee was appointed from each of the churches to make a house to house canvass [sic] . . . in order to determine to what extent loose family relations existed." Forty couples found to be living together "without the formality of a marriage ceremony" were prevailed upon to "marry within a certain length of time or . . . be prosecuted." Most married; some left. And in contrast to Charlotte and other southern towns, where race leaders had tried but failed to win the masses to prohibition, the sale of alcohol was banned by decree in Mound Bayou.[42]

Uplifters' attempts to regulate black working-class life extended into the workplace itself. Employers frustrated with their lack of success in anchoring black workers to steady, full-time industrial labor frequently solicited race leaders' advice, and many responded enthusiastically. Washington spoke on at least two occasions to orchestrated mass meetings at the Newport News Shipbuilding and Drydock Company, one of the largest employers of black industrial labor in the South. The first of these, in 1909, was hosted by "an efficient colored committee . . . ably and materially assisted by the white citizens who turned out in large numbers . . . and completely filled the lower floor of the local theater." A detailed report on the second such assembly, held three years later, sheds some light on the aim of Washington's intervention. The meeting originated in talks between R. R. Moton of the Hampton Institute and prominent local race leaders concerned with the "distinct need of having the 2250 colored men and boys co-operate with the general manager" in "getting [them] to work regularly."[43]

Prior to Washington's visit, the *Tuskegee Student* reported, the company's frustration with the undependability of its black workers had led to fears that "the introduction of foreigners" was imminent. A recent pay raise seemed to have made matters worse, it was alleged: "idleness and irregularity were increased" as a result. Speaking before a segregated audience that included black laborers and "those who [could] bring unusual influence upon them—mothers, wives, ministers, doctors, lawyers, teachers, and business men," Washington reportedly exhorted workers to "stick to their jobs and, instead of recklessly and foolishly spending their good wages, build better homes and churches." Urging them to "do their full duty and more than they were being paid for, to keep their word," and to "co-operate heartily with those in authority," Washington announced the opening of a company-run YMCA and night school, emphasizing that management would "do all that it can to keep its colored workers off the streets and give them an opportunity of becoming more efficient and reliable."[44]

The specter raised in the events at Newport News of the displacement of black workers with immigrant labor highlights another crucial point of convergence between southern capital and the accommodationist program. Integral to the outlook propounded by Washington and much of the middle-class race leadership was the conviction that only by proving themselves the most tractable, economical, and uncomplaining source of menial labor could the black masses secure a permanent monopoly over unskilled work in the South. This perspective led them not only to trim their demands for racial justice but, significantly, to oppose the occasional efforts of black workers to assert their rights through trade unions or other forms of collective organization.

Disfranchisement, civil inequality, and racial violence were not incidental aspects of the black southern experience in the years straddling the turn of the century, but their function is best understood when considered in the full, and distinctive, framework of New South labor relations. Although no stratum of the black South was immune from racial animosity during this period, as Nell Painter insists, its effects were felt disproportionately by "poor black men, the foundation of the southern working class." The "victimization of prosperous black men," she writes, was "almost incidental to the immobilization of millions of black workers." Voting restrictions targeted the same class, in many places leaving the privileges of black elites largely unaffected.[45]

The strategy pursued by accommodationists in the face of mounting reaction was predicated on emphasizing this distinction between themselves and the black masses: they countered Jim Crow in transportation with an argument for physical separation along class lines, insisting that respectable blacks should not have to endure traveling in the same coach as the dregs of the race;[46] they accepted educational and property qualifications in voting as positive, remedial steps that would allow the intelligent element to lead;[47] they refrained from straightforward denunciation of the most despicable acts of violence for fear that speaking out would jeopardize their cherished partnership with the "better class" of whites. Washington's feeble rebuke to a white audience at the turn of the century that it was "unreasonable for any community to expect that it can permit Negroes to be lynched or burned in the winter, and then have reliable Negro labor to raise cotton in the summer" provides a particularly poignant reminder of the limitations of this approach.[48]

In a region where, as one editorial predicted, "long hours of labor and moderate wages will continue to be the rule for many years to come," black workers' vulnerability offered southern employers a powerful means with which to maintain stability. Disparaging occasional objections that pervasive "ignoran[ce], thriftless[ness], and inefficien[cy]" ruled out the general employment of black labor in industry, editors at the *Manufacturers' Record* noted that, despite its alleged shortcomings, "the Southern employer . . . shrinks . . . from having white labor introduced which will call for concessions and demand rights denied the negro." The "presence" of black workers "has prevented the spread of labor organizations in the South," another concluded, leaving the region "comparatively free from . . . futile interruption by strikes and other disturbances."[49]

Black elites by and large accepted these generalizations-indeed, they celebrated the tractability and conservatism of the black masses and believed that these qualities offered strategic leverage in developing close relations with leading whites. Herein lay the basis for sharp tensions between black workers and race leadership. "Notwithstanding the advice of conservative[s] who propagated Booker T. Washington's pro-industrialist philosophy," Eric Arnesen has written, "black workers were hardly strangers to classic forms of class conflict" during this period. In the lumber camps, the docks and levees, the mines and mills, black workers challenged, even if they could not disrupt completely, the accommodationists' pretense that they spoke for black Southerners generally.

Prominent accommodators opposed almost universally any attempt by black workers to raise their conditions through collective organization. Washington maintained an abiding hostility to trade unionism throughout his long public career, deriving less from (understandable) revulsion at organized labor's mostly horrendous record regarding black workers than from his strategic calculation that race progress would accrue through the masses demonstrating their utility to capital.[50] He had been deeply influenced by the antilabor outlook of his mentors at the Hampton Institute, and despite a generally positive experience as a coal miner in the Knights of Labor, consistently derided the intervention of "professional labor agitators" in language compatible with the employers' anti-unionism. His response to a 1914 letter from a Pullman porter representing seven thousand workers "persecuted on every side" exemplifies this approach. Evading the author's complaints that the Pullman Company was "afraid that we will have a union among ourselves to fight them" and that management "discharge every man who starts any helpful movement," Washington responded with a vague message of support for an organization that would "help in maintaining a higher standard of efficiency, not only as employees but as men."[51]

Evidence from throughout the South makes clear that race leaders played a prominent role in inoculating black workers against the contagion of trade unionism. Often they did so under the direct, paid supervision of white employers. An 1891 cotton pickers' strike revealed the potential fracture lines among rural blacks: Delta field hands and landless workers overwhelmingly supported the strike, whereas black landowners generally sided with white planters. A biracial posse dispatched to put down the strike in Arkansas's Lee and Crittenden counties killed fifteen black workers and jailed six others.[52] The collaboration between white and black elites in Alabama's Birmingham district was more dramatic: from the 1880s, prominent black Democrats directed "Negro welfare work" on behalf of local coal and iron bosses, a relationship formalized after the rise of Tuskegee. Under Washington's leadership, a steady stream of black teachers and welfare workers made their way to Birmingham's industrial mecca, carrying his explicitly anti-union message to black workers. During the 1908 coal strike—in which the mineworkers' union was subjected to vicious race-baiting in the local press—race leaders came out squarely on the side of the operators, and again in 1920, Labor Department officials noted that "all of the Negro preachers [were] subsidized by the companies and were without exception preaching against the negroes joining the unions."[53]

Planters anxious to frustrate a challenge to their prerogative, Birmingham coal operators and steel kings, North Carolina tobacco manufacturers and Louisiana and Texas lumber barons all seemed acutely aware of the importance of racial divisions in maintaining their hold over labor costs, and of the utility of accommodationist hegemony for advancing their own aims. Southern industry's invulnerability to trade unionism was widely attributed to the potency of these divisions, and employers showed deliberation in their efforts to maintain such a state of affairs. An especially forthright lumber company official, determined to counter efforts of the Brotherhood of Timber Workers (BTW) to organize Louisiana, in 1911 advised his superiors that "there is one strong point that could be used effectively against [the BTW], if properly handled, and that is the negro question. No order can succeed in this country or in this section . . . where the negroes and whites are allowed to affiliate together on an equal social basis and if this information was judiciously disseminated it would have a splendid effect in breaking it up." A year later, the *Lumber Trade Journal* was warning employers that the IWW (Industrial Workers of the World) "knows no race or color. It accepts the negro as a member on an equality with the white man, and the most ignorant foreigner is equally if not more welcome . . . than is the skilled worker."[54]

These remarks only expressed in candid terms the usually unspoken basis of labor relations among southern lumber operators. The Southern Pine Association—one of the two main employers' organizations in the industry—attributed the absence of union organization to "racial antagonism between whites and Negroes."[55] Internal records of the Southern Lumber Operators' Association (SLOA) teem with evidence of management's appreciation for the special vulnerability of black workers and their determination to prevent any tampering with the status quo. The response of a manager at Groveton, Texas, faced with a walkout over a missed payday is revealing in its delineation of the role reserved for black labor by the timber bosses: "Sixty-five men quit and are trying to get others to quit," he reported. "Perhaps we can corral enough Negroes to operate." Another reported in the midst of a campaign to root out union sympathizers that he was "not hiring any men at present but what I know, except for a few country niggers."[56]

The lumber operators' acute understanding that extant racial divisions enhanced their ability to resist unionization is unsurprising. What is remarkable is their ability to draw black community leaders into their designs. Relying on a substantial cadre of black ministers and educators, between 1910 and 1920, SLOA-sponsored speakers visited at least seven southern states in an attempt to neutralize union agitation and counter the black exodus out of the South. In the face of BTW attempts to organize in 1911, a manager from Browndell, Texas, orchestrated a series of mass meetings led by a local black teacher (reported to be "a great deal above the average intelligence among the colored population" and "wholly on our side") that passed resolutions renouncing the union and pledging loyalty to the company. Several years later, the Kirby Lumber Company contracted with I. W. Crawford to speak at employer-sponsored Emancipation Day celebrations and in 1917 offered him work "for at least twenty, and perhaps thirty days" lecturing black workers at twelve sawmills and five logging camps.[57]

The lumber operators dramatically intensified their efforts in the postwar period. They directly sponsored at least three "race" newspapers aimed at containing black militancy and curtailing migration. The short-lived *Voice of Colored Labor* was published out of the Pythians' Hall in Birmingham and circulated mainly in rural districts in Alabama and Mississippi. The *Negro Advocate,* printed in Arkansas (1917–22) under the direction of the employer-subsidized black minister Milton Hampton, would, SLOA officials hoped, "keep the colored laborers of the South satisfied with their conditions[,] advise against the exodus . . . [and] elevate their morals." Directors in New Orleans assured SLOA members that the newspapers' "articles and editorials will be closely scrutinized by this office." Their most remarkable feat involved the New Orleans–based *National Negro Voice,* however. A memo that circulated among SLOA members along with the first edition introduced the publication as "a Negro paper that is being sponsored and controlled by a few large organizations whose members are employers of Negro labor." The "aim and purpose of the paper," members were informed, was to "combat the evil influence of the radical Negro papers and magazines published in the North." It would be overseen by an employer-appointed financial secretary (to whom "all published material had to be submitted"), who would be "the only white man that will come in direct contact with the Negro editor and Manager [R. A. Flynn of New Orleans], who does not and will not know what organizations are financing the enterprise."[58]

The systematic attempt to inscribe racial divisions permanently into the contours of labor relations in lumber and maintain the continued exploitation of black workers at the heart of that system represented a highly sophisticated version of a strategy being pursued throughout the industrializing South. In their more candid moments, leading white elites acknowledged that cheap black labor was the cornerstone on which their New South would be raised. In that sense, at least, industrial exploitation and Jim Crow were organically intertwined. Reconciled for the foreseeable future to the imposition of white supremacy, imbued with a paternalist sense of moral guardianship over the less fortunate members of their race, and unapologetic about linking their fate to the ascendancy of the white "better classes," middle-class race leaders pursued an elitist strategy that led them inevitably to forsake the interests of the black masses for whom they claimed to speak.

The accommodationist formula has been criticized, both by Washington's contemporary critics and by present-day scholars, mainly for its renunciation of the struggle for civil and political equality, or at least for having forsaken the open pursuit of these aims. The outworn practice of juxtaposing protest and accommodation in an attempt to measure the tactical efficacy of each rests on the premise that one or the other might have delivered better results for the race as a whole. But this method ignores the shared class outlook embedded in the strategy espoused by both camps.[59] The critical issue about Washington and his cothinkers is not whether they acquiesced in or fought surreptitiously against specific aspects of racial oppression in the South, but whether in their role as intermediaries between southern capital and black labor they served—or could possibly advance— the best interests of the race. Alabama sharecropper Nate Shaw reminds us, eloquently, of Washington's limitations. Criticizing him for "lean[ing] too much on the white people that controlled the money," Shaw insisted that Washington "didn't respect his race of people enough to go rock bottom with them. . . . He wanted his people to do this, that, and the other, but he never did get to the roots of our troubles." Historians concerned with reconstructing African American life in the Age of Washington have for too long ignored conspicuous evidence of black working-class dissent: it is time to let the Nate Shaws have their say.[60]

Scholarship on relations between black elites and the black laboring majority masses during the Age of Washington stands today at an important crossroads. Although some of the recent literature, saddled by what Eric Foner has identified as a "desire for a history of celebration,"[61] indicates a continuing reluctance to lift the veil on intraracial tensions, the elements of a more penetrating interpretive approach are evident, dispersed throughout some of the most exciting new scholarship at the margins where labor, women's, and African American history intersect. Even where it has hesitated in drawing the conclusions suggested by its own evidence or stumbled upon intracommunal tensions as a minor aside in a larger story, a rich evolving literature has begun to expose the need for a forthright engagement with the significance of class in the African American experience under Jim Crow.

Notes

Note: The author wishes to acknowledge the generous support of the British Academy, the Academic Council at Queen's University Belfast, the John Hope Franklin Collection of African and African-American Documentation at Duke University, and the National Humanities Center in Research Triangle Park, North Carolina, for supporting the research and writing that made this article possible. An earlier version of this article appeared in *Labor History* 44:3 (August 2003): 337–58.

1. The most authoritative account of the rise of the PIC and the 1912 revolt appears in Aline Helg, *"Our Rightful Share": The Afro-Cuban Struggle for Equality, 1886–1912* (Chapel Hill: University of North Carolina Press, 1995). See also Alejandro de la Fuente, *A Nation for All: Race, Inequality, and Politics in Twentieth-Century Cuba* (Chapel Hill: University of North Carolina Press, 2001) and Louis A. Perez Jr., "Politics, Peasants, and People of Color: The 1912 'Race War' in Cuba Reconsidered," *Hispanic American Historical Review* 66:3 (Aug. 1986): 509–39.

2. Booker T. Washington, "Negro Leaders Have Kept Racial Peace," *The Continent* (Chicago) 43 (Oct. 3, 1912): 1382, in Harlan, ed., *Booker T. Washington Papers* (hereafter *BTW Papers*), vol. 11 (Urbana: University of Illinois Press, 1981), 33–34.

3. Adam Fairclough, *Better Day Coming: Blacks and Equality, 1890–2000* (New York: Viking, 2001), xiii; Heather Cox Richardson, *The Death of Reconstruction: Race, Labor, and Politics in the Post–Civil War North, 1865–1901* (Cambridge, Mass.: Harvard University Press, 2001), 5.

4. An abbreviated list of such scholarship would include Janette Thomas Greenwood, *Bittersweet Legacy: The Black and White "Better Classes" in Charlotte, 1850–1910* (Chapel Hill: University of North Carolina Press, 1994); Fon Louise Gordon, *Caste & Class: The Black Experience in Arkansas, 1880–1920* (Athens: University of Georgia Press, 1995); Kevin K. Gaines, *Uplifting the Race: Black Leadership, Politics, and Culture in the Twentieth Century* (Chapel Hill: University of North Carolina, 1996); Tera W. Hunter, *To 'Joy My Freedom: Black Women's Lives and Labors after the Civil War* (Cambridge, Mass.: Harvard University Press, 1998); Deborah Gray White, *Too Heavy a Load: Black Women in Defense of Themselves, 1894–1994* (New York: Norton, 1999); Lynne B. Feldman, *A Sense of Place: Birmingham's Black Middle-Class Community, 1890–1920* (Tuscaloosa: University of Alabama Press, 1999); Stephen G. N. Tuck, *Beyond Atlanta: The*

Struggle for Racial Equality in Georgia, 1940–1980 (Athens: University of Georgia Press, 2001); Karen Ferguson, *Black Politics in New Deal Atlanta* (Chapel Hill: University of North Carolina Press, 2002); Michael W. Fitzgerald, *Urban Emancipation: Popular Politics in Reconstruction Mobile, 1860–1890* (Baton Rouge: Louisiana State University Press, 2002); Steven Hahn, *A Nation under Our Feet: Black Political Struggles in the Rural South from Slavery to the Great Migration* (Cambridge, Mass.: Belknap Press, 2003); Paul Ortiz, *Emancipation Betrayed: The Hidden History of Black Organizing and White Violence in Florida from Reconstruction to the Bloody Election of 1920* (Berkeley: University of California Press, 2005).

5. Virtually all assessments of Washington, including my own, accept the conclusion reached in early studies by Louis Harlan and August Meier that he combined public submission to white supremacy with surreptitious attempts to challenge specific elements of the southern racial order. Harlan writes that Washington "clandestinely financed and directed a number of court suits challenging the grandfather clause, denial of jury service to blacks, Jim Crow service in transportation, and peonage. Thus, he paradoxically attacked the racial settlement he publicly accepted." See Louis R. Harlan, *Booker T. Washington: The Making of a Black Leader* (London: Oxford University Press, 1972), preface, n.p. See also August Meier, *Negro Thought in America, 1880–1915* (Ann Arbor: University of Michigan Press), 110–14.

6. Jacquelyn Dowd Hall, "Mobilizing Memory: Broadening Our View of the Civil Rights Movement," *The Chronicle Review* (July 27, 2001), www.chronicle.com/weekly/v47/i46/46fl00701.htm.

7. George Gordon Crawford, Tennessee Coal, Iron and Railroad executive, cited in George R. Leighton, *Five Cities: The Story of Their Youth and Old Age* (New York: Harper and Brothers, 1939), 129.

8. Judith Stein, "Black and White Burdens: Review of Willard B. Gatewood, Jr., 'Black Americans and the White Man's Burden, 1898–1903,'" *Reviews in American History* (March 1976), 89.

9. "The Negro as a Mill Hand," *Manufacturers' Record,* Sept. 22, 1893.

10. See Michael K. Honey, *Southern Labor and Black Civil Rights: Organizing Memphis Workers* (Urbana: University of Illinois Press, 1993), 214–77. Honey's argument is sharply challenged by Alan Draper in *Conflict of Interests: Organized Labor and the Civil Rights Movement, 1954–1968* (Ithaca, N.Y.: ILR Press, 1994), 10–13.

11. "Southern Bessemer Ores," *Manufacturers' Record,* Oct. 25, 1890.

12. For useful surveys of black labor activism in the industrializing South see Paul B. Worthman and James R. Green, "Black Workers in the New South, 1865–1915," in Nathan I. Huggins, Martin Kilson, and Daniel M. Fox, eds., *Key Issues in the Afro-American Experience* (New York: Harcourt Brace, 1971), 2:47–69; Eric Arnesen, "Following the Color Line of Labor: Black Workers and the Labor Movement before 1930," *Radical History Review* 55 (1993): 53–87; Rick Halpern, "Organized Labor, Black Workers, and the Twentieth-Century South: The Emerging Revision," in Stokes and Halpern, eds., *Race and Class in the American South since 1890* (Oxford, England: Berg, 1994), 43–76; Daniel Letwin, "Labor Relations in the Industrializing South," in John Boles, ed., *A Companion to the American South* (Oxford, England: Blackwell, 2002), 424–43. On black workers in the rural South during this period see Hahn, *A Nation under Our Feet.*

13. See Elsa Barkley Brown, "Negotiating and Transforming the Public Sphere: African American Political Life in the Transition from Slavery to Freedom," *Public Culture* 7:1 (Feb. 1994): 123–24, 130. On community reaction against black Democrats generally see Judith Stein, "'Of Mr. Booker T. Washington,'" 434–41; Meier, *Negro Thought in America,* 38–39; Peter Kolchin, *First Freedom: The Responses of Alabama's Blacks to Emancipation and Reconstruction* (Westport, Conn.: Greenwood Press, 1972), 132; Fitzgerald, *Urban Emancipation,* 211. August Meier writes that although initially "those who [stood] with the Democrats tended to be the old servant class or successful, conservative businessmen," the composition of Democratic supporters changed as southern blacks dejected by the desertion of their cause by Republicans began to tactically divide their votes. See Meier, "The Negro and the Democratic Party, 1875–1915," *Phylon* 17:2 (Fall 1956), 173–91, quote from page 174.

14. John C. Rodrigue makes a compelling case that it was the Louisiana "sugar plantations' centralized work routine [that] enabled freedmen to sustain a unity that their counterparts in the cotton South, dispersed . . . throughout the countryside, could not match," with collateral effects on the persistence of black political power. See Rodrigue, *Reconstruction in the Cane Fields: From Slavery to Free Labor in Louisiana's Sugar Parishes, 1862–1880* (Baton Rouge: Louisiana State University Press, 2001), 176–77.

15. *Galveston News,* Aug. 1, 1877; Aug. 5, 1877. Cuney had been recently dismissed from his position as inspector in the Custom House at Galveston and was "making an effort to have himself re-established" when the strike broke out. The *Galveston News* reported that Cuney's role in the strike won him the backing of "many of the best business men of this city, who commend his capacities for the position and vouch for his character as a man. . . . [B]y the part he bore in restoring order among the turbulent negroes who had given themselves to riotous measures," editors concluded, "he made many friends who have availed themselves of this occasion to speak a good word on his behalf." In contrast he was denounced by black washerwomen who, "emboldened by the liberties allowed their husbands and brothers," joined the strike, demanding a raise from $1.00 to $1.50 per day.

16. Although "calculations of personal benefit were always significant during Reconstruction," Michael Fitzgerald writes, "jobs and money became more obvious motivations afterwards." Fitzgerald, *Urban Emancipation,* 234.

17. Stein, "'Of Mr. Booker T. Washington,'" 432; Charles N. Hunter to Hon. J. C. Pritchard, "Strictly Confidential," April 21, 1902, *Charles N. Hunter Papers,* Box 2, Duke University Special Collections.

18. August Meier, "Negro Class Structure in the Age of Booker T. Washington," *Phylon* 23:2 (Fall 1962): 258.

19. Henry W. Grady, *The New South and Other Addresses* (New York: Charles E. Merrill, 1904), 53. Oliver Cromwell Cox writes that "[t]he Southern oligarchy proposed to use the best Negroes, the most gifted of them, to forestall the political aspirations of their own people." Cox, "Leadership among Negroes in the United States," in Alvin W. Gouldner, ed., *Studies in Leadership: Leadership and Democratic Action* (New York: Russell and Russell, 1950), 238.

20. Harlan, ed., *BTW Papers,* vol. 2, 321; Harlan, *Washington: Making of a Black Leader,* 166.

21. Harlan, ed., *BTW Papers,* vol. 4, 17, n. 1.

22. Booker T. Washington, *Up from Slavery* (New York: Doubleday, Page, 1901), 159; Washington, "The Educational and Industrial Emancipation of the Negro: An Address before the Brooklyn Institute of Arts and Sciences," Feb. 22, 1903, in Harlan, ed., *BTW Papers*, vol. 7, 94; *Southern States Farm Magazine*, Jan. 1898, in Harlan, ed., *BTW Papers*, vol. 4, 375.

23. See, for example, Washington, *Up from Slavery*, 158.

24. H. C. Harris of Birmingham quoted in *Proceedings of the National Negro Business League*, Boston (Aug. 23–24, 1900), 219.

25. See David W. Blight, "Quarrel Forgotten or Revolution Remembered? Reunion and Race in the Memory of the Civil War, 1875–1913," in Blight and Simpson, eds., *Union and Emancipation: Essays on Politics and Race in the Civil War Era* (Kent, Ohio: Kent State University Press, 1997), 162–63.

26. William J. Edwards, *Twenty-Five Years in the Black Belt* (Tuscaloosa: University of Alabama Press, 1993), 109, 110–11.

27. Gaines, *Uplifting the Race*, 20; Leon F. Litwack, *Trouble in Mind: Black Southerners in the Age of Jim Crow* (New York: Knopf, 1998), 148.

28. Testimony of Mrs. Ward, Nov. 15, 1883, *Report on Relations between in Labor and Capital*, vol. 4, (Washington, D.C.: Government Printing Office, 1885), 343, cited in Hunter, *To 'Joy My Freedom*, 59–60.

29. Speech of Oswald Garrison Villard, *Proceedings of the National Negro Business League*, Sixth Annual Convention (Aug. 16–19, 1905), 45–48, 52.

30. Councill in *Colored American*, Aug. 11, 1900, cited in Meier, *Negro Thought in America*, 210; Fanny Jackson Coppin cited in Cynthia Neverdon-Morton, *Afro-American Women of the South and the Advancement of the Race, 1895–1925* (Knoxville: University of Tennessee Press, 1981), 113. Article on the futility of education in "[a]rt and music for people who lived in rented houses and have no bank account" appears in *Tuskegee Student* 14 (May 1902); 1–3, cited in Harlan, ed., *BTW Papers*, vol. 6, 469. Chisum's early career is discussed in Harlan, ed., *BTW Papers*, vol. 7, 219, n. 1. Washington's comments on domestic training appear in *Colored Alabamian*, Jan. 23, 1909.

31. *Birmingham Age Herald*, Aug. 16, 1903; James W. Sloss cited in Daniel L. Letwin, "Race, Class and Industrialization: Black and White Coal Miners in the Birmingham District of Alabama, 1878–1897." Ph.D. diss. (New Haven, Conn.: Yale University, 1991), 55.

32. BTW to Glenn R. LeRoy, March 31, 1903, in Harlan, ed., *BTW Papers*, vol. 7, 109–10; editor W. C. Smith in the *Charlotte Messenger*, Feb. 24, 1883, cited in Greenwood, *Bittersweet Legacy*, 85.

33. Fon Louise Gordon notes that NNBL supporters "provided local, middle-class opposition to suffrage leagues, the Niagara Movement, and the NAACP." Gordon, *Caste & Class*, 78.

34. *Birmingham Reporter*, Aug. 9, 1919.

35. Ibid., Dec. 4, 1920, Aug. 9, 1919; Greenwood, *Bittersweet Legacy*, 85, 96; Hunter, *To 'Joy My Freedom*, 173, and chapter 8, "Dancing and Carousing the Night Away," 168–86. Hunter concludes the chapter by suggesting that "[m]uch was at stake for the black middle class in this struggle to contain and eradicate vernacular dance. The controversy over dancing occurred as a modern black bourgeoisie asserted its claim to define and direct racial progress. The black elite sought to impose its own

values and standards on the masses, to obliterate plebeian cultural expressions that, in its view, prolonged the degradation of the race" (186). Lynne B. Feldman contends, similarly, that "members of the middle class believed it was their duty to perform as role models for the downtrodden and that the crude behavior displayed by members of the lower classes was responsible for the race's problems, including Jim Crow legislation." See Feldman, *A Sense of Place*, 189.

36. *Birmingham Reporter*, Aug. 12, 1916.

37. White, *Too Heavy a Load*, 70.

38. William E. Montgomery argues that in the years following Reconstruction an "expanded [black] aristocracy," which included the "mulatto-dominated elite [and] blacks from the ranks of teachers, ministers, lawyers, and physicians . . . formed their own churches" in order, one contemporary observer suggested, "to get as far as possible from the ordinary Negro." Montgomery, *Under Their Own Vine and Fig Tree: The African-American Church in the South, 1865–1900* (Baton Rouge: Louisiana State University Press, 1993), 260.

39. Wayne Flynt, "Alabama White Protestantism and Labor, 1900–1914" *Alabama Review* (Oct. 1981), 206, 208.

40. Montgomery writes that as "the Baptist and Methodist churches became more conservative, with expanding bourgeois values, their services and congregations looked and sounded more like the Presbyterian, Congregational, and Episcopal churches of the black aristocracy" and "began to lose their appeal to poor, uneducated people who looked in growing numbers to the new holiness, pentecostal, and spiritual movements for the religious experiences that would elevate their lives." See Montgomery, *Under Their Own Vine and Fig Tree*, 345–46. Paul Harvey concurs, arguing that "[r]acial and cultural interchange figured importantly in early Holiness/Pentecostalism. A faith born not in the South, but attracting white and black southern folk disaffected by the embourgeoisment of dominant urban religious institutions, early Pentecostalism functioned much like the early national camp meetings." Harvey, "Racial Interchange in Early Southern Pentecostalism," paper delivered at the annual meeting of the Southern Historical Association, New Orleans, Louisiana, Nov. 16–19, 2001, p. 1.

41. "The Alabama Mining Camp," *The Independent*, Oct. 3, 1907, 790–91; J. B. Hodges to W. N. Sangster, Jan. 15, 1923, Box 47:4, "Church-Blox," *Kirby Lumber Company Collection*, RG D-034, Houston Metropolitan Research Center, Houston, Texas.

42. *World's Work* 14 (July 1907): 9125–34.

43. "An Address by William Taylor Burwell Williams on Washington's Tour of Virginia," July 4, 1909, in Harlan, ed., *BTW Papers*, vol. 10, 144. Williams was a Hampton graduate and later a member of the faculty at Tuskegee. The 1909 Newport News visit was followed up by a trip to Page, West Virginia, where Washington addressed a meeting of black miners (148). The 1912 meeting is reported in "An Account of a Speech in Newport News, Virginia," *Tuskegee Student*, Aug. 1, 1912.

44. "An Account of a Speech in Newport News, Virginia," *Tuskegee Student*, Aug. 1, 1912.

45. Nell Irvin Painter, "Social Equality, Miscegenation, Labor, and Power," in Numan V. Bartley, ed., *The Evolution of Southern Culture* (Athens: University of Georgia Press, 1988), 60.

46. Kevin K. Gaines writes that elites "opposed racism by calling attention to class

distinctions among African Americans as a sign of evolutionary race progress. . . . The self-help component of uplift increasingly bore the stamp of evolutionary racial theories positing the civilization of elites against the moral degradation of the masses." Gaines, *Uplifting the Race,* 20–21. Greenwood reports that Charlotte race leaders opposed Democratic Party legislation calling for segregation on the rails "chiefly on the grounds that it did not take into account class differences among blacks." They voiced "no objection to being separated from white people if they will place colored ladies and gentlemen in a coach where they can be protected against white and black roughs alike." Greenwood, *Bittersweet Legacy,* 204–5.

47. See Washington to John Elbert McConnell, Dec. 17, 1885, Harlan, ed., *BTW Papers,* vol. 2, 284.

48. Washington's speech cited in Basil Mathews, *Booker T. Washington: Educator and Interracial Interpreter* (College Park, Md.: McGrath, 1948), 223. Some measure of white elite satisfaction with the accommodationists' silence on racial violence can be gleaned in the satisfaction expressed by white observers at annual meetings of Washington's National Negro Business League. Reporting on the NNBL's 1900 Convention in Boston, *Gunton's Magazine* noted that although "[t]he New Orleans riots occurred while the preparations for the conference were being made," the "streets of New York resounded to the cries of negro-hunting mobs just at the time when many of the delegates were leaving their homes to come to Boston," and the "newspapers were filled with accounts of the disturbance at Akron," the proceedings passed without "one single reference to the riots or the conditions which gave rise to them." "These were business men, come to Boston for a definite purpose with which politics had no connection." The Boston press reported similarly that "There was no politics [or] clamoring for rights. There was as little sentimentality as in a meeting of stock jobbers or railroad directors." See Harlan, ed., *BTW Papers,* vol. 6, 76–77. In almost identical terms the *Manufacturers' Record* ("Negroes Who Work," Aug. 27, 1903) remarked on the NNBL's Nashville Convention in 1903 that it was "gratifying to hear so few complaints urged against the white people. . . . But two babblements were uttered against 'the oppressions' of the white man out of a delegation of 1500 representatives of the industrial negroes from every part of the country. This serves to show that that portion of the negro race which wishes to work had no cause for just complaint. It is the loafer, the idler, the fellow who wants the government to come to his assistance, the improperly educated, who want social equality and advantages that their merits do not justify."

49. "Cheap Southern Labor," *Manufacturers' Record,* Aug. 16, 1890; "The South and Labor," *Manufacturers' Record,* Aug. 10, 1905; "The Negro Problem," *Manufacturers' Record,* Oct. 28, 1898; Lorenzo J. Greene and Carter G. Woodson, *The Negro Wage Earner* (Washington, D.C.: Association for the Study of Negro Life and History, 1930), 252.

50. Harlan writes that Washington "all his life reflected the general viewpoint that Bryce [editor of Hampton's conservative *Southern Workman*] expressed. Cox concludes that the "essentially capitalist philosophy of individualism [led] Washington to take a consistently anti-labor position in the continuing struggle between capital and labor." See Harlan, *Washington: Making of a Black Leader,* 90–91; Cox, "Leadership among Negroes," 255.

Of course, not only accommodationists but black workers themselves had good reason to resent the racially exclusionary policies of mainstream organized labor, and those who chose to cross picket lines usually did so without any fear of sanction from within the black community. I remain unconvinced, however, either that black workers were exceptionally prone to strikebreaking in the New South or that when they undertook to do so it was with any cohesive, strategic deliberation.

51. Booker T. Washington, *Up from Slavery,* 62; F. E. Edmunds to Washington, July 4, 1914; Washington to Edmunds, July 8, 1914, in Harlan, ed., *BTW Papers*, vol. 13, 81, 84.

52. Gordon, *Caste & Class,* 117–18. See also William F. Holmes, "The Arkansas Cotton Pickers' Strike of 1891 and the Demise of the Colored Farmers' Alliance," *Arkansas Historical Quarterly* 32 (Summer 1973): 107–13.

53. For an extensive discussion of Birmingham race leaders and their involvement with industrial elites see my *Race, Class and Power in the Alabama Coalfields, 1908–1921* (Urbana: University of Illinois Press, 2001), 81–106. On Tuskegee's involvement in welfare work see Stein, "Of Mr. Booker T. Washington and Others," 447–48, and C. Vann Woodward, *Origins of the New South, 1877–1913* (Baton Rouge: Louisiana State University Press, 1951), 358–59. Labor Department observations on black preachers in the 1920 strike appear in Edwin C. Newdick, "Employers Foster Race Prejudice," Feb. 24, 1919, *Records of the Department of Labor,* RG 174, National Archives, Washington, D.C.

54. M. L. Alexander to M. L. Fleishel, Nov. 4, 1911, Box 205, *Kirby Lumber Company Records* (hereafter *KLCR*), Forest History Collection, East Texas Research Center, Stephen F. Austin State University, Nacogdoches, Texas; *Lumber Trade Journal,* Dec. 15, 1912.

55. "Special Report on Industrial Conditions in the Mills and Logging Camps of the Southern Pine Association," Aug. 1918, Box 67b, Southern Pine Association Records, Louisiana State University Archives, Baton Rouge, cited in James E. Fickle, "Management Looks at the 'Labor Problem': The Southern Pine Industry during World War I and the Postwar Era," *Journal of Southern History* 40:1 (Feb. 74): 68.

56. Cited in Thad Sitton and James H. Conrad, *Nameless Towns: Texas Sawmill Communities, 1880–1942* (Austin: University of Texas Press, 1998), 113; J. W. Herndon to C. P. Myer, Sept. 15, 1911, Box 197, *KLCR.*

57. W. T. Hooker to C. P. Myer, Aug. 14, 1911, Box 197, *KLCR;* Kirby Company to Crawford, June 6, 1917, Box 338, *KLCR.*

58. *Voice of Colored Labor,* 1923, Box 343, *KLCR;* SLOA to All Members, Nov. 5, 1918, Box 489, *Kurth Collection,* Forest History Collection, East Texas Research Center, Stephen F. Austin State University, Nacogdoches, Texas.

59. Despite their considerable differences, before the turn of the century both Washington and Du Bois pursued elitist solutions to the predicament of black southerners. But whereas Du Bois looked to a "Talented Tenth" to lead the black masses, he never pursued the alliance with white elites so central to Washington's outlook. After 1900, of course, the gulf between them widened further, and by World War I the cadre that would form the NAACP began to pay serious attention to the predicament of black laborers and to openly criticize southern white employers, an important shift precluded for Washington by his commitment to industrial accommodation. On the early symmetry between Washington and Du Bois, see Joel Williamson, *The Crucible*

of Race: Black–White Relations in the American South since Emancipation (New York: Oxford University Press, 1984), 73–75.

60. Theodore Rosengarten, *All God's Dangers: The Life of Nate Shaw* (New York: Knopf, 1974), 543.

61. Eric Foner, *Who Owns History? Rethinking the Past in a Changing World* (New York: Hill and Wang, 2002), xiv.

5 "We Must Live Anyhow": African American Women and Sex Work in Chicago, 1880–1900

In 1870, a *Chicago Times* reporter ventured into Chicago's largest red-light district to discover the thoughts of prostitutes and madams on a matter of great public concern—the sources of the "social evil." After greeting several white prostitutes from whom he elicited extended comments, the reporter made his way to what he described as a "dark and dank" area. Huddled together in this ominous terrain were the houses of prostitution in which black women labored and lived. He eventually approached one black prostitute and asked: "What shall we do with you women, eh?" Apparently unruffled by the disdain lurking behind his question, she responded frankly, "Well, boss, we must live anyhow."[1] With a matter-of-fact reply, this nameless black woman encapsulated the predicament that led some women to choose employment in Chicago's sex economy. Whereas disturbed city leaders regarded prostitution as a "social evil" that needed to be contained, regulated, or stamped out altogether, some working-class and working poor African American women in the late nineteenth-century city viewed prostitution as a means of survival.

In the last decades of the nineteenth century, African American women appear to have been disproportionately represented among Chicago's prostitutes. In 1880, when African Americans constituted 1 percent of the city's population, black women accounted for 15 percent of the prostitutes enumerated by federal census takers as living in the city's main red-light district. In 1890, African Americans still made up a meager 1 percent of the city's population, with black women constituting 2 percent of gainfully employed women. Yet, black houses of prostitution accounted for 12 percent of all brothels listed in an 1889 *Sporting and Club House Directory.* In 1900, black women accounted for 17 percent of women listed in the federal census as working in red-light-district "houses of ill-fame." However, in that year blacks made up only 2 percent of the city's overall population, and black women accounted for just 3 percent of all gainful female workers.[2]

These are high percentages, indeed. When it came to assessing the character of African American women, federal census enumerators and the compiler of the directory to Chicago's "sporting houses" were probably not unlike most white Americans at the end of the nineteenth century—primed by history and habit to see black women as innately sexually depraved. Widely held beliefs about black women's hypersexuality may have contributed to the frequency with which these investigators branded black women with the label of "prostitute." In fact, at the end of the century the commonplace usage of this characterization of black women by white politicians and political writers, journalists and historians North and South, galvanized African American women to organize a club movement that would eventually form the basis of the National Association of Colored Women.[3]

Yet, however imprecise, the data culled from the federal census and the *Sporting and Club House Directory* tell us much about race, prostitution, and the limits of black women's wage work in the nineteenth-century city. First, even if we assume that some overcounting occurred in both the census and in the brothel directory, the numbers point to the fact that, by however much, black women were overrepresented among sex workers and entrepreneurs. Second, African American women were highly visible inhabitants of Chicago's sex terrain. Whether they occupied the "dark and dank" recesses of the city, as characterized by the *Tribune* reporter, or shared the unruly streets at the center of the sex district, as reflected in the sporting directory, black women were noticeably active participants in Chicago's sex trade. Finally, for untold and perhaps unknowable numbers of African American women, sex work provided a viable, often necessary, means of earning money in an industrializing and rapidly expanding urban economy.[4]

This essay offers a close look at African American women's work in a remarkably public, widely disdained, and racially organized niche of the late nineteenth-century informal economy—the sex industry. Historically, the informal economy has been a vital arena of economic activity and represents an array of endeavors through which women and men have earned cash in urban economies that have otherwise limited their ability to make a living. Peripheral to an industrial economy structured by race and gender, and restricted to low-paying domestic employment, black working women were frequently forced to look beyond wage work to make ends meet. The sex economy was among the largest and perhaps the most visible sector of the urban informal economy, and unlike other informal pursuits such as gambling,[5] it offered a steady stream of jobs to women. Yet, like the wage economy from which many women sought refuge, the sex economy was organized in distinctive ways by race. In particular, in an industry in which a woman could earn as much as $20 or as little as 50 cents for her sexual services, black women found themselves consistently earning less than their white counterparts. No doubt aware of their concentration among the sex industry's lowest-paid workers, black prostitutes and entrepreneurs nonetheless hoped to take advantage of money-making opportunities within the sex trade. Significantly, black women's earnings from the informal sector were important not only for personal maintenance. Well into the twentieth century, the money women generated through prostitution (and as other informal pursuits) often provided necessary assistance to families and institutions in Chicago's growing black communities.

Although the urban informal sector provided many black women with critical opportunities for economic subsistence, African American women's work in urban sex economies and their participation in the informal economy more generally have gone largely unexplored. This essay seeks to fill in some of the gaps left by African American urban, labor, and women's histories that have ignored the full range of black women's work in industrializing northern cities. Moreover, it seeks to demonstrate the importance of black women's informal labor to the economic, social, and cultural life of urbanizing blacks in the late nineteenth and early twentieth centuries.

Prostitution and African American History

The lack of attention to the sex economy within histories of black urbanization and histories of black women's work has in part been an outcome of the frameworks that historians have used to understand black employment in the industrializing North and the cultural process of black urbanization. Beginning in the 1960s, historians turned their attention to the racial crisis developing in the nation's urban centers. Yet prostitution specifically and the informal economy more generally have been largely ignored as objects of historical analysis. Works published in the late 1960s and early 1970s, in particular Allan Spear's *Black Chicago,* Gilbert Osofsky's *Harlem,* and David Katzman's *Before the Ghetto,* were concerned with tracing the origins of a persistently vexing social problem—the urban ghetto. In an effort to demonstrate the tragic history and lingering consequences of de facto segregation in the North, these works painted the ghetto as a grim location characterized by its geographical isolation within the city and by the poverty and social alienation of its residents. In this rendering, black urban communities at the turn of the twentieth century were land-scapes of deprivation and despair from which "escape was impossible"[6] and where aberrant forms of economic behavior flourished. In these studies, the informal economy covered an assortment of economic endeavors, each marked by social deviance. From the "cons" of spiritualists, herb doctors, and "jackleg preachers," to the illegal endeavors of gamblers, bootleggers, and prostitutes, the informal economy uniformly symbolized the social and moral disintegration at the core of African American ghetto life.[7]

Subsequent work has challenged this representation of black community life in the North. Rather than focusing on the isolation and pathologies of African American communities, studies by Kenneth Kusmer, James Grossman, Richard Thomas, and Kimberly Phillips have examined the efforts of urbanizing blacks to build economically and institutionally sustainable communities within the context of limited opportunity in the urban North. As these works make clear, such efforts were repeatedly challenged—by the racial segmentation of the industrial labor force, by the reticence of white employers and the frequent resistance of white labor unions, and by the realities of spatial segregation. African American men and women battled against these barriers. In cities such as Chicago, Detroit, and Cleveland they created communities characterized not by despair, but by the hope of seizing the promise of urban industrial prosperity.[8] However, in the process of countering arguments of black urban pathology, recent studies have pushed black women's and men's work in the informal sex economy almost entirely out of view.[9]

Similarly, African American women's history has failed to give sustained attention to the work and earnings of prostitutes. Black women's sex work remains largely invisible even though feminist historians over the last two decades have energetically and creatively begun to explore African American women's distinctive position as wage earners within urban industrializing economies in the United States.[10] As many have shown, black women at the turn of the twentieth century were consigned largely to domestic work—as household servants, washerwomen, workers in commercial laundries, and cleaning women in hotels and office buildings. These studies offer kindred accounts of black women's sufferance of demeaning working conditions and unremitting drudgery. They also highlight the numerous acts of creative self-assertion, the resistance to the arbitrary domination of employers, and the instances of collective action that allowed African American women to wrestle some degree of self-respect from frequently demoralizing circumstances.

Uncovering African American women's experiences as workers remains an important undertaking, yet the focus on black women's labors in the wage economy tells only part of the story.[11] A more expansive — and accurate — definition of work must address the realities of economies marked by extreme racial and gender subordination. Such a broadened definition would necessarily include prostitution.

African American women's informal work within Chicago's sex industry should not be seen as an example of the social disorganization of urban black communities. Nor should it be dismissed as merely a deviation from the more central story of black women's struggles within the wage labor force. Rather, the story of prostitution is very much a part of the story of women's wage work. For black working women plagued by low pay and haunted by the insecurity of temporary, unskilled legitimate employment, sex work offered a means of personal and economic survival.

African American Women's Wage Work in Chicago

Chicago's African American community had been growing steadily since the 1860s, as had all segments of the city's population. Fueled by its reputation as the Midwest's center for industry and commerce, Chicago was a rapidly swelling metropolis. Between 1860 and 1900, its population increased from 109,000 to nearly 1,700,000. African Americans accounted for a small portion of this influx. Post–Civil War migrations quadrupled the black population from 955 in 1860 to 3,700 in 1870. In the next thirty years, blacks continued to move to Chicago at a steady rate, so that by 1900 they registered at just over 30,000. Yet, even though their rate of increase outstripped that of both native and foreign-born whites, blacks still made up just 2 percent of the city's total population at the turn of the century.[12]

Most migrants arriving in Chicago took up residence in the neighborhood enclaves that had been forming on the city's South Side since mid-century. In 1880, newcomers found inexpensive housing in the working-class district that extended for about a mile southward from the southern edge of downtown. Nearly half of Chicago's African Americans lived within this area. At the same time many black residents, especially those of some means and living in families, were establishing footholds in less congested white middle-class neighborhoods farther south. This trend would accelerate through the remainder of the century, so that by 1890, two-thirds of the city's blacks lived in the area stretching from Harrison Street to Thirty-Third Street. By 1900, 80 percent of Chicago's growing black population lived between Twelfth and Thirty-Ninth streets, with the center of the community steadily shifting southward.[13]

Successive waves of migrating men and women forged the residential paths and built the institutional structures of the neighborhood that after the turn of the century would be known as the Black Belt. These new-comers were eager to make new lives for themselves and their families. Coming from the farms and small towns of the upper South and Midwest, migrants were drawn to Chicago for a number of reasons. Fueled by word from northern visitors and lured by newspaper reports of the prosperity of Chicago's growing black community, men and women came to Chicago seeking the social and economic freedoms that the city had to offer in-dustrious individuals.[14] Many left southern homes to flee—and hopefully lessen—their families' economic hardship. Whether traveling with fam-ily or on their own, they departed a social climate that subjected them to increasingly repressive Jim Crow practices, escalating racial violence, and, for women, the ever-present threat of sexual abuse.[15]

Like the men and women who left the South for other northern des-tinations including Detroit, Pittsburgh, New York, and Cleveland, those who moved to Chicago hoped to escape the low pay and indignities of southern agricultural and domestic labor. However, migrants seeking em-ployment in Chicago confronted equally constricted, if better-paying, job opportunities. The majority of black men could secure only unskilled em-ployment, most often in service. In fact, in 1890 nearly half (47 percent) of black laboring men worked as waiters, butlers, coachmen, chauffeurs, barbers, and janitors in the homes, hotels, and businesses of the city's white middle-class and well-to-do. A smaller proportion, 15 percent, were em-ployed as unskilled laborers in Chicago's commercial establishments, fac-tories, and railroad yards. As one of the nation's fastest-growing industrial centers, Chicago had attracted men ready and willing to work in its diverse manufactories; yet few African American men made inroads into the city's industries other than as poorly paid and easily expendable day laborers.[16]

Women also confronted a labor market that consigned them to the lowest positions within the urban workforce. The majority of African American women could hope to find only domestic employment. In 1890, 77 percent of black women working in Chicago were concentrated in ser-vice work. In 1900, 71 percent of working black women were employed as servants. Even for those working women who made gains as semiskilled workers, most either partook of the expanding fields of mechanized do-mestic labor or made inroads into domestic fields previously closed to them. For example, of the 998 women classified as semiskilled in 1900, 55 percent were seamstresses and dressmakers, and another 26 percent were housekeepers in hotels, commercial rooming houses, or boardinghous-es. Unlike white women, who after 1880 gradually found their way into a broadening array of clerical and industrial occupations, black women found few paths into the diversifying economies of the city. At the turn of the century, black women remained largely sequestered in domestic and personal service.[17]

Black women's concentration in domestic work was rarely a comfortable fit. Whether employed as household domestics, as cooks or waitresses in restaurants, or as charwomen in downtown office buildings and hotels, black female service workers labored under adverse conditions. In the homes of middle-class and wealthy white families, black women endured long, grueling hours, limited free and family time, and, too often, sexual abuse. As cooks in downtown restaurants, they were given the least desirable and most strenuous tasks. As cleaning women in office buildings or as charwomen in hotels, black women worked under physical conditions more onerous than those suffered by their white female—both native-born and immigrant—coworkers. The casual or seasonal nature of some service jobs, such as hotel employment or laundering, added a degree of uncertainty to women's earnings. And, like all service workers, black women toiled for traditionally low pay.[18]

With notable ingenuity and often with some sacrifice, black women struggled to mold the limited occupations within and low wages of service work to suit their personal aspirations, familial obligations, and economic needs. However, the obstacles African American working women faced in their efforts to make a living and at the same time defend their independence and dignity led some to look elsewhere for their money.

For many African American women in the late nineteenth century, making money in Chicago's informal economy was an integral part of urban living. As historian Tera Hunter has argued in her study of black domestic workers in postemancipation Atlanta, women's "incessant effort to try to find better terms for their work" could lead them to "move in and out of the labor market."[19] Black women frequently used the act of quitting as a strategy to improve working condition; yet leaving the legitimate labor market did not necessarily mean that women had given up work. Rather, black women (and men) were often forced to create opportunities elsewhere in the urban economy. Black women's enterprising attempts to make ends meet beyond wage work could include home-based needlework, keeping boarders, or turning their homes into places for black women's hair grooming. Newspaper advertisements for female elocutionists, herbalists, and spiritual advisors reveal other ways that black women carved out niches for themselves in Chicago's commercial economy. Such advertisements also suggest that black women's informal work ranged from the respectable to the dubious.[20] Sometimes black women's efforts to make money could shade into the illegal and criminal. Several women turned, at least for a while, to Chicago's flourishing sex economy.

Although it was an illegal enterprise, for the women involved selling sexual services for money was primarily an economic endeavor. Yet, even as it provided an alternative to service work, sex work had its own indignities and hazards. All women took numerous risks when they engaged in prostitution. At a time when venereal diseases such as syphilis and gonorrhea were incurable, sex workers daily exposed themselves to potentially debilitating or even deadly health risks. Nineteenth-century records on rates of venereal disease in American cities are incomplete, but in one study 40 percent of prostitutes working in New York City disclosed that they had contracted syphilis or gonorrhea.[21] Sex workers also risked pregnancy. And whether pregnant or suffering from venereal infection, prostitutes could not count on adequate or regular medical care. They encountered other perils, as well, including theft, frequent arrest, and social ostracism.[22]

Prostitution was a system that sanctioned and commodified women's sexual subordination. If male sexual license was at the heart of the sex economy, sex workers had to regularly contend with varied enactments of male privilege. Prostitutes might have to suffer the disdain or verbal abuse of their customers; women also faced the possibility of physical assault and sexual violence.[23] For black women, the indignities, and at times brutalities, of sexual exploitation were compounded by the inescapable fact of racial subordination. For women who entertained white customers, prevailing racial ideologies and the history of white men's sexual violation of black women must have made sexual contact with white clients at best a psychically demanding proposition, and at worst a demeaning experience.

Given the trade's harsh realities, sex work would seem to be an unappealing alternative to even the most onerous kinds of service work. Even though prostitution was dangerous, in the eyes of some women, the financial benefits of sex work outweighed the job's negative aspects. Indeed, many prostitutes may not have seen prostitution as an arena of male privilege at all. As we turn our attention to the choices that black women made in Chicago's sex trade, we begin to see that sex work was defined as much by its race and gender inequalities as it was by women's active and sometimes creative attempts to avoid, ameliorate, or even subvert them. The choice of whether or not to enter the sex trade was no doubt a difficult one. Black women who made that choice did so because the sex economy offered them something they could not find in the wage economy—the possibility of escaping the endless grind of domestic work and the hope of earning a living wage.

Working the Sex Economy

Chicago's sex trade ostensibly peddled a single commodity—women's sexual services. Yet it offered black women a number of different ways to pursue economic security, and women working as prostitutes labored in a variety of settings. Most black prostitutes worked within Chicago's largest and most concentrated sex terrain, the Levee District. In existence between 1874 and 1904, the Levee was located just south of downtown, framed by Van Buren on the north and Twelfth Street on the south, State Street on the east and Clark on the west. The most visible sex institution within the Levee was the brothel, an institution that took many forms. Levee brothels ranged from the inconspicuous two-woman establishment to the raucous ten-prostitute enterprise, from the no-frills 50-cent house to the extravagant $20 resort. Most black women worked in the low-priced brothels that were strewn along the main thoroughfares of the Levee sex trade—Custom House Place, Plymouth Street, and Clark Street. Employing between two and five women, these brothels were usually located in apartment building flats or occupied the rooms above saloons, restaurants, and other businesses.

The majority of black prostitutes worked in brothels run by black women. These businesswomen, some more successfully than others, joined white madams to provide the institutional foundation for the late nineteenth-century sex trade. They provided the places—houses or apartments—where women worked and sex-seeking men pursued their desires. The line separating madam and prostitute was not always clear, though. Some women combined the roles of sex entrepreneur and sex worker, usually working on their own out of their apartments or private rooms in a rooming house. Not all black prostitutes worked in houses of prostitution, however. Many sold their services out of saloons or hotels, or in boardinghouses; others used the streets to secure trade. The variegated organization of the urban sex trade allowed black women to find a form of sex work that suited their individual financial needs and familial obligations and that best accommodated the length of time they anticipated working in the trade.[24]

Nevertheless, in the late nineteenth century the brothel was at the center of the Levee's sex economy. Looking at the circumstances of a few African American madams and prostitutes will illustrate the variety in brothel prostitution. At the age of thirty-eight, Elizabeth Morris operated a small house of prostitution at 116 Custom House Place.[25] Morris employed two younger women, nineteen-year-old Jennie White and twenty-year-old Minnie Carter. Next door, Elizabeth Moore, thirty-six, operated a larger brothel housing seven women, all between the ages of twenty-two and twenty-four. Georgia Styles, forty-five, kept an unassuming house of prostitution on South Clark Street that housed four women ranging in age from nineteen to forty-five. Whereas these brothels occupied individual flats in Levee buildings, an especially successful brothel could occupy an entire house or a three-story apartment building. Hattie Briggs ran two such resorts in the 1890s, both on Custom House Place. Resorts of this size employed as many as ten women.[26]

Black prostitutes working in the area's numerous affordably priced houses of prostitution took advantage of the traffic of black and white laborers who lived in the furnished rooms, boardinghouses, and residential hotels that shaped residential life in the Levee. Male Levee dwellers generally earned low or irregular wages in employments conveniently located nearby. Native-born or foreign-born white men found work in the light industries or freight yards near the Chicago River, or in downtown warehouses. A large proportion of African American men found work as servants in downtown hotels and restaurants. Some men found temporary jobs in neighborhood institutions and in the leisure resorts of the Levee, working as waiters in nearby restaurants, or as porters in neighborhood saloons, boardinghouses, hotels, and brothels. The majority of black women's customers were drawn from this pool of low-wage workers who after work sought out recreation in nearby saloons, pool halls, and brothels.[27]

For most black women, then, "working the sex economy" meant finding ways to get working-class men to spend their meager earnings on the sexual entertainments they provided. To attract working men, many black women ran what Timothy Gilfoyle has referred to as "public houses," raucous brothels whose ambiance mirrored the boisterous atmosphere of the Levee's working-class saloons and pool halls. For example, in the 1890s Hattie Briggs ran two unruly brothels, each attached to saloons. Police officers frequently descended on Briggs's places to quiet loud employees and drunk patrons.[28] After attracting workers to their doors, however, madams such as Briggs did not encourage men to linger. Whereas in more expensive houses, extended and sometimes elaborate services could translate into more money for a prostitute and her madam, in low-priced brothels, rapid turnover ensured increased earnings.[29]

For women facing severely restricted job prospects, even low-wage sex work could pay reasonably well. In an inexpensive house, a black woman earning $1 per customer and seeing only two men a day could generate $14 per week. It was customary for brothel keepers to take half of their employees' earnings. Even with this significant reduction in pay, a black brothel worker could earn $7 at the end of the week, roughly two times the wages black women earned as domestic workers whose income was at or below the poverty level. Yet some black prostitutes earned less than this. Only by regularly servicing a high volume of men could women in 50-cent houses earn more than most domestic servants. Financial desperation joined with the expectation of earning more money to keep some black (and white) women working at the least profitable phases of the sex trade.[30]

A handful of black prostitutes earned far more than women employed in the Levee's working-class sex resorts. These women worked in parlor houses, the ornate and expensive houses of prostitution for which the Levee was best known. Parlor houses catered to an exclusive white male trade—local men of wealth and pleasure-seeking business travelers. These institutions combined the attractions of the billiard hall, the concert saloon, and the brothel, placing them all within the confines of the magnificently decorated home.[31] During the 1880s and 1890s, the majority of the Chicago's parlor houses were located along Custom House Place and Clark Street between Harrison and Taylor streets. Although they entertained a clientele quite different from the customers who visited the area's humble brothels, parlor houses were not separate from cheaper resorts. In fact, the most extravagant sex resorts neighbored the humbler workplaces of most black prostitutes. The proximity of elite houses helped to bring inexpensive black resorts into the center of the Levee trade.[32]

The money needed to furnish these multiuse and multiroomed houses was beyond the means of the vast majority of African American madams and prostitutes. Yet a few black women were able to meet the criteria of refinement, domesticity, and exclusivity upheld in the most lavish white parlor houses. Out of sixty-seven parlor houses listed in the *Sporting and Club House Directory,* three (only 4 percent) were "colored houses."[33] Madam Vina Fields managed a large parlor house on Custom House Place in the center of the Levee. Madams Lillian Richardson and Ella White operated brothels outside the Levee, in a small sex district emerging near Twenty-Second Street on the city's South Side.[34]

Of the three elite brothels, Madam Fields's house was the most successful. In 1889, Fields was a well-known madam who after ten years in the city had turned the peddling of black women's sexual services into a prosperous and highly visible enterprise. Her parlor house was unusually large, occupying two adjoining houses. In fact in the 1880s and 1890s, Fields's House of Pleasure was among the city's largest brothels, with each house typically lodging fifteen women. When business was booming, as was the case during the 1893 World's Columbian Exposition, her parlor house employed more than sixty women.[35]

Lillian Richardson operated her brothel on Twenty-First Street. An

1889 guidebook writer described her resort as "the most quiet and retired colored house in the city." Ella White's brothel was located a few blocks away from Richardson's house. Each woman supervised small enterprises housing only four or five women. Although both Richardson and White were parlor house madams, neither appears to have achieved the success of Vina Fields. Much smaller than Fields's capacious brothel, their resorts were comparable to nearby elite white brothels, most of which employed between five and seven women.[36]

Whatever the size of the parlor house, certain amenities were crucial to its success — the artful blending of domesticity and festivity, and the interweaving of musical entertainment, wine, and attractive women into an atmosphere of refined male sociality. Yet given the ongoing capital investments needed to prosper in this tier of the sex industry, it is likely that Fields, Richardson, and White occupied places more modest in decor than their white sisters in the parlor trade. They nevertheless endeavored to construct sex resorts for white middle-class and well-to-do pleasure seekers. These women accomplished their goal by advertising the specific nature of their resorts' exclusivity. The individual entries for Fields, White, and Richardson in the *Sporting and Club House Directory* made it plain: "*No colored men admitted*" [emphasis in original]. (Similar notices were not in entries for white parlor houses, where the exclusion of black men was customary.)[37] The prohibition of black male customers assured middle-class white men that they would have exclusive access to black women's sexual favors. This, perhaps more than a lavish decor, guaranteed the status of black parlor houses.

In adopting this exclusionary practice, black madams hoped to profit from white men's presumptions of black women's hypersexuality and black men's sexual degeneracy, as well as their belief in their own racial and gender supremacy. Heedless of the warnings of late nineteenth-century journalists and guidebook writers who regularly warned middle-class men about "dangerous" black women lurking in the Levee, white men of means sought out the particular sexual delights they imagined black women could offer. Yet if racial myths lured some white men to the doors of black parlor houses, they also accounted for the comparatively low prices they paid for black women's sexual services. Both Lillian Richardson and Vina Fields charged between $3 and $5 for their workers' sexual services. Ella White's prices went as low as $2. White women working in elite brothels, however, could command from between $5 and $30 for their services.[38] The low prices white men paid to have illicit sex with black women highlight the economic consequences black women suffered working at the intersection of sexual desire and racial contempt.

In tone, price, and clientele, parlor houses were quite different from the resorts in which most black prostitutes worked. Parlor house madams usually imposed rigid standards of behavior on their workers. For example, Vina Fields was known to run her house with a firm hand, posting "the rules and regulations of the Fields house" in every room, thereby "enforc[ing] decorum and decency with pains and penalties which could hardly be more strict if they were drawn up for the regulation of a Sunday school."[39] Fields's rigidity may have been extreme, yet it is likely that other black parlor house keepers required similar conduct from their employees. Like Fields, they hoped to appeal to white men of means, most of whom did not want their associations with black prostitutes detectable beyond brothel walls. For the most part, such rules did not govern the work experiences of black women employed in working-class brothels. In fact, many brothels thrived by flouting the decorum expected in nearby parlor houses.

Racial exclusivity was also ignored in black working-class brothels. Indeed, black houses survived by entertaining black patrons unwelcome in white houses. Although many white prostitutes entertained black men — to the distress of moral reformers and police authorities — some white women worked in inexpensive resorts that, like parlor houses, refused to admit black men as customers. Additionally, some black men might have been reluctant to engage the services of white prostitutes. Male migrants from the Jim Crow South's sexually charged climate may have been wary of crossing racial boundaries the transgression of which very often brought violence to black men.[40] Together, some black men's reluctance to visit white houses and their exclusion from resorts frequented by white middle- and upper-class men created a niche for enterprising black brothel owners. Black sex workers had easy, although not exclusive, access to the earnings of laboring black men.

Many white men, on the other hand, refused to engage the services of black prostitutes. Some elite and working-class responded with revulsion rather than curiosity to the myth of black women's racial inferiority and sexual depravity and avoided black houses altogether. For black prostitutes in cheaper brothels, the refusal of some white men to patronize their establishments was offset by their black customers and by white workers who had few reservations about hiring black women's sexual services. Yet wherever they worked, the racial views of pleasure-seeking men shaped black women's economic prospects in the sex trade.

The Brothel Workplace

The appeal of the brothel to paying men was more or less straightforward — it catered to men's desire for unencumbered sexual play outside of marriage.

The brothel's appeal to working women might not be as apparent. Nonetheless, houses such as those run by Elizabeth Morris, Hattie Briggs, and Ella White did offer some attractions for black working-class women. Brothels were not only places of work; for the women who labored in them, they were also homes. At a basic level, brothels provided shelter for young single black women for whom it was frequently difficult to secure affordable room and board in the city. Because many brothels were designed to be attractive and comfortable to prospective customers, they provided homelike comforts to the women who staffed them. Meals and clothing were frequently provided by madams; even if the price of each was deducted from a prostitute's earnings, such an arrangement might appeal to women on their own in the city. Furthermore, this arrangement compared favorably to the prospect of live-in domestic service. Although food and shelter were provided by employers of live-in servants, low pay, isolation in the homes of white families, and severe limitations on a woman's free time made live-in work unappealing for many black women. Finally, the social context of the brothel must have been attractive to some black women, most of whom were young, unattached migrants. In brothels, women shared their living spaces with at least two other women of about the same age. Work requirements and competition for clients could lead to conflicts, but many women no doubt forged friendships through their shared experiences. These friendships could fortify individual women as each tried to make a life for herself in an economically and socially challenging city.[41]

Yet working in brothels had numerous drawbacks. The sexual and nonsexual labors that prostitutes had to perform within brothel-homes were demanding and repetitive: greeting and entertaining customers in the parlor; sexually entertaining a steady stream of men in private boudoirs; assuring clients of their attractiveness and desirability; and constant self-care required to produce appealing personal effects and reflect well on the establishment. Although many white brothels hired live-in help, few black brothels—with the exception of Vina Fields's House of Pleasure—employed servants to cook or clean; thus, black women's brothel work regularly included domestic chores.[42]

Working under a madam had its own challenges. The watchfulness of a brothel madam could constrain a prostitute's activities in both inexpensive and elite houses. It could also limit the amount of money a worker might earn from a customer. The standard procedure of splitting earnings from a night's labors with a madam meant that brothel prostitutes watched large portions of their hard-earned money drift away from them. Some women might secretly try to get tips from patrons, but a madam's vigilance could make it difficult for workers to conceal extra earnings. Some brothel

keepers forbade their employees from seeing men outside of the brothel, further constraining prostitutes' earning opportunities. The internal
workings of black brothels are difficult to discern from available sources,
yet black madams who strove to maximize their take from the earnings
of their employees no doubt adopted these common brothel practices.[43]
The wages of brothel work may not have fully compensated women for
the difficulties they endured as employees under a madam's supervision.

Furthermore, African American brothels were often short-lived enterprises haunted by financial insecurity. Only a handful of black houses stayed
in business for any length of time. Of the black-owned brothels that left
traces in the historical record, few lasted for more than a couple of years.
The exceptions included the resorts of Hattie Briggs, Vina Fields, and Black
Mag, a madam whose brothel survived into the twentieth century and was
famous for staging wild sex shows for a white male audience. The majority
of black brothel keepers felt the strains of the comparatively low earnings
of their workers. Economic vulnerability frequently led to business failure.
Like poor brothels housing white women, few black houses of prostitution
stayed at a single address for too long. In any given year, a survey of Chicago's
brothels might find several black houses in a particular block. The next year,
one or all of those houses might have moved on, replaced by white establishments, other black resorts, or by the residences of working-class families.
For example, the 1889 *Sporting and Club House Directory* counted fourteen
"coon dives" concentrated at the southern end of Custom House Place. Four
years later, a Hull-House investigator counted only two black houses along
the same stretch; another reformer found only one.[44]

Brothel employees felt this insecurity particularly acutely. Given the
often fragile economies of black sex institutions, black women were
forced to devise ways to stabilize or increase their own earnings. One way
was to move frequently from one house to another, continuing the search
for better terms of employment that initially led them into prostitution.
Even if they could temporarily find a better-paying or more stable job,
they usually encountered the same predicament. Struggling to counterbal-
ance the instability of brothels and thereby ensure their own income, most
working-class prostitutes tried to maximize their exposure to the traffic
of men along Levee District thoroughfares by incorporating street work
into their daily work routine.

The Street

Historians of turn-of-the-century prostitution have frequently associated
African American women with street prostitution. Black streetwalkers have

also been linked to the shabbiest confines and most dangerous sectors of the sex industry. Black women's apparent concentration in streets, cribs, and alleyways, it has been argued, demonstrates their fundamental degradation in the urban sex economy. Furthermore, some have assumed that the sex work that began in the streets invariably concluded in squalid brothels or exposed alleys—locations quite removed from the brothel circuit.[45] Yet a look at black women's street work in Chicago gives us reason to revisit these commonly held assumptions. As we have seen, at the end of the nineteenth century, black women were not concentrated in street prostitution but were highly visible in Chicago's brothel trade. Yet even when they solicited trade on the streets, they very often did so as representatives of black brothels.

Rather than being detached, sex district thoroughfares were drawn quite aggressively into the sex economy that was based in brothels and in nearby saloons and assignation houses. Brothel madams, saloon keepers, and prostitutes strategically used sex district streets to gain access to the pockets of the men who daily and nightly roamed through the Levee. One way was to solicit men as they passed by open brothel windows. One police detective recalled that most Custom House Place brothels in the 1890s aggressively solicited men from the streets:

> Here at all hours of the day and night women could be seen at the doors and windows, frequently half-clad, making an exhibition of themselves and using vulgar and obscene language. At almost all of these places there were sliding windows, or windows that were hung on hinges and swung inside. . . . The habitues of this place embraced every nationality, both black and white, their ages ranging from eighteen to fifty.[46]

On thoroughfares where houses of prostitution were thickly settled, competition was stiff, and many brothel keepers required that their employees make more active use of the streets. Men passing black resorts were frequently targeted for invitations to sexual pleasure. A. Rapp, a white man who lived in a middle-class enclave on the city's South Side, reported being "seized by a negro woman who attempted to force him into her house" of prostitution on Custom House Place.[47] Alice Green, Bell Parker, and Ida Snow were arrested for luring a white Wisconsin man into their Clark Street resort and for robbing him of over $50.[48]

Such aggressive self-promotion was a necessity for women who were likely to work in houses that could not compete with the extravagantly attractive fronts and window devices of larger or elite brothels. On the streets, they could advertise their lower rates and, in so doing, attempt to stem the traffic flowing to white resorts. Black women struggled to enhance their visibility precisely because of their depressed earnings in brothels and saloons.

However advantageous street work may have been to black prostitutes, it had its shortcomings. The constant pursuit of clients could be wearing. Black sex workers had to approach white men who may have been hostile to their solicitations. On the streets, they also were exposed to theft and physical assault by customers and thieves who could easily make a getaway. Among the greatest challenges faced by women who used the streets were the unexpected events that could interrupt their ability to earn money by slowing the traffic of men to the sex district. Women and resorts that relied on street-generated trade suffered, for example, when the police sweeps of district thoroughfares scared away potential clients.

Black women's visibility on the streets had other costs. Efforts to secure trade made women visible to policemen who were under orders to keep the sex traffic from public spaces. Officers were frequently dispatched to Clark Street, State Street, and Custom House Place to clear them of all "sidewalk sylphs" and "black women of bad character."[49] Because of their visibility on the streets, and because of popular assumptions about black female depravity, black prostitutes were subject to more frequent arrest than white women. They frequently faced harsh penalties for their public transgressions. In 1876, Dora Perry, described in the *Daily News* as "a black wench," was arrested and charged in police court for vagrancy. At a time when most arrested white prostitutes were given fines averaging $5, Perry was found guilty of being "a prostitute of the worst kind" and given a substantial $20 fine. She was also threatened with confinement to the bridewell if she was unable to pay. In the 1890s, several black street workers regularly received brutal treatment at the hands of a particularly zealous police detective.[50]

The difficulties of working on Levee streets notwithstanding, it appears that street work was useful to black sex workers at all but the highest levels of the trade. To be sure, black women were not alone in street soliciting; white brothel workers also generated trade by advertising their services on the streets. However, for black women, street work announced a unique economic vulnerability in Chicago's sex marketplace; it also indicated the insecurity of the brothels, bawdy saloons, and other leisure establishments out of which they worked. In the process of bolstering the fragile economies of these sex resorts, black women who used the streets hoped to ameliorate their own circumstances.

Out of the Sex Economy

Sex work was hard work. Although it offered women an alternative to menial domestic employment and could provide some material rewards and social comforts, few women stayed in the trade for extended periods of time. In 1880, most women working in Chicago's sex economy were younger than twenty-five. Among African American sex workers, 78 percent were between the ages of nineteen and twenty-four; 65 percent of white prostitutes fell in this age group. In 1900, the prime years for brothel employment remained between the ages of nineteen and twenty-four: 62 percent of black brothel workers and 58 percent of white workers were in their early twenties. Except for a handful of prosperous madams—such as Vina Fields and Black Mag—brothel prostitution was not a long-term means of accumulating income for either black or white workers.[51]

It is difficult to determine where women went after they left brothel employment. Some turned to other illegal activities. Such was the case with Flossie Moore, a prostitute who briefly worked in Vina Fields's resort. According to a police reminiscence, Moore was a "high-strung, restless," and "self-willed" woman who eventually tired of Fields's rules and regulations. After she left Fields's house, she became one of the "toughest thugs, footpads and pickpockets in Chicago." Minnie Shouse was another prostitute and pickpocket who worked the Levee streets. In the 1890s, Shouse was reported to have been arrested almost weekly for robbing men on the streets of the sex district. According to one source, "her victims were mostly strangers and traveling men found around the vicinity of the Polk street depot,"[52] which emptied traveling men and women directly onto the streets of the Levee. For some intrepid black women such as Flossie Moore and Minnie Shouse, brothel prostitution was just one of several methods by which a woman could hustle a man out of his money.

Although such thievery could bring swift profits, few black women actually chose this course. More women left brothels to work in other outlets of sexual entertainment. Especially important for black women were the black-owned "disorderly" saloons that began to multiply in Chicago in the 1890s. Blending the saloon atmosphere with musical entertainment, dancing, and sometimes gambling, disorderly saloons flouted the reserve of common "gentlemen's" saloons and some brothels. Sex workers openly circulated among patrons, or beckoned from doorways or curtains at the back of the saloon leading to private chambers or upstairs rooms. The incursions of black male saloon proprietors into the Levee sex economy worked to the benefit of black sex workers who wanted to work in the sex industry but who had little patience for the restrictions of the brothel or the risks involved in self-employment. By the turn of the century, black disorderly saloons had begun to challenge the brothel as the preeminent site of black women's sex work.[53]

Although some women chose to seek out nonbrothel opportunities within the Levee landscape, others, it appears, left the trade altogether. Working as a prostitute, it seems, did not necessarily lead to a life in the sex trade. Nor did a stint in the sex economy necessarily sever a woman's connections to Chicago's emerging African American community. Women could sometimes conceal their brothel employment from relatives and friends living at a distance from the Levee. After earning some cash in the sex economy, many young black women returned to less remunerative work, able to live among the family and friends who had initially eased their transition to life in Chicago. Turn-of-the-century reform and journalistic accounts nervously portrayed prostitution as a profession that inevitably took girls and women on a downward spiral to impoverishment, degradation, and death. Yet sex workers, black and white, experienced a considerable degree of mobility out of the economy.[54]

Conclusion

In the late nineteenth century, whether they worked as household servants, laundresses, hotel maids, or prostitutes, African American working women were peripheral to Chicago's industrializing economy. Yet the fortunes of black sex workers were very much tied to the earnings of businessmen, clerical workers, and a growing pool of white and black male laborers. Brothels, Levee streets, and disorderly saloons served as transfer points where money earned in the commercial and industrial sectors shifted to women with limited opportunities in the formal economy. For African American prostitutes, work in the informal sex economy bound them to Chicago's formal economy.

Although African American sex workers were dependent on men's variable earnings in the wage economy, they were generally paid more than "dependent daughters" or "attached" women—women financially sheltered by fathers or husbands. Like the white women beside whom they worked in Chicago's sex districts, black prostitutes were paid the comparatively high wages attainable almost exclusively within the underground economy. Black women's earnings, however, were depressed by powerful racialized sexual ideologies. The commodity that black women sold remained the least valued, and as a group they were the poorest among the city's prostitutes. The intersection of race, sexuality, and the economy must have been frustrating for even the best-paid black prostitutes and madams. Although paid as self-supporting women, black women who worked in Chicago's sex industry suffered the economic consequences of the era's racial–sexual hierarchy.

For African American women, working in the sex industry provided no escape from the severe racial prejudices that weighed so heavily on them in the formal economy. Indeed, it is hard to imagine that white fantasies of black women's inferiority did not dog them in every financial transaction and in their sexual interactions with customers. Given the sexual nature of the era's racial mythology, it might be difficult to fathom why black women in turn-of-the-century Chicago would willingly seek employment in the underground sex trade. Indeed, how could a group of women, most of whom arrived in Chicago between 1870 and 1900 in search of the economic opportunity and social freedoms that the urban North was storied to offer, engage in work that so publicly suggested acceptance of the personae of debased women?

Even though contemporary onlookers, as well as many paying customers, may have labeled black sex workers morally depraved and socially dangerous women, we should not view black prostitutes as either of these. Rather, participation in the sex trade was evidence of black women's profound economic marginalization. One need only recall their disproportionate presence among Chicago's prostitutes—between eight and twenty times their proportion of the general population—to be struck by the economic forces impelling black women to prostitution and the economic implications of black women's sexual labors.

Yet, black women were not passive victims of economic displacement. To be sure, turning to prostitution could bespeak desperation among poor black women, but it also exemplified their resourcefulness within Chicago's race- and gender-stratified industrial economy. The sparely worded assertion of the black prostitute that opened this chapter—"we must live anyhow"—evokes both the economic hardship and the personal resourcefulness of individual black women in the sex industry. Significantly, these words did not explain only one woman's predicament. This unnamed prostitute explicitly acknowledged a similarity of experiences and perhaps outlook that linked her to other black women working in the Levee sex trade.

For many black women, sex work could be an assertion of self-respect. Indeed, as Victoria Wolcott has argued, a prostitute's ability to support herself in the city reaped for her more immediate benefits than the discourse of virtuous womanhood ever could.[55] Although working in the sex economy offered no guarantees, prostitution could help to liberate black women from the meanest of circumstances in the city. In addition, the sex trade offered a concrete means of escaping dependence—on parents, other relatives, husbands, or even charitable agencies.

For all its remunerative potential, prostitution was a difficult and at times dangerous method of earning money. In the practice of their trade, women faced social ostracism from neighbors and religious and social re-formers. Many no doubt maintained a distance from relatives, shielding themselves from the disapproval of their own families. Relations with clients bore numerous hazards. There was the chance of pregnancy, the looming threat of contracting venereal disease, and the possibility of physical abuse. Even the financial compensations that made the rigors of sex work bearable were not always predictable. Police harassment could diminish a brothel's earnings. And as workers in the leisure economy, women were vulnerable to the economic fortunes of middle- and working-class men. An economic downturn could quickly shrink the Levee's customer base.

Black prostitutes were keenly aware of the job's shortcomings. Like all women working in the sex economy, they developed strategies to cope with the numerous problems and daily indignities they faced as sexual commodities. They shared many of these working conditions with white women laboring in the trade. Many indignities, however, were theirs alone.

For African American women, work in this branch of the informal economy entailed serious trade-offs. While earning more money than they could in the legitimate economy, black sex workers contended with a prevailing racial mythology that branded all black women as morally debased; they submitted to a sexual rate structure that blatantly devalued their bodies and their labors; and they acceded to an urban wage system that required that working women look beyond wage work if they hoped to be paid as other than extensions of working men. Even as they labored outside of the formal economy, African American sex workers did not escape the oppressive racial and gender order of the urban economy. Paradoxically, working on the fringes of a modernizing urban economy, they confronted its contradictions head-on.

Notes

This essay is part of a larger study of African American women and prostitution in turn-of-the-century Chicago. I would like to thank Amanda Lewis, Tyrone Forman, Bryant Marks, Michelle Boyd, and Peg Strobel for their insightful comments on earlier versions of this essay.

1. *Chicago Times,* November 27, 1870.
2. Allan H. Spear, *Black Chicago: The Making of a Negro Ghetto, 1890–1920* (Chicago: University of Chicago Press, 1967), 12; *The Sporting and Club House Directory* (Chicago: Ross and St. Clair, 1889); U.S. Bureau of the Census, Tenth Census (1880), Chicago Manuscript Schedules, Enumeration Districts 5, 8, and 9; U.S. Bureau of the Census, Twelfth Census (1900), Chicago Manuscript Schedules, Enumeration Districts 12, 21, 30, 42, and 43; Estelle Hill Scott, *Occupational Changes among Negroes in Chicago* (Chicago: Illinois Writers' Projects Administration, 1939), 38, 72.

3. See Dorothy Salem, *To Better Our World: Black Women in Organized Reform, 1890–1920* (Brooklyn, N.Y.: Carlson, 1990); Deborah Gray White, *Too Heavy a Load: Black Women in Defense of Themselves, 1894–1994* (New York: Norton, 1999).

4. Important general studies of prostitution in American cities at the turn of the century include Ruth Rosen, *The Lost Sisterhood: Prostitution in America, 1900–1918* (Baltimore: Johns Hopkins University Press, 1982), and Timothy Gilfoyle, *City of Eros: New York City, Prostitution, and the Commercialization of Sex, 1790–1920* (New York: Norton, 1992).

5. Ann Fabian, *Card Sharps, Dream Books, and Bucket Shops: Gambling in 19th-Century America* (Ithaca, N.Y.: Cornell University Press, 1990). For a discussion of gambling in African American communities in the early twentieth century see Victoria Wolcott, *Remaking Respectability: African American Women in Interwar Detroit* (Chapel Hill: University of North Carolina Press, 2001), 121–26.

6. David M. Katzman, *Before the Ghetto: Black Detroit in the Nineteenth Century* (Urbana: University of Illinois Press, 1975), 210.

7. Spear, *Black Chicago;* Katzman, *Before the Ghetto;* Kenneth B. Clark, *Dark Ghetto: Dilemmas of Social Power* (New York: Harper and Row, 1965); Gilbert Osofsky, *Harlem: The Making of a Ghetto* (New York: Harper and Row, 1966).

8. Kenneth L. Kusmer, *A Ghetto Takes Shape: Black Cleveland, 1870–1930* (Urbana: University of Illinois Press, 1976); James R. Grossman, *Land of Hope: Chicago, Black Southerners, and the Great Migration* (Chicago: University of Chicago Press, 1989); Richard W. Thomas, *Life for Us Is What We Make It: Building Black Community in Detroit, 1915–1945* (Bloomington: Indiana University Press, 1992). Recent studies such as Kimberly L. Phillips's *AlabamaNorth* have further expanded our understanding of the extent of self-activity among African American men and women in cities. Looking at cultural practices ranging from religious and family life to leisure activities, these studies offer forceful critiques of the "social disorganization" model of black urban study. *AlabamaNorth: African-American Migrants, Community, and Working-Class Activism in Cleveland, 1915–45* (Urbana: University of Illinois Press, 1999).

9. A notable exception is Victoria W. Wolcott, *Remaking Respectability: African American Women in Interwar Detroit* (Chapel Hill: University of North Carolina Press, 2001), 93–130.

10. See Jacqueline Jones, *Labor of Love, Labor of Sorrow: Black Women, Work, and the Family, from Slavery to the Present* (New York: Vintage Books, 1986); Joanne J. Meyerowitz, *Women Adrift: Independent Wage Earners in Chicago, 1880–1930* (Chicago: University of Chicago Press, 1988); Elizabeth Clark-Lewis, *Living In, Living Out: African American Domestics in Washington, D.C., 1910–1940* (New York: Kondansha International, 1996); Tera W. Hunter, *To 'Joy My Freedom: Southern Black Women's Lives and Labors after the Civil War* (Cambridge, Mass.: Harvard University Press, 1997).

11. A notable departure from the exclusive focus on wage employment is Victoria Wolcott's work on black women numbers runners, mediums, and spiritualists in Detroit between World Wars I and II. Victoria W. Wolcott, "The Culture of the Informal Economy: Numbers Runners in Inter-War Detroit," *Radical History Review* 69 (1997): 46–75; "Mediums, Messages, and Lucky Numbers: African-American Female Spiritualists and Numbers Runners in Interwar Detroit," in Patricia Yaeger, ed., *The Geography of Identity* (Ann Arbor: University of Michigan Press, 1996), 273–306.

12. Spear, *Black Chicago,* 12; Homer Hoyt, *One Hundred Years of Land Values in Chicago: The Relationship of the Growth of Chicago to the Rise in its Land Values, 1830–1933* (Chicago: University of Chicago Press, 1933), 284; Bessie Louise Pierce, *A History of Chicago,* vol. 3, *The Rise of the Modern City, 1871–1893* (New York: Knopf, 1957), 515–16, 519.

13. African Americans could still be found throughout the city: they accounted for at least 1 percent of the population in fourteen of the city's thirty-five wards. Spear, *Black Chicago,* 12–15; Chicago Commission on Race Relations, *The Negro in Chicago* (Chicago: University of Chicago Press, 1922), 107.

14. Newspaper announcements of the social activities and travels of northern blacks painted a vivid portrait not only of prosperity, but of mobility unavailable in southern towns or rural districts. The doings of the city's black middle class were reported in the *Chicago Conservator* and in the Chicago *Broad Ax,* local papers with circulation beyond Chicago. Regular visits of transplanted family members reinforced this image of social freedom.

15. Darlene Clark Hine, "Black Migration to the Urban Midwest: The Gender Dimension, 1915–1945," in Joe William Trotter Jr., ed., *The Great Migration in Historical Perspective: New Dimensions of Race, Class, and Gender* (Bloomington: Indiana University Press, 1991), especially 130–31. See also Hine, "Rape and the Inner Lives of Black Women in the Middle West: Preliminary Thoughts on the Culture of Dissemblance," *Signs* 14 (Summer 1989): 912–20.

16. Scott, *Occupational Changes,* 32, 41; Spear, *Black Chicago,* 29.

17. Scott, *Occupational Changes,* 38, 43, 47, 68, 72, 83–85. In 1890, black women constituted only 4.3 percent of all female servants. Foreign-born white women, the largest proportion of whom came from Germany, Ireland, Sweden, and Norway, made up 66 percent of all women so employed. Native-born white women made up the balance of women in domestic and personal service. By 1900, black women's proportion of the city's service workforce nearly doubled, to 8.2 percent.

18. Hunter, *To 'Joy My Freedom;* Clark-Lewis, *Living In, Living Out.*

19. Hunter, *To 'Joy My Freedom,* 58.

20. See advertisements in I. C. Harris, *Colored Men's Professional and Business Directory* (Chicago: I. C. Harris, 1885). See also newspaper listings for hairdressers, elocutionists, and furnished rooms in the *Broad Ax,* the *Conservator,* and, after the turn of the century, the *Chicago Defender.*

21. William Sanger, *History of Prostitution* (New York, 1876), discussed in Gilfoyle, *City of Eros,* 62; Marilynn Wood Hill, *Their Sisters' Keepers: Prostitution in New York City, 1830–1870* (Berkeley: University of California Press, 1993), 232–34; Rosen, *Lost Sisterhood,* 99; Allan M. Brandt, *No Magic Bullet: A Social History of Venereal Disease in the United States since 1880* (New York: Oxford University Press, 1985), 11–13, 31–37.

22. Rosen, *Lost Sisterhood,* 74, 83, 100–101; Hill, *Their Sisters' Keepers,* 232–39.

23. Rosen, *Lost Sisterhood,* 98; Hill, *Their Sisters' Keepers,* 229–30. See also Patricia Cline Cohen, *The Murder of Helen Jewett* (New York: Vintage Books, 1998).

24. On the different institutions of the nineteenth-century sex trade see Hill, *Their Sisters' Keepers,* 175–216; Gilfoyle, *City of Eros,* 197–250.

25. Many prostitutes were listed as "mulatto" in the census. I have designated these women as black for the purposes of counting. Mulattoes were not defined as a separate social category or a distinct class of people. However, for many white customers,

purchasing the sexual services of a mulatto woman was preferable to buying sex from a Negro woman. Although this distinction is visible in the late nineteenth century, it becomes clearer in the twentieth-century Levee District.

26. U.S. Bureau of the Census, Tenth Census (1880), Chicago Manuscript Schedules, Enumeration District 9; Clifton R. Wooldridge, *Hands Up! In the World of Crime* (Chicago: Police Publishing, 1901), 60. Between 1901 and 1906, several editions of *Hands Up!* were published, with some differences distinguishing each. In this study I have used two editions, both published in 1901. In subsequent notes, I will distinguish the two by referring to the publisher.

27. Working men—black, native white, and foreign-born—made up an overwhelming proportion of the residents of the First Ward, the district containing the Levee. In 1890, roughly two-thirds of the ward's population was male, and in 1900, that figure mounted to 72 percent across all groups of men. U.S. Bureau of the Census, *Eleventh Census, 1890, Population,* 884; *Eleventh Census, 1890, Compendium,* 674–75; *Twelfth Census, 1900, Population,* Part 1, 613; See also Cynthia M. Blair, "Vicious Commerce: African American Women's Sex Work and the Transformation of Urban Space in Chicago, 1850–1915 (PhD diss., Harvard University, 1999), 82–98, 124–45.

28. Wooldridge, *Hands Up!* (Chicago: Thompson and Thomas, 1901), 290.

29. Gilfoyle, *City of Eros,* 165; Rosen, *Lost Sisterhood,* 92; Wooldridge, *Hands Up!* (Police Publishing), 60.

30. Isabel Eaton, "Special Report on Negro Domestic Service in the Seventh Ward," in Du Bois, *Philadelphia Negro,* 449; Meyerowitz, *Women Adrift,* 40–41; Rosen, *Lost Sisterhood,* 76. Estimates of prostitutes' earnings are based on prices listed for Colored Houses in the *Sporting and Club House Directory,* 38–39.

31. Gilfoyle, *City of Eros,* 225, Rosen, *Lost Sisterhood,* 88–92.

32. Levee District brothels were found in U.S. Bureau of the Census, Tenth Census (1880), Chicago Manuscript Schedules (microfilm), Enumeration Districts 5, 8, and 9; U.S. Bureau of the Census, Twelfth Census (1900), Chicago Manuscript Schedules (microfilm), Enumeration Districts 12, 21, 24, 30, 38, 42, 43, and 161.

33. *Sporting and Club House Directory,* 42–46.

34. Ibid., 39.

35. William T. Stead, *If Christ Came to Chicago* (Chicago: 1894; repr. Evanston, Ill.: Chicago Historical Bookworks, 1990), 247; Bill of Indictment, Case File no. 2682; Criminal Case Files; United States District Court for the Northern District of Illinois, Northern Division (Chicago); Records of District Courts of the United States, Record Group 21; National Archives and Records Administration–Great Lakes Region (Chicago).

36. Of the fifty parlor house listings in the brothel directory designating number of boarders, most had between five and eight workers. *Sporting and Club House Directory,* 7–39 passim.

37. *Sporting and Club House Directory,* 38–39.

38. For example, Vic Livingston charged her guests $5, $10, and $15. A few white madams commanded even higher prices. The rates in the house of longtime Chicago madam Carrie Watson were between $5 and $50. *Sporting and Club House Directory,* 24, 32.

39. Stead, *If Christ Came to Chicago,* 247.

40. Martha Hodes, *White Women, Black Men: Illicit Sex in the Nineteenth-Century South* (New Haven, Conn.: Yale University Press, 1999), 147–208.

41. Hill, *Their Sisters' Keepers,* 293–319; Rosen, *Lost Sisterhood,* 86–111.

42. U.S. Bureau of the Census, Tenth Census (1880), Chicago Manuscript Schedules (microfilm), Enumeration Districts 5, 8, and 9; U.S. Bureau of the Census, Twelfth Census (1900), Chicago Manuscript Schedules (microfilm), Enumeration Districts 12, 21, 24, 30, 38, 42, 43, and 161.

43. Hill, *Their Sisters' Keepers,* 99–103; Rosen, *Lost Sisterhood,* 76; Paula Petrik, "Capitalists with Rooms: Prostitution in Helena, Montana, 1865–1900," *Montana: The Magazine of Western History* 21 (Spring 1991): 28–40.

44. Residents of Hull-House, *Hull-House Maps and Papers,* Wage and Nationalities Maps; Stead, *If Christ Came to Chicago,* 448–49; *Sporting and Club House Directory,* 43–45; *Lakeside Annual Directory for the City of Chicago,* 1879 through 1900. On Black Mag, see U.S. Bureau of the Census, Twelfth Census (1900), Chicago Manuscript Schedules, Enumeration District 42; U.S. Bureau of the Census, Thirteenth Census (1910), Chicago Manuscript Schedules, Enumeration District 162; *Chicago Record-Herald,* October 5, 1912; Herbert Asbury, *Gem of the Prairie: An Informal History of the Chicago Underworld* (Chicago: Knopf, 1940; repr. DeKalb, Ill.: Northern Illinois University Press, 1986), 264.

45. For examples, see Jacqueline Jones, *Labor of Love, Labor of Sorrow: Black Women, Work, and the Family from Slavery to the Present* (New York: Vintage Books, 1985), 182; Barbara Meil Hobson, *Uneasy Virtue: The Politics of Prostitution and the American Reform Tradition* (New York: Basic Books, 1987), 35–36; Rosen, *Lost Sisterhood,* 80–81, 94.

46. Wooldridge, *Hands Up!* (Thompson and Thomas), 482–83.

47. *Chicago Daily News,* January 19, 1892.

48. *Chicago Tribune,* June 5, 1880.

49. *Chicago Times,* July 17, 1880, December 19, 1880; *Chicago Tribune,* May 10, 1893.

50. *Chicago Daily News,* March 10, 1876; Wooldridge, *Hands Up!* (Thompson and Thomas), 48–49, 289–92.

51. Statistics derived from U.S. Bureau of the Census, Tenth Census (1880), Chicago Manuscript Schedules, Enumeration Districts 5, 8, and 9; Twelfth Census (1900), Chicago Manuscript Schedules, Enumeration Districts 12, 21, 30, 42, and 43.

52. Wooldridge, *Hands Up!* (Police Publishing), 237–38; Hill, *Their Sisters' Keepers,* 60–61.

53. Leisure institutions owned by African American men — saloons, wine rooms, cigar shops, billiard halls, and gambling dens — had long been conspicuous within the Levee. However, in the last decades of the century, black businessmen began to see in prostitution a means of augmenting profits from their other business endeavors. Gradually, the infusion of men's capital into the sex economy helped to extend black women's prostitution beyond the brothels of the Levee. This initiated a shift in the institutional and cultural contexts of black women's sexual labor. Blair, "Vicious Commerce," 322–85.

54. See Rosen, *Lost Sisterhood,* 38–50; Judith Walkowitz, *Prostitution in Victorian Society: Women, Class, and the State* (Cambridge, England: Cambridge University Press, 1980).

55. Wolcott, *Remaking Respectability,* chapter 3.

6   The Great War, Black Workers,
     and the Rise and Fall of
     the NAACP in the South

The United States' entry into Europe's Great War posed fundamental challenges to white supremacy. Yet the war merely created the conditions for change. It took a surge of black activism to give those conditions the potential to undermine the legitimacy of segregation, disfranchisement, and economic subordination. A series of national movements from migration north to union drives; the expansion of national black advocacy groups such as the National Association for the Advancement of Colored People (NAACP) and the Universal Negro Improvement Association (UNIA); and the wide circulation of periodicals such as the NAACP's *Crisis,* A. Philip Randolph and Chandler Owen's *The Messenger,* and Robert Abbott's *Chicago Defender* all expressed the activist spirit of possibility on the rise during the war years. What remains less understood by historians is how ordinary African Americans on the ground tried shape these national movements and organizations to local circumstances, particularly in the South. Beginning in 1917, for example, the NAACP launched a nationwide campaign to increase its membership, especially in the South, where it hoped to establish "a real first line defense facing the enemy at proper range."[1] But if northern organizers proclaimed the ambitions of the national association, southern grassroots activists seized the initiative and transformed the national association from a small northern reform group into a popular working-class-based "movement against race prejudice" that comprised some 50,000 men and women in more than 140 branches. From St. Rose, Louisiana, to Falls Church, Virginia, branch activists aspired to transform America's Great War into a reconstruction of American society and democracy.[2]

This mobilization of black politics reveals the centrality of black resistance in these years in particular and to the political culture of Jim Crow more generally. In the past decade, a new political history of the Jim Crow South has emerged that questions older assumptions about white supremacist rule. Rather than seeing the rule of segregationists as absolute, these historians have pointed to the contingencies, complexities, and contradictions that haunted those regimes. Many adopt an expansive understanding of politics that deemphasizes the electoral process to illuminate struggles for power that raged outside voting booths. This new revisionism places black resistance at the center of the narrative. As Jane Dailey, Glenda Gilmore, and Bryant Simon explain in the introduction to a recent collection of essays, "the continuous contest between southern blacks determined to assert their civil rights and whites determined to deny blacks that power" defined the political culture of Jim Crow.[3]

This essay extends that understanding of black politics through an exploration of the travails of the wartime NAACP in the South. Branch organizers did not work simply at the behest of northern administrators but instead acted amid the deepening social conflicts generated by wartime mobilization. The southern black response to the draft, military service, expanding employment opportunities, and the increased federal presence in the region signaled a determination to capitalize on the forces unleashed by war. Activists seized on these conditions to enlist recruits, and thousands of African Americans in scores of communities responded, seeking to harness the influence and prestige of the national association to meet their own dreams, concerns, and aspirations. As black politics mobilized for reconstruction, white supremacists reacted to meet that challenge. Commenting on the political significance of the draft, the editors of *The New Republic* captured the challenges America's entry into the war posed to the white South. Doubting that black soldiers would "accept the facts of white supremacy" upon their return from France, the editors warned that unless segregationists overhauled their "scheme of racial relationships" and assumed "greater responsibility for the negro's civil and economic welfare," black soldiers would return as "fomenter[s] of unrest." If white supremacists resisted such moderate reforms, reasoned the editors, they would reveal to the world that coercion, not consensus, governed their social and political institutions.[4] Much was at stake, then, in how southern whites responded to black activism. Although only a part of the broader mobilization of black politics during the war years, the effort by ordinary blacks to build the NAACP at the local level and the white response to it reveals that a struggle over the social and political effects of wartime mobilization defined the American home front in the South.

As the United States mobilized for war in Europe, the implementation of the Selective Service threatened to disrupt the color line in the South. Uncertain how to conscript blacks into military service without jeopardizing their own political authority, white southerners pursued a draft policy toward blacks filled with unresolved tensions, "a compound of fear and contempt," in the apt phrase of historian David Kennedy. On the one hand, some southern draft boards conscripted blacks "for cannon fodder" and to spare local whites from being "heavily drawn upon." By drafting blacks over whites and faithfully acting on their assumption that black lives were cheap, local exemption boards undermined another, no less important foundation of the Jim Crow South: the supply of cheap black labor. Fearful that the draft would further weaken their control over black labor already aggravated by the Great Migration, southern planters and employers used their political influence to intervene in the administration of the draft. According to an attorney from Little Rock, Arkansas, blacks who worked "for some influential white men" could "'get by the board' as they put it. The Negro who is somewhat independent, has his own farm or business, is the one who is hard hit." Planters and employers also persuaded draft boards to fill their "colored" quotas with men who clearly suffered disabilities. Reports that southern states sent physically unfit black males to training camps in disproportionate numbers convinced federal draft officials that some local boards colluded with influential planters to reject healthy black men.[5]

Exempting en masse hardworking black sharecroppers and low-wage industrial workers from military service, others feared, would do little to preserve white supremacy. Complaining that too many draft boards throughout the South disqualified "large numbers of negroes" because of flat feet, one white Floridian accused the Navy of complicity in sparking an impending black uprising. If the military continued to drain the South of its white men while leaving behind "the bulk of the negroes," it ought to expect, he warned, "the most serious sort of trouble." More forthright, an anonymous resident of Longview, Texas, saw nothing less than the purity of the white race at stake in the Selective Service's failure to adopt a consistent policy regarding the conscription of blacks. If "the young white men go off to the war," blacks "will kill off all of the old white men and women [and] children and take the pretty white maidens for wives." He pleaded President Wilson to either "make them join the army or navy" or "banish them from our shores."[6]

Not all segregationists concurred that black conscription would ensure the safety of white women or preserve the rule of white men. Black veterans "inflamed their people with stories of race equality in Europe," cautioned one southern newspaper, "especially the lack of discrimination in social intercourse." One "million NEGRO SOLDIERS in the south would be a constant menace," warned one distressed white man in a letter to President Wilson. Blacks were no longer the "docile people of antebellum days." They harbored "political and RACIAL ambitions" and "want the ballot," which whites "can not AFFORD" to grant in the South, where blacks outnumbered whites. Nevertheless, he advised the president to place all African Americans "under military rule," where they would be "less of a menace" than if left to "vent their animosity on the helpless Southern people of both sexes who would have to be left here."[7]

This tension among white supremacists, who were never certain whether blacks posed a greater threat in uniform or at work on the home front, reveals deep anxieties about the security of their rule. Commenting on a report circulating in Richmond that once black soldiers returned from Europe, blacks intended "to force the white man to give them equal rights," the editors of the black weekly the *New York Age* perceptively remarked that southern whites should expect a "good many nightmares." These were not premeditated acts on the part of blacks, mused the *Age,* but the work of "an uneasy conscience dreaming of some of the things the owner of the conscience would do if he were in the Negro's place." Indeed, white supremacists' imaginations ran wild throughout 1917 and 1918 with fanciful tales of impending black insurrection.[8]

The case files of the Department of Justice's newly created Bureau of Intelligence read like a confession of southern whites' worst nightmares. A North Carolina real estate man reported that he had it on the good word of a credible black man who had slipped into one of "several nightly meetings" among local blacks that a preacher enjoined the assembled "mob" to dodge the draft and withhold their labor "until the white men were gone to the war" so they could "slip in and kill the whites remaining at home." A white attorney told of blacks in Texarkana "drilling with sticks as guns" in preparation for joining "the German cause." Federal agents warned of a black café operator in Nashville who held "daily meetings to formulate plans against the United States" and to instill among blacks "an Anti-American spirit." Even those blacks whom whites trusted most, such as waiters in the first-class clubs of Richmond, fell under suspicion of "eavesdropping while waiting on their diners" to collect information about the war to pass along to German agents. For all of southern whites' legendary pretension to "know their Negroes," these reports convey considerable suspicion and ignorance of what transpired in those black social spaces that whites seldom had the capacity to penetrate. In the context of war, whites sensed themselves unable to control what happened on the other side of the color line that they themselves had created.[9]

Despite the scope of these allegations, all informants attributed the discontent they detected to outsider agitators. According to this agitator theory of black discontent, the majority of southern blacks had no grievances and had no thought of using the war to reconstruct power relations. To have acknowledged otherwise, white supremacists would have admitted to the illegitimacy of the social order. Hence, to maintain the fiction of consent, they targeted agitators who spread unrest, such as preachers, labor organizers, and German spies believed to have infiltrated the South disguised as saloon keepers, Lutheran priests, and traveling Bible salesmen. A Virginia planter suspected that someone had infiltrated his black tenants to put "the idea into their silly head that social equality will follow German occupation." A woman in rural Mississippi assured herself that "negroes around here are mainly ignorant," yet her assumption that they were "easily led" had her fearful that they had "something up their sleeve." Two whites supposed to be representing the Wisconsin Orphan Home addressed "crowds of negroes at night" in York, Alabama, "urging them to leave and go to Mexico." White authorities tended to give credence to black informants who confirmed the agitator theory. When a black lecturer hired by the Justice Department detected an "unnatural" "undercurrent" in the "thickly settled colored communities" of central Texas, for example, he reported to his superiors that "the negroes have been tampered with." Thus, even as white southerners confronted evidence that shattered the fiction of consent, they continued to deny the authenticity of grassroots black dissent, assuring themselves that the path to restoration lay in targeting agitators rather than in a reconstruction of society.[10]

If southern white fears of a black uprising greatly exaggerated the means by which African Americans sought to challenge Jim Crow, they should not obscure how blacks nevertheless saw in the social dislocations generated by the war an opportunity to challenge white supremacy. Black discontent was not merely the stuff of white racist imaginations nor the handiwork of a few outside agitators and German spies. African Americans' own determination to respond to the war emergency on their own terms heightened southern whites' anxieties about the social and political impact of mobilization.

Blacks understood the political significance of military service. The southern black press chronicled the heroics of black troops in France and drew explicit links between the participation of black soldiers to the expansion of democracy in America. A keen sense of history informed these stories. Just as African American soldiers transformed the Civil War into a war of emancipation, black doughboys would expand the Great War into a fight to abolish Jim Crow. Just as black soldiers liberated four million slaves in the 1860s, declared the *Star of Zion,* the official organ of the African Methodist Episcopal Church, now a new generation of courageous veterans will demand their "citizen and manhood rights." Black servicemen themselves gave substance to these grandiloquent claims. "When we cross the Rhine, there'll be no color line," rang a popular chant among black servicemen in France. Shall we come back "to be ostraci[z]ed as pariahs and serfs, or as equal fellow citizens," wondered one black private. "I have but one desire," announced another; "and that is to be able to go all over our land and tell of my experiences in the democratic France, and [of] the manly qualities displayed by our soldiers under conditions so very foreign to those at home."[11]

Not all blacks so readily accepted these optimistic connections between wearing the uniform and an expansion of citizenship. As in America's past wars, many blacks insisted that they remain neutral until the nation pledged its commitment to democracy at home. As the historian Herbert Aptheker noted long ago, black opposition to the American war effort was extensive and politically motivated. By the spring of 1918, when the army began to call up black conscripts, the military reported high rates of desertion among southern blacks. Southern whites, in denying the political significance of draft evasion, attributed the desertion rates either to black illiteracy and ignorance of the law or to plots by German agents—outside agitators—to stir an insurrection. When federal agents, at the behest of fearful southern whites, investigated rumors of black uprisings, they uncovered ample evidence of black unwillingness to fight in the war, even if fantastic tales of a black uprising proved unfounded. Whether blacks embraced military service for its political possibilities or evaded the draft as one of the few means of political expression open to people without power, African Americans across the South resisted white attempts to make sure that the draft restricted rather than expanded black mobility.[12]

African Americans also responded to wartime mobilization widening their search for working conditions that permitted greater autonomy and control over their economic lives. As war curtailed European immigration, northern employers increasingly recruited southern blacks to meet labor shortages. Numerous historians have demonstrated that African Americans were not merely pulled by the impersonal forces of labor markets but generated their own social movement of "Northern fever." "[L]etters, rumors, gossip, and black newspapers carried word of higher wages and better treatment in the North," historian James Grossman explains. Between 1916 and 1919, roughly 500,000 African Americans left the South for the promised lands of Chicago, New York, Cleveland, and Pittsburgh.[13]

Although historians have taught us much in recent years about the experiences of black migrants, we remain less knowledgeable of the Great Migration's impact on the lives of black workers who remained in the South.[14] Migration and the draft created labor shortages in the South throughout the war years that improved the bargaining position of many black workers. "Unusually high wages," concluded the U.S. Employment Bureau (USEB), enabled "laborers to knock off from work for considerable periods," causing a "general scarcity of common labor in the cities, towns, mines, and fields of the South." Mississippi farmers complained of having to pay "fancy wages," employers in Atlanta decried the "nonchalant air of a millionaire" among the city's blacks, and managers in Mobile despaired that Alabama's blacks had become "indisposed to activity." Stories abounded in the black press about African American farmers prospering from wartime cotton prices. In one case, a black farmer and his three sisters purchased a 600-acre plantation in the Mississippi Delta for $90,000. In addition to farming, these buyers intended to establish a school for blacks where they would teach, among other things, "use of the ballot pending the annulment of the disfranchisement clause," suggesting that they anticipated new political freedoms to accompany economic prosperity. To bolster their case for imposing tighter restrictions on black mobility, planters blamed the labor shortage for the thousands of acres that lay fallow in 1918 and made ominous predictions that they would be able to cultivate only about 20 percent of their land in 1919. One agricultural commentator even speculated that unless something were done, landlords would soon turn to mechanization to compensate for labor shortages. "It never again will be the Black Belt it was in 1914," he lamented.[15]

Southern black women seized new labor opportunities generated by mobilization. The decision to draft black married men, for example, created prospects for black women to control, to some degree, the terms of their employment. Those wives and mothers who received government support payments for the military service of their sons and husbands were freed from dependency on wage work, which for black women was generally confined to domestic service. A chorus of white complaints about the "servant question" soon rang throughout the South. In Americus, Georgia, whites accused black women of cheating the military by claiming allotments from "soldiers to whom they have never been married" or for deviously marrying three or four men "simply to receive their allotments." Elsewhere, women used these new circumstances to negotiate better wages and working conditions. Domestic servants in Atlanta refused to work for less than $9.00 a week; cooks in New Orleans formed a union to demand a minimum wage of $25.00 a month and an eleven-hour day;

household workers in Tulsa, Oklahoma, refused to work unless their employers provided meals, travel fare, and electric wash machines to "lighten their labors." Reports of secret organizing among black domestic laborers and tales of untrustworthy servants embedding glass in loaves of bread frustrated white employers who denounced the "condition of sullenness and unrest" among black women.[16]

Black workers looked to a newly responsive federal government to embolden their bargaining position with southern employers. The U.S. Department of Labor created the Division of Negro Economics (DNE), which put the power of the federal government behind efforts to open new employment opportunities for black workers and to improve working conditions. As the Wilson administration recognized the necessity of black labor to the war effort, other federal agencies such as the USEB, the U.S. Railroad Administration (USRA), and the National War Labor Board (NWLB) at times intervened on the side of black workers in labor disputes. Few government investigators considered themselves champions of racial justice, but as historian Robert Zieger explains, they found workplace discrimination in the South "so blatant and irrational as to impede the war effort." Federal agencies also sought to regulate wages and working conditions to promote labor stability and prevent workers from migrating in search of higher wages. Those black workers who could appeal to this pragmatic logic had the best chance of securing federal intervention. Black women in Little Rock, Arkansas, for example, won a case before the NWLB that secured them equal pay with white women employed in commercial laundries that serviced nearby military installations. Thus even if pragmatism rather than racial justice motivated federal agents, their presence in the field, investigating charges of discrimination and having the power to ameliorate conditions, gave black workers reason to hope that the war might initiate a lasting reconstruction of southern labor relations.[17]

Quick to recognize the potential power the federal government could wield over their labor practices, southern employers strove to weaken the impact of these agencies. Lumber operator John Henry Kirby spoke for many southern employers when he affirmed his objections to working with George Haynes, the black director of the DNE. In the South, he maintained before a gathering of southern industrialists, "we do not accept [blacks] as our equals. . . . [W]e tell them what to do, and we do not sit in conference with them and accept their suggestions." Responding to rumors that a DNE field officer was unionizing black sawmill workers in Florida, the state's governor, Sidney Catts, demanded that the administration withdraw the DNE from his state. Comparing the DNE to the Freedmen's Bureau and its agents to carpetbaggers and scalawags, Catts advised

Secretary of Labor William Wilson that the DNE and its agents did not "understand the Florida people" and served no other purpose than to inflame "the minds of the negroes against the white people." Insisting that white Floridians would not submit to the egregious demands of blacks, Catts warned of impending trouble, implying that he would have neither the authority nor the desire to intervene if whites attacked blacks.[18]

As Catts was well aware, southern whites resorted to violent measures to restrict the labor mobility of southern blacks throughout the war years. A local Council of Defense in the Arkansas Delta passed a resolution fixing the price of cotton picking at $1.50 per 100 pounds and forcing all cotton pickers to work six days a week. When blacks refused to heed the demands, vigilantes retaliated with ferocity. In southwestern Arkansas, for example, a white mob dynamited an all-black town after blacks there refused to sell the choice lands they owned in that section of the Ouachita Valley. This attack, perpetrated to force blacks to sell out and leave, was part of a larger reign of terror leveled against blacks prospering or taking advantage of wartime conditions. Whites in Vicksburg reportedly dressed themselves in blackface and then raped white women of the community with the intent of creating violent prejudice against black men earning good wages in an industrial plant. A black minister in Yazoo City, Mississippi, narrowly escaped the wrath of a terrorist mob for organizing an effective boycott of a series of lectures sponsored by the town's business interests that advised black residents to "stay in the South among their friends." Discovering that the minister distributed the *Chicago Defender* and the *Crisis* among the city's residents, a white mob kidnapped him, pushed them into the trunk of a car, and sped out of town toward the river. The minister managed to secure his knife, cut himself loose, thrust open the trunk of the car, and leap to safety. He scurried back to his house, grabbed his rifle, and walked forty-six miles to Jackson and caught a train out of the South to Philadelphia.[19]

As mobs resorted to terrorism, southern blacks sought to enlist the power and moral authority of the federal government on their behalf. Inspired in part by the idealistic war rhetoric of President Wilson, they appealed for federal protection of their civil rights as just reward for wartime sacrifices. P. G. Cooper, a black attorney from Mississippi, pleaded with the U.S. attorney general to find a way to enforce the president's public denunciation of lynching. Cooper received only a polite but legalistic rejection. If constitutional arguments did not persuade, others hoped biblical ones might. As one man from Tulsa wrote to the president, the Great War was God's retribution for Jim Crow. Drawing an extensive analogy between the story of Exodus and the plight of America's former slaves, he explained to Wilson how God had compelled President Lincoln to free the slaves "by the result of a cruel civil war" in the same way God freed the slaves of Egypt with the Death Angel. But the South, through its cruel treatment of the former slaves, continued to pursue them for the past fifty years just as Pharaoh and his forces pursued Moses and the Israelites. The evil of Jim Crow, he insisted, "blindfolded the whole nation" and brought it down to the trenches of Europe just as the Israelites brought Pharaoh to the Red Sea. "Now your only hope," he declared, was "to let the Negroes go and restore to them all you have robbed" of them and make them citizens. But if Wilson failed to act, he warned, the nation would suffer the fate of Pharaoh, this time to be swept away by winds of war rather than drowned by the waves of the Red Sea.[20]

With wartime mobilization strengthening the political resolve of black southerners, many began to organize branches of the NAACP as the vehicle for effecting social change rather than wait for the federal government to respond to their appeals. Praising the NAACP as the greatest organization "in the world," one black Georgian envisioned his branch joining with not only ten million American blacks, but with every American citizen and every man who "lives on the face of the earth . . . in the great fight to help tear down the forces of rong and [in]judict [*sic*]." "The general tension down here reminds me" of the events that "caused the French Revolution," proclaimed Margaret Dorris McCleary of Jacksonville, Florida. Affirming "that any race of people who have wrenched from their oppressors their inalienable rights . . . had to do so by the greatest sacrifices and sufferings," she vowed to prepare a new generation of black Jacobins "to also pay the price" in the struggle for "life and liberty."[21]

As mobilization for war intensified social conflicts across the South, a growing and radicalized segment of black professionals emerged to support organized political action. Endless mob violence convinced many to break their silence. "Hasn't this gone far enough," cried self-described "friend of the South" and conservative educator J. E. Boyd of Longview, Texas. Citing the recent wave of lynchings, Boyd urged President Wilson in a "frank" letter to "do an act that will bring a halt to these awful and heart-rendering atrocities." In Jacksonville, Florida, General Leonard Wood's proposal to put black enlisted men to work as farmhands on southern plantations drew the ire of the established black leadership. "It was a little surprising," reported the branch secretary, "yet intensely gratifying, to hear [the] conservative men" of the city's black community denounce the "injustice of putting our young men on farms." Striking a similar chord, southern black newspaper editors revised their once cautious stance and composed a chorus of civil-rights demands. "Cullings from race papers everywhere," reported the *Nashville Globe,* were "brim full of burning editorials" that linked the war effort with a wide-ranging program of democratic possibility—fair and impartial trials, the right to sit on juries, decent wages, public investment in black neighborhoods, abolition of Jim Crow, and an end to mob violence.[22]

If mobilization for war radicalized certain segments of the southern black middle class, it even more dramatically inspired widespread militancy among the southern black working class. As numerous historians have shown in recent years, black workers played an instrumental role in the postwar confrontation between labor and capital as American workers "fought at home to define the content of their own democracy."[23] During this period, tens of thousands of black southerners joined unions in the region's docks, steel mills, coal mines, railroads, commercial laundries, and plantations. In some workplaces, such as the southern railroads, blacks "charted an independent course," in historian Eric Arnesen's phrase, in pursuit of "their unique interests as *black* workers." In the New Orleans waterfront and the coal mines of the Birmingham District in Alabama, black unionists joined with whites in uneasy yet determined biracial alliances. These interracial alliances were seldom committed to racial egalitarianism, and unionists framed their struggle as a demand for industrial, rather than social, equality. In the Arkansas Delta, black tenant farmers organized into the Progressive Farmers and Household Union to circumvent planter authority by challenging evictions, demanding fair prices for their cotton, and pooling their resources to purchase government land. Black unionists followed no single approach or trajectory, but the trend toward an upsurge in black worker militancy in these years was unmistakable and formed a critical component of the broader political mobilization of African Americans during the World War I era. In the apt words of historian Brian Kelly, "the 'new Negro' that struck fear in the hearts of white racists and black conservatives alike was by and large a proletarian."[24]

Some of these black trade unionists drew on their skills as labor activists to embolden local NAACP initiatives in the South. Knowing "the value of organization" in "protecting ourselves industrially," declared one Galveston waterfront unionist, we are "not afraid to take another step and protect ourselves as a race." He promised to build a local branch filled with the names of "representatives of organized labor." "We are making our greatest appeal to the masses of the race," declared the branch secretary from Falls Church, Virginia, "because we believe that in the awakening of the proletariat lies our mightiest strength." The NAACP's executive secretary, John R. Shillady, attributed the phenomenal growth of the association in the South to the efforts of "not only the professions but the common people," on whom the movement depended "for its strength and salvation." By Shillady's standard, the association appeared strong. Indeed, membership rolls from southern branches reveal a strong working-class presence. Miners and steelworkers in Ensley, Alabama; lumber workers in Munson, Florida; cigar makers in Tampa, Florida; longshoremen in Galveston, Texas; and railroad shopmen in Graham, Virginia, to cite just a few examples, joined with "farmers, longshoremen, people working at everything" to become NAACP members.[25]

By 1919, a majority of the NAACP's members were not only southern, but working class, as well. As historian Judith Stein has explained, this groundswell from below pushed the NAACP "ideologically to the left, toward working-class methods of protest" that were "franker in [their] pursuit of racial power." NAACP chairman Major Joel E. Spingarn recognized in the participation of the black working class the path to new possibilities for political action. In his speech before the association's annual conference in June 1919, Spingarn advised the audience not to "rest content until the 10,000,000 colored workmen in the south . . . stand ready to stop work at a moment's notice." A general strike in which "not a single black man" did "a stroke of work" would leave the "Southern aristocracy" no choice but to recognize their demands.[26]

This trend toward radicalization of outlook and tactic on the national level played out time and again on a local level during the war years. The initiatives of hundreds of local activists to establish branches and to link their efforts to an increasingly aggressive northern civil-rights group eroded the authority of so-called conservative race leaders in scores of communities across the South. Organizers informed association headquarters of a conservative campaign to portray branch executives as "strife breeders" and to use "pull with the white ruling element" to dismantle branches. Many worried of the chilling effect this opposition would have on the expansion and resolve of branches. James Weldon Johnson, the first black field secretary of the NAACP, encouraged branch activists to use the conflict as an opportunity to "smoke out these 'go betweens'" who looked after only "their own individual welfare." And branch activists did not give in easily, fighting off charges and countercharges of sexual impropriety and misappropriation of the hard-earned money of local black residents. Whatever the ultimate resolution of these local conflicts, they showed that the advent of the NAACP and its confrontational approach in the fight against Jim Crow did much to challenge the prewar approach to racial progress in the South, isolate conservative leadership, and create a forum for new approaches and possibilities. As one Augusta, Georgia, activist embroiled in "uphill work" against "reactionary Negroes" noted with optimism in 1917, the city had transformed into "another town. The old spirit of humble introspection . . . is just dying out."[27]

Itinerant organizers spread the new spirit of activism deep into the southern countryside. Convinced of his ability to enlist black recruits across the Arkansas Delta, one Memphis Branch activist pledged to "organise a branch whire [*sic*] ever I find my race needing help." A Shreveport, Louisiana, man with "great influence" over the area's rural black residents promised to establish branches in the forests of western Louisiana's piney woods. Caesar F. Simmons, a refugee from political violence in Texas, carried his fight "for my rights, civil and political" to rural eastern Oklahoma, where he organized more than a half a dozen branches in a month. Despite "doing three people's work," Simmons vowed "to keep at it till every Negro race loving and disfranchised tax paying citizen of my race is a member of this organization." Itinerant organizers broadened the base of the movement and established branches, as John R. Shillady put it, in places "whose names we never knew."[28]

It took enormous political courage to launch a branch of the NAACP in the Deep South. Letters from organizers reported case upon case of white attempts to harass their initiatives, intercept their mail, and even threaten their lives. Yet local activists persevered, and their letters conveyed more hope and promise than fear and despair. "Our branch is alive," asserted a man from Raleigh, North Carolina, despite the fact that "war conditions have made the white people . . . sensitive to every Negro movement." A faith in the ability of NAACP national officers to bring their struggles and travails to national attention and coordinate their demands for justice fueled much of this optimism. Reporters from the field conveyed a belief in deliverance, redemption, and an impending new day of emancipation that emboldened them to act. "God hasten the time when the Colored man may have a *real* chance in life," read one typical letter. Many believed the long-awaited day of reckoning had finally arrived. Now was the time, wrote one organizer, "to force in to the nation liberty, freedom, equality."[29]

Black participation in the military sustained the optimism of this growing, popular movement as branch publicists drove home comparisons of mobilization for war to the broader political mobilization of African Americans. E. M. Dunn of the New Orleans branch drew on war metaphors to enlist the city's blacks to the cause of the NAACP. With phrases such as "Let us go over the top" and "Don't be a slacker" for we can build "neither a Race" nor a "well-sustained organization" with "talk or promises," Dunn insisted that the same discipline required for victory on the battlefields of Europe would be needed "in our great civic fight" at home. Returning soldiers themselves acted as agents of change, bringing home lessons of discipline, and many played a crucial role in enlisting recruits in the fight for "political freedom," as one branch secretary put it. Branches featured public screenings of the films *Our Colored Fighters* and *Hell Fighters' Return,* which were effective in building membership. Branches convened panel discussions on topics such as "What Awaits Your Boy Home on his Return from the War," organized official welcomes for "the returning heroes of the race," and sponsored lectures by ex-soldiers. In one typical meeting, two veterans aroused a standing-room-only crowd with tales of their experiences "on the blood-soaked fields of the war ground of the world." The Reverend Jeems Lewis concluded the spirited session with a "roof raising speech right behind the fighting men, demanding the rights of the race which had been bought by blood."[30]

Mobilization for war mobilized black support for the NAACP in other ways. During the war, black churches, fraternal orders, labor unions, and women's clubs across the South organized Liberty Loan drives by canvassing their communities, staging rallies, and building networks to peddle the government's war savings bonds. Many of these local leaders translated their talents at selling the war to building the NAACP. One former Four-Minute Man reasoned that he could "make use of the ability he . . . acquired" as a speaker to "boost the membership" of the NAACP "for our own racial benefit." National Field Secretary James Weldon Johnson instructed branch organizers to model their membership drives after Liberty Loan rallies. Holding "well-advertised" mass meetings with speakers who could make "short, snappy addresses" combined with musical numbers that encouraged the assembled to sing, he advised, added "zest" to gatherings and guaranteed a large membership. These orators now appropriated messages of patriotism, sacrifice, and duty to banners, posters, and leaflets demanding the fulfillment of democracy at home.[31]

Activists went beyond merely capitalizing on the spirit of patriotism to envision organizing as a form of political education. T. G. Garrett's B & B Café in Shreveport, for example, served not only meals and drinks, but a good deal of politics on the side. Garrett, the local branch's vice president, became something of a "special reporter" to the national office by combing a wide range of black periodicals for news about conditions confronting blacks in the South, then clipping and mailing the articles to New York. By sharing these newspapers with his customers, Garrett converted the B & B into a kind of reading room. Diners no doubt learned of civil-rights initiatives occurring beyond Shreveport, argued over whether to display their patriotism or support the government's war effort, pondered how best to bring lynch mobs to justice, contributed money to legal defense funds, and signed petitions to the governor pleading for the release of blacks falsely accused of crime. E. M. Dunn of the New Orleans branch published a weekly sheet, *The Vindicator,* as a means of communicating to the city's black population the branch's message of defending "the right of the down trodden" and demanding a "square deal regardless of race." Relying on branch members and black businesses to distribute the penny paper, Dunn informed his readers about police brutality, the racial bias of the white press, and the benefits of union organizing efforts among black workers. Here was "the race's greatest opportunity since the emancipation," he proclaimed. Using short, simple, direct prose in the style of Four-Minute speakers, he urged readers to seize the moment and work for the defeat of autocracy in Europe and the triumph of a democracy "that will give to every man his just deserts." Both Garrett's restaurant and Dunn's cheap paper illustrate the innovative methods activists deployed to create what one Virginia organizer called "intelligent unrest" among a poor, semiliterate population.[32]

Through lecture circuits, rallies, neighborhood canvasses, and political education, branch activists began to build a nascent, yet growing, broad-based social movement unified by a culture of political opposition and racial solidarity. Two "very able speakers" thundered before the Nashville, Tennessee, branch on "the unchristian spirit of the south in dealing with the Negro," enthusing "the assembly to a high pitch." Such defiant tones about democracy, mob violence, Jim Crow, suffrage, and justice created an air of opposition to these sessions, aiding in the enrollment of "new names to our list at every meeting." Patriotic hymns lent "enchantment to the spell of race pride" at the Fort Worth, Texas, branch, creating an atmosphere "so joyous, so uplifting, and so full of real enthusiasm" that it united all in "one solid phalanx in a movement for the uplift of humanity." Expressions of unity and possibility such as these poured into the national office from all corners of the South. They suggest that the rapid embrace of the NAACP in the South grew from an emerging insurgent culture among the region's African Americans that blended patriotism, preaching, protest, and race pride. "Effective insurgent cultures," the historian Lawrence Goodwyn argued in his classic study of America's agrarian revolt of the 1880s and 1890s, "offer people hope. And from this starting point, political movements are possible." In similar fashion, NAACP activists built their own insurgency that not only grew out of the social tension generated by wartime mobilization, but gained its momentum from its ability to transform the ideals of Wilson's war aims into a vision of political change.[33]

Activists and recruits translated this movement culture of opposition into a wide-ranging program of political action. Branches organized efforts through petitions and rallies to protest police brutality, fight Jim Crow ordinances, demand improvements in municipal services in black neighborhoods, defend the rights of black civil-service applicants, and insist that local school boards hire black teachers and implement a series of reforms in black schools. Most branches established legal committees that defended blacks accused of crime, insisted that state and local authorities investigate lynchings and arrest whites responsible for mob violence, and, when officials balked, conducted their own investigations. Many initiatives made an impact. Because of local NAACP efforts, several cities and small towns pulled the racist film *Birth of a Nation,* overturned the implementation of residential segregation ordinances, and allowed blacks to sit on juries. The Columbia, South Carolina, branch assisted in the prosecution of a series of criminal cases involving white attacks on black citizens. As the branch secretary explained, city officials had done nothing to apprehend the accused "until we had warrants issued for their arrest." Despite working within this "hotbed of entrenched prejudice," these activists tended to close their reports by pledging not to tire nor fear in persevering in the work of the national association.[34]

"If the Negroes would learn their political lesson properly," insisted W. G. Young of Graham, Virginia, "we could, in any city or county election, determine the face of" officeholders, "from the prosecuting attorney and high sheriff [on] down." Young insisted that his branch's greatest achievement in this small industrial town in the mountainous southwestern corner of the state involved politics. The branch secured the appointment of sixteen delegates to the ninth congressional district convention, the first blacks to attend that body in more than twenty years. The branch also conducted a voter registration drive that increased the number of registered blacks in the Graham precinct from 9 to 150, a not insignificant accomplishment considering the entire county had fewer than 900 black men over the age of twenty-one. Because blacks in his precinct not only registered but voted, Young boasted that town and county authorities now informed the Graham branch of all matters affecting African Americans. Voting initiatives such as the one in Graham involved the participation of all branch members, not just those who served on committees. In Columbia, South Carolina, branch activists occupied the office of the registrar to demand the rights of black women to register to vote. Although not challenging the educational and property requirements needed to register, hundreds of Columbia's black women, many college-educated and employed as schoolteachers, refused to be turned away on technical grounds and returned day after day to demand that the registrar fairly assess their applications. Stories of black women being refused registration spread through town. Without any organized effort, a rising sentiment of outrage compelled black women to insist on their rights. Despite attempts by the registrar to insult these black women by forcing them to read sections from the criminal code on sodomy, incest, and miscegenation, they persevered and crowded the registrar's office, some waiting in line from six to eight hours.[35]

The thousands of black workers who joined the effort to establish branches in the South infused the movement with a spirit of labor activism. As historian Eric Arnesen has argued, "class and class strategies proved central to black workers' thought and behavior" in the era of World War I. Those branches composed of a working-class base and leadership, in particular, pursued an agenda that placed an emphasis on eradicating job discrimination and attaining higher wages and better working conditions. Many black workers saw commanding control over their working lives as equally essential to reclaiming their citizenship as was regaining the right to vote. Thus, we must do more than merely note the presence of black workers in the southern NAACP but also recognize how workers themselves sought to define the fight against Jim Crow.[36]

Some activists envisioned their branches as independent labor associations that would combat the peculiar conditions confronting black workers. Railroad workers who constituted the bulk of the branch membership at Jackson, Tennessee, and Graham, Virginia, for example, placed a high priority on fighting employment discrimination on southern railroads. The focus of their protest was not against working conditions, as appalling as they were, or to demand access to all-white jobs on the railroads, such as conducting and engineering. Rather, they sought to preserve the racial division of labor that provided them access to jobs such as firemen, which had come under assault by hostile white unionists. The practical effect of this white union offensive, observed A. R. Bell of Jackson, who served on the executive committee of the local NAACP and as the secretary of the all-black Grand United Order of Locomotive Firemen of America, would lead to white firemen gaining eventual control of all work. Or as W. G. Young, the energetic leader of the Graham branch, put it in his appeal for congressional intervention on behalf of black railroaders, the all-white Brotherhood of Railroad Trainmen (BRT) sought nothing less than to compel "an honest group of Americans into enforced idleness." Fears of impending unemployment were of profound political significance. Earning along with voting, the political scientist Judith Shklar has argued, are the key "attributes of an American citizen," and those thrust into "enforced idleness" are "expelled from civil society, reduced to second-class citizenship." As the Colored Association of Railroad Employees recognized, "our right to earn an honest living—our constitutional rights"—were at stake in the battle to preserve black jobs on the railroads. For Bell and Young, as well as thousands of other black labor activists, the enforcement of justice at the workplace was essential to the larger project of reconstructing a more democratic postwar America.[37]

The effort by some black labor activists to transform southern NAACP branches into vehicles that would pursue the distinct interests of black workers ran into multiple obstacles. Labor activists in Jackson and Graham looked to the NAACP and to the federal government to meet these challenges. Branch committees protested in person and by letter and petition to the general superintendents of the railroad companies and to federal authorities, but to little avail. Convinced that the fate of black trainmen had worsened since the USRA took charge of operating the nation's rail network in 1917, Bell pleaded that the NAACP come to their aid in securing "seniority rights, regardless of color." Young, too, lobbied both industry executives and Congress. He urged the president of the railroad to spurn the demands of the BRT as a threat to good business sense that would not only "heap injustice upon injustice," but also "stifle competition, destroy efficient service, and establish mob rule in industry." Despite their efforts, these groups lacked the power, the organizational reach, and the network of supporters necessary to gain influence with employers or federal regulators. Consequently, the USRA time and again deferred to the demands of organized white workers over the needs of blacks.[38]

Labor activists also encountered opposition from within the ranks of the NAACP. In some branches, black professional elites—those who referred to themselves as their community's "substantial citizens"—tried to block working-class initiatives. In Selma, Alabama, for example, a group of ministers and professionals circumvented John Garrett's efforts to organize a branch among the city's black workers. This group alerted the national office of their own intention to organize a branch and, by acting swiftly, received authorization from New York before Garrett could enlist the fifty members needed to apply for a charter. They accused Garrett of scheming to "array the working class" against the professional men and portrayed him as a devious labor organizer who enriched himself at the expense of the rank and file. Garrett defended his plans, claiming that as an eight-year veteran lecturer for the Masons who knew the real condition of blacks in the rural districts, he would create the kind of branch that Selma needed. As he put it, "it will take the masses not the classes to make the association succeed here."[39]

The organizational conflicts in Selma illustrate how, despite the emergence of a more confrontational black elite and the spread of an insurgent political culture, critical divisions rooted in class experience continued to fracture black communities. Although a sharpened racial consciousness attracted blacks of all walks of life to the NAACP, black workers experienced racial oppression in ways that made their interests distinct from people such as Selma's "substantial citizens." In more than a few cases, black working-class members had difficulty convincing executive committees composed of professionals to adopt strategies for change that addressed the specific needs of black workers. In Little Rock, for example, black railroad shop workers, some of whom were members of the established branch, petitioned the national office for the right to establish "a branch to our sels [*sic*]," because the regular branch would not actively help the nearly 900 "colored working people at this place" fight job discrimination. Rather than encourage the formation of a splinter group of workers that might function like a union, Walter White of the national office urged the shopmen to meet with the branch president to open a dialogue that would promote and preserve the greater good of racial unity. In separate correspondence with the executive board, White made no mention of the shopmen's request or of the conditions that black shopmen endured at the workplace.[40]

The cool reception to the requests of the black shopmen in Little Rock reflects the larger difficulty that local grassroots groups had in securing support from New York. By encouraging grassroots groups to organize, expand their membership, and report to the national office incidents of discrimination, Jim Crowism, and racial violence, the NAACP became overwhelmed by desperate pleas for help. Branch correspondence is replete with requests that a representative from the national office come visit the branch to witness firsthand conditions in their communities, to advise them on a course of action, or to assist in boosting membership. But New York seldom had the resources, ability, and, at times, even desire to respond. Working-class initiatives, in particular, received only limited support, as other issues, such as lynching, dominated the national agenda. Shillady, for example, apologized for his inability to assist the Jackson branch in its fight against employment discrimination on the railroads, explaining that the national office was in the midst of relocating its headquarters and that most of its "small force" was preoccupied with what benefits it could secure "for the race" at the Paris Peace Conference. Similarly, the national office rejected the proposal of a Louisiana branch that the NAACP operate as a farming cooperative in the South. These activists envisioned that branches could, under the supervision and financial support of the national office, loan farmers money and help them secure credit. When branch members in Sapulpa, Oklahoma, sought the NAACP's assistance in challenging the blacklisting of some seventy-five African American railroad workers who had joined a strike, James Weldon Johnson replied that it was "hardly a question which the Association can handle." Thus even as black workers energized the political culture of the movement to establish the NAACP in the South during the war years, they nevertheless were limited in their capacity to define the racial agenda.[41]

Whatever the resolution of these debates, they unfolded in a climate of intensifying hostility during the infamous Red Summer of 1919. Long a familiar topic in both African American and urban history, the racial violence of 1919 is most often associated with the dramatic riots that erupted in Chicago, Washington, D.C., and some twenty-five other American cities and towns, because of racial friction generated by white hostility to the influx of black migrants into America's urban industrial centers. What remains less familiar is that a wave of white terrorism, which was political in origin and purpose, also swept the South during the same time. In communities as diverse as Anderson, South Carolina; Leggett, Texas; Vicksburg, Mississippi; Greensboro, Florida; and Okmulgee, Oklahoma, white mobs took up arms explicitly to destroy the NAACP's capacity to function in the South. By the early 1920s, it would become clear that the wartime mobilization of black politics—and the intraracial debate it inspired over the trajectory of political activism—would be among the many casualties of the Red Summer of 1919.

True to their unwavering commitment to the agitator theory of black unrest, southern whites targeted returning black soldiers as the catalyst that spread a militant, revolutionary zeal among southern blacks. Alarmists in the Division of Military Intelligence lent credence to this perception, warning that "strutting" black soldiers consumed by "new ideas and social aspirations" would spark "numerous racial clashes" as they attempted "to carry those ideas back into the South."

Such "childish forgetfulness of races not yet ready for any sort of equality," reasoned the *Birmingham News,* "must be met by stern parental repression" by the "more conscient and dominant race." An Arkansas newspaper warned Delta blacks to "beware of new prophets and strange teachers" returned from Europe who "preached" that blacks were "deprived of certain inalienable rights" and spread the doctrine "that less work and more wages is the solution for all troubles." The clearest path to security and happiness, counseled the editor, lay in patience and "standing fast for the old ways of doing things." For segregationists, the restoration of order rested on their ability to discredit black veterans and other prophets of political change.[42]

It did not take long for such calls for "stern parental repression" to lead to antiblack hostility. "Before [I] give a Negro his rights, [I] would kick, kill, burn, and lynch the men and rape the black women," declared one white resident of Selma, Alabama. This man expressed no isolated sentiment.

Across the South, whites acted to remind black veterans that the uniform had changed nothing. Many southern communities, according to reports in the black press, gave returning black veterans a "cold reception." At a parade honoring returning veterans, the white children of Birmingham reportedly jeered black soldiers and poked fun at their uniforms. Other black veterans encountered hostility that ran deeper than mere insults. White police accused black soldiers of all sorts of crimes, from vagrancy and loitering to rape and murder. Police in Atlanta, for instance, raided a pool hall and arrested and fined two black soldiers for loitering, even as the alleged offenders protested that they were "just enjoying a little rest." In Tuscaloosa, a white man shot a black soldier who reportedly had made "himself objectionable to the white people" and "insulted several white women." In Petersburg, Virginia, a bus driver shot a black soldier in the head when the veteran questioned whether he received proper change. As one black veteran from Georgia put it, "ever since I came from France I have been picked at by white folks" who try to put "every colored man that has ever served in the army in France . . . in prison or run him off from his home."[43]

As the tensions over returning veterans mounted throughout 1919, southern whites turned their attention to the emerging network of NAACP branches in the South. The "most dangerous class of agitators ever brought together in this country" dominate the NAACP," bellowed the *Charlotte Observer* in an editorial syndicated in southern newspapers. These "gatherings of extremists," continued the *Observer,* desired "not so much the welfare of the negro as the disruption of the friendly relations so long existing between the whites and the blacks of the south." Such sentiment soon turned violent. In January 1919, the president of the Vicksburg branch reported that the branch had "been suppressed" and that he and two others had been "banished from the state" and one of them even tarred and feathered for organizing the NAACP. "Under the guise of patriotism," he explained from the safety of Chicago, "we were called disloyal citizens because we asked for a reform, a real democracy." In August, whites in Leggett, Texas, convened a citizens' council to put local blacks "under control." Fearing that the newly organized NAACP branch would force "white folks do what [blacks] wanted them to do," the council ordered T. S. Davis, the branch president, to leave town, established a curfew for blacks, prohibited them from holding meetings of any kind, and banned them from the railroad depot. The council enforced its orders with violence, attacking Davis in broad daylight. Later that night they encircled his brother's house, firing rounds of rifle shots into it. Davis escaped to Ohio, but persistent white intimidation forced the local branch to disband.[44]

The same pattern of violent intimidation followed by banishment unfolded in Anderson, South Carolina, two months later. Under the leadership of a school principal, Baptist minister, and editor of a black newspaper, some fifty black farmers and tradesmen chartered a branch of the NAACP in March 1919. From its inception, the local branch encountered the hostility of the *Anderson Daily Tribune,* which "labored overtime to stir to a white heat racial hatred." A typical editorial blamed the branch's "preaching of social equality" and "the intermarriage of the two races" for the "ever increasing insolence of many Negroes in the city." Undeterred by such inflammatory rhetoric, the local branch persevered in its fight for racial justice. It took up the case of a black schoolteacher, who had been accused of stealing from the town's Woolworth store. When she denied the charge, the white store clerks choked and beat her until the police arrived to arrest her. After the city court acquitted her, the Anderson branch sued Woolworth's for $10,000 in damages. In response, white civic leaders met and decided to force the three branch leaders into exile rather than allow them to organize blacks for the protection of their legal rights. A mob quickly convened to carry out the directive and stormed the homes of these men, giving them less than eight hours to pack and leave or "suffer the penalty of death." As in Vicksburg and Leggett, white intimidation of blacks in Anderson persisted. Terror achieved its purpose. The Anderson branch ceased its operations.[45]

Federal and state authorities responded with a mix of indifference and hostility. The Justice Department turned a cold shoulder to the flood of personal appeals and petitions it received from black southerners pleading for federal action to suppress mob violence, protesting that lynching was something over which the federal government had no jurisdiction. The actions of the Justice Department, however, reveal that it was more persuaded by southern elites' interpretation that militant blacks, not recalcitrant whites, were the principal cause of unrest. Accordingly, the Justice Department targeted black political activism as part of its larger postwar Red Scare to root out subversive and revolutionary threats. The Bureau of Investigation planted informants in black organizations, uncovered alleged plots by blacks to stockpile weapons, and coordinated with state and local officials to suppress the NAACP. In Texas, where the governor believed the NAACP had stirred blacks into "a frenzy against the government," state officials sought to suppress the branches, contending that they were operating in violation of state law because they lacked a charter to "do business." John R. Shillady rushed to Austin, Texas, to defend the NAACP, explaining that as a nonprofit organization, the NAACP did not require a state charter. State officials did not let such legal technicalities deter their objective. A county judge, accompanied by a band of thugs, attacked Shillady outside his hotel, striking him in the face until it was a mass of blood and bruises. As the judge explained, Shillady intended to "sow discontent among Negroes, and I thought it was my duty to stop him."[46]

Violence had a domino effect. News of terrorist attacks on one branch spread fears to others about the wisdom of continuing. Texas's bogus legal challenge to the NAACP's branch network and the subsequent assault on Shillady left many in doubt about the legality of the NAACP in the South. In Texas, South Carolina, and elsewhere, branches disbanded under the pressures of legal intimidation. By early 1920, it was clear that the NAACP in the South would not recover. One traveler for the association found the NAACP "practically dead" in Marshall, Texas, "inactive" in Fort Worth, and in disarray in Muskogee, Oklahoma. He found a few surviving stalwarts, such as George Lewis of Louisiana, but because Lewis had "been warned repeatedly," he feared that one "may expect anything to happen to him."[47]

The few branches that persisted risked retaliation. When branch activists in Greensboro, Florida, organized a voter registration drive in 1920, local whites doctored the registration books and threatened bloodshed if blacks voted. Many went "to the pole [sic] that day regardless of the consequence." But the ensuing "devilment," reported the branch president, "got our peeples afred," forcing the majority of members to quit. "Threats and violence toward our group" compelled into exile two women from the branch in Okmulgee, Oklahoma, in May 1921. They attributed the hostilities to the emergence of the NAACP, as well as to a growing following in town for Marcus Garvey's UNIA and another black nationalist group. Blacks suspected that whites targeted these groups because they underwrote black economic prosperity and independence. Town authorities reportedly jailed any "poverty-stricken" blacks who applied to these groups for assistance or membership. White employers ceased hiring blacks, even for jobs of "the most menial kind." But most important, blacks in town believed that the mob targeted property, owned by members of the NAACP, recently discovered to be rich in oil and gas reserves. A mob poured molasses and hog fat on one such landowner, then set him ablaze, dragged him through the streets, and murdered his sons. Another mob burned the home of one of the town's wealthiest black residents and forced Lizzie Johnson, another property owner and NAACP branch member, and her five children out of town. Fearful for the safety of the relatives they left behind, these refugees must have experienced unimaginable horror the following week when news surfaced that just thirty miles north of Okmulgee, a frenzied white mob torched the black district of Tulsa in one of the nation's most gruesome race riots.[48]

Political violence, legal intimidation, and economic terrorism destroyed what chance the NAACP had of becoming a popular movement rooted in the South. In the wake of the Red Summer, black southerners were reluctant to renew their membership in the NAACP, resulting in a precipitous decline in the organization's following, especially in the rural South. By 1923, the national office reported that most of the southern branches organized since 1917 were either dead or dormant. Efforts by the national office to revive branches had met with only sporadic and modest success, partly because of New York's insensitivity to the conditions confronting rural organizers. One branch activist from rural Texas proposed that the national office could better sustain and expand its following in the South if it permitted people to join for an annual fee of fifty cents rather than the required minimum dues of one dollar. By making membership affordable, he argued, rural branches would rapidly add members and expand their treasury, enabling them to "demand Justice much quicker and with less expense." The national office balked, claiming that those "sufficiently interested in the welfare of the race" would willingly pay one dollar a year. New York's inflexibility on dues foreshadowed its postwar shift away from rebuilding and sustaining its southern branches. In 1923, after three years of unsuccessful membership drives, the board of directors agreed to focus future drives on raising funds rather than on expanding membership. The directors recommended that field-workers solicit members who would pay five dollars or more dues annually and discourage people from pledging only the minimum one dollar. The directors even voted to suspend publication of *The Branch Bulletin,* an action symbolic of their abandonment of the once extensive branch network.[49]

The rapid decline of the NAACP in the aftermath of the war unfolded amid a larger retreat from the reconstruction that so many progressive reformers and activists, black and white, had imagined in 1918. The broader social insurgencies of the war years shared a similar fate as a combination of federal surveillance, government repression, and vigilantism vanquished other radicals, labor militants, and unionists.[50] Yet even as the forces of reaction overwhelmed the demands for reconstruction, hope endured. The fortunes of Caesar F. Simmons, long the guiding spirit behind the NAACP in rural central Oklahoma, reflect that persistence. No stranger to white intimidation, Simmons, an overworked local postmaster, branch president, and itinerant NAACP organizer, collapsed from a nervous breakdown in early 1922. Although the war years took their toll on him, he continued to dream of the day when "the fires of law and order and freedom will burn to the gulf and sweep across the Mississippi River" to liberate "the enslaved Negroes" of the South. "In the midst of all," he vowed, "we must not falter, but labor on."[51]

Notes

1. Roy Nash, "The Heart of the South," *Branch Bulletin,* Apr. 1917.

2. Nash, "The Heart of the South"; "Association's President Expresses Preference for Increased Membership as Testimonial," *Branch Bulletin,* Feb. 1918. Progressive reformers of various stripes saw the immediate postwar period as a new "reconstruction" that not only envisioned the expansion of citizenship rights for African Americans, but realized what they called industrial democracy. For example, see Mary White Ovington, "Reconstruction and the Negro," *Crisis,* Feb. 1919. On the use of the term *reconstruction* by reformers in this period, see Joseph A. McCartin, *Labor's Great War: The Struggle for Industrial Democracy and the Origins of Modern Labor Relations, 1912–1921* (Chapel Hill: University of North Carolina Press, 1997), 187–91.

3. Jane Dailey, Glenda Elizabeth Gilmore, and Bryant Simon, eds., *Jumpin' Jim Crow: Southern Politics from Civil War to Civil Rights* (Princeton, N.J.: Princeton University Press, 2000), 5. Despite the breadth of the sampling of the revisionist approach in that volume, it slights the important contributions that labor history has made to the new political history; for example, see Nan Elizabeth Woodruff, *American Congo: The African American Freedom Struggle in the Delta* (Cambridge, Mass.: Harvard University Press, 2003); Robin D. G. Kelley, "'We Are Not What We Seem': Rethinking Black Working-Class Opposition in the Jim Crow South," *Journal of American History* 80 (June 1993): 75–112; Steven A. Reich, "Soldiers of Democracy: Black Texans and the Fight for Citizenship, 1917–1921," *Journal of American History* 82 (Mar. 1996): 1476–1504; Stephen H. Norwood, "Bogalusa Burning: The War against Biracial Unionism in the Deep South, 1919," *Journal of Southern History* 63, no. 3 (Aug. 1997): 591–628; Paul Ortiz, *Emancipation Betrayed: The Hidden History of Black Organizing and White Violence in Florida from Reconstruction to the Bloody Election of 1920* (Berkeley: University of California Press, 2005); Brian Kelly, *Race, Class, and Power in the Alabama Coalfields, 1908–1921* (Urbana: University of Illinois Press, 2001). Two exemplary monographs of revisionist southern political history are Glenda Gilmore, *Gender and Jim Crow: Women and the Politics of White Supremacy in North Carolina, 1896–1920* (Chapel Hill: University of North Carolina Press, 1996); and Steven Kantrowitz, *Ben Tillman and the Reconstruction of White Supremacy* (Chapel Hill: University of North Carolina Press, 2000).

4. "Negro Conscription," *The New Republic,* 20 Oct. 1917.

5. David Kennedy, *Over Here: The First World War and American Society* (New York: Oxford University Press, 1980), 157; "The Negro and the World War," *Richmond Planet,* 5 Oct. 1918, in Tuskegee Institute News Clippings File (hereafter TINCF), reel 244, frame 343; Jeanette Keith, *Rich Man's War, Poor Man's Fight: Race, Class, and Power in the Rural South during the First World War* (Chapel Hill: University of North Carolina Press, 2004), 129; Gerald E. Shenk, "Race, Manhood, and Manpower: Mobilizing Rural Georgia for World War I," *Georgia Historical Quarterly* 81 (Fall 1997): 629–34.

6. S. W. Cauley to Mr. Bielaski, 21 Aug. 1917, in Casefile OG 3057, RG 65, Federal Bureau of Investigation, Federal Surveillance of Afro-Americans (1917–1925): The

First World War, the Red Scare, and the Garvey Movement (hereafter FSAA), reel 8, frame 602; Texas Citizen (Longview, Texas) to Woodrow Wilson, 10 Apr. 1917, ibid., frame 256.

7. "Race War," *Crisis* (Sept. 1919), quoted in Adam Fairclough, *Better Day Coming: Blacks and Equality, 1890–2000* (New York: Viking, 2001), 102; H. D. Cocka to President Woodrow Wilson, 29 Mar. 1917, in Casefile OG 3057, RG 65, FSAA., reel 8, frame 148.

8. "Uneasy Consciences at Work in Virginia," *New York Age,* 30 Nov. 1918, in TINCF, reel 244, frame 386.

9. T. J. Curran to Charles Owen, 8 Apr. 1917, in Casefile OG 3057, RG 65, FSAA, reel 8, frame 297; "Local White Slave Officer," Report, 25 May 1917, ibid., frame 500; Benjamin H. Littlestep, Report, 14 Apr. 1917, ibid., frame 238; T. W. Leonard to Newton D. Baker, 3 Apr. 1917, ibid., frame 172. On federal surveillance of African Americans during the war years, see Theodore Kornweibel, *Seeing Red: Federal Campaigns against Black Militancy, 1919–1925* (Bloomington: University of Indiana Press, 1998); Mark Ellis, *Race, War, and Surveillance: African Americans and the United States Government during World War I* (Bloomington: University of Indiana Press, 2001).

10. H. W. Kinney to Department of Justice, 31 Mar. 1917, in Casefile OG 3057, RG 65, FSAA, reel 8, frame 169; A. B. Hargrove to Inspector in Charge, 19 April 1917, ibid., frame 301; Ella Morris to Postmaster General, 31 Mar. 1917, ibid., frame 156; Albert Nuenhoffer, Report, 24 Sept. 1917, ibid., frame 659. On the alleged German plots to undermine the loyalty of black Americans, particularly in the South, see Ellis, *Race, War, and Surveillance,* 5–12, 65–72.

11. "The Soldier's Return," *The Star of Zion,* 12 Dec. 1918, in TINCF, reel 244, frame 388; "Horizon Clouds," *Macon Telegram,* 13 Dec. 1918, ibid., frame 954; Private Dalzell, letter to the editor, *Dayton* (Ohio) *Journal,* 23 Oct. 1918, ibid., frame 321; Horace G. Burke, letter to the editor, *Houston Observer,* 19 Oct. 1918, ibid., frame 659.

12. Herbert Aptheker, "The Afro-American in World War I," in *Afro-American History: The Modern Era* (Secaucus, N.J.: Citadel Press, 1971), 159–72; Jeanette Keith, "The Politics of Southern Draft Resistance, 1917–1918: Class, Race, and Conscription in the Rural South," *Journal of American History* 87 (Mar. 2001), 1335–61.

13. James R. Grossman, *Land of Hope: Chicago, Black Southerners, and the Great Migration* (Chicago: University of Chicago Press, 1989), 3. Other key works on the Great Migration include Peter Gottlieb, *Making Their Own Way: Southern Blacks' Migration to Pittsburgh, 1916–1930* (Urbana: University of Illinois Press, 1987); Joe William Trotter, ed., *The Great Migration in Historical Perspective: New Dimensions of Race, Class, and Gender* (Bloomington: University of Indiana Press, 1991); Kimberley L. Phillips, *AlabamaNorth: African-American Migrants, Community, and Working-Class Activism in Cleveland, 1915–45* (Urbana: University of Illinois Press, 1999); Carole Marks, *Farewell—We're Good and Gone: The Great Black Migration* (Bloomington: Indiana University Press, 1989); Eric Arnesen, *Black Protest and the Great Migration: A Brief History with Documents* (Boston: Bedford/St. Martin's, 2003); and Steven A. Reich, ed., *The Encyclopedia of the Great Black Migration,* 3 vols. (Westport, Conn.: Greenwood Press, 2006).

14. Labor historians have done the most to study changes in black life in the South; two examples include Eric Arnesen, *Waterfront Workers of New Orleans: Race, Class, and Politics, 1863–1923* (New York: Oxford University Press, 1991), 219–22, 225–28; and Kelly, *Race, Class, and Power in the Alabama Coalfields,* 132–202. But these studies and

others like them concern certain occupational groups rather than agriculture or the region as a whole. Much work remains to be done that explores blacks who remained in the South during the era of the Great Migration.

15. "Those Who Refuse to Work," *Montgomery Advertiser,* 8 Mar. 1919, in TINCF, reel 9, frame 896; "Fancy Wages Paid Negro Field Hands," *Mobile Register,* 6 July 1919, ibid., frame 944; "Loafers Caught in Big Roundup Have Plenty of Money," *Atlanta Georgian,* 30 Jan. 1919, ibid., frame 904; "Negroes Buy Second Big Plantation with Help of Land Bank," *New Orleans Item,* 21 Oct. 1919, ibid., frame 416; "Buy Big Plantation; Confront Labor Problem," *Chicago Defender,* 13 Dec. 1919, ibid., frame 411; "The Black Belt and Farm Labor," *Montgomery Advertiser,* 2 Feb. 1919, ibid., frame 414. The U.S. Employment Bureau was a federal agency charged with finding employment for and looking after the general welfare of returning veterans from the European war.

16. "Negro Women Collecting Allotments from as Many as Three or Four Husbands," *Atlanta Constitution,* 21 August 1918, in TINCF, reel 244, frame 536; "Man Is Trying to Stir Up Negroes in Atlanta," *Atlanta Journal,* 6 April 1918, ibid., frame 625; Agent report, 17 July 1917, in Casefile OG 83071, RG 65, FSAA, reel 8, frames 882–83; *New Orleans Times Picayune,* 21 May 1918, clipping, in New Orleans Branch File, box G-81, Papers of the N.A.A.C.P., Library of Congress (hereafter NAACP Papers); "Negro Washwomen in Tulsa Demand Electric Support," *Oklahoma City Times,* 23 Oct. 1920, in TINCF, reel 11, frame 672; "Negress Admits Putting Glass in Bread," *Montgomery Advertiser,* 23 April 1918, in TINCF, reel 244, frame 619; A. D. Dabney, report, 19 March 1918, in Casefile OG 159218, RG 65, FSAA, reel 10, frames 262–63. On the resistance strategies of black domestic servants in Atlanta during World War I, see Tera Hunter, *To 'Joy My Freedom: Southern Black Women's Lives and Labors after the Civil War* (Cambridge, Mass.: Harvard University Press, 1997), 219–38.

17. Robert Zieger, *America's Great War: World War I and the American Experience* (New York: Rowman and Littlefield, 2000), 131–34; Elizabeth Haiken, "'The Lord Helps Those Who Help Themselves': Black Laundresses in Little Rock, Arkansas, 1917–1921," *Arkansas Historical Quarterly* 49 (Spring 1990): 20–50. For more on the federal government's ambiguous impact on the working lives of African Americans during the war see McCartin, *Labor's Great War,* 114–19; and Eric Arnesen, *Brotherhoods of Color: Black Railroad Workers and the Struggle for Equality* (Cambridge, Mass.: Harvard University Press, 2001), 48–56.

18. "Southern Bunk," *New York Age,* 19 April 1919, in TINCF, reel 9, frame 838; George Haynes to William Wilson, 22 March 1919, in Chief of Clerk's Files, 8/102D, RG 174, Department of Labor, Black Workers in the Great Migration [hereafter BWGM], reel 14, frame 202; Sidney J. Catts to William Wilson, 7 April 1919, ibid., frames 210–11; Catts to Wilson, 22 April 1919, ibid., frame 14. Under pressure from Catts, Wilson suspended all work on behalf of blacks in the state of Florida; see William B. Wilson to Dabney M. Scales (Biloxi, Miss.), 17 May 1919, Chief of Clerk's Files, 8/102E, in BWGM, reel 14, frames 295–96.

19. Anonymous to Secretary of War, 23 Sept. 1918, Chief of Clerk's Files, 8/102E, in BWEGM, reel 14, frame 269; "Reign of Terror Is Staged Near Hot Springs," *Chicago Defender,* 7 June 1919, in TINCF, reel 11, frame 42; John R. Shillady to A. J. Brown, 8 Nov. 1919, in Vicksburg Branch File, box G106, NAACP Papers; "Ku Klux Busy in Mississippi," *The Christian Recorder,* 27 March 1919, in TINCF, reel 9, frame 824.

20. P. G. Cooper to A. Mitchell Palmer, 8 March 1919, in Casefile 158260, Section 1, RG 60, Department of Justice, FSAA, reel 14, frame 20; E. Johnson to Dept. of Justice, 4 Sept. 1918, ibid., frames 42–43. Although he issued a proclamation against lynching in August 1918, Wilson did so after the lynching of a German American in Illinois. He opposed mob violence on the pragmatic grounds that it aided the work of German propagandists, not on the moral grounds that it was a gross violation of racial justice. He made no case for a federal role in eliminating lynching.

21. G. C. Callaway (Athens, Ga.) to Roy Nash, 3 June 1917, in Athens Branch File, box G44, NAACP Papers; Margaret Dorris McCleary (Jacksonville, Fla.) to James Weldon Johnson, 16 Aug. 1917, in Jacksonville Branch File, box G41, NAACP Papers.

22. J. E. Boyd (Longview, Tex.) to Woodrow Wilson, 19 Nov. 1920, in Casefile 158260, section 2, RG 60, FSAA, reel 14, frames 296–301; Margaret Dorris McCleary to James Weldon Johnson, 16 Aug. 1917, in Jacksonville Branch File, box G41, NAACP Papers; "What the Negro Expects Out of the Recent War," *Nashville Globe,* 9 Feb. 1919, in TINCF, reel 10, frame 288.

23. McCartin, *Labor's Great War,* 2.

24. Arnesen, *Brotherhoods of Color* and *Waterfront Workers of New Orleans;* Daniel Letwin, *The Challenge of Interracial Unionism: Alabama Coal Miners, 1878–1921* (Chapel Hill: University of North Carolina Press, 1997); Hunter, *To 'Joy My Freedom,* 224–25; Kieran Taylor, "'We Have Just Begun': Black Organizing and White Response in the Arkansas Delta, 1919," *Arkansas Historical Quarterly* 58, no. 3 (1999): 264–84; and Kelly, *Race, Class, and Power,* 11.

25. Jonathan T. Maxey (Galveston, Tex.) to James Weldon Johnson, 8 Dec. 1918, in Jackson (Tenn.) Branch File, box G198, NAACP Papers; E. B. Henderson (Falls Church, Va.) to Mary White Ovington, 2 April 1920, in Falls Church (Fairfax County) Branch File, box G207, ibid.; John R. Shillady, Address to the Annual Conference, 23 June 1919, Annual Conferences File, Box B2, ibid. Applications for branch charters included a list of names and occupations of charter members, which reveal a substantial working-class presence in many of the southern branches.

26. Judith Stein, *The World of Marcus Garvey: Race and Class in Modern Society* (Baton Rouge: Louisiana State University Press, 1986), 58–59; "Enemies of Negro Welfare," *Greenville (SC) News,* 2 July 1919, TINCF, reel 10, frame 226.

27. T. L. McCoy to John R. Shillady, 20 May 1918, in Raleigh Branch File, box G148, NAACP Papers; McCoy to James W. Johnson, 21 Oct. 1918, ibid.; Johnson to McCoy, 23 Oct. 1918, ibid.; Wilson Jefferson (Augusta, Ga.) to Roy Nash, 11 April 1917, in Augusta Branch File, box G44, ibid.; Jefferson to James W. Johnson, 3 May 1917, ibid. For a particularly acrimonious fight between a newspaper editor and the Knoxville, Tennessee, branch, see correspondence in Knoxville Branch File, box G198; on intraracial conflicts within the Houston branch, see Reich, "Soldiers of Democracy," 1496–97.

28. George Bell (Memphis) to James Weldon Johnson, 4 April 1919, in Memphis Branch File, box G199, NAACP Papers; George E. Lewis (Shreveport) to John R. Shillady, 17 Feb. 1919, in Shreveport Branch File, box G83, ibid.; Caesar F. Simmons (Boley, Okla.) to James W. Johnson, 15 July 1919, in Boley Branch File, box G172, ibid.; Shillady, Address to Annual Conference, 23 June 1919.

29. T. L. McCoy (Raleigh) to John R. Shillady, 20 May 1918, in Raleigh Branch File,

box G148, NAACP Papers; J. T. Page (Danville, Va.) to O. G. Villard, 5 Jan. 1918, in Danville Branch File, box G206, ibid.; G. C. Callaway (Athens, Ga.) to Roy Nash, 3 June 1917, in Athens Branch File, box G44, ibid.

30. *The Vindicator,* 3 Sept. and 12 Sept. 1918, in New Orleans Branch File, box G81, NAACP Papers; Butler W. Nance, Notes from the Columbia Branch, 20 May 1919, box G196. ibid.; Joseph Robinson (Darlington, S.C.) to John R. Shillady, 23 May 1919, in Darlington (S.C.) Branch File, box G197, ibid.; Mary White Ovington to Joseph A. Robinson, 28 May 1919, ibid.; Progamme, New Orleans Branch, 19 May 1918, in New Orleans Branch File, box G81, ibid.; E. B. Henderson (Falls Church, Va.) to John R. Shillady, 21 Nov. 1918, in Falls Church Branch File, box G207, ibid.; *Dallas Express,* 19 Apr. 1919.

31. Jonathan T. Maxey to James Weldon Johnson, 8 Dec. 1918, in Jackson (Tenn.) Branch File, box G198, NAACP Papers; James Weldon Johnson to Aaron Jefferson, 23 July 1918, in Beaumont Branch File, box G200, ibid.; *Branch Bulletin,* Feb. 1918, Feb. 1919, Mar. 1919. Workers and trade unionists also proved adept at coopting the language of patriotism to serve their own political ends; see McCartin, *Labor's Great War,* 104–6; Arnesen, *Brotherhoods of Color,* 55–56.

32. Various of letters of T. G. Garrett in Shreveport Branch File, box G83, NAACP Papers; *The Vindicator,* 20 Aug. 1918, 3 Sept. 1918, and 12 Sept. 1918, in New Orleans Branch File, box G81, ibid.; and E. B. Henderson (Falls Church, Va.) to Mary White Ovington, 2 Apr. 1920, in Falls Church (Va.) Branch File, box G207, ibid.

33. P. F. Hill and J. W. Grant, Report of Nashville Branch, 5 Apr. 1919, in Nashville Branch File, box G200, NAACP Papers; G. N. T. Gray and J. Gentry Horace, Minutes of the Fort Worth Branch, 20 Apr. 1918, in Fort Worth Branch File, box G202, ibid.; Lawrence Goodwyn, *The Populist Moment: A Short History of the Agrarian Revolt in America* (New York: Oxford University Press, 1978), 61.

34. Rev. J. R. Cooper, Monthly Report of Danville, Virginia, Branch, in Danville Branch File, box G206, NAACP Papers; S. C. Snelson, Report of the Oklahoma City Branch, 8 Jan. 1920, box G173, ibid.; Butler W. Nance, Notes from the Columbia Branch, 20 May 1919, in Columbia Branch File, box G196, ibid.; Edwin A. Harleston (Charleston) to John R. Shillady, 2 Nov. 1918, in Charleston Branch File, box G196, ibid. The branch files are filled with examples of these initiatives that are far too numerous to summarize or cite. For further examples of the activities of the Texas NAACP branches in these years, see Reich, "Soldiers of Democracy," 1494–96.

35. W. G. Young to R. W. Bagwell, 27 Dec. 1922, in Graham (Va.) Branch File, box G207, NAACP Papers; Butler W. Nance to Walter F. White, 12 Sept. 1920, in Columbia Branch File, box G197, ibid.; D. B. Brooks to Catherine Lealtad, 20 Sept. 1920, ibid.

36. Eric Arnesen, "Charting an Independent Course: African-American Railroad Workers in the World War I Era," in Eric Arnesen, Julie Greene, and Bruce Laurie, eds., *Labor Histories: Class Politics, and the Working-Class Experience* (Urbana: University of Illinois Press, 1998), 285.

37. A. R. Bell to John R. Shillady, 7 Nov. 1918, in Jackson (Tenn.) Branch File, box G198, NAACP Papers; Bell to Shillady, 31 Dec. 1918, ibid.; W. G. Young to C. B. Slemp, 13 Dec. 1920, in Graham (Va.) Branch File, box G197, ibid; Judith Shklar, *American Citizenship: The Quest for Inclusion* (Cambridge, Mass.: Harvard University Press, 1991), 3, 93; Colored Association of Railway Trainmen quoted in Arnesen, "Charting an

Independent Course," 294. For more on the struggles and travails of black railroad unionists during World War I, including an analysis of the various tactics that black trainmen pursued, see Arnesen, *Brotherhoods of Color,* 56–83.

38. Bell to Shillady, 31 Dec. 1918, in Jackson (Tenn.) Branch File, box G198, NAACP Papers; Young to N. V. Maker, NW Ry., 11 Dec. 1920, in Graham (Va.) Branch File, box G197, ibid. On the limitations of the protests of black railroad activists during the war years, see Arnesen, "Charting an Independent Course," 298–303.

39. A. H. Reagin to James Weldon Johnson, 5 Nov. 1918, in Selma Branch File, box G8, NAACP Papers; Rev. M. A. Talley to James W. Johnson, 26 Nov. 1918, ibid.; Johnson to Reagin, 20 Nov. 1918, ibid.; Johnson to Talley, 2 Dec. 1918, ibid.; John L. Garrett to James W. Johnson, 15 Nov. 1918, ibid.

40. John W. White to Moorfield Storey, 24 Sept. 1918, in Little Rock Branch File, box G12, NAACP Papers; Walter F. White to John W. White, 15 Oct. 1918, ibid.; Walter F. White to J. H. McConico, 8 Oct. 1918, ibid.

41. John R. Shillady to A. R. Bell, 22 Nov. 1918, in Jackson (Tenn.) Branch File, box G198, NAACP Papers; George E. Lewis to Mary White Ovington, 1 Oct. 1919, in Shreveport Branch File, box G83, ibid.; S. L. James to James Weldon Johnson, 10 July 1922, in Sapulpa (Okla.) Branch File, box G175, ibid.; Johnson to James, 17 July 1922, ibid.

42. F. Sullens to Major Brown, 30 Nov. 1918, in Casefile 10218–289, RG 165, War Department: General and Special Staffs — Military Intelligence Division, FSAA, reel 21, frame 175; "Birmingham Is Inadequately Protected against Mob Violence and Race Disorders," *Birmingham News,* 10 Oct. 1919, in TINCF, reel 10, frame 883; *Blytheville (Ark.) Reports,* 9 Oct. 1919, ibid., frame 235.

43. Letter to the Editor, *The Guardian,* 18 Apr. 1919, in TINCF, reel 10, frame 339; "The Returning Soldiers," *Atlanta Independent,* 22 Mar. 1919, ibid., reel 244, frame 940; "Birmingham Is Inadequately Protected against Mob Violence and Race Disorders," *Birmingham News,* 10 Oct. 1919, ibid., reel 10, frame 883; "Discharged Soldiers Are Sent to Jail," *Atlanta Constitution,* 15 Feb. 1919, ibid., reel 244, frame 944; "Man Shoots Soldier on Flimsy Excuse," *St. Louis Argus,* 8 Feb. 1919, ibid., reel 9, frame 805; "Negro Soldier Shot in the Head by Conductor," *Petersburg (Va.) Index Appeal,* ibid., frame 812; John R. McCloud (Claxton, Ga.) to Warren G. Harding, 15 Mar. 1921, in Casefile 158260 Section 2, RG 60, FSAA, reel 14, frames 275–77.

44. "Enemies of Negro Welfare," *Greenville (S.C.) News,* 2 July 1919, in TINCF, reel 10, frame 226; D. D. Foote to James Weldon Johnson, 30 Jan. 1919, in Vicksburg Branch File, box G106, NAACP Papers; T. S. Davis to John R. Shillady, 11 Aug. 1919, in Leggett (Tex.) Branch File, box G203, ibid.; Davis to James Weldon Johnson, 24 Oct. 1919, ibid.; "Prosperous Farmers Driven from Their Polk County Homes," *Houston Informer,* 16 Aug. 1919, in TINCF, reel 10, frame 404.

45. Application for Charter, Mar. 1919, in Anderson (S.C.) Branch File, box G196, NAACP Papers; "Have Negroes the Right to Organize?" *Daily Herald,* 16 Oct. 1919, in TINCF, reel 10, frame 255; "Immediate Cause of the Anderson (S.C.) Outrages," *Daily Herald,* 27 Oct. 1919, ibid., reel 9, frame 995; Butler W. Nance to James Weldon Johnson, 26 Oct. 1919, in Columbia Branch File, box G197, NAACP Papers.

46. Reich, "Soldiers of Democracy," 1498–1501; Mary White Ovington, *The Walls Came Tumbling Down* (1947; reprint, New York: Arno Press, 1969), 172–75, and "Is

Mob Violence the Texas Solution to the Race Problem?" *The Independent,* 6 Sept. 1919; Fairclough, *Better Day Coming,* 104–6. On federal surveillance of black activists in the immediate postwar years, see Ellis, *Race, War, and Surveillance,* 101–40.

47. Reich, "Soldiers of Democracy," 1500–1501; Butler W. Nance to James Weldon Johnson, 26 Oct. 1919, in Columbia Branch File, box G197, NAACP Papers; N. B. Brooks to John R. Shillady, 8 Nov. 1919, ibid.; W. H. Holman to Shillady, 25 Apr. 1920, in Shreveport Branch File, box G83, ibid.

48. Branch President to NAACP, 23 Oct. 1920, in Greensboro (Fla.) Branch File, box G40, ibid.; Branch President to James Weldon Johnson, 19 Oct. 1923, ibid.; and Prince L. Edwoods to Walter F. White, 24 May 1921, in Okmulgee (Okla.) Branch File, box G175, ibid.

49. T. C. Smith to NAACP, Dec. 1919, in Mumford (Tex.) Branch File, box G205, NAACP Papers; John R. Shillady to T. C. Smith, 27 Jan. 1920, ibid.; Minutes, Board of Directors, in Administration Files, 10 Sept. 1923 and 12 Nov. 1923, box A1, ibid.

50. Stein, *The World of Marcus Garvey;* Arnesen, *Brotherhoods of Color,* 83; James Green, *Grass-Roots Socialism: Radical Movements in the Southwest, 1895–1943* (Baton Rouge: Louisiana State University Press, 1978), 345–95.

51. Caesar F. Simmons (Boley, Okla.) to Mary White Ovington, 26 Jan. 1922, in Boley (Okla.) Branch File, box G172, NAACP Papers; Simmons to Robert W. Bagnall, 17 June 1922, ibid.

NAN ELIZABETH WOODRUFF

7   The Organizing Tradition among
African American Plantation Workers
in the Arkansas Delta in the Age of Jim Crow

The Arkansas Delta was home to a rich rural political culture that preceded the better known post–World War II civil rights movement. African American sharecroppers in the region organized, in the first half of the twentieth century, two labor unions to secure economic justice within the plantation economy of sharecropping. The Progressive Farmers and Household Union, organized in 1919 in Elaine, Arkansas, resulted in the wholesale massacre of untold numbers of African American men, women, and children. Later, during the depression of the 1930s, black and white sharecroppers and tenant farmers organized the Southern Tenant Farmers' Union, which sought to secure a fair share of New Deal agricultural programs. In both cases, black people drew from a rural political culture based on the church, the family, and fraternal organizations. Through these institutions and in their daily encounters with the planters and their minions, rural black people fought to secure their fair share of the cotton crops and to protect their families from the violence and terror that underwrote the plantation system and white supremacy. The post–World War II civil rights movement cannot be understood outside the context of these earlier struggles for justice.[1]

Sharecropping, and the violence that underwrote it, shaped rural black politics and the struggle for economic and political rights in the age of Jim Crow. In the Delta, this struggle was rooted in earlier conflicts that grew out of, and were circumscribed by, the plantation society and polity as it had developed in the late nineteenth and early twentieth centuries. The age of Jim Crow began with the simultaneous creation of segregation and disfranchisement and the expansion of the plantation economy of sharecropping and tenant farming into the vast alluvial lands of the Arkansas and Mississippi deltas. From the 1880s through World War I, lumber companies, some of them northern-owned, cleared the swamplands and erected plantations that encompassed thousands of acres. As Harold D. Woodman has shown, this region became the center for large-scale business plantations, worked by African American sharecroppers and day laborers whose activities were strictly supervised by a plantation manager. After the cotton was harvested, sharecroppers settled either with the manager or the planter, who added up their commissary bill and combined it with production costs such as fertilizer, seed, and supervisory fees. Most fell deeper into debt and either renewed contracts or moved to another plantation.[2]

The modern alluvial empire was characterized by a polity that defined citizenship in terms of race and that drew a weak distinction between the functions of the state, or government, and those of civil society.[3] Legal disfranchisement, sanctioned by the United States Supreme Court, forced African Americans to negotiate with employers for whatever social space they could get. Planters controlled the political offices that bore directly on their interests. Wherever African Americans turned, they encountered a world circumscribed by constables and justices of the peace who constantly harassed them by arbitrarily enforcing vagrancy laws, by sheriffs who either ignored or engaged in peonage, by plantation managers who also served as deputies, by planters who had the power to protect their workers from arrests or to send them to the state penitentiary, and by enough lynchings to remind them of the costs involved in defying the brutal instruments of domination. To survive, workers depended on the precarious goodwill of employers for protection from local authorities and the courts.[4]

By removing African Americans from the realm of citizenship through segregation and disfranchisement, employers could intervene in areas of their workers' lives that in liberal democracies are the preserve of civil society. Planters extended their authority into workers' private or cultural space, into their families, homes, churches, and lodges. Through commissaries, planters determined what croppers ate, wore, or purchased for their homes, and lien laws allowed them to seize the laborer's every possession.[5] Employers built the churches and the schools and paid the preachers and the teachers. And most croppers received their mail through the commissary, allowing regulation of what they read and of the people with whom they corresponded. Planters even withheld mail until the crops were gathered, to ensure that workers remained on the plantation through the harvest.

Although the weak separation between state and civil society shaped the contours of black rural politics, it did not destroy African Americans' efforts to challenge their oppression and to seek justice on the plantation. Plantation workers, including sharecroppers as well as day laborers paid in wages by the day, formed a political culture in opposition to the harsh world they came to inhabit. Their daily encounters with planters and their minions shaped how they fought the injustice and terror that they lived under even as they sought to preserve their own humanity and dignity. Their political struggles at times broke out into armed resistance and organized rebellion in the form of labor unions, but most of the time, their battles were launched on a more personal basis in the form of confrontations with plantation managers, commissary operators, cotton weighers, and local law officers over issues of daily living, such as getting a just return on a cotton crop, having the right to move freely around the community, protecting oneself and one's family from physical harm and rape, securing the privacy of one's home, the right to raise and keep livestock, the protection of one's property—both in land and in material possessions—from theft, and securing a decent education for one's children.

These daily challenges to the plantation system received a boost during times of national crises, such as a world war or an economic depression, that allowed individual struggles to merge with broader collective interests. Thus, events outside the region created possibilities for African American workers to test the limits of planter authority and to press forward their inclusive demands for citizenship that comprised challenges to segregation, the sharecropping system, and disfranchisement.

World War I created for Delta black people new opportunities and possibilities that threatened planter dominance. Wartime industries and military service opened new economic opportunities for southern African Americans. As a number of scholars have shown, southern workers went north in search of not only economic improvement, but better education, housing, and a chance to exercise their civil rights.[6] Laborers left the countryside and the towns for the factories as soon as there were jobs. The effect on labor relations was immediate, for the migration of thousands of agricultural workers improved the bargaining power of those who remained. On many plantations, sharecroppers insisted on and received weekly cash settlements for crops. Planters also were forced to pay higher wages as workers withheld their labor, driving daily earnings from the usual $1.50 to as high as $4.50.[7]

The newly acquired economic leverage rural laborers achieved during the war had ramifications that transcended the issues of wages and hours. As sharecroppers gained greater economic independence, they made broad demands that challenged planters' control over their lives. For example, employers spent as much time complaining about their workers' purchasing of new cars as they did about paying high wages. Car ownership gave African Americans the mobility to travel wherever they pleased, back and forth across the Mississippi River, in search of higher-paying jobs. Driving also allowed workers to participate in leisure activities in towns, such as playing in pool halls or attending minstrel shows and circuses. Or workers could simply hang out in public places as a provocative reminder of their refusal to bend to planter demands for cheap labor. They could also exercise their consumptive independence by shopping outside the plantation commissary.[8]

Women gained some economic independence. According to one observer in Desha County, Arkansas, "the worst feature of the labor question is the domestic, or Negro women labor," who had "practically quit work" because of increased earnings of menfolk or because of allotments from relatives in the military. This travesty, he continued, had undermined the war efforts of women who had worked for the Red Cross, Liberty Loan drives, and other wartime organizations. "It looks hard that the white women who are striving so hard to assist in the war should sacrifice so much and undergo so many hardships and the Negro women live in ease and idleness." Moreover, African American women refused to work in other jobs they considered demeaning. For the first time, small businesses such as steam laundries employed white women. To the consternation of employers, they could not compel African American women to work; their independent incomes sheltered them from vagrancy laws.[9]

Rural laborers' refusal to work on planter-defined terms, and their determination to claim their family and leisure time as their own, concerned not only employers, but also the federal government. National wartime mobilization spawned a liberal state apparatus that touched southern life in ways not experienced since Reconstruction.[10] The decentralized nature of government agencies handed authority for administering the wartime programs to the planter elite, who made vital decisions through the state and local councils of defense, which were composed of landowners, businessmen, bankers, and agricultural extension agents. These councils mobilized labor, aided local draft boards in securing inductees, conducted Liberty Bond drives and food conservation campaigns, instilled loyalty, and monitored communities and plantations for subversion.[11]

Such an all-encompassing mission allowed planters and local officials to further extend their power into isolated plantation communities. In Arkansas, the state council sent an African American agent, P. L. Dorman, into the countryside to enlist the support of ministers and schoolteachers in organizing Liberty Bond drives, food conservation campaigns, and patriotic ceremonies.[12] Such activities, however, were often ignored or resisted. In a letter to one preacher, an Arkansas Council official complained that "we have not heard of any active steps that the colored ministers have been taking to forward any war movement." He insisted that all ministers must preach a monthly loyalty sermon and teach their flocks to sing "America." He warned that "a man's loyalty is sometimes questioned by his silence."[13]

African Americans' commitment to the war effort worried both the federal government and Delta civic leaders, especially when 66 percent of those drafted in Arkansas did not answer the call.[14] Arkansas governor Charles H. Brough argued that the failure of African Americans to enlist resulted not from disloyalty but from ignorance, illiteracy, and their "moving disposition."[15] A local postmaster may have been closer to the truth when he observed that many men had simply left their notices in their mailboxes, hoping that "through ignorance they . . . will not be drafted."[16]

Many African Americans undoubtedly failed to report for duty because of ignorance of the draft, but resistance to the draft was high enough in both Arkansas and Mississippi to suggest that more was involved than limited access to information. The massive efforts of local defense councils to control both the labor and the personal and cultural realms of their workers' lives implied that rural peoples contested not only the war, but also the power relations governing them at home. A government that simultaneously called on people to participate in patriotic ceremonies and purchase war bonds and required all field laborers to work six days a week for no more than $1.50 per day, or that invoked "work or fight laws" and forced people to carry employment cards, surely led African Americans to question whether the war would make the Delta safe for democracy.[17]

Although the actions of the state and local defense councils impressed on African Americans the importance of the war, rural peoples had other channels of information about wartime realities that shaped their views and expectations. Through the *Chicago Defender*, the NAACP's publication the *Crisis*, and letters from kin and friends up north and in the military, families on isolated plantations heard of the political struggles occurring outside the South. W. E. B. Du Bois, editor of the *Crisis*, urged his readers to support Woodrow Wilson's war to make the world safe for democracy. In return, Du Bois hoped that the president would reward African Americans' participation by supporting their struggle at home to achieve full citizenship. By reading the *Crisis*, rural peoples learned of their troops' military achievements—and of the discriminatory treatment to which they were subjected. Readers also obtained news describing the anticolonial movements that were sweeping Africa. The knowledge of struggles outside the South strengthened the contest for justice in the Delta.[18]

The awareness of developments outside the South encouraged political actions at home, especially the organization in the Delta of NAACP chapters. In Mississippi, the first chapter was organized in Vicksburg in

1918, and in the following year, another was formed in the African American community of Mound Bayou.[19] The Arkansas branches embraced both towns and plantation communities. By 1918, important chapters coalesced in Little Rock and Pine Bluff, a Delta commercial center; one year later, 101 members belonged to the chapter in Edmundson and affiliates emerged in Grand Lake and Jonesboro. Immediately following the war, sharecroppers formed a chapter in the town of Democrat. Sharecroppers from several communities wrote to the national office during and after the war to inquire about organizing branches. Although these attempts often failed, the letters indicated that poor people knew that outside agencies existed to secure their rights.[20]

Even though most chapter offices were located in towns or cities, rural workers still had access to the NAACP's activities. The seasonal nature of plantation work required men and women to seek employment in nearby towns. Fraternal orders, churches, and kin networks also yoked the countryside to the towns. Even if rural people did not join the NAACP, they might know of the organization and its goals through literature that circulated among their various networks. It would be logical to assume, then, that branches organized in Arkansas Delta commercial centers such as Pine Bluff and Jonesboro, or in the Yazoo Delta town of Vicksburg, would have links to plantation communities.

The politically awakened and assertive "New Negro" of the urban North, then, had followers in the plantation South. Delta leaders anxiously observed an increasingly defiant attitude among their workers. According to a member of the Arkansas Council of Defense, "We have noticed for some time, a very perceptible difference in the hitherto respectful demeanor of the colored people of this locality." Despite arguing that German propaganda was partly responsible for "upsetting the racial situation," the member was sure that the widespread circulation of the Chicago *Defender* was a major cause of unrest.[21] Continued reports of organizational activity in the Delta by the radical labor union the Industrial Workers of the World (IWW) caused additional anxiety.[22]

African American servicemen provided further tension, especially when they arrived home. Having offered their lives in service to the nation, the soldiers expected their citizenship would be reinstated—that they would have equal access to public accommodations and the vote. Delta leaders suspected as much and saw in these uniformed men the erosion of social relations. Consequently, P. L. Dorman carefully instructed community leaders "to take all precautions to see that our soldiers be rightly informed and encouraged to maintain at all times the correct deportment and attitude that should be theirs, to carefully avoid doing anything that might bring reproach upon them or the community in which they are." He noted that numerous incidents had been avoided because of "prompt and conservative action on the part of some of us." Ministers had been instructed to see that at all times the "proper kind of speakers appear before their people, who will give sober and wholesome advice, rather than the radical agitator."[23]

Fears about the dispositions of returning veterans arose well beyond the Delta. In other southern states, civic leaders argued that African American veterans should not receive a homecoming, but should return individually, so as not to call attention to them as a group. They also sought to prevent discharged African Americans from exercising the right to wear uniforms for three months.[24] Military intelligence in the South found a profound fear that returning soldiers would spread the social aspirations and political ideas they had acquired in their service abroad.[25] Mississippi governor Theodore Bilbo spoke for most southern leaders when he warned that those servicemen who had been "contaminated with Northern social and political dreams of equality" need not return: "we have all the room in the world for what we know as N-i-g-g-e-r-s, but none whatsoever for 'colored ladies and gentlemen.'"[26]

Not all Delta leaders followed this heavy-handed approach. Some acknowledged that African Americans had genuine grievances. The Mississippi Welfare League was formed by prominent planters and businessmen, including members from New Orleans and Memphis. It aimed to halt the flight of labor by encouraging planters to pay decent wages, improve living conditions and schools, and oppose lynching and other forms of violence directed against African Americans.[27] As one member observed, however, efforts to mold public opinion in support of "negro uplift" would take time. "Of course," wrote the secretary of the league, "we are, going to have, from time to time, instances where the negro will be imposed upon, lynched in some cases. This revolution cannot be brought about in the minds of our people in a short while."[28] The league sought to improve economic conditions without changing the power relations that governed plantation society; however, rural workers intended to extract broader changes, as events in Elaine, Arkansas, revealed.

The violence and terror that swept across the country in the Red Summer of 1919 occurred in the Arkansas Delta, as well. As corporate heads and their government partners crushed workers in the strikes of 1919 and sought to rein in the wartime aspirations and political assertiveness of the New Negro, racial confrontations swept the nation and the cities erupted into massive violence directed at black people. In the Arkansas Delta, African Americans, emboldened by the war that intended to make the world safe for democracy, returned to their plantations, towns, and villages to demand, with their families and friends who had remained at home, justice and a fair return on their crops. This struggle triggered a horrific response that led to an extensive massacre of African American men, women, and children.

The struggle for justice in Phillips County was intertwined with the rapidly developing cotton and timber economy that had swept the countryside during the war years. Soldiers returning to the region surrounding the town of Elaine found friends and family who had reaped the benefits of wartime wages in the lumber industry and sharecroppers and tenants who had shared in higher cotton prices. Black veterans, having fought in Europe, brought back to their plantations a determined sense that life could and would be different. Born from the ravages of war and the respect their sacrifices had won in Europe, the politicization of black veterans forged, together with the wartime aspirations engendered among their family and friends left behind, a collective will to secure a more just life in the Delta.

With men returning from the war and others coming home from their wartime jobs, landowners braced themselves for a more assertive working class. Many sharecroppers and tenants, although never making a just return on their crops, had made some money during the war, accumulating property in terms of livestock, furniture, pianos, and automobiles. Some had purchased Liberty Bonds, and others had acquired land. For example, Ed Ware and his wife had cultivated 120 acres of cotton and owned a Ford car that he drove daily to Helena as a taxi service when his crops were laid by. The Wares owned 2 mules, 1 horse, a Jersey cow, a farm wagon, all of their farm tools, a harness, 8 hogs, and 135 chickens. Another sharecropper, Ed Hicks, farmed 100 acres with his brother. He and his wife owned 4 mules, a wagon, and farming tools. Frank Moore, just returned from the war, worked with his wife 14 acres of cotton and 5 acres of corn, and they owned $678 worth of household goods.[29]

The acquisition of property and money threatened planter dominance, for many of their tenants had traveled to the nearby city of Helena to buy cars and goods, bypassing the commissary. Still others, like Ed Ware, refused to accept the planters' offer of 24 cents per pound for cotton in 1919 when the market price had risen to 40 cents. Ware decided to bypass his landlord and sell his cotton independently, thus violating the age-old rule of the plantation South that sharecroppers must market their crops through their planters. Aiming to retain control over the wartime surplus, planters moved to steal both the crops and the property of their croppers.[30]

In the fall of 1919, planters drove their croppers from the fields after the workers had planted and nurtured the crop. Landowners thus avoided settling with the croppers yet obtained their labor during planting season for the price of subsistence-level furnishings. They then hired day laborers to pick the cotton. The workers challenged the evictions and demanded a fair price for their cotton. In late September, men and women in the villages surrounding Elaine joined the Progressive Farmers and Household Union with the aim of hiring a lawyer to represent their claims against the planters for evicting them and stealing their crops. The union also sought to help its members buy government lands that had been set aside for World War I veterans. The union drew from the local Masonic orders in its use of rituals, secret passwords, and the collection of dues to purchase real estate for its members. Armed guards stood at the church doors during union meetings to protect the deliberations, a necessary precaution, as plantation managers and owners had spread the word that sharecroppers had formed an organization with the goal of murdering all of the planters and seizing the land for themselves. Thus when the Hoop Spur local of the union met in a church in early October 1919, a group of white men fired into the meeting in an effort to terrify the members. Black guards returned the fire, killing one man and wounding another.[31]

Word quickly spread of a black uprising that threatened to murder the planters. The county sheriff deputized men for a posse, and the mayor called the governor, who then led a machine-gun battalion of more than 500 federal troops to suppress what planters called an insurrection. The troops and posse were joined by landowners, plantation managers, sheriffs, and veterans who came from all over the Mississippi Delta to combat the rebellion. Vigilantes and soldiers roamed a 200-mile radius, mowing down hundreds of men, women, and children, and burning alive many others. Troops rounded up hundreds of people, interrogated them, and held them in custody until a planter vouched for their trustworthiness. Eventually, 122 men and women were indicted for various offenses, and 12 men were convicted for the murder of three white men, their confessions secured by torture. Among the 12 were Frank Moore and his brother, Ed Hicks, and Ed Ware. (Their convictions were overturned in 1924 when the U.S. Supreme Court ruled the defendants had been deprived of the due process clause of the Fourteenth Amendment.)[32]

The actual number of deaths will never be known, for the slaughter of African Americans continued long after the troops had withdrawn. Tallies of the dead ranged from 25 to over 800 African Americans.[33] Part of Red Summer, the Elaine Massacre represented the efforts of a regional elite to destroy their workers' wartime aspirations and to steal whatever material gains they had made. Planters rightly feared their workers, for the war had opened enough political space for them to assert their demands for citizenship and justice, which entailed economic justice. Although the members of the union aimed to hire a lawyer and to work through the legal process, as citizens normally do in a democratic society, they were also prepared for a different scenario. Born and raised in the violent world of sharecropping and Jim Crow, Delta black people knew that their efforts would not be met with kindness. Like their forebears and their later descendants, the sharecropping families in Phillips County armed themselves and prepared for the worst. It was said that the women in the Hoop Spur church carried automatic pistols concealed in their stockings and that soldiers found guns hidden on many women they captured. Surely others carried pistols, as did freedom fighter Fannie Lou Hamer's mother across the river in Mississippi, concealed in their food buckets when they went to pick cotton in the fields. Black people in Phillips County knew their rights and acted accordingly.[34]

Rumors spread of potential revolts in other parts of the Delta. In January 1920, 130 troops were called into Dumas, Arkansas, when 10 men forced a deputy sheriff to relinquish a man he had arrested for stealing hogs from a nearby plantation. Although the soldiers did not uncover another plot, their deployment demonstrated Delta leaders' continued fears regarding African American militance.[35] Measures were taken throughout the region to outlaw the distribution of the *Crisis* and the Chicago *Defender*. Mississippi passed a law in 1920 making it a misdemeanor to "print or publish or circulate" literature favoring social equality."[36] In Arkansas, Delta counties sought to ban the sale of firearms and ammunition to African Americans. And the planters of Phillips County requested from the federal government more than 100 regulation army rifles and 25,000 rounds of ammunition, plus six Browning rifles with 5,000 rounds of ammunition, to help preserve order.[37]

Civic leaders became especially concerned with banning fraternal orders, often referred to as *secret societies*. Fraternal lodges alarmed planters because they had become, at least during the war, a locus for political activity. Many of the members of the union in Phillips County had also belonged to the Masons. Further, because lodges were part of national organizations, they served as conveyers of outside information. Many had organized entire communities for the migration northward, and some had contributed the first members to local NAACP chapters. Their secretive nature fueled planter anxieties in the wake of the Elaine Massacre.[38] Indeed, a man whose work involved calling on funeral homes in several southern states had written to the Department of Justice in April 1919, regarding the forming of secret African American societies in Arkansas and Mississippi. He had predicted at that time "that there would be a race war in the States within six months. . . . That race war has happened," he continued, "only it happened in Arkansas in place of Mississippi where I thought the outbreak would occur." The writer urged the Justice Department to send investigators to determine how extensive these organizations had become.[39]

Fears of fraternal lodges continued among the planter society throughout the 1920s. The sheriff of Pine Bluff, Arkansas, reported in 1920 that he closely watched local African Americans in anticipation of an uprising. Another officer reported that "negro lodges at Pine Bluff are very strong and their leaders were known to advocate equal wages, political offices and social equality for the colored people."[40] And in 1921, an Odd Fellows lodge was blamed for two murders near Wilson, Arkansas. When lodge member Henry Lowry went to his landlord on Christmas Day to demand a settlement, he was met by gunfire. Lowry fired back, killing the planter and his daughter and wounding one of two sons. Afterward, Lowry briefly escaped to Texas, apparently with the help of fellow lodge members. Eventually, Lowry was apprehended and lynched; several of his fraternal brothers and their wives were arrested. Soon afterward, a local newspaper called for the destruction of all African American secret societies because they had been "inciting the southern negro" and "getting what money they could out of him."[41]

The Elaine Massacre cast a long shadow over the following decades. Planters had witnessed black people acting not in the stereotypical ways of dependence and fear, but as a people making their rightful claims for the fruits of their labor and the rights guaranteed them under the Constitution. For black people, the massacre left a legacy of fear and intimidation that permeated their everyday lives. Planters initiated a new reign of terror in the 1920s that sought to destroy black institutions and to rein in black people's wartime aspirations. Numerous lynchings followed the war and the Elaine Massacre. Beginning in January 1919, when an African American soldier was lynched in Memphis, Tennessee, people were tortured and burned all over the Delta. At least eighteen lynchings of men and women in Arkansas and Mississippi were reported to the NAACP in 1919, some involving the murder of more than one person. Some of the men were killed for alleged actions taken against white women, but most instances centered on crop disputes—as in the case of Henry Lowry, who had demanded a settlement from his landlord—or the actions of returning veterans.[42]

Planters tightened their control over labor in the 1920s. In 1922, numerous letters from the Democrat, Arkansas, NAACP chapter in St. Francis County, described the violence and terror sharecroppers experienced. "In June," wrote one cropper, "mr. Johnson take a Iron Single Tree (the cross-bar to a draft harness) and beat a man and taken his mule and hogs and chickens and household goods that he brought from Miss.," while "Mr. E. Williams, he has got all of his people starving and in debt to his day hands and won't pay off . . . now they want to run the hands off from their crops and take them." The landowner did not pay his workers last year, according to one writer, "and now they are having high power rifles shipped out here and is trying to find out when we hold our meetings." He concluded that "they are aiming to do us as it was dun at Elaine." Other members wrote that they were prohibited from attending church services and funerals, and that men and women were driven to the fields at gunpoint. Some sharecroppers complained that their children continued to attend classes only four months out of the year.[43]

African Americans, even in their darkest hour, found ways of fighting back. In the 1920s, some continued migrating to northern cities, leaving those behind to continue their struggle with the planters and their minions. Although lynching, peonage, and theft of their property and crops continued, black people kept the pressure on the landowners and defied planter authority. They formed NAACP chapters and locals of Marcus Garvey's Universal Negro Improvement Association (UNIA), and in the remotest places. The letters they wrote to the national offices revealed the issues on their minds and also indicated their growing determination to fight for their rights and justice. The local chapters linked rural peoples to events outside the region by providing them with information regarding the fate of people of color all over the world. And the national offices created venues for rural black people's political aspirations, making them part of national political campaigns. Thus, Delta NAACP chapters raised money to aid in the passage of the Dyer Anti-Lynching Bill, which floated in the Congress throughout the decade, and they helped to raise money for the Scottsboro Boys in Alabama. Delta branches wrote to the national office asking for copies of the *Crisis* to obtain lynching statistics, to report murders, rapes, peonage, and other injustices in their communities. And they used guns when necessary to fight planter oppression.[44] Black people's struggles against poverty, peonage, violence, and the sharecropping system during the postwar years were not in vain. From the villages and plantations where croppers and tenants had organized NAACP and UNIA chapters, and had directly challenged planter abuse and authority, came in 1934 the Southern Tenant Farmers' Union (STFU). Some of the members of the interracial union had either been at Elaine or had family members who had. Born of immediate issues engendered by the New Deal agricultural programs, the movement soon focused on the overall inequities and abuses of the sharecropping system, and the changing relationship of farmworkers to the rapidly transforming plantation economy from one based on labor to one of mechanization. The initial founders of the union, two white men from Tyronza, may have had connections to the Socialist Party, but the union drew strength from the earlier struggles of African Americans—in its collective form of organization, in the inclusion of both men and women as members, and in the use of churches and fraternal orders for organizational structure.

As in Elaine, planters used violence and terror to combat the union. However, this time, the sharecroppers encountered not only the familiar face of planter oppression, but the more foreign face of a federal government that gave with one hand while taking away with another. The Agricultural Adjustment Act of 1933 paid planters to plow less than a third of their cotton to raise prices and to control production. However, planters used the measure to collect the parity payments and drive their sharecroppers off the land. The STFU sought to secure for the farmworkers their share of the parity payments and to introduce collective bargaining into the plantation system. Although the union did raise wages briefly through a strike, it failed to secure collective-bargaining rights for its members. The federal government's decision to support the planters in their evictions undercut the STFU's efforts to secure decent wages and working conditions for the workers. Planter violence, with the help of the federal government, defeated the depression-era challenge to the plantation system.[45]

On some level, the weight of history was against the efforts of the STFU, as mechanization eventually rendered sharecropping and tenant farming obsolete. However, mechanization of the cotton crop did not complete its course in the Delta until the mid-1960s. Thus, black people continued to press their claims for economic justice within the plantation system until that time. Lynching and convict labor may have largely disappeared by the 1960s, but when the next wave of the freedom struggle came with the Student Nonviolent Coordinating Committee and the Congress of Racial Equality, the organizers found that black people in the Arkansas and Mississippi deltas still confronted landowners over questions of wages and access to federal programs such as the food commodity program, the right to welfare benefits, agricultural subsidies, theft of black people's land, and police brutality. The organizers also discovered that black people in the Delta had a long history of political struggle, as they encountered seasoned freedom fighters such as Mrs. Carrie Dilworth of Gould, Arkansas, who had been an organizer for the STFU.[46]

In short, black people in the Delta had a long history of political struggle in the twentieth century, one marked by assertions of human dignity and demands for economic justice. Both men and women engaged in this battle for human rights, and both carried and used guns whenever their lives were threatened. Their daily experiences with the planters and their minions often led them into piecemeal struggles over the use of certain tools or the ownership of livestock and farming equipment. However, given the necessary broader historical circumstances, usually manifested as a national crisis—a war, a depression—these confrontations over the work process and the terms of daily living broke out into major organized contests, which included armed men and women, over the plantation economy itself. Not for nothing had the men, women, and children of Elaine given their lives.

Notes

1. Nan Elizabeth Woodruff, *American Congo: The African American Freedom Struggle in the Delta* (Cambridge, Mass.: Harvard University Press, 2003); Donald H. Grubbs, *Cry from the Cotton: The Southern Tenant Farmers' Union and the New Deal* (Chapel Hill: University of North Carolina Press, 1971); John Dittmer, *Local People: The Struggle for Civil Rights in Mississippi* (Urbana: University of Illinois Press, 1994); and Charles M. Payne, *I've Got the Light of Freedom: The Organizing Tradition and the Mississippi Freedom Struggle* (Berkeley: University of California Press, 1995).

2. Harold D. Woodman, "Postbellum Social Change and Its Effects on Marketing and the South's Crop," *Agricultural History* 56 (January 1982), 215–31; Harold Woodman, "Post–Civil War Southern Agriculture and the Law," *Agricultural History* 53 (January 1979), 319–37; Harold Woodman, *New South, New Law: The Legal Foundations of Credit and Labor Relations in the Postbellum Agricultural South* (Baton Rouge: Louisiana State University Press, 1995). For a discussion of the Delta, see James C. Cobb, *The Most Southern Place on Earth: The Mississippi Delta and the Roots of Southern Identity* (New York: Oxford University Press, 1992); Jeannie M. Whayne, *A New Plantation South: Land, Labor, and Federal Favor in Twentieth-Century Arkansas* (Charlottesville: University of Virginia Press, 1996); and John C. Willis, *Forgotten Time: The Yazoo-Mississippi Delta after the Civil War* (Charlottesville: University of Virginia Press, 2000).

3. I am drawing on the distinction made by Antonio Gramsci between the state, or political society, and civil society. According to Gramsci, civil society is composed of the educational, religious, and associational institutions, whereas the state, or political society, consists of the courts, legislature, and elections. In bourgeois democracies, the latter are theoretically separate from the former. Gramsci argued that the elaborate structure of liberal democracy—elections, legislatures, courts—created a facade of popular control and participation and served as the means through which consent to be governed was obtained. However, in the plantation South, planters removed African Americans from political society. Moreover, they collapsed political and civil society, for the same people controlled both. See Joseph V. Femia, *Gramsci's Political Thought: Hegemony, Consciousness, and the Revolutionary Process* (London: Oxford University Press, 1987), 26–29; and Antonio Gramsci, *Selections from the Prison Notebooks of Antonio Gramsci,* Quinton Hoare and Geoffrey Nowell Smith, eds. and

trans. (New York: Monthly Review Press, 1971), 206–78. The finest application of Gramsci's work to explaining a society's specific historical development remains Eugene Genovese's masterful *Roll, Jordan, Roll: The World the Slaves Made* (New York: Pantheon, 1972).

4. For a discussion of peonage and various measures to limit labor mobility, see Pete Daniel, *The Shadow of Slavery: Peonage in the South, 1901–1969* (Urbana: University of Illinois Press, 1971); William Cohen, *At Freedom's Edge: Black Mobility and the Southern Quest for Racial Control, 1861–1915* (Baton Rouge: Louisiana State University Press, 1991).

5. Woodman, "Post–Civil War Southern Agriculture and the Law," 319–37.

6. Peter Gottlieb, *Making Their Own Way: Southern Blacks' Migration to Pittsburgh, 1916–1930* (Urbana: University of Illinois Press, 1987); James Grossman, *Land of Hope: Chicago, Black Southerners, and the Great Migration* (Chicago: University of Chicago Press, 1989); Joe William Trotter, *Black Milwaukee: The Making of an Industrial Proletariat, 1915–1945* (Urbana: University of Illinois Press, 1990); Neil McMillen, *Dark Journey: Black Mississippians in the Age of Jim Crow* (Urbana: University of Illinois Press, 1989). See also U.S. Department of Labor, Division of Negro Economics, *Negro Migration in 1916–1917* (Washington, D.C., 1919), and Emmett J. Scott, "Letters of Negro Migrants of 1916–1918," *Journal of Negro History* 4 (July 1919), 290–340; Emmett Scott, "Additional Letters of Negro Migrants, 1916–1918," *Journal of Negro History* 4 (October 1919), 412–75.

7. G. B. Ewing to Arkansas Council of Defense, October 23, 1918, Arkansas State Council of Defense Papers, Folder 57, located in the Arkansas History Commission, Little Rock, Arkansas. (Hereafter referred to as ACD.) For the best discussion of similar conditions in Mississippi, see Charles S. Johnson, "Migration Study: Mississippi Summary," 1917, National Urban League Papers, ser. 6, Box 86, Manuscripts Division, Library of Congress, Washington, D.C.

8. Minutes of the Arkansas State Council of Defense, January 21, 1918, RG 62, Council of National Defense, State Councils, General Correspondence, Box 692, National Records Center, Suitland, Maryland; Johnson, "Mississippi Summary."

9. G. B. Ewing to Arkansas State Council of Defense, October 3, 1918, ACD, Folder 57. For similar complaints in Mississippi, see Johnson, "Mississippi Summary."

10. For the creation of wartime agencies, see David M. Kennedy, *Over Here: The First World War and American Society* (New York: Oxford University Press, 1980). For a thoughtful discussion of the liberal state during this time, see Alan Dawley, *Struggles for Justice: Social Responsibility and the Liberal State* (Cambridge, Mass.: Harvard University Press, 1991).

11. Arthur H. Flemming to the Several Southern State Councils of Defense, "Organization of Negroes," July 24, 1918, RG 62, Council of National Defense, Field Division, Winterbotham Correspondence, 15–A, Box 859.

12. Report of P. L. Dorman of Work Done, Field Man For Council of Defense, Month Ending November 30, 1918, ACD, Folder 249.

13. Chairman of the Arkansas Defense Council to Reverend A. J. Rooks, September 2, 1918, ACD, Folder 85.

14. Provost Marshal General E. H. Crowder to Governor Charles H. Brough, November 6, 1918, RG 163, U.S. Selective Service System, 1917–1919, State Files, Arkansas, Box 86, National Records Center, Suitland, Maryland.

15. C. H. Brough to Provost Marshal General E. H. Crowder, November 2, 1917, RG 163, ibid., Box 88. For similar complaints in Mississippi, see Senator John Sharp Williams to President Woodrow Wilson, October 21, 1918, ibid., Box 178.

16. J. W. Johnston to Provost Marshal General E. H. Crowder, November 8, 1917, ibid., Box 89.

17. R. A. Nelson to Arkansas State Council of Defense, October 9, 1918, Folder 89; Wallace Townsend to Judge G. B. Ewing, November 1, 1918, Folder 57; Townsend to Ouachita County Council of Defense, August 2, 1918, folder 95, all in ACD.

18. For a discussion of Du Bois's position on the war and for his criticisms of the treatment of returning soldiers, see Elliot Rudwick, "W. E. B. Du Bois: Protagonist of the Afro-American Protest," in John Hope Franklin and August Meier, eds., *Black Leaders of the Twentieth Century* (Urbana: University of Illinois Press, 1982), 75–77.

19. McMillen, *Dark Journey,* 314–15.

20. During the 1920s, the national office received several letters from sharecroppers seeking to organize chapters. See applications for charters in NAACP Papers, Group I, Series G. Branch Files, 1913–1939, Boxes 11–12. There is an extensive correspondence with sharecroppers from Democrat, Arkansas, in Group I, Series, Box 11, 1919, all located in the Manuscripts Division, Library of Congress, Washington, D.C.

21. D. Whipple to A. M. Briggs, July 5, 1917, RG 65, Department of Justice, Bureau of Investigations, *Federal Surveillance of Afro-Americans, 1916–1925,* ed. Theodore Kornweibel (Bethesda, Md.: University Publications of America, 1986), reel 9.

22. The Arkansas State Council and the local councils of defense constantly referred to the IWW's presence. For examples, see C. T. Carpenter to Chairman, Arkansas State Council of Defense, July 25, 1917, Folder 98, and Lloyd England and Wallace Townsend to Chairmen, County Councils of Defense, February 16, 1918, Folder 1, both in ACD.

23. P. L. Dorman to the State Council of Defense, December 31, 1918, Folder 1, ACD.

24. Military regulations made it illegal to prevent any honorably discharged soldier from wearing his uniform from the place of his discharge to his home for up to three months. *War Department Bulletin Number* 16, June 22, 1916, 83. I thank John Slonaker, chief reference historian, U.S. Army Military History Institute, for finding this reference for me.

25. Captain F. Sullens, Memo to Major Brown, November 30, 1918, RG 65, Department of Justice, Bureau of Investigations, Kornweibel, *Federal Surveillance of Afro-Americans,* Reel 22.

26. McMillen, *Dark Journey,* 305–6.

27. The Mississippi Welfare League had thirteen branches in 1919 and included such prominent planters as LeRoy Percy, O. F. Bledsoe, Alex Y. Scot, and Alfred Holt Stone. Charter of Welfare League included in Jack C. Wilson to Moorfield Story, February 27, 1919, NAACP, Group I-C, Box 2.

28. Jack C. Wilson to John R. Shillady, April 11, 1919, NAACP, Group I-C, Box 2.

29. Ida Wells-Barnett, *The Arkansas Race Riot* (Chicago: Hume Job, 1920), 13–18.

30. U. S. Bratton to Frank Burke, November 6, 1919, Arthur I. Waskow Papers, State Historical Society of Wisconsin, Madison.

31. O. S. Bratton to U. S. Bratton, November 5, 1919, Waskow Papers; Wells-Bar-

nett, *The Arkansas Race Riot;* For an extensive account of the Elaine Massacre, see Woodruff, *American Congo.*

32. There are a number of articles on the massacre. For a more recent account, see Grif Stockley, *With Blood in Their Eyes: The Elaine Massacre of 1919* (Fayetteville: University of Arkansas Press, 2001), and Richard C. Courtner, *A Mob Intent on Death: The NAACP and the Arkansas Riot Cases* (Middletown, Conn.: Wesleyan University Press, 1988).

33. Walter White, "The Real Causes of Two Race Riots," *Crisis* 19 (December 1919), 61; U. S. Bratton to Walter White, January 11, 1923, Waskow Papers.

34. Chana Kai Lee, *For Freedom's Sake: The Life of Fannie Lou Hamer* (Urbana: University of Illinois Press, 1999), 11. For a discussion of armed self-defense, see Greta de Jong, *A Different Day: The African American Freedom Struggle and the Transformation of Rural Louisisana, 1900–1970* (Chapel Hill: University of North Carolina Press, 2002); and Timothy B. Tyson, *Radio Free Dixie: Robert F. Williams and the Roots of Black Power* (Chapel Hill: University of North Carolina Press, 1999).

35. Major Robert Q. Poage to Director of Military Intelligence, January 22, 1920, RG 60, Department of Justice Files, Glasser File, Kornweibel, *Federal Surveillance of Afro-Americans,* Reel 16.

36. McMillen, *Dark Journey,* 174.

37. Cortner, *A Mob Intent on Death,* 15.

38. For the role fraternal orders played in the Great Migration, see Grossman, *Land of Hope,* 92

39. C. T. Schade to Department of Justice, RG 65, Department of Justice, Kornweibel, *Federal Surveillance of Afro-Americans,* Reel 12.

40. F. W. Lynch, "Negro Activities throughout the South-Arkansas," December 31, 1920, RG 165, Department of War, General and Special Staffs, Military Intelligence Division, Kornweibel, *Federal Surveillance of Afro-Americans,* Reel 19.

41. "An American Lynching: Being the Burning at Stake of Henry Lowry at Nodena, Arkansas, January 26, 1921, as Told in American News Papers," and William Pickens, "The American Congo: Burning of Henry Lowry," *Nation* 23 (March 1921), both in RG 59, U.S. Department of State, Kornweibel, *Federal Surveillance of Afro-Americans,* Reel 18.

42. For the numerous lynchings in both Arkansas and Mississippi, see the NAACP Papers, Group I-C, Boxes 349, 350, 360,389.

43. H. L. Henderson to Joel Spingarn, August 26, 1922. See also Jim Coleman's report to Spingarn, August 12, 1922; J. C. Coleman to Spingarn, August 29, 1922; Lucious Holiday to Spingarn, August 11, 1922; L. B. Sanford to NAACP, June 12, 1922; Josie Coleman, Report of Chairman of Democrat Branch of NAACP, June 12, 1922; all in NAACP Papers, Group I-C, Box 386.

44. Woodruff, *American Congo,* 110–51.

45. Ibid., 152–90.

46. Dittmer, *Local People;* Lee, *For Freedom's Sake;* Payne, *I've Got the Light of Freedom.*

8   Mobilizing Black Chicago:
    The Brotherhood of Sleeping Car Porters
    and Community Organizing, 1925–35[1]

Despite a tradition of activism by black workers, the majority of African Americans rarely joined labor unions until the mid-1930s. The situation changed dramatically during the New Deal as large numbers of black workers joined the trade union movement. Explanations for this historic shift include New Deal labor laws, communist organizers within the Congress of Industrial Organization (CIO), and black activists who challenged the racial status quo on several fronts during the depression decade.[1]

Activities initiated and carried out by the Left helped erase doubts and suspicions harbored by black leaders toward organized labor and were a significant force in bringing about changes in relations between the black community and organized labor. Those efforts were reinforced by the New Deal's Wagner Act, which legally established the right to organize. Although this interpretation explains part of the process that led to the dramatic increase in black memberships within organized labor, it fails to account sufficiently for the role black activists from diverse political persuasions played in bringing about this change. What influence did those activists have in cultivating a climate within the black community that was receptive to radical labor organizers? And what happens to the narrative when we include the shifting dynamics within the black community during the 1920s that laid the groundwork for changing attitudes toward labor unions?[2] Often lost in the discussion of the rise of industrial unionism is the ferment of black protest that was reshaping politics within the black community before many of the communists and Leftists entered black neighborhoods in significant numbers in the urban North.

The question is not whether the left and communists, through the promotion of black equality, contributed to the rise of the industrial union movement in the 1930s, but why did a large cross-section of the black community in cities such as Chicago welcome the communists? Despite the important role played by communists and CIO organizers within the black community, how successful would the labor organizers have been had the larger black community—leaders, clergy, newspapers editors, members of women's clubs, social and fraternal orders, and politicians—placed roadblocks in their path? Without the welcome black leaders showed CIO organizers in Chicago, would the ability of the Left to find outlets for meetings or form alliances within the black community have been greatly restricted? New Deal labor polices, the Communist Party, and CIO activism do not explain the rising sentiment favoring organized labor that predated the Great Depression and collaborative interracial efforts of the industrial union movement. To assess the success left-leaning organizers had in getting black workers to sign union cards, careful attention must be paid to the predepression social and labor-based movements led by black activists themselves. One such movement was led by the Brotherhood of Sleeping Car Porters (BSCP). Through its community-based organizing campaign in the late 1920s and early 1930s, the BSCP nurtured an ideological shift within the black community that helped pave the way for CIO organizers.

For decades, black Americans had been devising strategies both at work and within the community to expand their economic opportunities, challenge restrictions in the job market, and increase job security. There was, however, considerable division over the appropriate means for opening up the labor market to African Americans. During World War I, African Americans' interest in unionization intensified, but the appeal was largely restricted to black workers and black radicals.[3] African American leaders, for the most part, remained neutral, stood outside the discussion of unionization, or encouraged cooperation with those employers who hired black workers while white unions locked blacks out of employment.

In the 1920s, when organized labor lost more than a million members and unions conceded demands to employers, many black workers, toiling in the urban North, established their place in the industrial heartland. They did so by adapting to prevailing circumstances and the demands of welfare capitalism, a paternalistic system initiated by employers who wanted to avoid disruptive labor unrest and limit the growth of unions. The majority of Chicago's black steel and packinghouse workers, for example, adjusted to the anti-union designs of welfare capitalists, exchanging control over wages and hours for the security of employment.[4] Although black industrial workers tolerated welfare capitalism during the 1920s to make occupational gains, their interests did not overlap entirely with those of black leaders who had spent years building careers around a workable relationship with the white elite. The investment in welfare capitalism was greater and the stakes higher for entrenched African American leaders than for the black working class who had recently migrated north.

In Chicago, techniques and approaches developed by black leaders for negotiating with the white status quo took hold in the decades around the turn into the twentieth century. Because those patterns opened up greater political representation for black Americans in Chicago by the 1920s than anywhere else in the United States, black leaders vigorously guarded their connections to white corridors of power. Of special significance was the relationship that emerged between the managers of the Pullman Company and leaders of black Chicago. Pullman officials provided a measure of what the company thought of as uplift for the black community by pouring money into black institutions and hiring black workers as Pullman porters for its Pullman sleeping cars. When the Brotherhood of Sleeping Car Porters (BSCP) set out to organize black porters into a union in 1925, it confronted a chorus of opposition from leading voices in black Chicago who had come to believe that the Pullman Company had done more for the community than any labor union. To combat this opposition and win support from the black community, the BSCP questioned just how benevolent Pullman had been by exposing negative aspects inherent in the unequal relationship between the Pullman Company and black Chicago. While black leaders focused on the appearance of benevolence in the form of material benefits that accrued to the community, the brotherhood recast the debate in terms of the high cost of accommodating a system based on keeping black Americans in a subordinate position. The BSCP's struggle for the hearts and minds of black Chicago sheds light on how the question of labor and unions began to infuse the discussion of the larger black freedom struggle by the 1930s.[5] That discussion was part of the tangled relationship between the Pullman Company and Pullman porters that emerged in the aftermath of the Civil War.

George Pullman, founder and president of the Pullman Company, created the position of Pullman porter in the late 1860s for recently freed African American men. Pullman specifically wanted African American porters to serve his white patrons on his Pullman sleeping cars, which were, until the era of the airplane, the major means used by the wealthy to travel long distance across the country. Pullman's goal was to provide a luxurious setting to carry his clients in palatial comfort across the country. The cars featured brocaded fabrics, polished walnut woodwork, gilt-edged mirrors, plush carpets, and silver-plated metalwork. To complete the picture, black porters waited on and pampered white patrons in a manner once reserved for privileged gentry in the antebellum South. Porters were at the beck and call of customers to prepare berths, clean the cars, and render whatever services customers desired to make them comfortable.[6]

By the twentieth century, the Pullman porter was a national figure, perhaps the most easily recognized African American in white America. As early as 1913, Hollywood had such demand for Pullman porters in films that one actor made a good living—much better than actual porters—cast as a porter for nearly three decades. In the 1920s, more than 35 million passengers annually slept on Pullman sleeping cars, served by approximately 12,000 porters, making Pullman the single largest private employer of African American men in the United States. National recognition came at a terrible cost, for the association between African Americans and slaves carried forward by the Pullman porter position perpetuated the stereotype of the black man as servant. For this reason, the white public who patronized Pullman sleeping cars often regarded porters not as not fully formed, three-dimensional human beings, but as pieces of furniture or props to be used for their convenience. Indeed, customers called all porters "George"—after the founder of the Pullman Company.[7]

On the job, Pullman porters sustained a cloak of invisibility, smiling as though they were content with the racial status quo.[8] It was a protective mechanism that shielded them from the charge of stepping out of place—the place assigned by the white world—or "being uppity." Because $72.00 per month (the salary in the late 1920s) was not a living wage, porters learned to use their "invisibility" to attract tips.[9] Although pretending not to understand or be privy to conversations, for example, porters took mental notes of the likes and dislikes, interests, and habits of clients as a way of anticipating the patrons' needs. One ex-porter in Chicago explained that "Pullman made hustlers out of us. They had us constantly on our knees." Malcolm X, who once worked briefly for the New Haven railroad, not as a Pullman porter but as a dishwasher and sandwich man, noted that black service employees on railroads were both "servants and psychologists" for white people, who were "so obsessed with their own importance that they will pay liberally . . . for the impression of being catered to and entertained."[10]

Despite enjoying a relatively high social standing in the black community, porters discovered quickly that their drive to organize a union in 1925 sharply divided African Americans. The initial effort to organize a BSCP chapter in New York City was fairly successful, but the brotherhood needed to win support in Chicago, headquarters of the giant Pullman corporation and the city where the largest number of porters and maids lived (over one-third, or more than 4,000, of the company's porters and one-half, or 100, of its maids). When the BSCP arrived in Chicago, organizing stalled as officials of the Pullman Company unleashed an aggressive campaign against the brotherhood. Porters who openly supported the BSCP were fired, and company spies infiltrated brotherhood meetings, taking down the names of porters and maids in attendance and reporting back to officials, who subsequently discharged those on the list or threatened them with dismissal if they did not renounce the union and become loyal employees. Company managers, cashing in on Pullman's decades-long investment in black Chicago, pressured local black elites and leaned on the press, politicians, preachers, and loyal Pullman porters to praise the company, slander BSCP president A. Philip Randolph, and dismiss the foolish porters' union. Accordingly, "influential people and publications" in the community reminded those who challenged Pullman that the terms of the social contract did not include biting the hand that helped feed black Chicago.[11]

"Everything Negro was against us," concluded Milton P. Webster, general organizer of the Chicago division of the brotherhood, during the fall of 1925. Webster had approached some forty-five or fifty prominent and respected black citizens before the first meeting for the BSCP. "There was going to be a movement started to organize Pullman porters and I wanted them to come out and give us a word of encouragement," he recalled. "Lo and behold, only five agreed to come and speak, and when the time came only one showed up."[12] That one was Dr. William D. Cook, minister of the People's Church and Metropolitan Community Center. For the next two weeks, BSCP held its nightly meetings at Cook's community center. But the men in Chicago, Randolph later recalled, were "nowhere near as eager to sign up as the New York men had been." Porters in Chicago, unlike those in New York City, lived in the shadow of the giant Pullman Company. The roster of defenders of the Pullman Company in its campaign against the upstart union read like a who's who of black Chicago. It included Jesse Binga, head of Binga State Bank in Chicago (one of the nation's most successful black banks); Bishop Archibald Carey, bishop of the AME Church for the Chicago region; the Reverend Lacy Kirk Williams, minister of Olivet Baptist Church, the largest Baptist church in a community where more than half the population was Baptist; members of editorial staff of the *Chicago Whip;* and Robert S. Abbott, editor of the *Chicago Defender.*[13]

Despite what seemed like overwhelming odds, the BSCP's first significant breakthrough occurred between 1925 and 1927 when a small group of African American clubwomen, led by antilynching activist Ida B. Wells-Barnett, and several ministers joined forces with BSCP activists to question Pullman's paternalism and to secure opportunities for union porters to speak publicly. These clubwomen, who had been active in the fight for women's suffrage, shared with the BSCP a commitment to full citizenship rights for all black Americans. In December 1925, several Chicago club-women ignored black public opinion against the brotherhood and invited Randolph to address one of their meetings. Wells-Barnett tried unsuccessfully to secure the Appomattox Club, an important gathering place for Chicago's black leaders, but members informed her that they could not "afford to have Mr. Randolph speak" on its premises because so many of "the men who are opposing him are members here and it would embarrass them with the Pullman Company." Ultimately, Wells-Barnett held the meeting in her home. Randolph's talk on his union's aims prompted the women's group to endorse the BSCP. Subsequently, clubwomen's groups provided the union with membership lists for publicity purposes, urged members to attend BSCP meetings and educate other black Chicagoans, and otherwise served as a counter to the "hostility of our local newspapers against this movement."[14]

Using its alliance with Chicago clubwomen as a base, the brotherhood connected its campaign to broader community interests by tapping into aspirations unleashed by World War I when thousands of black Americans journeyed north for jobs in industry. In addition to creating jobs, the war raised the hope that the effort to make the world safe for democracy would make America a more democratic haven for black Americans. However, when black Americans exercised their rights of citizenship after World War I, many white Americans used violent tactics to keep them in second-class status. African Americans fought back during the racial strife of the postwar era, reflecting the impatience they felt with the slow pace of change.[15]

During and after the war, the quest for full citizenship rights was expressed through the New Negro movement, which celebrated a self-assertive black American committed to demanding rights. The New Negro, unlike the Old Negro, "cannot be lulled into a false sense of security with political spoils and patronage" from white America, declared Randolph, who helped shape the concept of the New Negro in the pages of the *Messenger*, a monthly magazine he coedited in Harlem. The New Negro demanded the right to "select his representatives." As a worker, the New Negro "advocates that the Negro join the labor union." When white unions discriminated against black workers, Randolph declared in the early twenties, "the only sensible thing to do is to form independent unions."[16]

For Randolph, the BSCP provided an opportunity to form an independent union and carry forward the spirit of the New Negro, which he translated into a call to complete the long-overdue "unfinished task of emancipation." Drawing from understandings of citizenship that had deep roots within African American history, Randolph appropriated the pages of the *Messenger* to conduct a massive educational campaign, challenging the politics of Pullman's paternalism. The effort was constructed around a conscious effort to reawaken the spirit that defined emancipation and Reconstruction, linking the impatience African Americans felt in the 1920s with the unfulfilled promise of citizenship issued in the 1860s.[17] The brotherhood expanded upon a traditional theme—independence from white control, a marker in the black freedom struggle and a stage on the way to gaining full "manhood rights"—to build on the legacy of nineteenth-century black freedom fighters who struggled to be regarded as adults, not as children of their former masters.[18] Union porters asked audiences in black neighborhoods to "re-dedicate" their "hearts and minds" to the spirit of Denmark Vesey, Nat Turner, Sojourner Truth, Harriet Tubman, and Frederick Douglass so they "shall not have died in vain." "We, who have come after these noble souls who suffered and sacrificed" to deliver their children from the "cruel oppression of the Slave Power" are "bound in duty" to complete what they began. Despite the passage of the Thirteenth Amendment, which the *Messenger* called a "dead letter," slavery had not entirely been abolished.[19]

To depict the difference between its union and that of the Pullman Company union, controlled by Pullman management, BSCP organizers cast the company union as a newer form of slave labor, one that robbed porters and maids of their "manhood," which stood for the ability to act as a free agent, as a human being free of servitude.[20] In contrast, the worker-controlled BSCP exemplified rights accorded to free labor. The Pullman Company opposed the BSCP union, organizers claimed, because the company officials regarded porters as children who possessed no rights the company was bound to respect. "So far as his manhood is concerned," the *Messenger* told its readers, "in the eyes of the Company, the porter is not supposed to have any." The campaign for manhood was to claim "the humanhood of the Negro race," starting with a company that demanded of its porters and maids the "submersion of their manhood by making public beggars of them." BSCP propaganda asked if porters and maids were "tired of being treated like children instead of men," and if so implored them to oppose the company union, raising questions related not just to porters and maids but the status and place of all African Americans.[21]

More than suffrage, manhood rights included the right to equal economic opportunity and the right to a place at the bargaining table of labor. The brotherhood implied that these rights were held by white Americans despite the fact that during the 1920s the rights of many white workers were also limited by company unions. Rhetorical flourishes of the BSCP are revealing not so much for what is *true* as for what they reveal about the perspective of those African Americans the propaganda was aimed at. Was the exclusion of black workers from the bargaining process open to white workers really a literal violation of citizenship rights? Were Pullman porters really slaves? The fact that many in the black community rallied around these interpretations suggests the degree to which slavery metaphors resonated with a population that felt excluded from full participation in American society.

To spread its message and to connect its movement for workplace rights to the broader concerns of Chicago's African American community, the BSCP formed alliances with clubwomen, sponsored labor conferences, and established a Citizens Committee open to prominent middle-class backers of the union. Indeed, the networks fostered by the BSCP proved to be a key factor in breaking down the resistance from anti-union or indifferent community leaders. In addition to Chicago clubwomen, a small number of black ministers aligned themselves with the union. One was Dr. William Cook, a "kind of outlaw preacher" ostracized by AME bishop Carey for his "political and social leanings," who opened his People's Church to Randolph in 1925.[22] Another was the Reverend Dr. Junius C. Austin, who welcomed Randolph and the BSCP in his Pilgrim Baptist Church, allowing them to conduct mass meetings there.[23]

In the fall of 1926, Irene Goins, a pioneer black clubwomen in the state of Illinois and a labor organizer, used her influence at the national level to convince the National Federation of Colored Women's Clubs to endorse the BSCP.[24] Mary McDowell, a trade unionist and the only white supporter during the BSCP's early days in Chicago, insisted that black workers must use their "power to organize" to promote their own interests. Until workers won the right to sign their own contracts, "we are not men and women."[25] Although the voice of the majority representing the black press and pulpit—most notably the *Chicago Defender*—continued to rebuke or ignore the message from BSCP supporters, seeds planted by this small network of activists began to take root.

By the fall of 1927, responding to declarations by Randolph that the *Chicago Defender* had surrendered to "gold and power," large gatherings of citizens at BSCP sponsored events, and a campaign to boycott the newspaper, the *Defender* did an about-face and began supporting the brotherhood. This was an important victory, for the *Defender* was the largest-selling black newspaper in the United States, with a national weekly circulation in the mid-1920s of well over 200,000 copies.[26] Soon, networks allied with the BSCP's Citizens' Committee carried the brotherhood's message to new sections of black Chicago. In 1928, Irene McCoy Gaines, a leading clubwomen and industrial secretary of the Young Women's Christian Association (YWCA), joined the Citizens' Committee, bringing the BSCP in contact with the Illinois Federation of Republican Colored Women's Clubs, a group Gaines presided over between 1924 and 1935. The Citizens' Committee also included George Cleveland Hall, a personal friend of Booker T. Washington who promoted black business in Chicago and became the president of the Chicago branch of Washington's National Negro Business League in 1912. Simultaneously, he was one of two active black members on the executive staff of the Chicago branch of the National Association for the Advancement of Colored People (NAACP) and was a cofounder of the Chicago Urban League. Although he may have subscribed to Washington's self-help message, he also believed that black Americans had to fight white prejudice and discrimination directly. Hall's support of the BSCP suggests that, even within the pro-employer Chicago Urban League, differences could be found on the issue of unionism. Claude Barnett, another active member of the league's board, adamantly opposed the BSCP and received money from the Pullman Company to publish a magazine opposing the brotherhood's philosophy.[27]

In January 1928, the brotherhood inaugurated its first Labor Conference in Chicago, laying the groundwork for a pro–labor union perspective by connecting its union drive to its vision for broader economic and civil rights for all African Americans. Labor conferences, a major arena for integrating the public's and the porter's struggles, focused on creating cross-class alliances within the community around demands for basic rights of citizenship. In the process, civil rights were inextricably fused to the labor agenda of the BSCP. Brotherhood activists and members of the Citizens' Committee led sessions on numerous topics of concern in the community, but all would emphasize cultivation of a pro-labor perspective, what organizers referred to as the "labor viewpoint."

A labor movement, claimed the brotherhood, would develop organizational skills needed to claim first-class status for all African Americans through effective organizations, just as white workers have done. Moreover, through the "process of self-organization and self-struggle, Negro workers will develop the necessary labor view-point, sense of responsibility, and labor union morale and technique." In this way, the development of a black labor movement would mark "the beginning of the period when the Negro earnestly begins to help himself instead of merely looking for his friends to help him."[28] As Randolph reminded the community, organizing for the rights of black workers carried "immeasurable" significance for the race. With the "recognition of our economic rights, privileges and power, will develop the initiative and ability to write our own economic contracts." That accomplishment was connected with ushering "the

Negro into the final cycle of race freedom. It is our next step as a group of workers and as a race, oppressed outraged and exploited. It is the final road to freedom of all oppressed peoples."[29]

At the first Negro Labor Conference in Chicago, the brotherhood declared that a worker's right to organize was an American right, an entitlement embedded in American citizenship. Winning the right to negotiate a labor contract with the Pullman Company was connected to the basic right of all Americans to pick their leaders. To clarify the link, union activists dismissed those they called the "mis-leaders" of black America, who worked not for the best interests of African Americans, but for individual white employers or politicians to whom they were eternally grateful. The brotherhood hoped to destroy the myth that "only white men are supposed to organize for power, for justice and freedom."[30] The BSCP's message challenged the prevailing pattern of petitioning the dominant culture for rights that, at least in theory, already belonged to black Americans, prescribing a new approach for conducting negotiations between black and white communities. In short, labor conferences served as a vehicle for reshaping how black Chicago approached and thought about the politics of patronage and citizenship rights.[31]

By the late 1920s, Abram L. Harris, professor of economics at Howard University, noted that African Americans in Chicago were "lining up almost solidly behind the new organization."[32] The large turnout at the labor conferences and other meetings arranged by the brotherhood suggests that the BSCP's prolabor perspective had captured the interest of the black community. The numbers may also reflect the fact that members of the community were more willing than they had been in the mid-1920s to be seen and heard at a brotherhood gathering, despite the persistence of Pullman Company spies.

In January 1929, close to 2,000 teachers, businessmen and -women, social workers, porters, and maids participated in discussions about mobilization for economic power, housing, and health of workers at the BSCP's three-day labor conference. The network reached out to the future business and professional class with the participation of the Intercollegiate Club, which represented the young, educated elite, who thought of themselves as "New Negroes," seekers of opportunity rather than philanthropy, "lover[s] of world brotherhood," and supporters of "human principles." These young college graduates, who prided themselves on advancing cross-class alliances, told students they ought to "quit criticizing workers and get in harmony with them." Frederic Robb, president of the Intercollegiate Club, spoke at several brotherhood mass meetings, and BSCP organizers took their case directly to Intercollegiate youth.[33]

By 1929, a prolabor perspective was taking shape in black Chicago through the efforts of the BSCP Citizens' Committee and labor conference networks. The participation of the Reverend Harold M. Kingsley, pastor of the Church of the Good Shepherd, which had largely white-collar members, suggests the nature of the shift that had emerged. The Reverend Kingsley, absent from brotherhood networks in the mid-1920s, had become actively involved in the BSCP's Citizens' Committee, labor conferences, and allied networks by the end of the decade. In his sermons he emphasized the virtue and value of labor. At the 1930 National Negro Labor Conference, with a turnout of over 3,000, the Reverend Kingsley challenged other clergy within the community to reexamine their relationship to organized labor and the black worker. He compared the black church of the late 1920s to the Russian church before the Russian Revolution of 1917, which was particularly blind to the needs of workers, perhaps reflecting his own limited vision in the mid-1920s. "The Church is the one institution that gets more of the people together than any other institution," he said, but it needed to be "educated up to the economic conditions of the workers." In the past, the church often told black workers whom to vote for; Reverend Kingsley was suggesting that workers educate the clergy, who had a responsibility to workers.[34]

The annual labor conferences of the BSCP focused on a broad range of topics, including organized labor, crime, the black family, black women in industry, and education. Congressman Oscar DePriest, representative from black Chicago, the first black member in the U.S. House of Representatives since 1901, and the first from the North, united all these topics at the 1930 conference by highlighting the importance of overcoming second-class status through the independent organization of black Americans. An entire afternoon was devoted to "The Woman in Industry," with sessions on the benefits of trade unionism for female workers and special problems of black women in industry. Jeanette Smith, president of the Chicago and Northern District Federation of Women's Clubs, noted the role clubwomen had to play educating recent southern migrants about the importance of organized labor for overcoming racial inequities. Aggressive approaches to organization were necessary, she said, if "significant change is to be brought about." Smith stressed the importance of cross-class alliances and unity, giving a militant interpretation to uplift philosophy. When a member of the National Negro Business League spoke at the Negro Labor Conference, Webster, head of the Chicago division of the BSCP, was pleased because he considered them a "hardboiled bunch," that is, not easy to win over to the brotherhood's side.[35]

The front pages of the *Chicago Defender* captured part of the central message of the 1930 Labor Conference in a large political cartoon that depicted the brotherhood awakening "workers" from slumber while an alarm rang out the necessity for "organization." Through the bedroom window, workers march into the sunrise of "economic freedom."[36] The prolabor message was aimed at all black Americans, especially the 98 percent defined as "workers of hand and brain who depend upon jobs and wages for life." The conference, both in its sessions and final resolutions, called on the "student, minister, doctor, lawyer, teacher, and business man" to unite in support of the "struggle of the black workers for the right to organize."[37]

By the end of the 1920s, social networks allied with the BSCP had introduced the brotherhood's message on labor into the civic discourse that guided many professional and leadership circles. BSCP networks made a pioneering effort to put workers' interests and unionization on the agenda of civic clubs, to help bridge the gap between the middle class and working class, and connect issues of labor with those for basic citizenship rights. With the labor conferences, the BSCP gained substantial support from black Chicago by linking the dependency inherent under paternalism and welfare capitalism to the social relations endemic in second-class status.

Community leaders who came together to support the brotherhood between 1925 and 1930 were part of what Randolph called a "new crowd" of leaders who, unlike the old guard, would assert rights and make collective demands rather than appeal to white benefactors on an individual basis for relief from subordinate status.[38] The new crowd gathered at the labor conferences were engaged in a community education project aimed at redefining how to gain a more equal place in society. Although not opposed to all alliances with white people, new-crowd activists and leaders condemned playing by the ground rules established by the dominant white culture when carrying out negotiations for equal access or greater economic opportunity. The legal approach of the NAACP, for example, did not go far enough because the politics of the new crowd called for applying direct pressure using the power of mass collective action. The *Chicago Defender* called the brotherhood labor conferences one of the "most ambitious efforts to influence race thinking."[39]

Although weak as a union during this period, the BSCP broadened its network and intensified its efforts within the community by forging alliances with other groups challenging the racial status quo. While continuing to hold labor conferences, the BSCP network organized against the nomination of Judge Parker to the U.S. Supreme Court, for solidarity of black, female domestic and industrial workers, and for the release from prison of the Scottsboro Boys (nine black men who had been falsely accused of raping two white women in Alabama). Mobilization around the restricted freedom of all black Americans and for the right to self-determination fueled the formation of cross-class alliances and strengthened the development of protest networks that operated outside political channels traditionally used to address grievances. As activities of protest networks overlapped, the politics of civility that permeated old-guard relations in black Chicago was increasingly called into question.

The diversity represented in new-crowd networks in black Chicago during the 1930s reflected, in part, the social and political ferment the depression had unleashed. Black and white Communist Party (CP) cadre often worked side by side with black workers, black middle-class professionals, and the black elite in alliances that were not imaginable during the 1920s. The Communist Party, which had been trying to establish a foothold in Chicago for several years, did not make much of an impression on the black community until it launched its Unemployed Councils during the winter and spring of 1931. Communists used Unemployed Councils, formed to directly address problems created by the depression, to struggle against landlords who evicted the unemployed and to gain the confidence of black Chicago.[40]

At one gathering, on August 3, 1931, nearly 2,000 people protected the furniture of seventy-two-year-old Diana Gross, an unemployed resident of the South Side. The police arrived, fired into the crowd, and killed three black men. An estimated 5,000 to 8,000 people joined a funeral procession, led by the Unemployed Council and Communists through the heart of black Chicago, while many thousands more looked on.[41]

After the shooting, a coalition of leaders from black Chicago—including the Reverends Junius Austin and Harold Kingsley—met with City officials to discuss ways to prevent bloodshed in the future. Austin and Kingsley informed the officials that they could not talk religion to men with empty stomachs; the appeal of the Communists would grow until the problem of hunger was taken care of. The two ministers wrote a statement calling for a temporary moratorium on evictions and additional funding for unemployment relief, which was adopted by the City of Chicago.[42] For Austin and Kingsley, the Unemployed Council was an opportunity to put into practice the brotherhood's call for black Americans to take the initiative and "organize for power, for justice and freedom."[43]

Although the Communists supervised the overall structure of branches of Unemployed Councils, the party's ability to make a mark on black neighborhoods depended on cooperation from an eclectic group—including Republicans, Democrats, black fraternal orders, and some ex-members of the all-black Eighth Infantry Regiment—who carried out operations at the local level.[44] As Paul Young has argued, the diverse background of black activists within the councils located in black neighborhoods "prevented the Party from exerting hegemony over Council branches." Party leadership even criticized the Chicago district for "following rather than leading" mass demonstrations in the black community, suggesting that the party gained influence when it was able to link its struggle with special concerns of black Americans in Chicago.[45]

Activists in the BSCP labor conferences and Citizens Committee networks who exploded the myth of Pullman benevolence, and who repudiated the politics of clientage and patronage between 1928 and 1931, also helped lay the foundation for the confrontation with the status quo led by Unemployed Councils during eviction marches. The minds of many middle-class members of the black community who had been active participants in the BSCP's movement—particularly ministers, teachers, and clubwomen—were opened to a perspective sympathetic to labor and working-class issues. In this sense, brotherhood networks helped pave the way for alliances in 1931 between the middle-class and black Communist organizers in Unemployed Councils.

Other alliances may have been forged in Washington Park, located on the edge of black Chicago. Longtime Chicago resident Dempsey J. Travis describes Washington Park as a place where someone could get "a liberal education" listening to black radicals, Zionists, white leftists, and others who held forth in open-air forums.[46] The Reverend Austin, an early supporter of the BSCP who spoke several times in Washington Park, exemplifies the diversity of activists interacting for change during the early 1930s.

The industrial secretary of the South Parkway Branch of the Chicago YWCA, which placed the interests of black female industrial workers high on its agenda in the early 1930s, further demonstrates the diversity of black activists working for change. Thelma Wheaton, who had just received her master's degree from Case Western Reserve, was hired in 1931 as South Parkway's industrial secretary, a position that included community outreach and education. Born on July 29, 1907, in Hadley Township, Illinois, Wheaton came from a family with a long history of protest. Her great-grandfather, Free Frank McWorter, had purchased his freedom, along with that of sixteen family members, from slavery between 1817 and 1854.[47]

Although Wheaton worked with both industrial and domestic service workers, she recalled that the majority "were full-time industrial workers who were very glad to have their jobs." "Their normal work day was ten hours." Because money was scarce, they "loved overtime; they needed the job; they desired any work they could get." Wheaton's boss, Arnetta Dieckmann, the metropolitan industrial secretary of the Chicago YWCA, encouraged a progressive approach to social and economic issues. With a nod from Dieckmann, Wheaton broadly interpreted her responsibility as teacher and mentor. The Y's approach did not advocate joining any particular union, but it did teach "the value of the unions. How you get in and participate." Wheaton's personal goal was to facilitate participation by giving workers the tools needed to understand procedures for negotiating and conducting business meetings. The most important thing Wheaton recalled trying to teach the industrial workers was self-confidence. "We tried to teach the women to learn to speak up for yourself."[48]

Few household and industrial workers, the majority of them recent migrants from the South, knew much about their rights as workers, according to Wheaton. To encourage a fresh look at their role as both citizens and workers, she not only taught about labor laws, but put laws and rights into historical context by introducing the women to labor history, the history of women workers, and problems women workers faced in various occupations. The Chicago YWCA supplemented its labor education program by selecting a few potential leaders each year and sending them to Bryn Mawr's Summer School in Pennsylvania, an institute for workers devoted to labor economics, politics, and history. A larger group attended the University of Wisconsin School for Workers. She recalled that as a community organizer she was aware of the significance of her work, for trade unions in the early 1930s were making "no effort to get the women to join."[49]

Although the women Wheaton worked with were not especially averse to the idea of unions, they were not aware of the "benefits in belonging." Some of the women were workers in the garment factory jobs at the Sopkins apron and dress plants on the South Side. Once they understood the benefits unions offered in terms of increased control over and security of jobs for black workers, the next hurdle was overcoming the fear most of her students felt about losing their jobs. To allay that fear, the other component of her curriculum emphasized rights and entitlements, which she backed by building trust among the group and teaching the importance of collective action.[50]

Wheaton worked closely with the BSCP, which also promoted organization among black female domestic and industrial workers. The two organizations collaborated in 1932 when Irene McCoy Gaines, secretary of the BSCP Citizens' Committee, brought Wheaton into her communitywide cooperative effort to advance the interests of black workers. Randolph, Webster, and activists from the BSCP Citizens' Committee discussed problems black labor faced in a discriminatory economic marketplace. From that base, the Wheaton and Citizens' Committee networks reached deeper into the community by holding more meetings to spread the gospel of unionism—for both men and women—and present labor organization as a tool to advance civil rights. Strategy sessions were often held at BSCP headquarters in Chicago.[51] Although in 1932 Gaines had introduced Wheaton and Helena Wilson, president of the Colored Women's Economic Council (WEC), the women's auxiliary for the BSCP, Wilson did not participate in the alliance with Wheaton and the BSCP Citizens' Committee until some time later. Wheaton lectured on Saturdays and Sundays to the WEC of the BSCP between 1933 and 1935 and recalled that the wives of BSCP members were "very conscious" of the meaning of unions." But at that time the WEC restricted its efforts largely to keeping the BSCP as a union intact.[52]

To encourage participation in labor schools, an important avenue for expanding a prolabor perspective, Wheaton had to raise a considerable amount of money to pay the students' way. The South Parkway YWCA industrial committee addressed the difficulties in depression-era fundraising by intensifying its own efforts, pooling resources with other organizations, and drawing on the assistance from the BSCP and its Citizens Committee. The relationship was mutually beneficial, for by helping Wheaton with interested volunteers, the BSCP's networks were able to act on their interest in promoting black women in the role of labor organizer.[53]

Wheaton gave one of the YWCA's scholarships to Katheryn Williams, who attended Bryn Mawr Summer School in 1936. After studying at the labor college, Williams returned to Chicago and became an organizer for the Upholsterers International Union. Williams recalled in 1937 the importance of combating the fear workers have when talking with organizers on the job. When she approached workers on the street with pamphlets, they might avoid her. But "they will talk," she said, "in their homes." Indeed, "most of our work has been done in the homes. It slows the progress but is quite effective."[54] Although the process was slow, overlapping educational networks helped spread the idea of workers' rights.

The life of Thyra J. Edwards, a social worker, community organizer, and journalist who directed the Lake County Children's home at Gary, Indiana, during the 1920s, was transformed through her alliance with the brotherhood and other new-crowd networks in the Chicago area in the 1930s. In 1931, Edwards's activities as a social worker first brought her in contact with Wheaton and the BSCP's Citizens' Committee.[55] From 1932 to 1933, Edwards attended Brookwood Labor College at Katonah, New York. Afterward, she spent several months in the mining district of southern Illinois, studying conditions among black and white miners.[56]

Edwards remained active as a community organizer and popular lecturer for the brotherhood on issues of labor and manhood rights throughout the 1930s.[57] In 1933, she helped found the Abraham Lincoln Center, an educational community organization under the auspices of the Illinois Emergency Relief Commission, to address problems "dealing with discrimination in housing, restaurants and attempted discrimination in bathing beaches." She organized a diverse group of activists that included Claude Lightfoot and Mary Dalton of the League for Struggle for Negro Rights, an organization for young Communists; BSCP Citizens' Committee member Lulu E. Lawson; and A. L. Foster of the Chicago Urban League. Even the Chicago branch of the NAACP cooperated with Edwards, reflecting the broad-based coalitions that were emerging.[58]

"Injustice, not Reds," proclaimed the *Chicago Defender*, was stirring up workers. For "black men, like all other men, will find interest in any organization, whether it be red or blue, that promises them better opportunities for life and livelihood for themselves and dependents." The problem, according to the *Defender*, was that although the black man "believes in the American Constitution; . . . the American Constitution does not believe in the black man."[59] During the heady days of the early 1930s, when African Americans in Chicago and elsewhere exercised their constitutional rights, it was often in cooperation with Communists. The case of Angelo Herndon, a black worker and Communist sentenced to eighteen years in prison for exercising his right of free speech in Atlanta, illustrates an alliance with the Left that captured the attention of black Chicago. Communists defended Herndon when he was convicted in 1932.[60] The Chicago BSCP raised funds for Herndon's defense, and Randolph declared that "Herndon deserves the unstinted, definite, and aggressive moral and financial support of every Negro with any pride of race, regardless of his political philosophy."[61]

After Herndon was released from a Georgia prison, he went on a national tour that included a stop in Chicago. The Reverend Austin of the BSCP Citizens' Committee invited Herndon to speak in his church but was warned, presumably by other, cautious community leaders, "not to allow" Communists and their allies use his church for the Herndon gathering. Undeterred, Austin opened his church to Herndon and over 3,000 others who filled every available seat and stood in the aisles to hear Herndon speak about his two years in prison. The audience cheered Herndon, but they "went wild" when Austin declared, "any man who does not want freedom is either a fool or an idiot, and if to want freedom is to be a Communist, then I am a Communist, and will be till I die." Communism, he explained, "means simply the brotherhood of man and as far as I can see

Jesus Christ was the greatest Communist of them all." His church, Austin announced, would always be open to "any group that stood for the universal brotherhood of man." The *Defender* reported that deafening applause followed Austin's speech. "For fully five minutes the crowd stood and cheered." The following day, the *Defender*'s front page carried a banner headline exclaiming, "'I'm a Communist,' Shouts Rev. Austin as Herndon Tells of Prison Horrors."[62]

Austin brought the BSCP Citizens' Committee and other new-crowd networks into his church and sanitized Communist rhetoric for middle-class congregations by connecting it to Christianity, which helped forge a new relationship between the black middle class and the left. Thelma Wheaton did not think it was strange that the Communist Party was able to win the confidence of so many black Americans during the 1930s. She recalled years later that "I never knew a Communist who was not also a Christian. I'll bet over a third of my church was communist." Although that figure may be high, Wheaton claims it was the perception that Communists were independent of control by the dominant white culture that was the key issue.[63] Randolph, considered among the more vocal opponents of the Communists during the 1920s, shifted his position on the issue of working with Communists by the early 1930s. He may have changed his position because he sensed the political possibilities that could emerge from an alliance with the Left, or he may have been persuaded by the argument that black Americans needed more allies.[64]

Both the Communists and the BSCP emphasized self-determination. When the brotherhood addressed the issue, it challenged the black community to sever ties with patronage politics and black leaders who approached white benefactors with a posture of deference. When the Communists raised the issue, they captured the attention of the black community and, no doubt, hoped the slogan would help them recruit new members into the party. Although African Americans did not flock to the CP in huge numbers, the theme of self-determination did, as Robin Kelley reminds us, "create an opening" for black Americans "to promote race politics."[65] The national government reinforced the opening when it failed to provide effective leadership for the first three years of the depression to stem layoffs and evictions or provide direction for the millions adrift in what seemed like an economic wasteland.[66] When the Communists rushed into black Chicago, they found not a void of leadership, but new-crowd activists promoting black protest politics who were receptive to their self-determination slogan and their fight against racism and for the unemployed and the working poor. African Americans in Chicago were not waiting in the wings for a chance to play a leading role in labor organization in the 1930s. Black activists had already assumed leading roles by preparing the community for the main event—the coming of the CIO.

The CIO, which came along in the mid-1930s, emerged from a dispute raised within the mainstream American Federation of Labor (AFL) over the question of how to organize the tens of thousands of unskilled workers within mass-production industries such as steel, autos, and meatpacking. Clinging to its traditional approach, the AFL advocated organizing workers according to skill or craft within an industry. Others, arguing that new industries demanded a new approach to organizing, wanted to organize by industry rather than craft, mobilizing skilled and unskilled alike in an all-inclusive organization. Unable to turn around the AFL, the insurgents split from the AFL and formed the CIO. To succeed in organizing industrial unions, the CIO needed the support of thousands of black workers who labored in steel, auto, and meatpacking plants. In Chicago, the community organizing effort of the BSCP provided important preconditions for widespread unionization of black workers. When CIO activists approached black workers in mass-production industries, organizers relied on new-crowd networks formed during the previous decade to open doors in the black community. The new-crowd networks that overlapped with efforts of the BSCP's cadre of activists were not the only groups contributing to a new outlook toward labor, but the brotherhood's struggle for manhood rights, aimed at gaining the confidence of middle-class leaders as well as workers, planted its labor rhetoric firmly in the soil of rights denied African Americans as citizens.[67]

The National Negro Congress (NNC), founded in 1936 by a group of new-crowd activists including Randolph, BSCP activists, black intellectuals, and Communists, illustrates how new-crowd networks in Chicago carried forward the new outlook toward labor. Bringing labor unions, fraternal orders, religious and civil groups, and political organizations under one umbrella, the NNC encouraged militant grassroots organizing within black communities across the nation. Several brotherhood activists assumed leadership positions within the NNC, linking local Chicago BSCP and NNC networks with the national organization. Randolph served as president of the NNC for its first three years. The Chicago branch of the NNC, called the Chicago Council, formed in 1936 by men and women from the ranks of organized labor, the Communist Party, and the BSCP's Citizens' Committee, was headed by Charles Burton, president of the BSCP's Citizens' Committee in Chicago, who also was on the national executive council of the NNC. Similarly, Thyra Edwards, organizer for both the International Ladies Garment Workers' Union (ILGWU) and the BSCP, was a member of the national executive council of the NNC.

The Chicago Council brought in churches, trade unions, and social organizations to work together on local issues such as police brutality, economic discrimination, and jobs for black Chicagoans. Most of the work was channeled through Eleanor Rye, secretary of the labor committee. As a member of the executive board of the Fur Workers Union; a member of the Communist Party, active in the Chicago Federation of Labor; and a supporter of the BSCP, Rye had established contacts within both white and black working-class communities of Chicago. She also relied on the work of Henry Johnson, a labor organizer who contacted more than 600 black organizations in Chicago and Gary, Indiana.[68]

The NNC alliance extended further into black Chicago as Rye, Johnson, and other NNC activists collaborated with the Urban League, the Interclub Council of Chicago, the South Side Garment Workers Club (members of the ILGWU), women's clubs, and the Freight Handlers Union. Horace Cayton, a University of Chicago scholar, along with other "prominent people," helped the Chicago Council raise funds and educate the community. But collaboration was built on the foundation laid by other organizations and individuals active on the South Side before the NNC local council or the CIO was formed. Wheaton's work as a paid community organizer for the YWCA, for example, helped prepare many female industrial and domestic workers for the NNC message in 1936, including laying the foundation for what later became the Domestic Workers' Association.[69]

The NNC labor committee published and distributed 10,000 leaflets to white and black trade unionists, used the Chicago Federation of Labor radio station, WCFL, to broadcast the NNC labor message, established labor forums and the Southside Citizens Committee to support the steel-organizing drive in the greater Chicago area, wrote articles published in the *Chicago Defender,* and demanded that black men and women buy union-made products.[70] As the NNC local connected disparate new-crowd networks, it developed a mutually beneficial relationship with activists organizing for the CIO.[71]

The first collaboration between the CIO and the NNC grew out of overlapping interests of the Steel Workers Organizing Committee (SWOC), formed in June 1936, and the NNC. A mutually beneficial relationship emerged as Randolph and NNC activists received financial backing from SWOC and the CIO, and new-crowd activists who had worked with the brotherhood served as an advance guard within the community, helping break down resistance to organizing labor. Often in the privacy of people's homes, activists met with representatives of black and white women's clubs, with ministers, and with other community figures. After gaining support from key groups within the community, they brought group pressure on clergy still in the pockets of steel companies. The efforts paid off when they set up an NNC-SWOC women's auxiliary with a black vice president and treasurer, won the allegiance of several black ministers, and successfully established an interracial union at the Inland Steel Company in Indiana Harbor.[72]

Without this collaboration and communitywide support, it is questionable whether SWOC would have made the connections in the black community that led to signing up large numbers of black workers in the new union movement. SWOC's success in the Chicago-Indiana steel mills served as a model for the Packinghouse Workers Organizing Committee (PWOC), helping to organize black packinghouse workers, who made up 25 percent of the Chicago workforce. The PWOC, as Roger Horowitz demonstrates, was built on the "highly visible welcome extended to black steelworkers by the SWOC."[73] The leadership, participation, and money supplied by CIO and Left organizers were extremely important. But so were ideas planted by the BSCP during the 1920s that helped assure a positive reception for the Left in the 1930s. When the brotherhood initiated its campaign in 1925, it was considered pure foolishness by the majority of black leaders. By the late 1920s, the BSCP's prolabor arguments had won the support and respect of many leading figures within the community. By connecting the history of social and labor activism in black Chicago during the 1920s with the efforts of the Left in the 1930s, we can better understand why such a large cross-section of the community placed a welcome mat in front of the doors they opened to CIO organizers. The cross-fertilization that occurred between the Left and new-crowd protest networks in the early 1930s cultivated alliances that shaped much of the labor and social history of the decade.

In June 1935, the BSCP won, through a union election, the right to represent Pullman porters and maids in labor negotiations with the Pullman Company. It took two more years before the company signed its first contact with the BSCP. Well before that historic occasion, Randolph, a leading figure in the new crowd of black Americans, became know as Mr. Black Labor and union Pullman porters and maids could do little wrong in the eyes of black Americans. Although winning a contract from the Pullman Company secured a prominent place for Randolph and union porters and maids in labor history, the BSCP's larger significance lay in providing important preconditions for widespread unionization of all black workers.

Notes

1. Historians who have shed light on the role the Communists played in bringing black workers into the industrial union movement include Robin D. G. Kelley, *Hammer and Hoe: Alabama Communists during the Great Depression* (Chapel Hill: University of North Carolina Press, 1990); Michael K. Honey, *Southern Labor and Black Civil Rights: Organizing Memphis Workers* (Urbana: University of Illinois Press, 1993); Nell Irvin Painter, *The Narrative of Hosea Hudson: His Life as a Negro Communist in the South* (Cambridge, Mass.: Harvard University Press, 1979); Rick Halpern, *Down on the Killing Floor: Black and White Workers in Chicago's Packing Houses, 1904–54* (Urbana: University of Illinois Press, 1997); Roger Horowitz, *"Negro and White, Unite and Fight!": A Social History of Industrial Unionism in Meatpacking, 1930–1990* (Urbana: University of Illinois Press, 1997). Other explanations of the historic shift include the struggle by black railroad workers to fight racism and exclusion by powerful railroad unions, by Eric Arnesen, *Brotherhoods of Color: Black Railroad Workers and the Struggle for Equality* (Cambridge, Mass.: Harvard University Press, 2001); the role of new-crowd activists, which included black workers promoting unions and a labor agenda in the black community, by Beth Tompkins Bates, "A New Crowd Challenges the Agenda of the Old Guard in the NAACP, 1933–1941," *American Historical Review* 102:2 (April 1997): 340–377; the role consumer culture played in creating new alliances within the black community, by Elizabeth Cohen, *Making a New Deal: Industrial Workers in Chicago, 1919–1939* (New York: Cambridge University Press, 1990); and black elites and unions in the 1930s, by August Meier and Elliott Rudnick, *Black Detroit and the Rise of the UAW* (New York: Oxford University Press, 1979).

2. This is not to imply that many of the books cited in the previous footnote pay no attention to the influence of black activists. This essay merely seeks to expand the discussion of the historic shift by bringing the African American community more prominently into the foreground while examining the 1920s and 1930s in tandem. On scholars calling for more attention to African American communities, see comments of Eric Arnesen and Kimberley L. Phillips, "Symposium on Halpern and Horowitz: Packinghouse Unionism," in *Labor History* 40:2 (1999): 211–212, 223, 225.

3. Arnesen, *Brotherhoods of Color,* 42–83; Eric Arnesen, "Charting an Independent Course: African-American Railroad Workers in the World War I Era," in *Labor Histories: Class, Politics, and the Working-Class Experience,* ed. Eric Arnesen, Julie Greene, and Bruce Laurie (Urbana: University of Illinois Press), 284–308; Eric Arnesen, *Waterfront Workers of New Orleans: Race, Class, and Politics, 1863–1923* (New York: Oxford University Press, 1991), 217–52; Earl Lewis, *In Their Own Interests: Race, Class, and Power in Twentieth-Century Norfolk, Virginia* (Berkeley: University of California Press, 1991), 48–61.

4. Halpern, *Down on the Killing Floor,* 44–72.

5. For more on the relationship between the Pullman Company and black Chicago, see Beth Tompkins Bates, *Pullman Porters and the Rise of Protest Politics in Black America, 1925–1945* (Chapel Hill: University of North Carolina Press, 2001), 40–62.

6. Stanley Buder, *Pullman: An Experiment in Industrial Order and Community Planning* (New York: Oxford University Press, 1967), 15–17; Jervis Anderson, *A. Philip Randolph: A Biographical Portrait* (New York: Harcourt Brace Jovanovich, 1973), 159–64.

7. For images of Pullman porters, see Janet L. Reiff and Susan E. Hirsch, "Pullman

and Its Public: Image and Aim in Making and Interpreting History," *The Public His-*
torian 11 (Fall 1989): 102; for Martin Turner's story as a veteran film Pullman porter,
see *Detroit News,* April 9, 1941; for perpetuation of black porters as slaves, see Joseph
Husband, *The Story of the Pullman Car* (Chicago: A. C. McClurg, 1917), 155–56; for
customers referring to porters as George, see Murray Kempton, *Part of Our Time:*
Some Ruins and Monuments of the Thirties (New York: Simon and Schuster, 1955), 259.

8. Kempton, *Part of Our Time,* 259.

9. William Hamilton Harris, *Keeping the Faith: A. Philip Randolph, Milton P. Webster,*
and the Brotherhood of Sleeping Car Porters, 1925–1937 (Urbana: University of Illinois
Press, 1977). Officials of the Pullman Company admitted in 1915 to the federal Commission on Industrial Relations that porters were underpaid and "obliged" to secure
tips from the public in order to live, Commission on Industrial Relations, *Final Re-*
port, Vol. 1, 76.

10. For making hustlers out of porters, see Anderson, *A. Philip Randolph,* 162. For
Malcolm X quote, see David D. Perata, *Those Pullman Blues: An Oral History of the*
African American Railroad Attendant (New York: Twayne, 1996), xxviii.

11. Frank R. Crosswaith, "Porters Smash a Company Union," *Labor Age* 17 (January
1928): 15–16; Greg LeRoy, "The Founding Heart of A. Philip Randolph's Union: Milton P. Webster and Chicago's Pullman Porters Organize, 1925–1937," *Labor's Heritage* 3
(July 1991): 27–31; Harris, *Keeping the Faith,* 40–48; Arnesen, *Brotherhoods of Color,* 96–
97; interview of Thelma Wheaton by author in Chicago, September 1, 1994; James R.
Grossman, *Land of Hope: Chicago, Black Southerners, and the Great Migration* (Chicago:
University of Chicago Press, 1991). The phrase "biting the hand that feeds you" appeared in newspapers and in Brotherhood of Sleeping Car Porters' correspondence,
and it was mentioned by St. Clair Drake and Horace R. Cayton, *Black Metropolis: A*
Study of Negro Life in a Northern City (Chicago: University of Chicago Press, 1945),
370. It was commonly used by both black and white politicians as a way of reminding
patrons about the terms of the social contract. See also Frank L. Hayes, writing on
the BSCP Chicago Division for the *Chicago Daily News,* November 5, 1929, found in
BSCP Papers, Chicago Division.

12. Anderson, *A. Philip Randolph,* 183, 171.

13. *The Messenger* 8 (January 1926): 24; Anderson, *A. Philip Randolph,* 171.

14. Branham, "Transformation of Black Political Leadership in Chicago, 1864–
1942" (Ph.D. diss., University of Chicago, 1981), 452; *Chicago Defender,* December 19,
1925, pt. 2, p. 4; for brief history of Ida B. Wells's club, *Chicago Defender,* December
5, 1934, p. 22; Milton P. Webster to Ida Wells-Barnett, September 15, 1926; Webster
to Dad Moore, May 16, 1926; A. Philip Randolph to Webster, August 3, 1926; Randolph to John C. Mills, August 3, 1926; Randolph to Webster, January 28, 1927, p. 2,
BSCP Papers, Chicago Div.; on Wells-Barnett's request to use Appomattox Club, see
S.W.O. 193, report on the Woman's Forum, December 21, 1925, File: History of BSCP,
Box 10, A. Philip Randolph Papers (hereafter APRP).

15. W. E. B. Du Bois, "Close Ranks," *Crisis* 16 (July 1918): 111; William M. Tuttle,
Race Riot: Chicago in the Red Summer of 1919 (New York: Atheneum, 1970), 208–22;
Grossman, *Land of Hope,* 161–80.

16. Editorial, "The New Negro—What Is He?" *The Messenger* 2 (August 1920).

17. *The Messenger* 8:4 (April 1926): 114.

18. BSCP poster, Propaganda folder, Box 633–a, Pullman Company Papers, New-berry Library. For discussion of independence from white control, see Eric Foner, *Reconstruction: America's Unfinished Revolution, 1863–1877* (New York: Harper and Row, 1988), 60–123. See also Eric Foner, "The Meaning of Freedom in the Age of Emanci-pation," *Journal of American History* 81:2 (September 1994): 457–58; Mark D. Naison, "Black Agrarian Radicalism in the Great Depression: The Threads of a Lost Tradi-tion," *Journal of Ethnic Studies* 1:3 (Fall 1973): 52–55.

19. *The Messenger* 8:4 (April 1926): 114; and *The Messenger* 9:6 (June 1927): 207.

20. BSCP poster, Propaganda folder, Box 633–a, Pullman Company Papers, New-berry Library.

21. *The Messenger* 7:8 (August 1925): 312; Frank W. Crosswaith, "Toward the Home Stretch," *The Messenger* 8:7 (July 1926): 196; *The Messenger* 7 (September 1925): 314, 336.

22. Greg LeRoy, "The Founding Heart of A. Philip Randolph's Union," 27; Milton P. Webster to Ida Wells-Barnett, September 15, 1926, BSCP Papers, Chicago Division; Ida B. Wells, *Crusade for Justice: The Autobiography of Ida B. Wells,* as told to Alfreda M. Duster (Chicago: University of Chicago Press, 1970).

23. For the Pittsburgh phase of Austin's activism, see Joe W. Trotter Jr., *River Jordon: African American Urban Life in the Ohio Valley* (Lexington: University Press of Kentucky, 1998), 120–21; "Twentieth Century Churches (Chicago): Pilgrim Baptist Church," pp. 1–2, Box 17, Folder 25, Vivian G. Harsh Research Collection, Woodson Branch of Chi-cago Public Library (hereafter VGHC); *Pittsburgh Courier,* December 26, 1925, p. 1; Frederick H. Robb, *The 1927 Intercollegian Wonder Book, or, The Negro in Chicago, 1779–1927* (Chicago: Atlas Printing, 1927), 163, 167 (hereafter *The Negro in Chicago, 1927*).

24. *Chicago Defender,* March 16, 1929, p. 7, May 4, 1929, part 2, p. 6; "List of News-papers and Organizations on the South Side," Box 345a, Folder 1, Claude Barnett Papers, Chicago Historical Society; Alice Henry, *The Trade Union Woman* (New York: Lenox Hill, 1973; reprint from University of Minnesota Library, n.d.), 75.

25. "Speech Made by March McDowell," Sunday, October 3, 1926, Chicago, re-printed in *The Messenger* 8 (December 1926): 375.

26. Webster to Dad Moore, November 8, 1927, BSCP Chicago Div.; *The Messenger* (January 1926): 15; Roi Ottley, *The Lonely Warrior: The Life and Times of Robert S. Ab-bott* (Chicago: Henry Regnery, 1955), 138–39, 263–65; E. Franklin Frazier, "Chicago: A Cross-Section of Negro Life," *Opportunity* 7:3 (March 1929): 71; *Chicago Defender,* August 20 and November 19, 1927; Harold Gosnell, *Negro Politicians: The Rise of Negro Politics in Chicago* (Chicago: University of Chicago Press, 1935), 101.

27. Webster to Randolph, December 17, 1927, BSCP Papers, Chicago Div.; Entries in "Datebook," Irene McCoy Gaines, for January 13, 17, 25, 29, 1921, box 8, Irene McCoy Gaines Papers, CHS; "Extensive Work of Dr. G. C. Hall," in *Broad Ax* (Feb-ruary 17, 1912): 3; obituaries on Dr. Hall, *Chicago Defender,* June 21, 1930, pp. 1, 12, 14; Arvarh E. Strickland, *History of the Chicago Urban League* (Urbana: University of Il-linois, 1966), 28; LeRoy, "The Founding Heart of Randolph's Union," 29.

28. Editorial, "The Need of a Labor Background," *Messenger* 9:8 (August 1927): 256.

29. A. Philip Randolph, "State and Policy of Brotherhood," *Messenger* 8:4 (April 1926): 186.

30. *Messenger* 9 (January 1927): 17.

31. *Chicago Defender,* January 7, 1928, p. 2; invitation to "Chicago's First Negro Labor

Conference," sponsored by "a Committee of Chicago Citizens and the Brotherhood of Sleeping Car Porters, January 23, 1928, BSCP Papers, Chicago Div.; Harold Simmelkjaer, "Civil Rights," *Messenger* 8:3 (March 1926): 74.

32. Abram L. Harris, "Why the Brotherhood of Sleeping Car Porters Should Organize under Separate International Charter," I-C-413, NAACP Papers, p. 17.

33. St. Clair Drake and Horace R. Cayton, *Black Metropolis: A Study of Negro Life in a Northern City* (Chicago: University of Chicago Press, 1945), 365–74; Branham, "Transformation of Black Political Leadership," 241–45; Robb, *The Negro in Chicago, 1927,* 16; Robb, *The Wonder Book: The Negro in Chicago, 1779–1929* (Chicago: Washington Intercollegiate Club of Chicago, 1930), 69, 72, 73 (hereafter *The Negro in Chicago, 1929*); *Chicago Defender,* March 2, 1929, p. 7, part 2, p. 6.

34. Herbert Morrisohn Smith, "Three Negro Preachers in Chicago" (M.A. thesis, University of Chicago), 2–5, box 17, VGHC; Robb, *The Negro in Chicago, 1929,* 70–71, 74; *Chicago Defender,* January 25, 1930, p. 9.

35. Drake and Cayton, *Black Metropolis,* 365–74; Branham, "Transformation of Black Political Leadership," 241–45; Robb, *The Negro in Chicago, 1929,* 68–73; *Chicago Defender,* March 2, 1929, p. 7, part 2, p. 6 and February 1, 1930, p. 18. For NNBL, see Webster to Randolph, August 20, 1928, BSCP Chicago; *The Black Worker,* March 1, 1930, p. 2.

36. *Chicago Defender,* January 25, 1930, p. 1.

37. "Address Delivered before National Labor Conference," by Jeanette Smith, *Chicago Defender,* February 1, 1930, p. 18; Robb, *Negro in Chicago, 1929,* 198; Webster to John Fitzpatrick, April 25, 1930, BSCP Papers, Chicago Div.

38. For Randolph's depiction of the new crowd and old guard, see *The Messenger* (May–June 1919): 9, 26–27.

39. For more on development of the new crowd, see Bates, "A New Crowd Challenges the Agenda of the Old Guard," *Chicago Defender,* January 25, 1930, p. 1.

40. *Chicago Whip,* July 25, 1931; Gosnell, *Negro Politicians,* 329–31; Drake and Cayton, *Black Metropolis,* 85–87. For more on the history of Unemployed Councils, see Roy Rosenzweig, "Organizing the Unemployed: The Early Years of the Great Depression, 1929–1933," *Radical America* 10 (July–August 1976): 37–62; Daniel Leab, "'United We Eat': The Creation and Organization of the Unemployed Councils in 1930," *Labor History* 8 (1967): 300–315; Christopher Robert Reed, "A Study of Black Politics and Protest in Depression-Decade Chicago: 1930–1930" (Ph.D. diss., Kent State University, 1982), 50–54, 173–74.

41. *Chicago Defender,* August 8, 1931; Reed, "A Study of Black Politics," 182; Harry Haywood, *Black Bolshevik: Autobiography of an Afro-American Communist* (Chicago: Liberator Press, 1978), 443; Harold D. Lasswell and Dorothy Blumenstock, *World Revolutionary Propaganda: A Chicago Study* (New York: Knopf, 1939), 73, 203. There is much dispute about the numbers that marched and the numbers that looked on from the sidelines. The *Chicago Tribune* said "several thousand," August 9, 1931; Haywood claimed 30,000; the *Defender* estimated between 5,000 and 8,000, August 15, 1931.

42. Mark Solomon, *The Cry Was Unity: Communists and African Americans, 1917–1936* (Jackson: University Press of Mississippi, 1998), 158; *Chicago Tribune,* August 6 and 7, 1931; *Pittsburgh Courier,* August 8, 1931; Frances Fox Piven and Richard Cloward, *Poor People's Movements: Why They Succeed, How They Fail* (New York: Pantheon Books, 1979), 62–63.

43. *The Messenger* 9 (January 1927): 17.

44. Reed, "A Study of Black Politics," 174, 182.

45. My thanks to Paul Young for sharing with me his research findings on the Chicago Unemployed Councils. See Young, "Race, Class, and Radical Protest: Chicago Unemployed Council 1930–1934," paper presented at Organization of American Historians, San Francisco, April 19, 1997, 11–12.

46. Dempsey Travis quote is from ibid., 6; Cayton and Drake, *Black Metropolis,* 603.

47. The biography of Thelma McWorter Kirkpatrick Wheaton is drawn from interviews of Thelma Wheaton by author in Chicago, Ill., between September 1, 1994, and January 5, 1995. I am also grateful for information provided by historian Juliet E. K. Walker in "The Afro-American Woman: Who Was She?" *Black Women's History: Theory and Practice,* Vol. 2, ed. Darlene Clark Hine (Brooklyn, N.Y.: Carlson, 1990), 659–69.

48. *Chicago Defender,* June 24, 1933, p. 4, July 1, 1933, pp. 1, 3, 4, and July 15, 1933, p. 4; Gosnell, *Negro Politicians,* 334; interviews of Thelma K. Wheaton by author, September 1 and 14, 1994.

49. Interview, Wheaton by Bates, September 14, 1994.

50. Interviews, Wheaton by Bates, September 1 and 14, 1994.

51. "Women Civil Leaders Hold Labor Confab," *Chicago Defender,* March 12, 1932, p. 2.

52. Interview, Wheaton, January 5, 1995, by author. See also "Women's Council to Present Program," *Chicago Defender,* March 25, 1933; and Melinda Chateauvert, *Marching Together: Women of the Brotherhood of Sleeping Car Porters* (Urbana: University of Illinois Press, 1998), 61–66.

53. "Scholarship for Women in Industry Given by YWCA," *Chicago Defender,* March 18, 1933, p. 20, April 15, 1933, p. 21.

54. Katheryn Williams, interviewed by Robert Davis, August 6, 1937, Folder 3, Box 34, VGHC.

55. Information on Thyra Edwards from Thelma Wheaton, interview by author, January 5, 1995. Information verified through interviews with Ishmael P. Flory, a co-worker with Edwards in the Chicago branch of the National Negro Congress, by author, August 31, 1994, and January 7, 1995. See also "Professional History," Box 1, Thyra Edwards Papers, CHS.

56. "Lecturing: Thyra Edwards," *Chicago Defender,* April 1, 1933, p. 20; "Friends Gather at Poro College," *Chicago Defender,* April 22, 1933, p. 21.

57. For the popularity of Thyra Edwards as a speaker and lecturer, see Ishmael P. Flory, interview, April 11, 1995, with author.

58. "Near South Side Gets Interracial Committee," *Chicago Defender,* June 3, 1933, p. 4.

59. Editorial, "Injustice, Not Red, Stirring Up Workers," *Chicago Defender,* June 16, 1934, p. 14.

60. *Nation* 139 (August 1, 1934): 127–28; Harvard Sitkoff, *A New Deal for Blacks: The Emergence of Civil Rights as a National Issue: The Depression Decade* (New York: Oxford University Press, 1978), 150–51.

61. *Chicago Defender,* July 6, 1935, p. 4.

62. Ibid., September 22, 1934, pp. 1, 2.

63. Thelma K. Wheaton interviewed by author, January 5, 1995, Chicago, Illinois.

64. Randolph may also have agreed with Charles Houston, legal counsel for the NAACP, who praised the militant activities of Communists that inspired mass struggle. See Genna Rae McNeil, *Groundwork: Charles Hamilton Houston and the Struggle for Civil Rights* (Philadelphia: University of Pennsylvania Press, 1983), 99, 121. For Randolph becoming convinced that "cooperation with Communists was possible," see Solomon, *The Cry Was Unity,* 274.

65. Robin D. G. Kelley, *Freedom Dreams: The Black Radical Imagination* (Boston: Beacon Press, 2002), 49.

66. Steve Babson, *The Unfinished Struggle: Turning Points in American Labor, 1877–Present* (Lanham, Md.: Rowman and Littlefield, 1999), 60; Robert H. Zieger, *The CIO, 1935–1955* (Chapel Hill: University of North Carolina Press, 1995), 13–21.

67. For more on cross-class interracial alliances that formed during the 1930s in Chicago, see Bates, "A New Crowd Challenges the Agenda of the Old Guard."

68. For the relationships between NNC and community organizations, see Charles Wesley Burton to residents of Chicago, May 12, 1936; Eleanor Rye to John P. Davis, May 13, 1936; John Davis to Eleanor Rye, March 26, 1936; and Davis to Rye, May 18, 1936, all in Box 7, NNC Papers. On Communist affiliation, see interview by author in Chicago with Ishmael P. Flory, colleague of Eleanor Rye in the 1930s, August 29, 1994. On organizers for NNC, see John Davis to Van A. Bittner, July 14, 1936, Box 4, NNC Papers; Chateauvert, "Marching Together," 148, 159. For a discussion of the role of the National Negro Congress (NNC) in opening doors for the CIO in the black community, see Bates, "A New Crowd Challenges the Agenda of the Old Guard," 362–67.

69. Thelma Wheaton, September 1 and 14, 1994, interview by author, Chicago, Illinois; John Davis to Marion Cuthbert, January 18, 1936, mentioned his concern regarding organizing black female industrial and domestic workers and suggested that Marion Cuthbert contact Mrs. Kirkpatrick in Chicago. Mrs. Thelma Kirkpatrick's name later changed to Thelma Wheaton. Box 4, NNC Papers.

70. Ralph Bunche, "Extended Memo on the Programs, Ideologies, Tactics, and Achievements of the Negro Betterment and Interracial Organizations," Carnegie-Myrdal Study of the Negro in America Papers, Schomberg Center for Research in Black Culture, New York Public Library; Eleanor Rye to John Davis, October 3, 1936, and John Davis to A. Philip Randolph, June 6, 1936, Box 7, NNC Papers; *Pittsburgh Courier,* July 31, 1937. For contemporary articles, see *Chicago Defender,* September 12, 1936, p. 4.

71. Elmer W. Henderson, "Political Changes among Negroes in Chicago during the Depression," *Social Forces* 19 (October–May 1941): 545. The Committee for Industrial Organization, formed within the AFL in 1935, launched the effort to organize industrial unions. It did not formally become the Congress of Industrial Organizations until 1938; Zieger, *The CIO,* 90.

72. Bates, "A New Crowd Challenges the Agenda of the Old Guard," 363–65.

73. On contribution to PWOC's campaign, see Horowitz, *"Negro and White, Unite and Fight!"* 71. For more on meatpacking, see Halpern, *Down on the Killing Floor,* 137–38; for more on black workers and the CIO, see Zieger, *The CIO,* 80–83.

ROBERT KORSTAD AND
NELSON LICHTENSTEIN

9 Opportunities Found and Lost: Labor, Radicals, and the Early Civil Rights Movement

Most historians would agree that the modem civil rights movement did not begin with the Supreme Court's decision in *Brown v. Board of Education*. Yet all too often the movement's history has been written as if events before the mid-1950s constituted a kind of prehistory, important only insofar as they laid the legal and political foundation for the spectacular advances that came later. Those were the "forgotten years of the Negro Revolution," wrote one historian; they were the "seed time of racial and legal metamorphosis," according to another. But such a periodization profoundly underestimates the tempo and misjudges the social dynamic of the freedom struggle.[1]

The civil rights era began, dramatically and decisively, in the early 1940s when the social structure of black America took on an increasingly urban, proletarian character. A predominantly southern rural and small-town population was soon transformed into one of the most urban of all major ethnic groups. More than two million blacks migrated to northern and western industrial areas during the 1940s, while another million moved from farm to city within the South. Northern black voters doubled their numbers between 1940 and 1948, and in the eleven states of the Old South, black registration more than quadrupled, reaching more than one million by 1952. Likewise, membership in the National Association for the Advancement of Colored People (NAACP) soared, growing from 50,000 in 355 branches in 1940 to almost 450,000 in 1,073 branches six years later.[2]

The half-million black workers who joined unions affiliated with the Congress of Industrial Organizations (CIO) were in the vanguard of efforts to transform race relations. The NAACP and the Urban League had become more friendly toward labor in the depression era, but their legal and social-work orientation had not prepared them to act effectively in the workplaces and working-class neighborhoods where black Americans fought their most decisive struggles of the late 1930s and 1940s. By the early forties it was commonplace for sympathetic observers to assert the centrality of mass unionization in the civil rights struggle. A Rosenwald Fund study concluded, not without misgivings, that "the characteristic movements among Negroes are now for the first time becoming proletarian," while a *Crisis* reporter found the CIO a "lamp of democracy" throughout the old Confederate states. "The South has not known such a force since the historic Union Leagues in the great days of the Reconstruction era."[3]

This movement gained much of its dynamic character from the relationship that arose between unionized blacks and the federal government and proved somewhat similar to the creative tension that linked the church-based civil rights movement and the state almost two decades later. In the 1950s the *Brown* decision legitimated much of the subsequent social struggle, but it remained essentially a dead letter until given political force by a growing protest movement. In like manner, the rise of industrial unions and the evolution of late New Deal labor legislation offered working-class blacks an economic and political standard by which they could legitimate their demands and stimulate a popular struggle. The "one man, one vote" policy implemented in thousands of National Labor Relations Board (NLRB) elections, the industrial "citizenship" that union contracts offered once-marginal elements of the working class, and the patriotic egalitarianism of the government's wartime propaganda all generated a rights consciousness that gave working-class black militancy a moral justification in some ways as powerful as that evoked by the Baptist spirituality of Martin Luther King Jr. a generation later.[4] During the war, the Fair Employment Practice Committee (FEPC) held little direct authority, but like the Civil Rights Commission of the late 1950s, it served to expose racist conditions and spur on black activism wherever it undertook its well-publicized investigations. And just as a disruptive and independent civil tights movement in the 1960s could pressure the federal government to enforce its own laws and move against local elites, so, too, did the mobilization of the black working class in the 1940s make civil rights an issue that could not be ignored by union officers, white executives, or government officials.[5]

This essay explores two examples of the workplace-oriented civil rights militancy that arose in the 1940s—one in the South and one in the North. It analyzes the unionization of predominantly black tobacco workers in Winston-Salem, North Carolina, and the ferment in the United Auto Workers in Detroit, Michigan, that made that city a center of black working-class activism in the North. Similar movements took root among

newly organized workers in the cotton compress mills of Memphis, the tobacco factories of Richmond and Charleston, the steel mills of Pittsburgh
and Birmingham, the stockyards and farm equipment factories of Chicago
and Louisville, and the shipyards of Baltimore and Oakland.[6]

Winston-Salem in the War

Winston-Salem had been a center of tobacco processing since the 1880s,
and the R. J. Reynolds Tobacco Company dominated the life of the city's
80,000 citizens. By the 1940s, whites held most of the higher-paying ma-
chine-tending jobs, but blacks formed the majority of the workforce, concentrated in the preparation departments, where they cleaned, stemmed,
and conditioned the tobacco.[7] The jobs were physically demanding, the
air was hot and dusty, and, in departments with machinery, the noise was
deafening. Most black workers made only a few cents above minimum
wage, and benefits were few. Black women workers experienced frequent
verbal and occasional sexual abuse. Reynolds maintained a determined opposition to trade unionism, and two unsuccessful American Federation of
Labor (AFL) efforts to organize segregated locals had soured most black
workers on trade unionism.

But in 1943 a CIO organizing effort succeeded. Led by the United Cannery, Agricultural, Packing and Allied Workers of America (UCAPAWA),
a new union drive championed black dignity and self-organization, employing several young black organizers who had gotten their start in the
interracial Southern Tenant Farmers Union. Their discreet two-year organizing campaign made a dramatic breakthrough when black women in
one of the stemmeries stopped work on June 17. A severe labor shortage,
chronic wage grievances, and a recent speedup gave the women both the
resources and the incentive to transform a departmental sit-down into a
festive plantwide strike. The UCAPAWA quickly signed up about 8,000
black workers, organized a committee to negotiate with the company, and
asked the NLRB to hold an election.[8]

The effort to win union recognition at Reynolds sparked a spirited debate about who constituted the legitimate leadership of the black community in Winston-Salem. Midway through the campaign, six local black busi-
ness- and professional men—a college professor, an undertaker, a dentist,
a store owner, and two ministers—dubbed "colored leaders" by the *Winston-
Salem Journal*—wrote a long letter to the editor urging workers to reject
the "followers of John L. Lewis and William Green" and to remain loyal to
Reynolds. In the absence of any formal leadership, elected or otherwise,
representatives of Winston-Salem's small black middle class had served as

spokesmen, brokering with the white elite for small concessions in a tightly segregated society. The fight for collective bargaining, they argued, had to remain secondary to the more important goal of racial betterment, which could only be achieved by "good will, friendly understanding, and mutual respect and co-operation between the races." Partly because of their own vulnerability to economic pressure, such traditional black leaders judged unions, like other institutions, by their ability to deliver jobs and maintain a precarious racial equilibrium.[9]

The union campaign at Reynolds transformed the expectations tobacco workers held of the old community leadership. Reynolds workers responded to calls for moderation from "college-trained people" with indignation. "Our leaders," complained Mabel Jessup, "always look clean and refreshed at the end of the hottest day, because they work in very pleasant environments. . . . All I ask of our leaders is that they obtain a job in one of the factories as a laborer and work two weeks. Then write what they think." W. L. Griffin felt betrayed. "I have attended church regularly for the past thirty years," he wrote, "and unity and co-operation have been taught and preached from the pulpits of the various Negro churches. Now that the laboring class of people are about to unite and co-operate on a wholesale scale for the purpose of collective bargaining, these same leaders seem to disagree with that which they have taught their people." Others rejected the influence of people who "have always told us what the white people want, but somehow or other are particularly silent on what we want." "We feel we are the leaders instead of you," asserted a group of union members.[10]

Reynolds, the only major tobacco manufacturer in the country not under a union contract, followed tried-and-true methods to break the union. Management used lower-level supervisors to intimidate unionists and supported a no-union movement among white workers, whose organizers were given freedom to roam the company's workshops and warehouses. That group, the R. J. Reynolds Employees Association, sought a place on the NLRB ballot to delay the increasingly certain CIO victory. Meanwhile, the white business community organized an Emergency Citizens Committee to help defeat the CIO. In a well-publicized resolution, the committee blamed the recent strikes on "self-seeking representatives of the CIO" and warned that continued subversion of existing race relations would "likely lead to riots and bloodshed."[11]

In earlier times, this combination of anti-union forces would probably have derailed the organizing effort. But during World War II, black workers had allies who helped shift the balance of power. The NLRB closely supervised each stage of the election process and denied the company's request to divide the workforce into two bargaining units, which would have weakened the position of black workers. When local judges sought to delay the election, government attorneys removed the case to federal court. In December 1943, an NLRB election gave the CIO a resounding victory. But continued federal assistance, from the United States Conciliation Service and the National War Labor Board, was still needed to secure Reynolds workers a union contract in 1944.[12]

That first agreement resembled hundreds of other wartime labor-management contracts, but in the context of Winston-Salem's traditional system of race relations it had radical implications, because it generated a new set of shop-floor rights embodied in the seniority, grievance, and wage-adjustment procedures. The contract did not attack factory segregation—for the most part, white workers continued to control the better-paying jobs—but it did call forth a new corps of black leaders to defend the rights Reynolds workers had recently won. The 100 or so elected shop stewards were the "most important people in the plant," remembered union activist Velma Hopkins. They were the "natural leaders," people who had "taken up money for flowers if someone died or would talk to the foreman [even] before the union." Now the union structure reinforced the capabilities of such workers: "We had training classes for the shop stewards: What to do, how to do it. We went over the contract thoroughly." The shop stewards transformed the traditional paternalism of Reynolds management into an explicit system of benefits and responsibilities. They made the collective bargaining agreement a bill of rights.[13]

The growing self-confidence of black women, who constituted roughly half of the total workforce, proved particularly subversive of existing social relations. To the white men who ran the Reynolds plants, nothing could have been more disturbing than the demand that they negotiate on a basis of equality with people whom they regarded as deeply inferior—by virtue of their sex as well as their class and race. When union leaders like Theodosia Simpson, Velma Hopkins, and Moranda Smith sat down at the bargaining table with company executives, social stereotypes naturally came under assault, but the challenge proved equally dramatic on the shop floor. For example, Ruby Jones, the daughter of a railway fireman, became one of the most outspoken shop stewards. Perplexed by her newfound aggressiveness, a foreman demanded, "Ruby, what do you want?" "I want your respect," she replied. "That's all I ask."[14]

By the summer of 1944, Local 22 of the reorganized and renamed Food, Tobacco, Agricultural and Allied Workers (FTA) had become the center of an alternative social world that linked black workers together regardless of job, neighborhood, or church affiliation. The union hall, only a few blocks from the Reynolds Building, housed a constant round of meetings, plays, and musical entertainments, as well as classes in labor history, black history, and current events. Local 22 sponsored softball teams, checker tournaments, sewing circles, and swimming clubs. Its vigorous educational program and well-stocked library introduced many black workers (and a few whites) to a larger radical culture few had glimpsed before. "You know, at that little library they [the city of Winston-Salem] had for us, you couldn't find any books on Negro history," remembered Viola Brown. "They didn't have books by Aptheker, Dubois, or Frederick Douglass. But we had them at *our* library."[15]

The Communist Party was the key political grouping in FTA and in Local 22. FTA president Donald Henderson had long been associated with the party, and many organizers who passed through Winston-Salem shared his political sympathies. By 1947, party organizers had recruited about 150 Winston-Salem blacks, almost all tobacco workers. Most of these workers saw the party as both a militant civil rights organization, which in the 1930s had defended such black victims of white southern racism as the Scottsboro Boys and Angelo Herndon, and as a cosmopolitan group, introducing members to the larger world of politics and ideas. The white North Carolina Communist leader Junius Scales recalled that the "top leaders [of Local 22] . . . just soaked up all the educational efforts that were directed at them. The Party's program had an explanation of events locally, nationally, and worldwide which substantiated everything they had felt instinctively. . . . It really meant business on racism." The party was an integrated institution in which the social conventions of the segregated South were self-consciously violated, but it also accommodated itself to the culture of the black community. In Winston-Salem, therefore, the party met regularly in a black church and started the meetings with a hymn and a prayer.[16]

The Communist Party's relative success in Winston-Salem was replicated in other black industrial districts. In the South a clear majority of the party's new recruits were black, and in northern states like Illinois and Michigan the proportion ranged from 25 to 40 percent. The party's relative success among American blacks was not based on its programmatic consistency: during the late 1940s, the NAACP and other critics pointed out that the wartime party had denounced civil rights struggles when they challenged the Roosevelt administration or its conduct of the war effort, but that the party grew more militant once Soviet-American relations cooled.[17] However, the party never abandoned its assault on Jim Crow, and unlike the NAACP, which directed much of its energy toward the courts and Congress, the Communists or their front groups more often organized around social or political issues subject to locally initiated protests, petitions, and pickets. Moreover, the party adopted what today would be called an affirmative action policy that recognized the special disabilities under which black workers functioned, in the party as well as in the larger community. Although there were elements of tokenism and manipulation in the implementation of that policy, the party's unique effort to develop black leaders gave the Communists a special standing among politically active blacks.[18]

Tobacco industry trade unionism revitalized black political activism in Winston-Salem. Until the coming of the CIO, NAACP attacks on racial discrimination seemed radical, and few blacks risked associating with the organization. A 1942 membership drive did increase branch size from 11 to 100, but most new members came from the traditional black middle class and were mainly teachers and municipal bus drivers. The Winston-Salem NAACP became a mass organization only after Local 22 conducted its own campaign for the city branch. As tobacco workers poured in, the local NAACP reached a membership of 1,991 by 1946, making it the largest unit in North Carolina.[19]

Unionists also attacked the policies that had disenfranchised Winston-Salem blacks for more than two generations. As part of the CIO Political Action Committee's voter registration and mobilization drive, Local 22 inaugurated citizenship classes, political rallies, and citywide mass meetings. Union activists challenged the power of registrars to judge the qualifications of black applicants and insisted that black veterans vote without further tests. The activists encouraged the city's blacks to participate in electoral politics. "Politics IS food, clothes, and housing," declared the committee that registered some 700 new black voters in the months before the 1944 elections.[20] After a visit to Winston-Salem in 1944, a *Pittsburgh Courier* correspondent wrote, "I was aware of a growing solidarity and intelligent mass action that will mean the dawn of a New Day in the South. One cannot visit Winston-Salem and mingle with the thousands of workers without sensing a revolution in thought and action. If there is a 'New' Negro, he is to be found in the ranks of the labor movement."[21]

Organization and political power gave the black community greater leverage at city hall and at the county courthouse. NAACP and union officials regularly took part in municipal government debate on social services for the black community, minority representation on the police and fire departments, and low-cost public housing. In 1944 and 1946, newly enfranchised blacks helped reelect Congressman John Folger, a New Deal supporter, against strong conservative opposition. In 1947, after black registration had increased some tenfold in the previous three years, a minister, Kenneth Williams, won a seat on the Board of Aldermen, becoming the first black city official in the twentieth-century South to be elected against a white opponent.[22]

Civil Rights Militancy in Detroit

The social dynamic that had begun to revolutionize Winston-Salem played itself out on a far larger scale in Detroit, making that city a center of civil rights militancy in the war years. Newly organized black auto workers pushed forward the frontier of racial equality on the shop floor, in the political arena, and within the powerful million-member United Auto Workers. Despite increasing racism among white workers, union goals and civil rights aims largely paralleled each other in the 1940s.

In 1940 about 4 percent of all auto workers were black; the proportion more than doubled during the war and rose to about one-fifth of the auto workforce in 1960. Although proportionally less numerous than in Winston-Salem, blacks were nevertheless central to the labor process in many of Detroit's key manufacturing facilities. Excluded from assembly operations and skilled work, blacks dominated the difficult and unhealthy, but absolutely essential, work in foundry, paint shop, and wet sanding operations.[23]

Ford Motor Company's great River Rouge complex contained the largest concentration of black workers in the country. More than half of its 9,000 black workers labored in the foundry, but Henry Ford's peculiar brand of interwar paternalism had enabled blacks to secure some jobs in virtually every Ford department. The company therefore proved a mecca for black workers. Those who worked there proudly announced, "I work for Henry Ford" and wore their plant badges on the lapels of their Sunday coats. Ford reinforced his hold on the loyalty of Detroit's black working class by establishing what amounted to a separate personnel department that recruited new workers on the recommendation of an influential black minister. That policy, which continued until the early 1940s, strengthened the procompany, anti-union attitude of most churchmen and reinforced the hostility shown the early CIO by leaders of the Detroit Urban League and the local NAACP branch.[24]

UAW leaders recognized that unless black workers were recruited to the union, they might undermine efforts to consolidate UAW power in key manufacturing facilities. The danger became clear during the racially divisive 1939 Chrysler Corporation strike when management tried to start a back-to-work movement spearheaded by black workers, and it proved even more apparent during the 1940–41 Ford organizing drive, when black workers hesitated to join the union. During the April 1941 Ford strike, several hundred scabbed inside the plant. In response, UAW leaders made a concerted effort to win over elements of the local black bourgeoisie, who were not directly dependent on Ford's patronage network. The ensuing conflict within the Detroit NAACP chapter was only resolved in favor of the UAW after Ford's unionization. Thereafter black workers, whose participation in union activities had lagged well behind those of most whites, became among the most steadfast UAW members. The UAW itself provided an alternative focus of power, both cooperating with and challenging the black church and the NAACP as the most effective and legitimate spokesman for the black community.[25]

Many talented, politically sophisticated black officers and staffers emerged in the UAW during the mid-1940s, although never in numbers approaching their proportion of union membership. Blacks were a majority in almost every foundry and in most paint shops, so locals that represented manufacturing facilities usually adopted the United Mine Workers formula of including a black on the election slate as one of the top four officers. Locals with a large black membership also elected blacks to the annual UAW convention, where the 150 to 200 black delegates in attendance represented about 7 or 8 percent of the total voting roll. And almost a score of blacks also secured appointment as highly visible UAW international representatives during the early 1940s.[26]

Ford's River Rouge complex overshadowed all other Detroit-area production facilities as a center of black political power. Although most blacks had probably voted against the UAW in the NLRB elections of May 1941, the unionization process, particularly radical in its reorganization of shop-floor social relations at the Rouge, helped transform the consciousness of these industrial workers. With several hundred shop committeemen in the vanguard, workers intimidated many foremen, challenged top management, and broke the company spy system. "We noticed a very definite change in attitude of the working man," recalled one supervisor. "It was terrible for a while . . . the bosses were just people to look down on after the union came in." For the next decade, Rouge Local 600 proved a center of civil rights militancy and a training ground for black leaders. The Rouge foundry sent more than a score of black delegates to every UAW convention, provided at least half of all black staffers hired by the UAW, and customarily supplied Local 600 with one of its top officers. Foundryman Shelton Tappes, a 1936 migrant from Alabama, helped negotiate a then-unique antidiscrimination clause into the first UAW-Ford contract and went on to serve as recording secretary of the 60,000-member local in the mid-1940s.[27]

The Rouge was also a center of Communist Party strength in Detroit. The radical tradition there had remained unbroken since World War I, when the Industrial Workers of the World and other radical union groups had briefly flourished. Skilled workers from northern Europe had provided most members during the difficult interwar years, but after 1941 the party recruited heavily among blacks, and at its peak in the late 1940s it enrolled

450 workers, almost half from the foundry. The Rouge was one of the few workplaces in the country where Communists, black or white, could proclaim their political allegiance without immediate persecution. As late as 1948, Nelson Davis, the black Communist elected vice president of the 9,000-man Rouge foundry unit within Local 600, sold several hundred subscriptions to the *Daily Worker* every year. But even here, Communist influence among black workers rested on the party's identification with civil rights issues; indeed, many blacks saw the party's foundry department "club" as little more than a militant race organization.[28]

With almost 100,000 black workers organized in the Detroit area, black union activists played a central role in the civil rights struggle. They demanded the hiring and promotion of black workers in metropolitan war plants, poured into the Detroit NAACP chapter, and mobilized thousands to defend black occupancy of the Sojourner Truth Homes, a federally funded project that became a violent center of conflict between white neighborhood groups and the housing-starved black community. In those efforts, black activists encountered enormous resistance not only from plant management and the Detroit political elite, but also from white workers, midlevel union leaders under direct pressure from white constituents, and conservatives in the black community. But as in the civil rights movement of the early 1960s, black militants held the political initiative, so that powerful white elites—the top officeholders in the UAW, company personnel officers, and the government officials who staffed the War Labor Board and War Manpower Commission—had to yield before this new wave of civil rights militancy.[29]

As in Winston-Salem, mass unionization transformed the character of the black community's traditional race advancement organizations. Under pressure from Local 600 leaders like Tappes, Horace Sheffield (his rival for leadership of the foundry), and the pro-union minister Charles Hill, the NAACP and the Urban League became more militant and activist. Black community leadership still came largely from traditional strata—lawyers, ministers, doctors, and teachers—but the union upsurge reshaped the protest agenda and opened the door to new forms of mass struggle. The NAACP itself underwent a remarkable transformation. In the successful effort to keep the Sojourner Truth housing project open to blacks, NAACP officials had for the first time worked closely with the UAW militants who organized the demonstrations and protests that forestalled city or federal capitulation to the white neighborhood groups that fought black occupancy. That mobilization in turn energized the local NAACP, as almost 20,000 new members joined, making the Detroit branch by far the largest in the nation. Black workers poured in from the region's recently unionized foundries, tire plants, and converted auto/aircraft facilities, and from city government, streetcar lines, restaurants, and retail stores.[30]

By 1943, the Detroit NAACP was one of the most working-class chapters in the country. Its new labor committee, the largest and most active group in the branch, served as a forum for black workers to air their grievances and as a pressure group, urging companies and the government to advance black job rights. With UAW support, the labor committee sponsored an April 1943 march and rally that brought 10,000 to Cadillac Square to demand that managers open war-industry jobs to thousands of still-unemployed black women in the region. Although the NAACP old guard repulsed a direct electoral challenge from UAW members and their sympathizers, the chapter added two unionists to its executive board and backed protest campaigns largely shaped by UAW militants: mass rallies, picket lines, and big lobbying delegations to city hall, Lansing, and Washington. By the end of the war, the ministerial leadership of the black community was in eclipse. Horace White, a Congregational minister, admitted, "The CIO has usurped moral leadership in the [Negro] community."[31]

On the shop floor, black workers sought to break out of traditional job ghettos in the foundry and janitorial service, precipitating a series of explosive "hate" strikes as white workers walked off the job to stop the integration of black workers into formerly all-white departments. The strikes were almost always failures, however, not only because federal officials and UAW leaders quickly mobilized to cut them off, but also because they failed to intimidate most black workers. During the war there were probably as many demonstrations and protest strikes led by black workers as racially inspired white walkouts.[32] For example, at Packard, scene of one of the most infamous hate strikes of the war, black workers eventually triumphed over white recalcitrance. A racialist personnel manager, a divided union leadership, and a heavily southern workforce heightened racial tensions and precipitated several white stoppages that culminated in June 1943 when more than 25,000 whites quit work to prevent the transfer of three blacks into an all-white department. But black workers were also active. Under the leadership of foundryman Christopher Alston, a Young Communist League member, they had earlier shut down the foundry to demand that union leaders take more forceful action against recalcitrant whites; and in the months after the big wildcat hate strike, those same blacks conducted strikes and protests that kept the attention of federal officials and local union leaders focused on their problems. Their militancy paid off; by the end of 1943 about 500 blacks had moved out of the Packard foundry and into previously all-white production jobs.[33]

Although newly assertive second-generation Poles and Hungarians had come to see their jobs and neighborhoods as under attack from the equally militant black community, top UAW officials championed civil rights during the war. In the aftermath of the great Detroit race riot of 1943, in which the police and roving bands of whites killed twenty-five blacks, the UAW stood out as the only predominantly white institution to defend the black community and denounce police brutality. During the hate strikes, UAW leaders often sought the protection of a War Labor Board back-to-work order to deflect white rank-and-file anger onto the government and away from themselves. But officials like UAW vice president Walter Reuther made it clear that "the UAW-CIO would tell any worker that refused to work with a colored worker that he could leave the plant because he did not belong there."[34]

Intraunion competition for black political support encouraged white UAW officials to put civil rights issues high on their agenda. During the 1940s, black staffers and local union activists participated in an informal caucus that agitated for more black representatives in the union hierarchy and more effort to upgrade black workers in the auto shops. Initially chaired by Shelton Tappes of Local 600, the group was reorganized and strengthened by George Crockett, an FEPC lawyer the UAW hired to head its own Fair Employment Practices Committee in 1944. The overwhelming majority of UAW blacks, however, backed the caucus led by Secretary-Treasurer George Addes and Vice President Richard Frankensteen, in which Communists played an influential role. The Addes-Frankensteen caucus endorsed the symbolically crucial demand for a Negro seat on the UAW executive board and generally supported black-white slates in local union elections. The other major UAW faction was led by Walter Reuther and a coterie of ex-socialists and Catholics, whose own internal union support came from workers in the General Motors plants (Flint and Western Michigan), in the South, and in the aircraft fabricating facilities of the East and Midwest. Support for Reuther's faction was particularly strong among the more assimilated Catholics and Appalachian whites in northern industry. Reuther denounced proposals for a black executive board seat as "reverse Jim Crow," but his group also advocated civil rights, not so much because they expected to win black political support, but because the rapid growth of a quasiautonomous black movement had made militancy on civil rights the sine qua non of serious political leadership in the UAW.[35]

A Moment of Opportunity

By the mid-1940s, civil rights issues had reached a level of national political salience that they would not regain for another fifteen years. Once the domain of Afro-American protest groups, leftist clergymen, and Communist-led unions and front organizations, civil rights advocacy was becoming a defining characteristic of urban liberalism. Thus ten states established fair employment practice commissions between 1945 and 1950, and four major cities—Chicago, Milwaukee, Minneapolis, and Philadelphia—enacted tough laws against job bias. Backed by the CIO, the Americans for Democratic Action spearheaded a successful effort to strengthen the Democratic Party's civil rights plank at the 1948 convention.[36]

In the South, the labor movement seemed on the verge of a major breakthrough. *Fortune* magazine predicted that the CIO's "Operation Dixie" would soon organize key southern industries like textiles. Black workers proved exceptionally responsive to such union campaigns, especially in industries like lumber, furniture, and tobacco, where they were sometimes a majority of the workforce. Between 1944 and 1946, the CIO's political action apparatus helped elect liberal congressmen and senators in a few southern states, and organizations that promoted interracial cooperation, such as the Southern Conference for Human Welfare and the Highlander Folk School, experienced their most rapid growth and greatest effectiveness in 1946 and 1947.[37]

The opportune moment soon passed. Thereafter, a decade-long decline in working-class black activism destroyed the organizational coherence and ideological élan of the labor-based civil rights movement. That defeat has been largely obscured by the brilliant legal victories won by civil rights lawyers in the 1940s and 1950s, and by the reemergence of a new mass movement in the next decade. But in Winston-Salem, Detroit, and other industrial regions, the time had passed when unionized black labor was in the vanguard of the freedom struggle. Three elements contributed to the decline. First, the employer offensive of the late 1940s put all labor on the defensive. Conservatives used the Communist issue to attack New Deal and Fair Deal reforms, a strategy that isolated Communist-oriented black leaders and helped destroy what was left of the Popular Front. The employers' campaign proved particularly effective against many recently organized CIO locals with disproportionate numbers of black members. Meanwhile, mechanization and decentralization of the most labor-intensive and heavily black production facilities sapped the self-confidence of the black working class and contributed to high rates of urban unemployment in the years after the Korean War.

Second, the most characteristic institutions of American liberalism, including the unions, race advancement organizations, and liberal advocacy organizations, adopted a legal-administrative, if not a bureaucratic, approach to winning citizenship rights for blacks. The major legislative goal of the union-backed Leadership Conference on Civil Rights in the 1950s was revision of Senate Rule 22, to limit the use of the filibuster that had long blocked passage of a national FEPC and other civil rights legislation. The UAW and other big unions cooperated with the NAACP in the effort, but the work was slow and frustrating and the struggle far removed from the shop floor or the drugstore lunch counter.[38]

Finally, the routinization of the postwar industrial relations system precluded efforts by black workers to mobilize a constituency independent of the leadership. Focusing on incremental collective-bargaining gains and committed to social change only if it was well controlled, the big unions became less responsive to the particular interests of their black members. By 1960, blacks had formed oppositional movements in several old CIO unions, but they now encountered resistance to their demands not only from much of the white rank and file, but also from union leaders who presided over institutions that had accommodated themselves to much of the industrial status quo.[39]

Postwar Reaction: Winston-Salem

Like most labor-intensive southern employers, R. J. Reynolds never reached an accommodation with union labor, although it signed contracts with Local 22 in 1945 and 1946. Minimum-wage laws and collective-bargaining agreements had greatly increased costs of production, especially in the stemmeries, and the black women employed there were the heart and soul of the union. Soon after the war, the company began a mechanization campaign that eliminated several predominantly black departments. When the factories closed for Christmas in 1945, new stemming machines installed in one plant displaced over 700 black women. The union proposed a "share the work plan," but the company was determined to cut its workforce and change its racial composition by recruiting white workers from surrounding counties. The black proportion of the manufacturing labor force in Winston-Salem dropped from 44 to 36 percent between 1940 and 1960.[40]

The technological offensive undermined union strength, but by itself Reynolds could not destroy Local 22. When contract negotiations began in 1947, the company rejected union demands for a wage increase patterned after those won in steel, auto, and rubber earlier in the spring. Somewhat reluctantly, Local 22 called a strike on May 1. Black workers and virtually all of the Negro community solidly backed the union, which held out for thirty-eight days until a compromise settlement was reached. But, in a pattern replicated throughout industrial America in those years, Communist influence within the union became the key issue around which management and its allies mounted their attack. The *Winston-Salem Journal* soon denounced Local 22 as "captured . . . lock, stock and barrel" by the Communist Party, warning readers that the strike would lead to "open rioting." This exposé brought Local 22 officers under the scrutiny of the House Committee on Un-American Activities (HUAC), which held a highly publicized hearing on the Winston-Salem situation in the summer of 1947.[41]

Communist Party members contributed to the volatility of the situation. In the late 1940s, Local 22 found itself politically vulnerable when foreign-policy resolutions passed by the shop stewards' council followed Communist Party pronouncements. The party's insistence on the promotion of blacks into public leadership positions sometimes put workers with little formal education into union leadership jobs they could not handle. Moreover, the party's obsession with "white chauvinism" backfired. After the 1947 strike, Local 22 made a concerted effort to recruit white workers. Some young veterans joined the local, although the union allowed most to pay their dues secretly.[42] The party objected, remembered North Carolina leader Junius Scales: "'If they got any guts,' they would say, 'let them stand up and fight,' not realizing, as many black workers and union leaders realized, that for a white worker to just *belong* to a predominantly black union at that time was an act of great courage."[43]

With its workforce increasingly polarized along racial and political lines, Reynolds renewed its offensive in the spring of 1948. Black workers remained remarkably loyal to the union leadership, but the anticommunist campaign had turned most white employees against the union and eroded support among blacks not directly involved in the conflict. The company refused to negotiate with Local 22 on the grounds that the union had not complied with the new Taft-Hartley Act. The law required union officers to sign an affidavit swearing they were not members of the Communist Party before a union could be certified as a bargaining agent by the NLRB. Initially, all the CIO internationals had refused to sign the affidavits, but by 1948 only Communist-oriented unions such as FTA still held out. When Reynolds proved intransigent, there was little the union could do. FTA had no standing with the NLRB, and it was too weak to win another strike.[44]

At the same time, Local 22 began to feel repercussions from the conflict within the CIO over the status of unions, like the FTA, that had rejected the Marshall Plan and endorsed Henry Wallace's Progressive Party presidential campaign in 1948. A rival CIO union, the United Transport Service Employees (UTSE), sent organizers into Winston-Salem to persuade black workers to abandon Local 22. In a March 1950 NLRB election, which the FTA requested after complying with the Taft-Hartley Act, UTSE joined Local 22 on the ballot. The FTA local retained solid support among its black constituency, who faithfully paid dues to their stewards even after the contract had expired and in the face of condemnation of their union—from the company, the CIO, and HUAC. Even the black community leader Alderman Williams asked workers to vote against the union and "send the Communists away for good." Yet Local 22 captured a plurality of all the votes cast, and in a runoff two weeks later, it won outright. But when the NLRB accepted the ballots of lower-level white supervisors, the scales again tipped against the local.[45]

Local 22 disappeared from Winston-Salem's political and economic life, and a far more accommodative black community leadership filled the void left by the union's defeat. Beginning in the mid-1940s, a coalition of middle-class blacks and white business moderates had sought to counter the growing union influence within the black community. They requested a study of local race relations by the National Urban League's Community Relations Project (CRP). Largely financed by Hanes Hosiery president James G. Hanes, the CRP study appeared in late 1947 and called for improved health, education, and recreational facilities, but it made no mention of workplace issues. The Urban League foresaw a cautious, "step by step approach" and proposed that an advisory committee drawn from the black middle class discuss community issues with their white counterparts and help city officials and white philanthropists channel welfare services to the black community. The *Winston-Salem Journal* called the CRP's recommendations a "blueprint for better community relations" but one that would not alter "the framework of race relations."[46]

The Urban League's program helped make Winston-Salem a model of racial moderation. Blacks continued to register and vote in relatively high numbers and to elect a single black alderman. The city high school was integrated without incident in 1957, while Winston-Salem desegregated its libraries, golf course, coliseum, and police and fire departments. But the dynamic and democratic quality of the black struggle in Winston-Salem would never be recaptured. NAACP membership declined to less than 500 in the early 1950s, and decision making once again moved behind closed doors. When a grievance arose from the black community, a group of ministers met quietly with Hanes; a few phone calls by the white industrialist led to desegregation of the privately owned bus company in 1958.[47]

A similar story unfolded in the plants of the R. J. Reynolds Tobacco Company. After the destruction of Local 22, the company blacklisted several leading union activists, yet Reynolds continued to abide by many of the wage standards, benefit provisions, and seniority policies negotiated during the union era. The company reorganized its personnel department; rationalized procedures for hiring, firing, and evaluating employees; and upgraded its supervisory force by weeding out old-timers and replacing them with college-educated foremen. To forestall union activity, Reynolds kept its wages slightly ahead of the rates paid by its unionized competitors.[48]

In February 1960, when sit-ins began at segregated Winston-Salem lunch counters, the voices of black protest were again heard in the city's streets. But the generation of blacks who had sustained Local 22 played little role in the new mobilization. College and high school students predominated on the picket lines and in the new protest organizations that confronted white paternalism and challenged the black community's ministerial leadership. NAACP membership rose once again; more radical blacks organized a chapter of the Congress of Racial Equality (CORE). Public segregation soon collapsed.[49]

The subsequent trajectory of the freedom struggle in Winston-Salem was typical of that in many black communities. Heightened racial tensions set the stage for a 1967 riot and a burst of radicalism, followed by the demobilization of the protest movement and years of trench warfare in the city council. The political career of Larry Little, the son of Reynolds workers who had been members of Local 22, highlighted the contrasts between the two generations of black activists. Little moved from leadership of the North Carolina Black Panther Party in 1969 to the position of city alderman in 1977, but despite the radicalism of his rhetoric, crucial issues of economic security and workplace democracy were not restored to the political agenda in Winston-Salem. Because black activists of his generation confronted the city's white elite without the organized backing of a lively mass institution like Local 22, their challenge proved more episodic and less effective than that of the previous generation.[50]

The Limits of Liberalism in Postwar Detroit

A similar demobilization took place in Detroit after the war. There the union, as well as the companies, helped undermine the independent working-class base black activists had built in the six years since UAW organization of the Ford Motor Company. Racial issues were not of primary importance in the factional conflict of 1946 and 1947 that brought Walter Reuther to the presidency of the UAW. The victory of his caucus was based both on rank-and-file endorsement of Reuther's bold social vision, especially as exemplified in the General Motors strike of 1945–46, and in the Reuther group's anticommunism, which struck an increasingly responsive chord after passage of the Taft-Hartley Act.[51] Nevertheless, the Reuther victory greatly diminished black influence and independence within the UAW and the liberal-labor community in which the union played such an important role. Reuther was as racially egalitarian as his opponents, but the political logic of his bitterly contested victory—he won less than 10 percent of black delegate votes in 1946—meant that Reuther owed no organizational debt to the growing proportion of union members who were black.

When the Reuther group consolidated their control of the union in 1947, there was a large turnover in the Negro UAW staff. Blacks with ties to the opposition, such as John Conyers Sr. and William Hardin, two of the first black staffers, and the articulate lawyer George Crockett, the de facto leader of the UAW's black caucus, were ousted from their posts. The young dynamo Coleman Young lost his job with the Wayne County CIO council. Tappes was hired as a UAW international representative in the early 1950s, but only after he had broken with the Communists and lost his base of support in the Rouge plant.[52]

During the 1950s and 1960s, the Reuther group understood that civil rights was a litmus test of labor liberalism. Reuther sat on the board of directors of the NAACP, and the UAW probably contributed more funds to that organization than all other trade unions combined. The UAW also proved a ready source of emergency funds for the Montgomery Improvement Association, the Southern Christian Leadership Conference (SCLC), and Students for a Democratic Society's early community organizing activities. Reuther was outraged that the AFL-CIO did not endorse the 1963 March on Washington; his union had provided much of the early funding, and he would be the most prominent white to speak at the interracial gathering.[53]

Reuther also maintained a high profile on civil rights issues within the UAW. As president, he appointed himself codirector of the union's Fair Employment Practices Department (FEPD) and used the FEPD post to denounce racial discrimination and identify himself with postwar civil rights issues. Reuther pushed for a fair employment practices bill in Michigan and led the successful UAW effort to integrate the American Bowling Congress. During the crucial months after he had won the UAW presidency, but before his caucus had consolidated control of the union, such activism helped defuse black opposition; when Reuther was reelected in 1947, he won about half of all black delegate votes.[54]

Despite this public, and well-publicized, appearance, the emergence of a more stable postwar brand of unionism undermined civil rights activism in the UAW. As in many unions, the Reuther regime sought to eliminate or to coopt potentially dissident centers of political power. Local 600 was such a center of opposition, where black unionists still within the Communist orbit continued to play an influential, if somewhat muted, role well into the 1950s. Immediately after the 1952 HUAC hearings in Detroit, which publicized the continuing presence of Communists in Local 600, the UAW

International Executive Board put the huge local under its direct administration. Six months later, tens of thousands of Rouge workers reelected their old officers, but the influence and independence of the giant local nevertheless waned in the next few years. Leaders of the UAW defused much of the local's oppositional character by appointing many of its key leaders, including Tappes and Sheffield, to the national union staff.

Equally important, Ford's postwar automation and decentralization slashed the Rouge workforce in half, eliminating the predominantly black production foundry. The same phenomenon was taking place in many of Detroit's other highly unionized production facilities, so that by the late 1960s a ring of relatively small and mainly white manufacturing facilities surrounded Detroit's million-plus black population. Meanwhile, high levels of black unemployment became a permanent feature of the urban landscape after the 1957–58 recession. Not unexpectedly, the size and social influence of the unionized black working class ceased to grow, although this stagnation was masked by the militance of inner-city minority youth late in the 1960s.[55]

The UAW's Fair Employment Practices Department also defused civil rights activism in the union. After 1946. the department was led by William Oliver, a black foundryman from Ford's Highland Park factory. Unlike the politicized blacks from the Rouge, Oliver had no large reservoir of political support in the UAW, nor did he attempt to build one. During Oliver's tenure, the FEPD had a dual role: it represented the UAW to the national civil rights community, the NAACP, the Urban League, and the more liberal federal agencies and congressmen; and it processed discrimination complaints as they percolated up from black workers in the locals. Rather than serve as an organizing center for UAW blacks, the FEPD bureaucratized the union's civil rights activities. "We are a fire station," admitted Tappes, who served in the department during the 1950s and 1960s, "and when the bell rings we run to put out the fire."[56]

A UAW retreat from civil rights militancy also became evident in politics. From 1937 to 1949, the UAW sought to reshape Detroit's formally "nonpartisan" electoral politics along interracial class lines. Thus in 1945 and 1949, Richard Frankensteen and George Edwards, both former UAW leaders, fought mayoral campaigns that helped move integrated housing and police brutality to the center of local political debate. Both were defeated by conservative incumbents, but their labor-oriented campaigns nevertheless provided a focus around which civil rights forces could mobilize. However, after the CIO's "bitterest political defeat in the motor city," in 1949, the UAW ceased to expend its political capital in what many of its leaders now considered fruitless campaigns to take over city hall. The UAW continued to back the liberal governor G. Mennen Williams, but in the city proper, the union made peace with conservatives like Albert Cobo and Louis Miriani, who had built much of their political base on segregationist homeowner movements.[57]

Neither the Communist Party nor the NAACP was able to fill the void opened up by the UAW default. In the early 1950s, many erstwhile leaders of the union's black caucus joined the Detroit Negro Labor Council (NLC), a Communist front organization. But the NLC faced relentless pressure from the NAACP, HUAC, and the UAW, which denounced the council as a "Communist-dominated, dual unionist organization which has as its sole objective the disruption and wrecking of the American labor movement."[58] Both the UAW and the NAACP made exclusion of Communists from civil rights coalition work a high priority in the early 1950s, and the NLC dissolved in 1956. The NAACP, of course, maintained a cordial relationship with the UAW, but it also declined in postwar Detroit. After reaching a wartime peak of 24,000 in 1944, membership dropped to 6,000 in 1950, when there was much discussion of the need to "rehabilitate" what had once been the organization's largest unit. In the early 1950s, national NAACP membership also fell to less than half its wartime level.[59]

When civil rights reemerged as a major issue in union and city politics in the late 1950s, the Reuther leadership often found its interests counterposed to the forces mobilized by the freedom movement of that era. By 1960, Detroit's population was about 30 percent black, and upward of a quarter of all auto workers were Mexican or black. At the Rouge plant, between 50 and 60 percent of production workers were nonwhite.[60]

Reuther's mode of civil rights advocacy seemed increasingly inadequate as the fears and conflicts of the early Cold War era receded. Two issues seemed particularly egregious. First, black participation in UAW skilled trades apprenticeship programs stood at minuscule levels, 1 percent or less. Second, no black sat on the UAW executive board, although blacks had been demanding that symbolically important post in UAW convention debates since the early 1940s. Failure to make progress on those problems genuinely embarrassed white UAW leaders, but Reuther and his colleagues were trapped by the regime over which they presided. Reuther hesitated to take on the militant and well-organized skilled trades, then in the midst of a long-simmering craft rebellion against the UAW's industrial unionism. Nor could a black be easily placed on the UAW executive board. In no UAW region did blacks command a majority of all workers; moreover, Reuther loyalists held all existing posts. Creating a new executive board slot seemed the only alternative, but that would dilute the power of existing board members and flatly repudiate Reuther's long-standing opposition to a specifically black seat on the executive board.[61]

In this context, and in the immediate aftermath of the Montgomery Bus Boycott, an independent black protest movement reemerged in Detroit politics with the founding of the Trade Union Leadership Council (TULC) in 1957. Initially, TULC was little more than a caucus of UAW black staffers, but under the leadership of Horace Sheffield, the organization challenged Reutherite hegemony. Despite the UAW's good reputation, Sheffield explained in 1960, a black-led organization was needed because "the liberal white trade unionists had long been 'mothballed,' . . . by the extensive growth of 'business unionism.'"[62] TULC opened a new chapter in Detroit politics in the 1961 mayoralty race. The incumbent mayor, Miriani, had the support of virtually all elements of the Detroit power structure, including the UAW, but he was hated by most blacks and not a few whites because of his defense of Detroit's increasingly brutal and racist police department. Sheffield used the mayoral campaign of Jerome Cavanagh, a young liberal lawyer, to establish his own network among Detroit's black trade union officials and make the TULC a mass organization of more than 7,000 members in 1962 and 1963. Thereafter, a number of black activists whose political roots went back to the anti-Reuther forces of the 1940s won elective office, sometimes over bitter UAW protest. They included John Conyers Jr., who took Detroit's second black congressional seat in 1964; George Crockett, who won election as Recorders Court judge in 1966 and later went on to Congress; and Coleman Young, who became mayor in 1973.[63]

TULC proved less successful in remolding UAW politics. The organization's mushroom growth, combined with the growth of the civil rights movement, forced the UAW to put a black on its executive board in 1962. But for this position the Reuther leadership chose none of the blacks prominently associated with TULC militancy, but instead the relatively little-known Nelson Jack Edwards, a black staff representative. Although black appointments to the UAW staff increased markedly in the 1960s, TULC failed to generate a mass movement among rank-and-file black workers. TULC represented the generation of black activists politicized in the 1940s, but many had spent the intervening years on union staffs or in local office, so they no longer enjoyed an organic link with the younger black militants who were flooding into Detroit's auto shops.[64]

When the Dodge Revolutionary Union Movement (DRUM) and other black insurgencies swept through the auto industry in the late 1960s, the new generation had come to see UAW liberalism as indistinguishable from corporate conservatism. They were mistaken, but in 1968, that year of great expectations and smashed hopes, such distinctions seemed beside the point. Many TULC veterans found DRUM's wholesale condemnation of the UAW irresponsible, while the young militants thought their elders merely a reformist wing of Reuther's union leadership. A reported exchange conveys DRUM members' impatience with TULC veterans' loyalty to the union. Shelton Tappes is said to have told a group of black Chrysler workers who had been fired for staging an outlaw strike and were picketing Solidarity House, the UAW's official home: "If the TULC had done what it was organized for there wouldn't be any such development as DRUM." And one of the young pickets reportedly answered, "And if Reuther and the other bureaucrats had done what the *union* was organized for, there wouldn't have been any need for TULC."[65]

Conclusion

E. P. Thompson once asserted that most social movements have a life cycle of about six years. And unless they make a decisive political impact in that time, that "window of opportunity," they will have little effect on the larger political structures they hope to transform.[66] For the black freedom struggle, the mid-1940s offered such a time of opportunity, when a high-wage, high-employment economy, rapid unionization, and a pervasive federal presence gave the black working class remarkable self-confidence, which established the framework for the growth of an autonomous labor-oriented civil rights movement. The narrowing of public discourse in the early Cold War era contributed largely to the defeat and diffusion of that movement. The rise of anticommunism shattered the Popular Front coalition on civil rights, while the retreat and containment of the union movement deprived black activists of the political and social space necessary to carry on an independent struggle.

The disintegration of the black movement in the late 1940s ensured that when the civil rights struggle of the 1960s emerged, it would have a different social character and an alternative political agenda, which eventually proved inadequate to the immense social problems that lay before it. Like the movement of the 1940s, the protests of the 1960s mobilized a black community that was overwhelmingly working class. However, the key institutions of the new movement were not the trade unions, but the black church and independent protest organizations. Its community orientation and stirring championship of democratic values gave the modern civil rights movement a transcendent moral power that enabled a handful of organizers from groups like the Student Nonviolent Coordinating Committee, SCLC, and CORE to mobilize tens of thousands of Americans in a series of dramatic and crucial struggles. Yet even as this Second Reconstruction abolished legal segregation and discrimination, many movement activists, including Martin Luther King Jr., recognized the limits of their accomplishment. After 1965, they sought to raise issues of economic equality and working-class empowerment to the moral high ground earlier occupied by the assault against de jure segregation.[67] In retrospect, we can see how greatly they were handicapped by their inability to seize the opportunities a very different sort of civil rights movement found and lost twenty years before.

Notes

The authors wish to thank Eileen Boris, William Chafe, Charles Eagles, Sara Evans, Jacquelyn Hall, Alice Kessler-Harris, Steven Lawson, Susan Levine, Leslie Rowland, Harvard Sirkoff, David Thelen, Seth Wigderson, and several readers for the *Journal of American History* for their helpful comments.

This essay first appeared in the *Journal of American History*, 75.3 (Dec. 1988), 786–811. Copyright © Organization of American Historians. Reprinted with permission.

1. Richard M. Dalfiume, "The 'Forgotten Years' of the Negro Revolution," *Journal of American History*, 55 (June 1968), 90–106; Steven Lawson, "The Second Front at Home: World War II and Black Americans," paper delivered at the Sixth Soviet-American Historians Colloquium, Sept. 24–26, 1986, Washington (in Nelson Lichtenstein's possession). This view has recently been reinforced by the television documentary *Eyes on the Prize*, which begins abruptly in 1954. Juan Williams, *Eyes on the Prize: America's Civil Rights Years, 1954–1965* (New York, 1986). However, a few sociologists have broken with the orthodox periodization: Aldon Morris, *The Origins of the Civil Rights Movement Black Communities Organizing for Change* (New York, 1984); and Jack Bloom, *Class, Race and the Civil Rights Movement* (Bloomington, 1987).

2. Harold M. Baron and Bennett Rymer, "The Negro in the Chicago Labor Market," in *The Negro in the American Labor Movement*, ed. Julius Jacobson (New York, 1968), 188. See also Gavin Wright, *Old South, New South: Revolutions in the Southern Economy since the Civil War* (New York, 1986), 239–57. For a discussion of black proletarianization, see Joe William Trotter Jr., *Black Milwaukee: The Making of an Industrial Proletariat, 1915–1945* (Urbana, 1985); Steven Lawson, *Black Ballots: Voting Rights in the South, 1944–1969* (New York, 1975), 134; Henry Lee Moon, *Balance of Power: The Negro Vote* (Garden City, 1949), 146–96; and Dalfiume, "'Forgotten Years,'" 99–100.

3. Dalfiume, "'Forgotten Years,'" 100; Harold Preece, "The South Stirs," *Crisis*, 48 (Oct. 1941), 318.

4. James A. Gross, *The Reshaping of the National Labor Relations Board: National Labor Policy in Transition, 1937–1947* (Albany, 1981), 5–41; Gary Gerstle, "The Politics of Patriotism: Americanization and the Formation of the CIO," *Dissent*, 33 (Winter 1986), 84–92. Racist discrimination in hiring, promotion, and seniority were hardly eliminated by the new CIO unions; see Robert Norrell, "Caste in Steel: Jim Crow Careers in Birmingham, Alabama," *Journal of American History*, 73 (Dec. 1986), 669–701.

5. Herbert R. Garfinkel, *When Negroes March: The March on Washington Movement in the Organizational Politics of FEPC* (Glencoe, 1959); Louis Kesselman, *The Social Politics*

of FEPC: A Study in Reform Pressure Movements (Chapel Hill, 1948); William Harris, "Federal Intervention in Union Discrimination: FEPC and West Coast Shipyards during World War II," *Labor History*, 22 (Summer 1981), 325–47.

6. Horace Huntley, "Iron Ore Miners and Mine Mill in Alabama: 1933–1952" (Ph.D. diss., University of Pittsburgh, 1977); Michael Honey, "Labor and Civil Rights in the South: The Industrial Labor Movement and Black Workers in Memphis, 1929–1945" (Ph.D. diss., Northern Illinois University, 1987), 422–75; Nell Irvin Painter, *The Narrative of Hosea Hudson: His Life as a Negro Communist in the South* (Cambridge, Mass., 1979); Rick Halpern, "Black and White, Unite and Fight: The United Packinghouse Workers' Struggle against Racism," paper delivered at the North American Labor History Conference, Oct. 1985, Detroit (in Lichtenstein's possession); Dennis C. Dickerson, "Fighting on the Domestic Front: Black Steelworkers during World War II," in *Life and Labor: Dimensions of American Working-Class History*, ed. Charles Stephenson and Robert Asher (Albany, 1986), 224–36; Toni Gilpin, "Left by Themselves: A History of United Farm Equipment and Metal Workers, 1938–1955" (draft, Ph.D diss., Yale University, 1988, in Toni Gilpin's possession).

7. Nannie M. Tilley, *The Bright-Tobacco Industry, 1860–1929* (Chapel Hill, 1948); Nannie M. Tilley, *The R. J. Reynolds Tobacco Company* (Chapel Hill, 1985).

8. Robert Korstad, "Those Who Were Not Afraid: Winston-Salem, 1943," in *Working Lives: The Southern Exposure History of Labor in the South*, ed. Marc Miller (New York, 1980), 184–99; and Robert Korstad, "Daybreak of Freedom: Tobacco Workers and the CIO, Winston-Salem, North Carolina, 1943–1950" (Ph.D. diss., University of North Carolina, Chapel Hill, 1987), 2–50; Tilley, *R. J Reynolds Tobacco Company*, 373–414.

9. *Winston-Salem Journal*, July 14, 1943, p. 6, July 25, 1943, p. 6; Horace R. Caron and George S. Mitchell, *Black Workers and the New Unions* (Chapel Hill, 1939), 372–424.

10. *Winston-Salem Journal*, July 14, 1943, p. 6, July 16, 1943, p. 6, July 17, 1943, p. 6, July 25, 1943, p. 6.

11. Robert A. Levert to David C. Shaw, Aug. 22, 1944, in R. J. Reynolds Tobacco Company, Case 5–C-1730 (1945), Formal and Informal Unfair Labor Practices and Representation Cases Files, 1935–48, National Labor Relations Board, RG 25 (National Archives); *Winston-Salem Journal*, Nov. 17, 1943, p. 1.

12. "Directive Order, R. J. Reynolds Tobacco Company and the Tobacco Workers Organizing Committee," Oct. 18, 1944, Case No. 111–7701–D, Regional War Labor Board for the Fourth Region, RG 202 (National Archives).

13. "Discussion Outline for Classes in Shop Steward Training," Highlander Folk School, n.d. (in Robert Korstad's possession); Velma Hopkins interview by Robert Korstad, March 5, 1986, ibid.

14. Ruby Jones interview by Korstad, April 20, 1979, ibid.

15. *Worker's Voice*, Aug. 1944, Jan. 1945, p. 2, April 1945, p. 2; Viola Brown interview by Korstad, Aug. 7, 1981 (in Korstad's possession). The United Cannery, Agricultural, Packing and Allied Workers of America (UCAPAWA) changed its name to reflect the increasing number of tobacco locals within it.

16. Junius Scales interview by Korstad, April 28, 1987 (in Korstad's possession); Ann Matthews interview by Korstad, Feb. 1986, ibid. See also Junius Irving Scales and Richard Nickson, *Cause at Heart: A Former Communist Remembers* (Atlanta, 1987), 201–19; and Robin D. G. Kelley, "Hammer N' Hoe: Black Radicals and the Commu-

nist Party in Alabama, 1929–1941" (Ph.D. diss., University of California, Los Angeles, 1987), 296–311.

17. Roger Keeran, *The Communist Party and the Auto Workers Unions* (Bloomington, 1980), 234; Painter, *Narrative of Hosea Hudson*, 306–12; Nat Ross, "Two Years of the Reconstituted Communist Party in the South," *Political Affairs*, 26 (Oct. 1947), 923–35; Wilson Record, *Race and Radicalism: The NAACP and the Communist Party in Conflict* (Ithaca, 1964), 84–168; Irving Howe and B. J. Widick. *The UAW and Walter Reuther* (New York, 1949), 223–25.

18. Saul Wellman interview by Lichtenstein, Nov. 10, 1983 (in Lichtenstein's possession); Mark Naison, *The Communist Party in Harlem* (Urbana, 1984), 23–34.

19. William H. Chafe, *Civilities and Civil Rights: Greensboro, North Carolina, and the Black Struggle for Freedom* (New York, 1980), 29–30; Lucille Black to Sarah March, March 28, 1945; Winston-Salem, 1945–55, file, box C140, National Association for the Advancement of Colored People Papers (Manuscripts Division, Library of Congress): Gloster Current to C. C. Kellum, Nov. 19, 1947, ibid.; Memorandum, Feb. 9, 1942, North Carolina State Conference file, box C141, ibid.; Membership Report, July 31, 1946, ibid.

20. *UCAPAWA News*, Aug. 1, 1944, p. 2., Sept. 1, 1944, p. 5; *Worker's Voice*, Oct. 1944, p. 3, March 1946, p. 4. For politics in the preunion era, see Bertha Hampton Miller, "Blacks in Winston-Salem, North Carolina, 1895–1920: Community Development in an Era of Benevolent Paternalism" (Ph.D. diss., Duke University, 1981), 6–74; *Worker's Voice*, Oct. 1944, p. 3.

21. *Pittsburgh Courier*, June 3, 1944.

22. Board of Aldermen, Winston-Salem, North Carolina, Minutes, vol. 30, p. 278 (City Hall, Winston-Salem, N.C.); ibid., vol. 32, p. 555.

23. Herbert R. Northrup, *Organized Labor and the Negro* (New York, 1944), 186–88; August Meier and Elliott Rudwick, *Black Detroit and the Rise of the UAW* (New York, 1979), 3–7.

24. Meier and Rudwick, *Black Detroit*, 8–22.

25. Ibid., 39–87.

26. Shelton Tappes interview by Herbert Hill, Oct. 27, 1967, Feb. 10, 1968 (Archives of Labor History and Urban Affairs, Wayne State University, Detroit, Mich.).

27. Robert Robinson interview by Lichtenstein, Oct. 9, 1983 (in Lichtenstein's possession); Ed Lock interview by Peter Friedlander, Dec. 1976, ibid.; Walter Dorsch interview by Lichtenstein, Oct. 14, 1982, ibid.; Meier and Rudwick, *Black Detroit*, 106–7.

28. Wellman interview; Paul Boatin interview by Lichtenstein, Oct. 12, 1982 (in Lichtenstein's possession); Keenan, *Communist Party and the Auto Workers Unions*, 33–67; U.S. Congress, House Committee on Un-American Activities, *Communism in the Detroit Area*, 82 Cong., 2 sess., March 10–11, 1952, pp. 3036–45, 3117–35.

29. Meier and Rudwick, *Black Detroit*, 175–206; Alan Clive, *State of War: Michigan in World War II* (Ann Arbor, 1979), 144–51.

30. "20,000 Members in 1943," *Crisis*, 50 (May 1943), 140–41; Dominic J. Capeci Jr., *Race Relations in Wartime Detroit: The Sojourner Truth Housing Controversy of 1942* (Philadelphia, 1984), 75–99, 111–13.

31. "20,000 Members in 1943," 141; "All Out for Big Demonstration against Dis-

crimination," file 1943, box C86, NAACP Papers; Meier and Rudwick, *Black Detroit,* 114–17; Howe and Widick, *UAW and Walter Reuther,* 103.

32. Meier and Rudwick, *Black Detroit,* 136–56.

33. Richard Deverall to Clarence Glick, "UAW-CIO Local 190 Wildcat Strike at Plant of Packard Motor Co.," Richard Deverall Notebooks (Catholic University of America, Washington); "Negro Workers Strike to Protest 'Hate Strike,'" *Michigan Chronicle,* Nov. 18, 1944, Fair Employment Practices vertical file (Archives of Labor History and Urban Affairs); Meier and Rudwick, *Black Detroit,* 162–74.

34. Capeci, *Race Relations in Wartime Detroit,* 78–82, 164–70; Meier and Rudwick, *Black Detroit,* 164.

35. "Addes-Frankensteen to Support Proposal for UAW Board Member," Sept. 25, 1943, *Michigan Chronicle,* Fair Employment Practices vertical file (Archives of Labor History and Urban Affairs); "[Reuther] Slaps Addes for Stand on Race Issues," Oct. 2, 1943, ibid; "UAW Leaders Assail 1,400 Hate Strikers;" April 29, 1944, ibid.; "Split in Ranks of Officials Aid to Cause," Sept. 16, 1944, ibid.; "Reuther Urges Support of NAACP Membership Campaign," *Detroit Tribune,* June 1, 1946, ibid.; George Crockett interview by Hill, March 2, 1968 (Archives of Labor History and Urban Affairs); William Dodds interview by Lichtenstein, June 12, 1987 (in Lichtenstein's possession); Martin Halpern, "The Politics of Auto Union Factionalism: The Michigan CIO in the Cold War Era," *Michigan Historical Review,* 13 (Fall 1987), 66–69.

36. Harvard Sirkoff, "Harry Truman and the Election of 1948: The Coming of Age of Civil Rights in American Politics," *Journal of Southern History,* 37 (Nov. 1971), 597–616. See also Peter J. Kellogg, "Civil Rights Consciousness in the 1940s," *Historian,* 42 (Nov. 1972), 18–41.

37. "Labor Drives South," *Fortune,* 34 (Oct. 1946), 237; *Wage Earner,* April 12, 1946, p. 3; *New York Times,* April 21, 1946, p. 46; *Final Proceedings of the Eighth Constitutional Convention of the Congress of Industrial Organizations, November 18, 19, 20, 21, 22, 1946, Atlantic City, New Jersey* (Washington, n.d.), 194; Barbara Sue Griffith, *The Crisis of American Labor: Operation Dixie and the Defeat of the CIO* (Philadelphia, 1988).

38. Paul Sifton to Victor G. Reuther, "Revised Civil Rights Memorandum," June 13, 1958, Civil Rights Act of 1958 file, box 25, Joseph Rauh Collection (Library of Congress).

39. Sumner Rosen, "The CIO Era, 1935–55," in *The Negro in the America Labor Movement,* ed. Julius Jacobson (New York, 1968), 188–208; Herbert Hill, "The Racial Practices of Organized Labor: The Contemporary Record," ibid., 286–357.

40. *Worker's Voice,* Jan. 1947, p. 2; Tilley, *R. J. Reynolds Tobacco Company,* 485–88; Everett Carll Ladd, *Negro Political Leadership in the South* (Ithaca, 1966), 61. See also Howell John Harris, *The Right to Manage: Industrial Relations Policies of American Business in the 1940s* (Madison, 1982), 96, 157.

41. *Winston-Salem Journal,* May 19, 1947, p. 1; Tilley, *R. J. Reynolds Tobacco Company,* 400–401; U.S. Congress, House, Committee on Un-American Activities, *Hearings Regarding Communism in Labor Unions in the United States,* 78 Cong., 1 sess. July 11, 1947, pp. 63–122; *Winston-Salem Journal,* July 12, 1947, p. 1.

42. Jack Fry interview by Korstad, Oct. 16, 1981 (in Korstad's possession).

43. Harvey A. Levenstein, *Communism, Anticommunism, and the CIO* (Westport, 1981), 286–87.

44. *Winston-Salem Journal*, July 15, 1947, p. 14; Robert Black interview by Korstad, March 4, 1985 (in Korstad's possession).

45. *Winston-Salem Journal*, March 18, 1950, p. I; March 22, 1950, p. 1, March 25, 1950, p. 1, April 6, 1950, p. 1; Tilley, *R. J. Reynolds Tobacco Company*, 404–12.

46. Reginald Johnson to Lester Granger, memorandum, Jan. 28, 1946, Community Relations Project, Winston-Salem, North Carolina, file, box 27, series 6, National Urban League Papers (Library of Congress); *Winston-Salem Journal*, Nov. 16, 1947, sec. 3, p. 1.

47. Ladd, *Negro Political Leadership*, 121–27, 134–35; Black to March, Jan. 25, 1950, 1946–55, file, box C140. NAACP Papers; Tilley, *R. J. Reynolds Tobacco Company*, 410; Aingred Ghislayne Dunston, "The Black Struggle for Equality in Winston-Salem, North Carolina: 1947–1977" (Ph.D. diss., Duke University, 1981), 59.

48. Tilley, *R. J. Reynolds Tobacco Company*, 412–14, 454–58, 463–71.

49. Dunston, "Black Struggle for Equality," 61–161.

50. Ibid., 270–71.

51. John Barnard, *Walter Reuther and the Rise of the Auto Workers* (Boston, 1983), 101–17; Martin Halpern, "Taft-Hartley and the Defeat of the Progressive Alternative in the United Auto Workers," *Labor History*, 27 (Spring 1986), 204–26.

52. Crockett interview; Tappes interview; Studs Terkel, *Division Street, America* (New York, 1971), 328–30.

53. Walter Reuther, "The Negro Worker's Future;" *Opportunity*, 23 (Fall 1945), 203–6; William Oliver to Roy Reuther, "Status of UAW Officers and NAACP Memberships," Feb. 21, 1961, file 24, box 9, UAW Citizenship Department (Archives of Labor History and Urban Affairs); Herbert Hill interview by Lichtenstein, June 20, 1987 (in Lichtenstein's possession).

54. Martin Halpern, "The Disintegration of the Left-Center Coalition in the UAW, 1945–1950" (Ph.D. diss., University of Michigan, 1982), 237–40, 273–74, 433–37; Tappes interview.

55. William D. Andrew, "Factionalism and Anti-Communism: Ford Local 600," *Labor History*, 20 (Spring 1979), 227–36; Dorach interview. See also Nelson Lichtenstein, "Life at the Rouge: A Cycle of Workers' Control," in *Life and Labor*, ed. Stephenson and Asher, 237–59.

56. Tappes interview; Oliver to Roy Reuther, "Ford Plant, Indianapolis," Dec. 20, 1957, file 29, box 8, UAW Citizenship Department (Archives of Labor History and Urban Affairs); Oliver to Walter Reuther, "Preliminary Analysis of Allegations Made against UAW by the NAACP Labor Secretary Which Were Unfounded," Nov. 1, 1962, file 10, box 90, Walter Reuther Collection, ibid.

57. Dudley W. Buffa, *Union Power and American Democracy: The UAW and the Democratic Party*, 1935–72 (Ann Arbor, 1984), 133–73; B. J. Widick, *Detroit: City of Race and Class Violence* (Chicago, 1972), 151–55.

58. *Proceedings, Fourteenth Constitutional Convention, International Union, United Automobile, Aerospace, and Agricultural Implement Workers of America (UAW), March 22–27, 1953, Atlantic City, New Jersey* (n.p., [1953]), 264; Philip Foner, *Organized Labor and the Black Worker* (New York, 1981), 295–309.

59. Herbert Hill to Roy Wilkins, Dec. 23, 1949, Hill-1949 file, box C364, NAACP Papers; "Graphic Representation of Detroit Branch NAACP Campaigns, 1941 to

1948," Detroit file, box C89, ibid.; "Memorandum for Gloster Current on Rehabilitation of Detroit Branch," April 20, 1950, ibid.; Record, *Race and Radicalism,* 132–231; Lerone Bennett Jr., *Confrontation: Black and White* (Chicago, 1965), 213.

60. Widick, *Detroit,* 138–40; "UAW Fair Practices Survey—1963," file 12, box 90, Reuther Collection; Robert Battle to James Brown, "RE: Civil Rights Hearing," Dec. 13, 1960, file 13, box 50, ibid.

61. William Gould, *Black Workers in White Unions* (Ithaca, 1977), 371–88; Jack Stieber, *Governing the UAW* (New York, 1962), 83–88; "UAW Fair Practices Survey—1963."

62. Horace Sheffield, "Bitter Frustration Gave Added Impetus to Trade Union Leadership Council," *Michigan Chronicle,* May 28, 1960, Horace Sheffield vertical file (Archives of Labor History and Urban Affairs); B. J. Widick interview by Lichtenstein, Aug. 6, 1986 (in Lichtenstein's possession).

63. Buffa, *Union Power,* 139–42; Widick, *Black Detroit,* 151–56; The UAW made an all-out, but ultimately unsuccessful, effort to stop George Crockett's reentry into mainstream political life. See Nadine Brown, "Crockett Supporters Charge Union 'Takeover' in First," *Detroit Courier,* Oct. 6, 1966, George Crockett vertical file (Archives of Labor History and Urban Affairs); and Morgan O'Leary, "Hectic '49 Trial Haunts Crockett's Bid for Bench," *Detroit News,* Oct. 7, 1966, ibid.

64. Nelson Jack Edwards and Willoughby Abner, "How a Negro Won a Top UAW Post," *Detroit Courier,* April 4, 1964, vertical file, Trade Union Leadership Conference (Archives of Labor History and Urban Affairs); "Reuther Outlines UAW Position on Sheffield Assignment," file 9, box 157, Reuther Collection; Hill interview; Widick interview.

65. Foner, *Organized Labor and the Black Worker,* 423.

66. Notes on E. P. Thompson, speech in support of European peace movement, July 8, 1983, Berkeley, California (in Lichtenstein's possession). The notion that protest movements have a limited time frame in which to make their impact felt is also put forward by Frances Fox Piven and Richard A. Cloward, *Poor People's Movements: Why They Succeed, How They Fail* (New York, 1977), 14–34.

67. David Garrow, *Bearing the Cross: Martin Luther King, Jr., and the Southern Christian Leadership Conference* (New York, 1986), 431–624.

10 "Simple Truths of Democracy": African Americans and Organized Labor in the Post–World War II South

In the spring of 1943, Elijah Jackson faced what must have seemed an impossible assignment. An African American union organizer, Jackson had been dispatched to Mobile, Alabama, to recruit black workers into the Congress of Industrial Organization's (CIO) shipbuilders' union during World War II. He had been in town just a few months when, on May 24, 1943, 4,000 young white men and women rampaged through the Alabama Dry Dock and Shipbuilding Company, using pipes, wrenches, and other weapons to drive black workers from the yard. The rioters were responding to the promotion of twelve black men to skilled welding jobs, a challenge to traditional hiring practices ordered by the Fair Employment Practice Committee (FEPC), a federal antidiscrimination agency established in response to black protest. White reaction to the FEPC in Mobile demonstrated the double-edged nature of racial politics during the war. Black activism and wartime labor shortages increased black workers' access to better jobs and federal protection of their political and legal rights. At the same time, white supremacists stoked white workers' anxieties over urbanization and the influx of women and African Americans into jobs traditionally segregated by race and gender. By pushing for skilled jobs and union membership for black workers at Alabama Dry Dock, Jackson risked provoking a backlash horrific enough to outweigh the gains of his activism.[1]

Jackson's dilemma epitomized the contradictions faced by black activists nationally, and especially in the South, during and shortly following World War II. The early 1940s represented a watershed moment in African American history, when black political, economic, and institutional power reached an apex not seen since Reconstruction. Much of this progress was based on an allegiance between civil rights activists and economic liberals, primarily within the CIO and the Democratic Party, who were at best moderate supporters of racial equality. The tension between racial and economic liberalism would come to a head in the years following the war, as a conservative backlash against the New Deal, the intensification of domestic Cold War politics, and racist entrenchment against a growing civil rights movement fractured liberal support for racial equality at the very moment when Jackson and other black activists seemed poised to reap the fruits of their wartime toils.

This essay illustrates that dynamic by analyzing a campaign to unionize mostly African American lumber workers on the eastern coast of North Carolina, where Elijah Jackson was transferred after white workers and union organizers protested his insistence on racial equality in Alabama. CIO officials interpreted the Mobile riot as a sign that white workers would not tolerate racial equality, and they subsequently backed away from their previous strategy of promoting racial equality as means of building solidarity between black and white workers. Jackson, however, continued to encourage black workers to join the CIO, and he sought alliances with civil rights organizations to deepen organized labor's commitment to both racial and economic justice. These competing strategies shaped the CIO's campaign to organize southern workers after World War II. Impressed by the support that black workers gave to Jackson and other organizers, CIO officials eventually rededicated themselves to the struggle for civil rights. Having backed off their insistence on interracial cooperation during the war, however, union leaders were unable to convince their white membership to follow them down that road.

Jackson's assignment to Mobile in 1943 represented the culmination of a decade-long struggle to unite black and white workers around a program for economic and racial equality in the South. As early as 1929, the civil rights journal *Opportunity* expressed dismay that leaders of the American Federation of Labor (AFL) had not included African American workers in their plans to support unions in the South. "Any attempt to organize the workers which ignores that presence of the two million black workers will be fraught with disaster," wrote the editor, pointing out that avoiding African Americans had crippled previous efforts to organize the South.[2] Industrial unionists, who built the movement that lead to the CIO's break from the AFL in 1937, also saw interracial cooperation as critical to their efforts. By focusing their energies on the largely white textile workforce and by underestimating black workers' ability to build and sustain unions in important interracial industries such as lumber and mining, however, even radical labor activists may have missed opportunities to build on a wave of interracial working-class activism that swept the South in the 1930s. At the end of that decade, when CIO leaders launched a second southern organizing campaign, they adopted the AFL's logic that white workers would be easier to organize in isolation from African Americans.[3]

CIO support for interracial unionism in the South grew not simply from the rise of industrial unionism in the 1930s, but also out of the confluence between increased black activism and a labor shortage brought on by World War II. The Brotherhood of Sleeping Car Porters and Maids (BSCP), an independent union of black railroad workers, initiated a solitary effort to build ties between civil rights and labor activism in the late 1920s, but it gained few allies until the late 1930s. Allies emerged initially among left-wing civil rights and labor activists, who converged to form the National Negro Congress in 1936. Their success encouraged CIO activists to confront rather than avoid racial tensions when the union set out to organize meatpacking and other industries in Chicago. "The CIO took every opportunity to advertise what a multiethnic community it had become" during those campaigns, according to historian Lizbeth Cohen, and worked "painstakingly" to hire union staff that reflected the racial and ethnic diversity of their membership.[4] By 1941, the BSCP had enough support among black civil rights organizations to convince United States president Franklin D. Roosevelt that it could bring 100,000 African Americans to the nation's capital in a massive protest against employment discrimination in the defense industry. In a legendary standoff, BSCP president A. Philip Randolph agreed to call off the march in exchange for Roosevelt's creation of the FEPC, which would be charged with investigating charges against both employers and unions. In addition to focusing attention on organized labor's own history of racial exclusion, the March on Washington movement provided CIO leaders with a clear illustration of the potential power that rested in black working-class communities. In that context, sociologists St. Clair Drake and Horace Cayton described the CIO as a "crusading movement" that made "racial equality . . . a component part of its ideology."[5]

Even before the United States entered World War II in December 1941, war mobilization created a demand for labor that significantly strengthened black workers' demands for jobs, better pay, and better working conditions in the South. CIO unions built on that strength by reaching out to black workers in northern auto and steel plants, and union leaders made explicit efforts to tie unionization to black demands for racial equality in the South. The CIO cannery workers' union initiated drives in majority-black workplaces in Memphis that year, and it was joined shortly thereafter by the CIO woodworkers' union. Success allowed those unions to expand operations to North Carolina and Mississippi, respectively, where they established significant beachheads in states that were notorious for their violent opposition to any unions, let alone interracial ones. The United Mine Workers remained outside of the CIO, but it, too, enjoyed rapid growth during the war because of its ability to balance interracial cooperation with black working-class militancy. The growth of black participation in CIO unions influenced not just the labor movement, but also civil rights activism. When sociologist Charles S. Johnson took a survey of African American activism in 1942, he found that "characteristic movements among Negroes are now for the first time becoming proletarian, as contrasted to upper class or intellectual influence that was typical of previous movements."[6]

Riots and hate strikes in 1943 had the effect of shattering the emerging alliance between labor and civil rights organizations. In industries such as tobacco and food processing, where black workers formed large majorities, unions could afford to sacrifice white support by pushing on civil rights. The Cannery Workers (renamed the Food, Tobacco, and Allied Workers of America), for example, united with the NAACP and other civil rights organizations in 1944 and 1945 to build "labor-based civil rights movements" in Memphis and in Winston-Salem, North Carolina.[7] Unions with large black minorities and histories of interracial unionism, such as the Packinghouse Workers, the Transport Workers, and the International Union of Mine, Mill and Smelter Workers, succeeded in maintaining some support among their white members for black job promotion, desegregation, and political equality later in the war.[8] These four unions represented the left wing of the CIO, which at least partially accounted for their leaders' commitment to racial equality. As both anticommunism and racial conservatism gained political potency in the late 1940s, radical unions found themselves isolated from most white workers and the mainstream of the CIO's leadership.[9]

Union leaders were not alone in their belief that racist violence was too great a price to pay for interracial unionism. Jackson's first assignment following the Mobile riot was to rebuild a CIO local in Wilmington, North Carolina, that had been discredited when leaders of the local National Association for the Advancement of Colored People (NAACP) launched a media campaign urging African Americans not to join the CIO.[10] NAACP field director Ella Baker was working to improve relations between unions and civil rights activists, and she explained to Jackson that local black leaders were convinced by the violence of 1943 that unionization would provoke a repeat of the Wilmington Massacre of 1898, when local whites had responded to black political activism after Reconstruction by destroying the black community.[11] Their fear grew more credible in the months following the Mobile riot, as whites attacked black communities in Beaumont and Brownsville, Texas; Detroit; Chicago; and Los Angeles. That same year, white workers staged hate strikes in Detroit, Chicago, Philadelphia, and Baltimore, refusing to work alongside black workers who had been promoted into previously all-white positions.[12] Frustrated by the number of African Americans who believed the CIO would inspire more such backlash, Baker wrote to Jackson that "So many of the old timers have the position that there is no need for such an organization and are quick to tell you what happened in Wilmington years ago."[13]

It was in this context of reaction that CIO leaders launched their third, and largest, campaign to unionize the South's major industries. Fearing a backlash against economic and political gains won during the war, and recognizing that the still largely unorganized South provided a refuge for northern firms seeking cheaper labor, leaders of the CIO concluded that the future of organized labor depended on their ability to organize the South. Rather than targeting interracial industries such as mining, lumber, or tobacco, as they had in 1941, the CIO focused "Operation Dixie" on textiles, an industry notorious for resisting both black employment and unionization. The focus on white textile workers was part of a conscious strategy to portray the CIO as a moderate force in southern society. CIO president Phillip Murray explained to the conservative *Saturday Evening Post* that he chose "practical" leaders for Operation Dixie, such as shipbuilders' union president William Smith, rather than "theorists who want a freshly laundered world next Monday morning." Operation Dixie's leaders "are hewing singly to the job of building unions," the magazine reported, "and they have no desire at the moment to undertake a crusading job on race relations. That, they think, is someone else's wrestling match."[14]

Taking a self-consciously conservative approach, leaders of Operation Dixie distanced themselves from the overtly antiracist rhetoric of the early 1940s. Rather than build a racially balanced staff for Operation Dixie, CIO officials actually discouraged black organizers from applying to work on the southern campaign.[15] William Smith, who headed Operation Dixie in North Carolina, denounced the tobacco worker union's "negro nationalist approach" on the grounds that appeals to racial equality would alienate white workers from the labor movement. He argued that organizers could have gained support from black workers "without the need of elaborating on the racial issue" and that civil rights campaigns only created "material [that] could very easily boomerang on us and be used" to rally white workers against the union.[16] In stark contrast to 1941, according to an article on Operation Dixie in *Fortune* magazine, similarities now "far outweighed the differences" between the CIO and the notoriously racist AFL.[17]

In keeping with the CIO's focus on white workers, Operation Dixie opened with an effort to organize the mostly white employees of Cannon Mills, the crown jewel of the North Carolina textile industry. A well-organized anti-union drive, coupled with a postwar boom market, allowed textile employers to raise wages and benefits while defeating unionization attempts. CIO leaders fired head textile organizer Dean Culver for lack of progress in October, and they replaced two others by the end of the year. The union lost more than half of the representation elections held in southern textile mills in 1946, and the majority of southern mills never even witnessed an election to determine representation. Despite their efforts to conform to southern racial mores, most union leaders agreed that the textile campaign failed even before it began.[18]

The lumber industry became "No. 2 on the CIO agenda," according to the *Saturday Evening Post.* Whereas textiles employed mostly "white skilled labor," lumber employed "a heavy percentage of Negro labor." Assuming that racial oppression would make black workers harder to organize than whites, the magazine asserted that "a quick look at traditional prejudice easily satisfies the neutral observer that lumber will be a tough ear to shuck."[19] The International Woodworkers of America (IWA) conducted the CIO lumber drive. Discussion at that union's 1946 convention focused on the potential difficulties of organizing black workers. Seeking to raise hopes for organizing in lumber, one organizer related his impression of an African American local union officer whom he had met at a meeting in Atlanta. He recalled her "devotion and diligence" and noted that she persisted despite a shortage of "facilities" and "abilities" enjoyed by white union activists. As if to dispel the pessimism that overshadowed the meeting, the organizer declared, "we don't have too many impossible problems after all!"[20] An organizer from Alabama pointed out that lumber and other industries had in fact been easier to organize than textiles during the war. "The relative slowness of the drive in textiles does not reflect the success of the drive as a whole in this state. Tremendous victories have been won in this state in wood, steel, and auto."[21]

For Elijah Jackson and other black activists, the turn to lumber renewed the possibility for building alliances between civil rights activists and the CIO. Jackson had continued to recruit black workers to the CIO following the Mobile riot, winning praise from union officials for "restoring to this group confidence in the CIO" and even winning acceptance among some white workers. After he joined an NAACP campaign to register black voters in Alabama, however, CIO leaders branded him a "fomenter of racial hatred" and accused him of being "under the [d]omination" of the civil rights organization. Jackson's transfer to North Carolina did not dampen his commitment to "the great work" that Ella Baker and the NAACP were "carrying on in the interest of our race." Upon his arrival in Wilmington, he may also have contacted Rosella Sessoms, a black woman who had been "working quietly" over the past year to organize the sawmills and logging operations that dotted the coastal plains near Wilmington. Based on her work, an Operation Dixie organizer reported that "Chances are very favorable" for organizing "several hundred woodworkers" in southern Virginia and the eastern Carolinas.[22]

Impressed by black workers' support for the CIO in eastern North Carolina, William Smith directed Jackson and two white organizers to coordinate a lumber campaign in the summer of 1946. In contrast to their experience in textiles, CIO organizers found the mostly African American lumber workforce eager to join the union. "Organization at the beginning was slow," the team reported to Operation Dixie headquarters, "but it picked up momentum as the campaign progressed." Jackson and his coworkers established an office in the fishing village of Elizabeth City, and they focused their organizational work on Elizabethtown, a county seat fifty miles inland where the Greene Brothers Lumber Company operated the largest sawmill in North Carolina. The team identified Greene Brothers as a potential "toughest customer," which according to Operation Dixie strategy they would target for a well-publicized campaign designed to inspire organization at other mills. By October 1946, the CIO had established shop committees in each division of the Elizabethtown plant.[23]

As they moved from textiles into the lumber industry, CIO organizers discovered how completely southern workers' lives were defined by race. Patterns of social and residential segregation that were rooted in custom in the North were strengthened in the South by the force of law. Most southern states forbade blacks and whites from using the same hospitals, schools, parks, and even cemeteries. Although stores and restaurants often served both blacks and whites, they did so through segregated counters and windows, or they simply required blacks to take their food and drink elsewhere rather than sit in whites-only dining areas. The realm of politics, which provided an important bridge between diverse working-class communities in the North, was effectively cut off from African Americans and many working-class whites in the South.[24] Poll taxes, literacy tests, intimidation, and overt laws kept all but 2 percent of voting-age black southerners from voting in the 1940 elections. Because many of these restrictions also disfranchised whites, fewer than 30 percent of all southern adults voted that year, compared to more than 50 percent in the North and the West.[25]

Whereas northern factories employed workers from many ethnic and racial communities, racial segregation often followed southerners to work. Even after a period of rapid urbanization and industrialization during World War II, just over half of all southerners worked on farms.[26] Sharecroppers and tenant farmers worked in family units with little daily contact with other workers or even employers. Paid and unpaid domestic work employed large numbers of black and white women and provided even less opportunity for interracial contact. Those southerners employed in less isolated settings often worked only alongside those of their own race. Leading southern industries were racially segregated, with textiles employing nearly all whites and other industries such as tobacco, steel, and paper separating blacks and whites by department and often even into distinct factories. African Americans held 60 percent of southern lumber jobs in 1945, but their heavy concentration in coastal mills meant that few had any white coworkers. Whereas Piedmont and Appalachian mills employed mostly white workforces, more than 75 percent of all lumber workers in eastern North Carolina were African American.[27]

Reflecting the racial segregation of the southern industrial workforce, black workers composed the vast majority of union membership at Greene Brothers and other eastern North Carolina lumber companies. Of 182 black workers in the Greenes' milling and logging operations, 133 joined the union in 1947. Only 7 of 48 white workers joined, and of those, only 1 paid his membership dues. In part, union support reflected the concentration of African Americans in more difficult, dangerous, and low-paid jobs where union support was strongest, but better-paid skilled black workers also joined the union. Of 24 black workers in the planing mill, 15 skilled machine operators joined the IWA, as did Solomon Owens, the Greenes' only black foreman.[28]

Even as they organized nearly all-black locals in southern lumber, CIO leaders went to absurd lengths to deny the racial character of the southern campaign. "We are not mentioning the color of people," Van Bittner declared, and he even insisted that "there was no Negro problem in the South."[29] Most CIO officials took a more moderate position, admitting that racial differences did exist but insisting that they could be overcome by appealing to white and black workers' common economic grievances. The *Saturday Evening Post* explained that Operation Dixie was being led by men who believed that "'You want your pay raised, don't you?' is a more effective gambit than a long talk about human equality and human rights."[30]

In their struggle to avoid racial conflict, CIO leaders valued diversity and the appearance of racial harmony over racial justice and democratic representation. An IWA representative reported with enthusiasm, for example, that one North Carolina local had elected a white president and treasurer and a black vice president and secretary. Despite the fact that the local was two-thirds African American, the organizer praised their selection of a white-dominated executive committee as "somewhat democratic."[31] The CIO lumber workers' newspaper encouraged readers to celebrate "Brotherhood Week" during Operation Dixie, a holiday based on vague appeals to "unity" and "tolerance" that according to historian Harvard Sitkoff "supplanted protests against white supremacy" after the racial violence of 1943.[32] Glossing over the difficult organizational work that had built multicultural solidarity in the late 1930s, the union newspaper *International Woodworker* asserted that Catholic, Jewish, Protestant, Greek, Negro, Yankee, and Swedish union members had learned the "simple truths of democracy" merely by working alongside each other in diverse workplaces. "Remember," the union instructed its members, "democracy begins in every day living."[33]

Democracy was not a part of daily life in postwar North Carolina, and for that reason, both blacks and whites viewed interracial unionism as an implicit attack on political and economic structures of Jim Crow society. By February 1947, organizers claimed support from a majority of Greene Brothers employees, and they petitioned the National Labor Relations Board to conduct an election to determine union representation at the mill. A routine procedure for union organizers, this election was likely the first time since Reconstruction that federal officials had defended African American voting rights in eastern North Carolina. The Greenes conceded to that intervention, agreeing to an election on April 18. Union organizers set similar processes into motion across eastern North Carolina that year when they won elections at three mills, filed for six elections, and initiated organizing drives at four others.[34]

Aware of the threat that unionization of black workers posed to local power relations, lumber employers wasted no time in attempting to destroy the new local. Southern lumber firms, including Greene Brothers, hired the anti-union attorney who had previously coordinated the wartime campaigns against unionization at the Wilmington shipyards. While the attorney organized anti-union efforts on a regional level, managers used violence and intimidation to defeat the union at their particular mills. Organizers reported that the company fired "several enthusiastic" union supporters before the election and transferred others to "unpleasant jobs."[35] On the day of the election, a foreman and superintendent beat a worker who left his job to vote, and then they had him arrested for assault and sentenced to ninety days on a chain gang.[36] Greene Brothers managers removed another worker from the voting line and warned him to "get away before he got in trouble with the white folks."[37]

Despite the company's efforts, 171 out of 230 workers at Greene Brothers voted in favor of the union on April 18.[38] Impressed by black workers' support for the union, William Smith put Elijah Jackson in charge of the organizing team. He increased the staff to six men that June and promised two more in the following weeks. Nine other elections had been won in North Carolina, and three more were pending. With four new drives under way in Fayetteville, the union moved its headquarters to Kinston, a more central location than Elizabeth City. "Things have progressed so well," the North Carolina director wrote to IWA headquarters, "that we have decided to extend our activities over the entire eastern part of the state and all the way up to the Virginia line."[39]

The pro-union vote in Elizabethtown strengthened organization at other mills, organizers reported, but employers' stalling gave "anti-union forces plenty of time to completely destroy and demoralize union members." State and federal officials provided little support for the rights of union members, and lumber firms avoided federal intervention in labor disputes by agreeing to negotiate with the CIO and then finding excuses not to meet with union representatives. The following year, workers voted for unions at twenty-five southern lumber companies, bringing the total number of southern woodworker locals to sixty-four.[40] Of the nineteen North Carolina locals that had won NLRB elections since the beginning of the lumber campaign, only six secured contracts with their respective companies before the end of 1948.[41] In April of that year, the organizing team reported that the election at Greenes' had "been won almost a year now and nothing has been accomplished."[42] Predicting a turning of the tables in the southern campaign, the employers' journal *Southern Lumberman* celebrated an August vote against the union at a Belhaven sawmill—"one of the first elections in eastern North Carolina where the company won."[43]

In the face of company resistance and government passivity, union organizers began to rely more heavily on the black workers who had from the start provided consistent support for their campaign. "Unless we were able to force the operators to sign good working agreements with our union," organizer Frank Evans explained to the IWA annual convention a few months later, "then we would have to simply forget about further organizational work." The day after losing the vote at Belhaven, union representatives planned a strike to force the Greene Brothers into negotiations. Elijah Jackson, another black organizer named Jimmie Compton, and Compton's wife moved into Elizabethtown, where they became trusted members of the black community.[44] "We were convinced that we had to pick out a key operation there, organize for a strike," and secure a contract that could serve as a model in other mills, Evans explained.[45]

Even as they prepared for a showdown, white organizers expressed doubts about black workers' ability to challenge their employers. "The Greene Brothers are awful big and powerful people in this little town and this strike is the first time anybody has ever stood up to them in any way," Dean Culver explained. "A lot of people were so beat down they wouldn't fight in open defiance of the Greene Brothers."⁴⁶ Striving to reduce racial tensions, Culver tried in vain to recruit white workers to official positions within the union. He wanted an overrepresentation of whites—four whites to three blacks on the strike committee and three to two on the relief committee—"if possible," which was unlikely because only seven whites had joined the union.⁴⁷ A few days after the strike began, Culver requested that fifteen to thirty white workers be sent from other locals to support the pickets. He also asked for assistance from a white organizer whose "soundness on the colored problem and his size and open friendly personality make him fit this situation perfectly."⁴⁸ Culver felt confident that he could win "a straight strike" but reported that he feared "a race riot" if the union did not earn "some white support."⁴⁹

Contrary to Culver's fears, black support for the strike proved strong enough to challenge what remained a solid wall of white opposition. At dawn on July 16, when they normally would have headed for work, union members gathered at the union hall and then "fell out in four groups behind the sound truck, carrying the signs, and . . . marched on the plant to the tune of the stars and stripes forever." Culver described the scene with glee—it was "wonderful," he wrote. "It looked like an army."⁵⁰ Solidarity extended far beyond the picket lines, as black community members gave money and other support to strikers and their families. Female relatives of many strikers worked in white homes, and some used their positions to monitor antistrike plans. One striker's sister-in-law overheard her employer discussing plans to dynamite a union organizer's car.⁵¹ Another striker's wife opened her beauty shop as a meeting place for strikers' wives, allowing union officials to leave relief baskets there for women to collect on their way home from work. Reverend Cotton lent his preaching skills, leading songs and coordinating marches at the company gates.⁵² William Smith celebrated the "splendid moral situation" maintained by picketers and praised their ability to "get the scabs out as fast as the company gets them in." His hopes raised by support for the strike, the North Carolina CIO director declared that "this strike MUST BE WON," and "we can win it."⁵³

Black defiance provoked a violent response from local whites, who perceived the strike as a direct attack on the race and class hierarchies that were so clearly aligned in eastern North Carolina lumber towns. Learning of the early morning march, Elizabethtown shop owner and former mayor Floyd Cross grabbed a shotgun and jumped in his car. "Run you car over the black son-of-a-bitch!" he screamed as he leaped out of his car and urged passing drivers to smash through the recently formed picket line.[54] Company managers urged delivery truck drivers to run down strikers on their way into the plant. "Don't ever stand there and wait on them," mill owner A. H. Greene demanded.[55] Culver reported that Elijah Jackson provoked particularly violent reactions and that it was "unsafe to leave the pickets out at any time without one white organizer there with them at all times."[56] The Bladen County Junior Chamber of Commerce (Jaycees) denounced the strike demands of a pay raise and collective bargaining as "excessive and absurd," and blamed the union for "fomenting prejudice and hate" and disrupting "not only race relations but also private enterprise which is the bulwark of this nation."[57]

As businessmen and aspiring employers, Cross and the Jaycees had a direct investment in labor relations in Elizabethtown, but white support for the Greenes extended far beyond immediate economic interests. One white millworker traveled throughout Bladen Country selling tobacco sticks that the mill produced during the strike. A white painter drove a log truck. "Everybody diversified," one manager recalled, noting that the painter's inexperience cost him a finger that he caught in a chain while helping to break the strike.[58] The Bladen County sheriff deputized plant managers to carry guns and make arrests during the strike. Local police drove deliveries and strikebreakers through the picket line, and they carried out a vow to "fill the jails full of strikers" by arresting nearly every union member over the course of the strike.[59] Local loggers and tobacco companies refused to hire strikers, and one local farmer claimed thirteen strikers as his full-time employees so that the Greenes could legally evict them from company housing.[60] One of the Greenes later described white opinion: "A strike against the mill was a strike against the town."[61]

This version of the "town" did not include African Americans, who would succeed in challenging the power of both the mill owners and the whites who supported them. After two months on strike, William Smith emphasized the need to maintain "present discipline and unity" by intensifying "picket line activity." He also recommended visiting nearby communities to dissuade workers from crossing the picket line, advising that "whenever possible, strikers should be used for this."[62] Frank Evans traveled in October to the IWA annual convention, where he urged delegates to send strike support funds from their respective locals.[63] As a result of his plea and regular reports on the strike in the *International Woodworker,* the Elizabethtown local received $500 a week from International and West Coast office of the IWA, as well as $3,300 from IWA locals in the Pacific Northwest.[64] Smith emphasized the importance of these efforts, as without a victory in Elizabethtown, the union would "not get any contracts in the North Carolina wood industry."[65]

As union leaders had hoped, a victory in Elizabethtown turned the tide in their effort to establish lasting organizations in other eastern North Carolina mills. Even with the support of local business, media, and police, the Greenes could not operate without access to the African American labor force. After starving the company of labor for four months, the *Woodworker* reported, the Elizabethtown local "tasted the sweet cup of victory" when their employers "suddenly capitulated and signed a contract" with the union. Building on that success, IWA organizers increased the number of southern locals from forty-eight to sixty-four in 1947 and to seventy-four in 1949. By 1950, six of the eleven IWA locals in North Carolina had secured contracts with their respective employers. The IWA's southern force peaked in 1952 when eighty-seven southern locals sent voting representatives to the union's annual convention in Portland, Oregon. Thirteen of those representatives traveled from North Carolina.

Black union members were not satisfied with simply joining the CIO, however, and they pushed the union to address their social and political grievances, as well as their economic ones. CIO organizers held classes in labor history and union management for new union members in 1950 and helped black members who were "determined to be qualified voters" to register for upcoming senatorial elections.[66] More than 1,000 lumber workers and their family members gathered for "fun" and "serious talk about labor's problems" at a 1951 IWA Labor Day celebration in Washington, North Carolina. Local newspapers noted the "political angle" taken by the "mostly colored" crowd at the event.[67] A few months later, nine black men and a black woman "took a leading role" in forming the North Carolina CIO Political Action Committee, which conducted registration and voter-education drives across the state.[68] The Carolinas Council of the IWA elected a black man to their only permanent office in 1952 and passed a resolution denouncing the Ku Klux Klan.[69]

Whereas union leaders had distanced the CIO from racial politics after the violence of 1943, the Elizabethtown victory drew their attention to the ways in which racial oppression shaped black workers' lives. Despite the work of "organized labor and race relations groups," the *International Woodworker* observed in 1951, black workers still faced "brutality, a peonage system, low pay and long hours," and they were often charged higher prices at company commissaries than were white workers. Emphasizing the extent to which unions had already aided "Negroes in the South," the union newspaper admitted that there was "still much to be done."[70]

The IWA's growing acknowledgment of the significance of race was apparent in its newspaper's reporting during and after the Elizabethtown campaign. Throughout the 1948 strike, the *International Woodworker* described the town's workers as "beat down" and impoverished, but it never clarified their racial identity. Readers learned of the Greenes' "attempts to create divisions among workers" but never discovered the nature of those divisions. Not until the strike was won did the newspaper print photographs that had been taken at several times throughout the course of the strike. Only then did readers see that the Elizabethtown local was entirely African American.[71] The newspaper's coverage of the victory was the first in an increasing number of stories that revealed and even analyzed racial differences between workers. Pictures of a 1951 Labor Day celebration showed mass meetings of African Americans similar to those that would become common in national newspapers during the civil rights movement of the late 1950s. A report from the Canadian Congress of Labor's 1951 convention highlighted a picture of Indian, Jewish, Korean, white, and black representatives discussing "mutual problems."[72] Readers learned of a 1952 southern regional IWA meeting, "attended by members of different races and creeds who thus gave conclusive proof that the fraternal spirit of democracy and justice is moving into the South along with the coming of the CIO woodworkers."[73]

CIO officials renewed their support for black civil rights in the 1950s, but the union had far less power to lend to civil rights causes than it had in the 1940s. Taking advantage of divisions within the CIO and the continued disfranchisement of southern African Americans, conservative politicians passed a barrage of anti-union legislation in the late 1940s and early 1950s. The most devastating of these were state "right to work" laws and the federal Taft-Hartley Act, which limited union political activity, weakened their bargaining position, and empowered employers to intervene against unionization. Even as the IWA gained southern members during Operation Dixie, anti-union laws prevented them from representing those members through collective-bargaining agreements.[74] "The picture is an ugly one," read a 1950 report from North Carolina. "We have lost over two thirds of the persons we organized. Consequently, over two thousand woodworkers who placed their confidence in the union have slipped away and have lost their faith in the organization through no fault of their own."[75]

Even in Elizabethtown, union supporters found it difficult to maintain their organization in the face of company opposition. After signing an initial contract, the Greenes returned to their early evasion by stalling on meetings and refusing to grant basic union demands in subsequent contracts. The local threatened a second strike in 1950, but union members had not yet recovered from the first and could hardly sustain another protracted struggle. The North Carolina legislature passed a "right-to-work" law during the first strike, which prevented the union from demanding that all workers pay dues to the union that had won pay raises at the mill. Demonstrating the continuing significance of racial loyalty, local president Jonnie D. Lewis complained that most "free riders" were white and that "It will take a white man to get them into the union."[76] The union maintained itself until Greene Brothers closed in 1958, but the company stopped negotiating years before that. Elijah Jackson left town in frustration, convinced that white organizers had not supported the local.[77] In 1957, the Elizabethtown Chamber of Commerce boasted that "There is no organized labor in Bladen County."[78]

African Americans continued to press for equality in Elizabethtown, but they did so without the support of labor unions. Adel McDowell and Leah Betty Lewis, whose husbands Thomas and Jonnie had led the Elizabethtown local, helped form a Bladen County branch of the NAACP in the late 1950s. In the early 1960s, both women led a series of school strikes that made Elizabethtown the focal point of what one scholar labeled "probably the most serious" school desegregation conflict in North Carolina's civil rights movement.[79] McDowell and Lewis traced the origins of this civil rights activism to the "different attitude" that emerged in the wake of the 1948 union drive. By confronting the Greenes and their supporters, another strike supporter explained, African Americans learned that they could "do something for themselves." Watching that defiance, whites also "learned that we're not going to take that kind of treatment now." By confronting both the economic and racial foundations of the Jim Crow order, Adel McDowell claimed, the Elizabethtown strikers "started the ball rolling" for the civil rights movement that would emerge in the following decades.[80]

Events in Elizabethtown paralleled the rise of the civil rights movement throughout the South, as African Americans mounted an assault on Jim Crow despite the fact that very few whites supported them. Having lost hope of winning white support for black civil rights, the NAACP focused in the late 1940s and early 1950s on court battles that were subject to legal arguments and international pressure rather than popular opinion.[81] The Supreme Court vindicated that strategy with its 1954 *Brown* decision, which outlawed racial segregation in public education, but then returned the struggle to the field of public opinion by allowing local governments to determine the pace of desegregation. The CIO merged with the AFL in 1955, and national leaders of the newly unified labor movement "wholeheartedly" endorsed the Supreme Court's ban on segregation. In southern communities where the fate of *Brown* would be decided, however, white union members demonstrated solid support for Jim Crow. "If we have to choose between staying in the union or see our segregated way of life being destroyed, we will pull out and form our own union," white Alabama steelworkers warned national union officers in 1956. Labor leaders quietly provided financial and political aid to the civil rights movement, but their support ended at the point where white union members felt threatened by racial equality. The movement that ultimately destroyed Jim Crow in the 1950s and 1960s was composed almost entirely of African Americans.[82]

The Mobile riot set the terms of organized labor's relationship to civil rights activism after World War II. By backing off demands for racial equality in order to maintain the support of white workers, CIO leaders broke away from a coalition that had brought both organized labor and civil rights organizations to unprecedented national influence in the early 1940s. Elijah Jackson and other black activists refused to accept that compromise, and by building solid support for the CIO in Elizabethtown and other North Carolina communities, they demonstrated that black southerners could organize themselves despite white opposition. Although Jackson's success impressed CIO leaders enough to win their support for black civil rights, they were unable to win white members' support in that stance. CIO unions left a legacy of organization and community leadership that aided civil rights battles in eastern North Carolina, but those battles were fought with only symbolic support from organized labor.[83] The evolution of interracial unionism in the 1940s demonstrated that there were few "simple truths" involved in the effort to build a democratic society in the twentieth-century South. On one hand, interracial cooperation did not grow automatically from the experience of working in an interracial work place. On the other hand, neither were black and white southerners permanently and essentially divided, as was indicated in the emergence of interracial unionism in 1941 and 1942. Between these two extremes lay a complex reality shaped by black and white working-class initiative, economic and political context, and the shifting strategies of both civil rights and labor leaders.

Notes

1. Bruce Nelson, "Organized Labor and the Struggle for Black Equality in Mobile During World War II," *The Journal of American History* 80 (December 1993): 952–88. See also Pete Daniel, "Going among Strangers: Southern Reactions to World War II," *Journal of American History* 77 (Dec. 1990): 899–908.

2. Elmer Anderson Carter, "The A.F. of L. and the Negro," *Opportunity* 7 (November 1929): 335–36.

3. On interracial unionism in the 1930s South, see William P. Jones, *The Tribe of Black Ulysses: African American Lumber Workers in the Jim Crow South* (Urbana: University of Illinois Press, 2005); and Michael K. Honey, *Southern Labor and Black Civil Rights: Organizing Memphis Workers* (Urbana: University of Illinois Press, 1993). On the CIO generally, see Robert H. Zieger, *The CIO, 1935–1955* (Chapel Hill: University of North Carolina Press, 1995).

4. Lizbeth Cohen, *Making a New Deal: Industrial Workers in Chicago, 1919–1939* (New York: Cambridge University Press, 1990), 338–39.

5. Beth Tompkins Bates, *Pullman Porters and the Rise of Protest Politics in Black America, 1925–1945* (Chapel Hill: University of North Carolina Press, 2001); St. Clair Drake and Horace Cayton, *Black Metropolis: A Study of Negro Life in a Northern City, Vol. I* (New York: Harper and Row, 1962), 313–14.

6. Honey, *Southern Labor and Black Civil Rights;* Jones, *The Tribe of Black Ulysses;* Robert R. Korstad, *Civil Rights Unionism: Tobacco Workers and the Struggle for Democracy in the Mid-Twentieth-Century South* (Chapel Hill: University of North Carolina Press, 2003); and Glenn Feldman, "Alabama Miners in War and Peace, 1942–1975, in Edwin J. Brown and Colin J. Davis, eds., *It Is Union and Liberty: Alabama Coal Miners and the UMW* (Tuscaloosa: University of Alabama Press, 1999). Johnson quoted in Richard M. Dalfume, "The 'Forgotten Years' of the Negro Revolution," *Journal of American History* 55 (June 1968): 100.

7. Korstad, *Civil Rights Unionism;* Honey, *Southern Labor and Black Civil Rights.*

8. Rick Halpern, "The CIO and the Limits of Labor-Based Civil Rights Activism: The Case of Louisiana's Sugar Workers, 1947–1966," and Alex Lichtenstein, "'Scientific Unionism' and the 'Negro Question': Communists and the Transport Workers Union in Miami, 1944–1949," in Robert H. Zieger, ed. *Southern Labor in Transition, 1940–1995* (Knoxville: University of Tennessee Press, 1997); Alan Draper, "The New Southern Labor History Revisited: The Success of the Mine, Mill and Smelter Workers Union in Birmingham, 1934–1938," *Journal of Southern History* 62 (February 1996): 87–108.

9. There is considerable debate on the significance of left-wing unions in the postwar South. See the works cited in notes 7 and 8, as well as Eric Arnesen, et al., "Symposium on Halpern and Horowitz: Packinghouse Unionism," *Labor History* 40, no. 2 (1999): 207–35.

10. Ella J. Baker, letter to Mr. E. J. George, September 9, 1943, Papers of the NAACP, Part I, Box C140, Library of Congress, Washington, D.C.; William Smith, letter to Walter White, December 23, 1943, Papers of the NAACP, Group II, Box A 347, Library of Congress, Washington, D.C. See also Barbara Ransby, *Ella Baker and the Black Freedom Movement: A Radical Democratic Vision* (Chapel Hill: University of North Carolina Press, 2003).

11. David S. Cecelski and Timothy B. Tyson, eds., *Democracy Betrayed: The Wilmington Race Riot of 1898 and Its Legacy* (Chapel Hill: University of North Carolina Press, 1998).

12. Thomas J. Sugrue, *The Origins of the Urban Crisis: Race and Inequality in Postwar Detroit* (Princeton, N.J.: Princeton University Press, 1996), 29.

13. Ella Baker, letter to Mr. E. Jackson, July 10, 1945, Papers of the NAACP, Part I, Box C140, Library of Congress, Washington, D.C.

14. Milton MacKaye, "The CIO Invades Dixie," *Saturday Evening Post* (July 20, 1946): 12, 94–99.

15. Zieger, *The CIO,* 234.

16. William Smith, letter to Frank Green, October 3, 1946, CIO Organizing Committee Papers, Box 56, Folder 8, Duke University Special Collections, Perkins Library, Durham, N.C.

17. "Labor Drives South: The CIO with the AFL in Full Pursuit, Sets Out for the Last US Labor Frontier," *Fortune* 34 (November 1946): 134–237.

18. Timothy Minchin, *What Do We Need a Union For?: The TWUA in the South, 1945– 1955* (Chapel Hill: University of North Carolina Press, 1997).

19. MacKaye, "The CIO Invades Dixie," 97.

20. Proceedings of the 10th Annual Convention of the International Woodworkers of America–CIO–Canadian Congress of Labor, Portland, Ore., September 10, 1946.

21. Edmund F. Ryan, letter to George Baldanzi, October 26, 1946, CIO Organizing Committee Papers, Box 53, Folder 1.

22. R. Wray Alt, letter to William Smith, June 10, 1946, CIO Organizing Committee Papers, Box 59, Folder 1.

23. "Synopsis of Incidents at Greene Brothers Lumber Company since the Beginning of Organization to the Present Date," CIO Organizing Committee Papers, Box 64, Folder 4.

24. See William H. Chafe, Raymond Gavins, and Robert Korstad, eds., *Remembering Jim Crow: African Americans Tell about Life in the Segregated South* (New York: The New Press, 2001). On race and working-class solidarity in the North, see Cohen, *Making a New Deal,* 256–61, 332.

25. Gunnar Myrdal, *An American Dilemma: The Negro Problem and Modern Democracy* (New York: Harper and Brothers, 1944), 475.

26. Morton Sosna, Introduction to Neil R. McMillen, ed., *Remaking Dixie: The Impact on World War II on the American South* (Jackson: University Press of Mississippi, 1997), xv.

27. For more on racial segregation of southern labor markets, see Jones, *The Tribe of Black Ulysses.*

28. Membership lists, Green [*sic*] Brothers Lumber Company, 1947, "Operation Dixie: The CIO Organizing Committee Papers, 1946–1953," Microfilm Edition, Reel 5.

29. Bittner quoted in Zieger, *The CIO,* 234.

30. Milton MacKaye, "The CIO Invades Dixie," *Saturday Evening Post,* July 20, 1946, 12, 94–99.

31. R. Wray Alt, letter to William Botkins, October 22, 1946, CIO Organizing Committee Papers, Box 59, Folder 1.

32. Harvard Sitkoff, "African American Militancy in the World War II South: Another Perspective," in McMillen, ed., *Remaking Dixie,* 87.

33. "Brotherhood Week," *International Woodworker,* February 24, 1948, 1. On liberal suspicion of racial politics in the wake of World War II, see Gary Gerstle, *American Crucible: Race and Nation in the Twentieth Century* (Princeton, N.J.: Princeton University Press, 2001), 128–86.

34. "Synopsis of Incidents," William Smith, letter to John Harkins, February 26, 1947, CIO Organizing Committee Papers, Box 59, Folder 1.

35. "Synopsis of Incidents," 4.

36. Jerry Ratcliff, Affidavit, October 26, 1948, "Operation Dixie," Microfilm Edition, Reel 5.

37. "Synopsis of Incidents," 4.

38. "Tally of Ballots," NLRB, ODP, Box 64, Folder 1.

39. William Smith, letter to Mr. J. E. Fadling, IWA, Portland, June 11, 1947, ODP Box 59, Folder 1.

40. Proceedings of the 11th Annual Constitutional Convention of the International Woodworkers of America–CIO–Canadian Congress of Labor, August 26 1947; St. Louis, Mo.

41. A. E. Boadle, Southern Pines Labor Information Service, letter to J. Clifford Miller, February 15, 1954, Southern Pine Association Records, Box 332, Folder 2–5.14.

42. "Synopsis of Events at Greene Brothers Lumber Company, Elizabethtown, N.C.," 10–12; "The Elizabethtown Story: How an Anti-Union Company Forced Their Workers to Strike," ODP Box 66, Folder 5.

43. "Company Wins Over Union," *Southern Lumberman,* August 1, 1948.

44. Leah Betty Lewis and Adel McDowell, interview with author, June 5, 1996, Southern Oral History Collection, Wilson Library, University of North Carolina at Chapel Hill.

45. Proceedings of the 12th and 13th Annual Constitutional Convention of the International Woodworkers of America–CIO–Canadian Congress of Labor, Portland, Ore., October 11–15, 1948.

46. "Strike Ends in IWA Victory," *International Woodworker,* December 29, 1948.

47. "Strike Plans — Greene Brothers — Elizabethtown," July 16, 1948, "Operation Dixie," Microfilm Edition, Reel 5.

48. Dean L. Culver, letter to William Smith, July 17, 1948, "Operation Dixie," Microfilm Edition, Reel 5.

49. Dean L. Culver, "Transcript of Telephone Report, July 21, 1948, "Operation Dixie," Microfilm Edition, Reel 5.

50. "Bargaining Rights at Issue: Elizabethtown Woodworkers Challenge Lumber Barons in Fight for Living Wage," *International Woodworker,* July 28, 1948, 1.

51. William Wagner Weiss, letter to Ted, October 5, 1948, "Operation Dixie," Microfilm Edition, Reel 5.

52. Orie and Louise Tyson, interview with author, September 1, 1996, Southern Oral History Collection, Wilson Library, University of North Carolina at Chapel Hill; Lewis and McDowell, interview with author.

53. William Smith, "Notes on Elizabethtown," September 14, 1948, "Operation Dixie," Microfilm Edition, Reel 5.

54. "Synopsis of Incidents."

55. Signed Statement, September 30, 1948, "Operation Dixie," Microfilm Edition, Reel 5.

56. "The Elizabethtown Story."

57. "Jaycees Hit Local Strike," *Bladen Journal,* July 22, 1948; "Jaycees Hit CIO Pamphlet," *Bladen Journal,* August 19, 1948.

58. Alvin Greene, interview with author, June 25, 1996, Southern Oral History Collection, Wilson Library, University of North Carolina at Chapel Hill.

59. Jerry Ratcliff, Affidavit, October 26, 1948; "Synopsis of Incidents," 18; William Weis, Affidavit, July 1948, "Operation Dixie," Microfilm Edition, Reel 5.

60. Solomon Owens, Affidavit, September–October 1948, "Operation Dixie," Microfilm Edition, Reel 5.

61. Ben Greene, interview with author, May 16, 1996, Southern Oral History Collection, Wilson Library, University of North Carolina at Chapel Hill.

62. William Smith, "Greene Brothers Lumber Company," September 14, 1948, "Operation Dixie," Microfilm Edition, Reel 6.

63. Frank Evans, Address to 12th Annual convention, IWA-CIO, "Operation Dixie," Microfilm Edition, Reel 5.

64. "North Carolina Strike Continues Solid Front," *International Woodworker,* August 18, 1948.

65. "Accounting of Strike Fund, Elizabethtown, NC, strike," August 22–September 30, 1948, "Operation Dixie," Microfilm Edition, Reel 5.

66. "North Carolina Locals Forging Ahead in 1950," *International Woodworker,* June 26, 1950.

67. "Talks Highlight Union Rally Here," *Washington Daily News,* September 1, 1951, 1; "Labor Day Celebration," *International Woodworker,* September 26, 1951, 16.

68. "PAC Meeting," *International Woodworker,* November 14, 1951.

69. *International Woodworker,* November 12, 1952.

70. "Labor Unions Aid Negroes in the South," *International Woodworker,* October 10, 1951, 3.

71. *International Woodworker,* July 28, 1948; August 18, 1948; December 24, 1948.

72. *International Woodworker,* October 10, 1951, 13.

73. *International Woodworker,* August 13, 1952.

74. "Southern Regional Conference, International Woodworkers of America," November 11, 1950, CIO Organizing Committee Papers, Box 59, Folder 4.

75. Bruce Davis, letter to Franz Daniel, November 9, 1950, CIO Organizing Committee Papers, Box 59, Folder 4.

76. Jonnie D. Lewis, letter to Franz Daniel, May 17, 1951, CIO Organizing Committee Papers, Box 59, Folder 5.

77. Waymond Tyson, interview with author, September 1, 1996, Southern Oral History Collection, Wilson Library, University of North Carolina at Chapel Hill.

78. Elizabethtown Chamber of Commerce, "Elizabethtown, North Carolina: An Invitation to Industry," 1957, Local History Room, Elizabethtown Public Library.

79. David S. Cecelski, *Along Freedom Road: Hyde County, North Carolina, and the Fate of Black Schools in the South* (Chapel Hill: University of North Carolina Press, 1994).

80. Lewis and McDowell, interview with author; and Tyson and Tyson, interview with author.

81. Mary L. Dudziak, *Cold War Civil Rights: Race and the Image of American Democracy* (Princeton, N.J.: Princeton University Press, 2000).

82. Quotes in Alan Draper, *Conflict of Interest: Organized Labor and the Civil Rights Movement in the South, 1954–1968* (Ithaca, N.Y.: ILR Press, 1994), 19, 23. There is a huge literature on black civil rights activism in the 1950s and 1960s. See, for example,

Charles Payne, *I've Got the Light of Freedom: The Organizing Tradition and the Mississippi Freedom Struggle* (Berkeley: University of California Press, 1995); and Ransby, *Ella Baker.*

83. On efforts to maintain alliances between civil rights and labor organizations, see John d'Emilio, *Lost Prophet: The Life and Times of Bayard Rustin* (New York: Free Press, 2003).

11 Managing Discontent:
The Life and Career of Leamon Hood,
Black Public Employee Union Activist

On March 28, 1977, the usually serene lobby of city hall in Atlanta, Georgia, was crowded with an angry throng of more than 300 of the city's blue-collar public employees, members of Local 1644 of the American Federation of State, County, and Municipal Employees (AFSCME). They had marched to city hall that day to protest two years of inaction by the administration of Mayor Maynard Jackson on their demands for a 50-cent-per-hour raise. They sought a wage increase to boost salaries that averaged only $7,000 annually, placing families of four with single breadwinners below the poverty line.[1] Failing to get relief from the mayor after repeated efforts, they decided to confront him in person. These workers, the vast majority of whom were African American, had good reason to be bitter, for their union had worked hard to elect Jackson as Atlanta's first black mayor in 1973. After a short honeymoon with labor, however, Jackson distanced himself from union allies and wooed Atlanta's once suspicious white business establishment. Thus, when he encountered inflationary pressures and a recession in the mid-1970s, Jackson decided to hold the line against wage increases for public employees. "Let there be no mistake about it," Mayor Jackson said. "The employees need a pay increase. The employees deserve a pay increase. But we don't have it."[2]

Jackson's stance infuriated Atlanta's poorly paid sanitation workers. On March 28, they went to the mayor to get an answer to their demands. Mayor Jackson recalled the scene this way: "Hearing the angry shouts and cursing in the second floor hall adjacent to my office, I immediately left a previously scheduled meeting to meet with the group outside. There, I was met with shouting, curses, insults, and a written demand for an economic package that, if acceded to, would have cost the taxpayers of the City of Atlanta between 8 and 10 million dollars, which money the city simply did not have."

Jackson told the crowd he could do nothing for them. This infuriated the workers. Cleveland Chappell, the president of Local 1644, called the restive group together. "Gather 'round," he said. "You see what the mayor thinks of us. He's not going to do anything." At that point, one of the sanitation workers yelled out, "I make a motion that we strike." Others cheered. After two years of frustration, the moment of truth had finally arrived.[3]

At that instant, many eyes in the crowd turned to the demonstration's organizer, Leamon Hood. Hood served as area director for AFSCME's southern region, the first black area director in the union's history. Six feet tall and a well-built 230 pounds, Hood was a commanding presence at the rally. His face was familiar to the city employees, as he had worked for years building AFSCME's ranks in Atlanta, spending countless hours visiting the sites where the sanitation workers, road crews, and waterworks employees toiled. As attention turned to Hood, as he later explained, he realized he "could have stopped that strike." And Hood thought about doing so. He, better than anyone, knew the difficulty of the workers' situation. Hood had led fruitless negotiations with the City over the past two years, and he realized how determined Mayor Jackson was to resist the union's demands. Taking financially strapped workers out on a prolonged strike against a determined opponent was risky. But Hood, a shrewd "manager of discontent," as sociologist C. Wright Mills might have called him, also understood his members.[4] They had been stretched to their breaking point, and a failure to act that afternoon might undermine their organization. "I knew those people," Hood recalled years later. "I knew they were going to walk out." Quickly, he expressed his approval. The strike vote was held on the spot, and only three of the roughly three hundred employees present voted against a strike.[5] "I was confident that we had enough support from the community," Hood later explained. The next morning, March 29, 1977, 1,300 city workers left their jobs, beginning one of the bitterest labor battles ever waged in Atlanta and leading to one of the most painful defeats in AFSCME's history.[6]

The road that led Leamon Hood to this particular confrontation in 1977 and the course of Hood's life as a union activist in the years since 1977 can teach us much about the complex interactions between class and race that have shaped black workers' lives in the postwar era. Leamon Hood's life in labor brought him into the mainstream of organized labor's most vital wing in the postwar years: public-sector unionism. As a black man, he participated in one of the most hopeful developments of the 1960s, the fusing of the union struggle with the aspirations of minority workers. And, as a leader of public employees, Hood fought many of the forces that enervated the labor movement in the years after the 1960s. His life thus provides a revealing lens through which to examine both the gains and the frustrations that characterized the lives of black workers in the union movement during the late twentieth century.

To date, historians have yet to grapple with life narratives like Hood's. In recent years, the field of labor history has seen a renaissance of labor biographies. Yet most of these books have treated union leaders who figured in organized labor's rise, from the late nineteenth century through the triumph of the Congress of Industrial Organizations (CIO). Such biographies have helped us understand what Warren Van Tine and Melvyn Dubofsky have called the "transformation of union leadership from a calling to a career." But they have shed less light on the forces that contributed to labor's decline in the years since the 1960s.[7] Even more glaring has been the lack of attention devoted to the lives of black labor leaders. Nor have the many outstanding recent biographies of African Americans redressed this neglect. Indeed, in the recent literature of African American biography, scholars have paid little attention to the lives of black workers and unionists.[8] For different reasons, then, both labor history and African American history have yet to fully explore the complex experiences of African American labor leaders.

To a great extent, this failure can be explained by the underrepresentation of blacks in the top ranks of union leadership, a reality that forces scholars to examine the lives of secondary-level leaders such as Leamon Hood to bring the experience of black labor leaders to life.[9] Yet for two reasons, scholars must begin to examine secondary-level leaders. First, as George Lipsitz has pointed out, without the work of grassroots activists, leaders would have "no followers and ordinary citizens have no means of translating their wishes and desires into coherent political contestation."[10] Second, as historians test new ways of conceptualizing the interconnection of class and race in U.S. working-class history, they have a greater need than ever to keep their discussions grounded in the realities of people's lived experiences.[11] As the story of Leamon Hood suggests, no simple theoretical formulation can evoke the rich complexity of the experience of black workers in the postwar union movement.

The Education of a Black Union Activist

Leamon Hood was born on April 20, 1937, in Jackson, Georgia, in Butts County, about forty miles southeast of Atlanta. He was the fifth child of I. B. and Ella Walton Hood, sharecroppers who raised seven surviving children. When Hood was a child, the family moved about twenty miles west to the small town of Williamson in Pike County. Census figures indicate just how impoverished the Pike County of Hood's youth was. At the end of World War II, when Hood was eight years old, more than 70 percent of the county's labor force was still engaged in agriculture; more than 60 percent of the county's farms were operated by tenants; fewer than half of farm dwellings were electrified; and fewer than 20 percent had running water. Only 11.5 percent of county residents over the age of twenty-five had completed high school educations. Although the population of Pike County was nearly one-half African American, blacks had no political voice and exercised little economic power.[12] Hood's family, however, partially escaped the relentless grip of agricultural poverty when Hood's father, I. B., took a job with the Southern Central Railroad in Griffin, in the more prosperous Spalding County a few miles to the north.[13] Hood's mother, Ella, supplemented the family income by taking jobs as a domestic worker for a short time.

The Hood family's precarious stability was upset in 1952 when Ella Hood succumbed to cancer. I. B. Hood immediately moved fifteen-year old Leamon and his siblings to Atlanta, where I. B.'s relatives helped with the children and friends found him construction work. The Hoods settled on the "poor end" of Thayer Avenue in the heart of the city's growing south-side black community. In moving to Atlanta from rural Georgia in 1952, the Hoods joined a stream of Georgians, more than half of whom were African Americans, leaving the state's agricultural counties for cities. During the decade of the 1950s, Atlanta's population grew by a staggering 47 percent. The city's black population alone leaped by 54 percent, as Atlanta received its share of the millions of African American migrants who fled impoverished cotton culture for cities north and south.[14] But Atlanta's growth, like urban growth elsewhere, did not benefit whites and blacks equally. Leamon Hood arrived in a segregated city where black neighborhoods lacked basic amenities: in 1954, the Atlanta Urban League reported that the city had 128 parks for whites only, and only 4 parks for blacks; 18 playgrounds for whites, and only 3 for blacks. Housing, garbage collection, police protection, and decent job opportunities were just as unequally distributed.[15]

Hood's arrival in Atlanta coincided with his entry into high school. He entered the segregated David T. Howard High School (where for a brief time his schoolmate was future Atlanta mayor Maynard Jackson). The Atlanta public school system was grossly unequal. In the 1948–49 school year, one study found, Atlanta spent an average of $570 on each white student, and only $228 on each black student.[16] Those inequities had scarcely been addressed by May 1954 when the Supreme Court handed down *Brown v. Board of Education,* a decision with which Atlanta officials did not willingly comply. "The City of Atlanta is now engaged in defense of segregation in the public schools of Atlanta," then-mayor William Hartsfield announced in response to the court's action.[17] Integration in Atlanta would await years of legal wrangling that ended long after Leamon Hood left high school. Yet the segregated education Hood received in Atlanta was far superior to the one available in Pike County. And in Atlanta, Hood first became aware of some courageous voices that challenged segregation. He found them among the black teachers in his schools, including his father's cousin LoVette Hood, who taught social studies at Luther J. Price High School, to which Hood transferred in 1954. He also found such a voice in the *Atlanta Constitution*'s liberal white columnist Ralph McGill, who championed the notion of "Tomorrow's South," freed from the bondage of racial backwardness. Decades later, Hood remembered McGill's defenses of the Supreme Court against the massive resistance crowd, recalling McGill as a "writer with real human compassion."[18]

Although he was a bright student, Hood never graduated from high school. He dropped out in the twelfth grade, in the fall of 1955, inspired by a friend's plan to join the service. After making his decision abruptly one day while walking to school, Hood was inducted into the U.S. Navy on December 13, 1955, at the age of eighteen. The navy provided more than a ticket out of segregated Georgia. It allowed him to get top-notch training as an aircraft mechanic; it exposed him to a wide range of experiences that he would draw upon later in his life; and it marked his entry into the largest nonsegregated institution in the United States of the 1950s, the military. Years later, he called his time in the navy as "one of the best things that ever happened to me."

In December 1955, Hood boarded a train for San Diego, California, where he was to undergo his basic training. He was thrilled as he watched a vast countryside roll by the window of his coach on the three-day journey westward, his first trip out of Georgia. Barely able to contain his excitement, he stayed up through the night, feeling the same rush of emotions shared by hundreds of thousands of blacks who had joined the Great Migration years earlier. The ride was "quite an adventure, quite exciting," he recalled.[19]

Perhaps no U.S. city was more deeply influenced by the desegregation of the U.S. Navy after World War II than San Diego. The city's black population had more than tripled during the war.[20] But African Americans hardly found social equality within San Diego or in the desegregated navy of the postwar years. What Hood himself encountered during basic training in San Diego was as traumatic as it was exciting. Added to the anxieties that any recruit had about physical conditioning or the badgering of the tough drill instructors, Hood found himself for the first time in a situation where he was in a distinct racial minority. Fewer than a dozen of the 287 recruits who trained with Hood were African American. And many of the whites inducted with him did not conceal their racism. Hood experienced a number of incidents of "direct racism," as he later put it. But he also made his first white friends from among the recruits in San Diego. Later, when stationed in Jacksonville, Florida, he became particularly close to two white sailors from the South. These guys would "go to hell and back for me," Hood recalled. While on weekend leaves from the Jacksonville base, Hood would give his white friends a lift up to Atlanta. They did not socialize in public there, however; once in Atlanta, they went their separate ways into segregated worlds.[21]

Although the navy had begun to abandon segregation more than a decade earlier, during World War II, Hood still encountered its legacy in the mid-1950s. After basic training in San Diego, he was assigned first to Norman, Oklahoma, and then to Memphis, Tennessee, where he trained as an aircraft mechanic, working with jet and turboprop engines. He excelled in his work, and at the conclusion of training in 1956 he shipped out to the Jacksonville, Florida, Naval Air Station. It was there that Hood experienced his first serious incidences of outright racism in the navy. At Jacksonville, he remembers, he was "running into racism all the way up to the captain's level." Although he was fully certified as an aircraft mechanic, and more thoroughly trained than several people working in the Jacksonville mechanic's shop (some of whom had no formal training), Hood was not assigned to the shop. Instead he was made a lineman, with menial duties that included washing airplanes. For a year, the racism of the officers and the men in the base's lily-white air mechanic's shop trapped Hood in the lineman's job. When he finally did gain a position in the shop thanks to a white chief petty officer's recommendation, he was initially shunned by most coworkers and found himself in "a couple of verbal altercations" with one particularly overt racist. It took a while for his white shopmates to adjust to his presence, but Hood's skills eventually won over most white mechanics. Soon, white coworkers were coming to him for advice. When Hood later shipped out to the Mediterranean, he was assigned to a prestigious crew that rescued and repaired disabled planes.[22]

Hood considered a career in the navy, tempted by an attractive reenlistment bonus. But a conversation with a Douglas Aircraft consultant persuaded him he could earn big money as a civilian airline mechanic. So, after four years in the service, Hood was honorably discharged in April 1960. That year he returned to Atlanta to search for the lucrative employment he believed awaited him in the nation's burgeoning airline industry.

He was soon bitterly disappointed. The first job notice Hood answered was for a position as aircraft mechanic for Delta Airlines. He arrived at the Delta personnel office excited by the prospect of such a well-paid job. Yet before he could even fill out an application, the receptionist told him that the position had been filled by someone who answered a notice that ran in the previous day's paper. Suspicious, Hood returned home, scanned the previous day's paper, and confirmed his fears: no such ad had run that day. This was Leamon Hood's first experience of outright civilian employment discrimination, but it was not his last. The next job notice that Hood answered advertised a mechanic's job at Southern Airlines. When Hood applied, he was again told that the job was filled. This time, however, the personnel agent added insult to injury by offering Hood a low-paying aircraft washer job. A thoroughly disgusted Hood got in his car and drove off, leaving behind forever his dreams of making big money as an airline mechanic.[23]

Unable to crack the color line in airline machine shops, Hood scrambled for work. The highly trained mechanic soon found himself unloading banana trucks, digging sewers, and delivering newspapers. In the late summer of 1960, he finally found a more stable job as a custodian at Atlanta's Pittsburgh Plate Glass Company plant. Thus settled into secure work, Hood married Gloria P. Gooden, whom he had met in high school, and prepared to start a family.

Hood was an ambitious worker. Ranging freely around the plant on his custodial rounds, he familiarized himself with all parts of its operation. He soon convinced his supervisors to elevate him to the position of paper baler, loading used empty bags for recycling. Shortly after this promotion, Hood bid on a vacancy in the higher-paying production department, confident that his knowledge of that department's machinery would win him the job. His desire for a better position was reinforced by the fact that his wife had been fired from her department-store job when her boss heard that she had married. Hood was sure he would get the job: he was the only employee to bid on it. But the plant's personnel director quickly deflated his hopes. Hood was qualified for the position, the manager allowed, but "Didn't anyone tell you that you can't get the job? We have a contract with the union that we can't hire Negroes in there." The Teamsters were organized at Pittsburgh Plate Glass at that time. Hood did not join the union, however, refusing to "get in it when I found out how they operated." The Teamsters, he found, excluded blacks from higher-paying jobs in the plant.[24]

Hood's refusal to knuckle under to the Teamsters' racist practices at Pittsburgh Glass did not endear him to union officials. Insisting that he cease his protests, the Teamsters "gave me an ultimatum," Hood says.

Hood did not back down. At precisely the moment when the student-led sit-in movement was challenging segregation in downtown Atlanta in the fall of 1960 (leading to the arrest of Martin Luther King Jr.), Leamon Hood made his own stand for justice.²⁵ He went to a meeting of the Teamsters' local and "raised hell." Not surprisingly, he soon found himself on the street. With the union's approval, the company laid off Leamon Hood.²⁶

This bitter affair was a turning point in Hood's life. Not only had this first encounter with organized labor made Hood keenly aware of the ways in which unions could frustrate racial justice, it also sent him into a different career. After losing his job at Pittsburgh Plate Glass, Hood became a public employee. In January 1961, Hood took a job with the Atlanta School Board as a school custodian. Public employment was certainly less remunerative than private industry had been: Hood saw his weekly pay drop from $72 to $25. With his first son born in 1961, Hood took on second jobs to supplement his income, eventually finding night work buffing the marble floors of the state capitol building in Atlanta. The school board job did not pay well, but it offered security and the hope that conditions would improve in time. His appetite for justice whetted by his experience at Pittsburgh Glass, Hood was determined to improve those conditions soon. That determination transformed him into a self-educated labor organizer.

Shortly after taking his new job, Hood joined with two colleagues in an effort to try to unionize Atlanta's 1,200 school custodians. Besides low pay, their grievances included what Hood called the "completely segregated" nature of the custodial workforce. At that time, all head custodians in the system were white; whites with little or no experience were often hired into supervisory positions over blacks who had years of seniority. Hood and his coworkers undertook their organizing effort without prior experience or the aid of any union staff. Mimeographing leaflets, issuing press releases, and holding meetings around the city, the activists quickly built a mass following. Within a few months, recruits were "coming out of the rafters," Hood recalls. More than 300 custodians attended the movement's first public meeting. Suddenly, Hood was leading a union. Only after their organizing work was nearly complete in late 1961 did the Georgia State Federation of Labor refer Hood and his colleagues to AFSCME, which chartered the school custodians' unit before later absorbing it into AFSCME Local 1644.

In taking his job with the Atlanta School Board and helping unionize custodians, Hood was participating in two processes that were changing the nation in the 1960s. Nationally, public employment increased dramatically in the decades after World War II, inducing millions like Leamon Hood into public-sector jobs. Between 1947 and 1967, public employment more than doubled, rising from 5.5 million to 11.6 million, most of that increase coming at the state, county, and municipal levels. By 1970, nearly 18 percent of the nation's workers labored in the public sector.[27] In organizing school custodians, Hood also participated in a process that was changing the labor movement. Between 1955, the year Hood left high school, and the early 1970s, union membership among public employees rocketed from 400,000 up to 4 million workers.[28]

Just as Hood was leading the school board custodians into AFSCME in 1962, public employee unionism was entering the decade of its most explosive growth. Two developments helped make this possible. The first came on January 17, 1962, when President John F. Kennedy signed an executive order giving 2.3 million federal workers the right to join unions and bargain collectively with the U.S. government. Later that year, the U.S. Supreme Court issued its *Baker v. Carr* decision, which promulgated the principle of one person, one vote. This decision prompted legislative redistricting in many states where sparsely populated rural districts once had dominated state legislatures at the expense of densely populated—and increasingly African American—cities. In conjunction with the Voting Rights Act of 1965, this process ended up giving urban and minority voters more control over the purse strings of state and local governments. Together these developments helped build a massive wave of public-sector unionization in the 1960s.

It is hard to imagine public employee unionism gaining the tremendous momentum that characterized it by the end of the 1960s had its rise not coincided with and drawn inspiration from the civil rights movement. Since the New Deal era, millions of African Americans had looked to government employment as a more promising alternative than private employment. By the 1960s, the number of African American public employees was rising faster than the number of whites in the public sector. Black workers played an important role in the upsurge of public employee unionism, infusing the labor movement with African American members at precisely the moment when the old industrial unions of the CIO to which black workers flocked in the 1930s and 1940s were entering periods of stagnation or decline. The influence of black workers' aspirations on the public employee union movement was significant, which helps explain why one of the most important symbolic stands of government unions in the 1960s was their effort to replace the condescending (and, for many, racially pejorative) title of "public servant" with the more dignified "government worker."[29] Nor is it surprising that public employee union militancy rose in tandem with civil rights militancy through the 1960s. The number of public employee strikes fluctuated between 28 and 36 per year before the 1963 March on Washington. But by 1970, the number had exceeded

400 annually.[30] For African American public employees, organizing meant more than improving wages; it meant winning dignity in the workplace to match the access won by the civil rights movement in the arenas of public accommodations, transportation, and schools.

The public-sector union that sought to link itself most directly with the aspirations of the civil rights movement was the union that Leamon Hood and the Atlanta custodians joined in 1962. One of the fastest-growing unions in the AFL-CIO in the 1960s, AFSCME contained some 500,000 members by 1973, more than double its membership when Hood joined it.[31] In the realm of collective bargaining, AFSCME helped eliminate favoritism, standardize job descriptions and promotion ladders, and establish grievance procedures, all achievements that had special significance for black workers who had been victimized by racial discrimination in their workplaces. In the realm of politics, AFSCME contributed large sums to civil rights campaigns, worked as a key player in the Democratic Party's left wing, and emerged by the early 1970s as one of the most racially progressive unions in the AFL-CIO (in 1972 an African American, William Lucy, achieved the post of secretary-treasurer, the union's second-highest position). The union played a key role in forging a coalition between labor and civil rights groups, which shared a common liberal political agenda.[32]

As the 1960s began, however, there was little indication that AFSCME would develop in this way. Chartered in 1936 by the American Federation of Labor, in the mid-1950s AFSCME was little more than "a genteel lobbying agent for small groups of technical and professional workers," as one historian put it. Arnold Zander had headed the union since its inception and developed an effective political machine to keep himself in power. To keep peace with the union's white members in the South, Zander tolerated segregated locals in the region.[33] The union that Leamon Hood joined in 1962 was thus neither very strong nor particularly committed to the concerns of African American workers. That was soon to change, however. And Leamon Hood would play his own role in bringing about this change.

Shortly after his organizing success, Hood left the Atlanta schools for a better-paying job as a plant operator in the water pollution division of Atlanta's public works department. When he took that job in February 1964, Hood became only the second black man hired in that category. Hood immediately joined the union of Atlanta's municipal employees, AFSCME Local 850. An active union member, Hood soon impressed James Howard, a black AFSCME staff representative in Georgia. With Howard's strong encouragement, Hood ran for president of his local in 1964. At that time, two-thirds of the roughly 1,200 members of the local were black, but all of the local's officers were white, as they had been since the local's inception. Hood waged a tough campaign to break the local's leadership color line in 1964, spending countless hours after work as well as vacation days leafleting shops and garages where his colleagues labored. In the end, a large proportion of black members did not vote, and he lost the election to the white incumbent.[34]

This defeat was in turn followed by another painful experience of racial discrimination. When an opening came up for a position as a pollution control operator, a supervisory job, Hood scored third highest on the application. Nonetheless, his superiors skipped over him to pick a white man for the job after the first and second applicants declined the position. In the past the union had ignored such practices. But this time Hood protested and AFSCME filed a grievance on his behalf. When Hood met with Atlanta's public works commissioner, however, it became clear that the grievance would go nowhere. "Don't you understand that the city of Atlanta is not ready for no Negroes to be supervising white folks?" the commissioner asked. "It didn't matter to me," Hood later recalled. "I applied for the job based on the increase in [pay] rate. I wasn't all that enthusiastic about the notion of who I had to supervise."[35]

As frustrating as his union election defeat and his fruitless grievance hearing were, these experiences nonetheless held positive consequences for Hood. They further impressed AFSCME representative James Howard with Hood's talent and led the black union staffer to encourage Hood to consider joining him in making union work his career. Hood was initially skeptical of Howard's entreaties. "I kept telling him the union was racist," Hood recalls. But Howard disagreed. "Not only is the union's leadership changing," Howard argued, "but you should join the staff and help to change it."[36]

The Burdens of Leadership

James Howard's interest in Hood came at a propitious time in the history of AFSCME. During the years when Hood was struggling to establish himself in the Atlanta public works department, AFSCME was undergoing a huge national shake-up with profound significance for Hood's future. At AFSCME's 1962 national convention, a coalition of reformers mounted an unsuccessful insurgency to unseat Arnold Zander as the union's president. Zander survived that effort. But over the next two years, a onetime protégé of Zander's, Jerry Wurf, emerged as the leader of the coalition. As the head of the huge District Council 37, which represented New York City's municipal workers, Wurf held the balance of power in AFSCME. Steeped in the world of Jewish socialist activism in his days as a college student in New York, Wurf was a feisty and combative trade unionist. Wurf was also progressive in his politics and particularly sensitive to the union's failure to reform its racial practices. At the 1964 convention, Wurf edged out Zander for the union's top post, and his victory initiated a sea change in AFSCME's culture. Wurf promptly desegregated AFSCME's southern locals and hired civil rights leader James Farmer, the longtime head of the Congress of Racial Equality, to organize hospital workers. He also devoted union resources to organizing unorganized public employees around the country. The evidence is overwhelming that blacks greeted these reforms with great enthusiasm.[37] One action that won wide support was Wurf's creation of a training program intended to identify members with leadership potential and train them to become full-time union staffers.[38]

In 1966, James Howard persuaded AFSCME's southern district director Mike Botello to nominate Hood for this new training program. "I can't give up my job to work for no union," Hood remembers telling Botello. "I don't have the vaguest notion of what I'd be doing." With encouragement, however, he eventually accepted the offer, joining a class of fifteen trainees. Indicative of AFSCME's new focus on minority workers, six of Hood's colleagues in that program were black and one was Hispanic. Hood excelled in his training and formally joined the AFSCME staff as a field representative on June 1, 1967.

Hood's first assignment was in Columbus, Ohio. As he drove north with his family to work with the members of the AFSCME local that represented employees of Ohio State University, Hood experienced the same feeling he'd had a dozen years before when he boarded the train westward from Atlanta to San Diego. "I was really, really excited," he remembers. What he found in Columbus, though, soon brought him back to earth and showed him that AFSCME had yet to shed the unwelcome racial baggage of its past. His task was to dissuade black dissidents in the Columbus local from decertifying AFSCME and bringing in another union. When Hood met with James Ervin, the leader of that movement, Ervin told him: "You don't understand, white people have come in here and they've been able to get jobs with the union, they've been able to get positions, they can move right up. I've been the one here carrying the load. If I'm the one carrying the load and I can't go anyplace, why should we stay in AFSCME?" Stung by his own past encounters with union racism, Hood had no answer for Ervin. The Ohio State workers left AFSCME, and Hood was happy to leave Columbus for a new assignment in New York City.[39]

Hood arrived in New York in time to participate in one of the most important public-sector union battles of the 1960s: the struggle to win representation rights for 150,000 workers employed by New York State. During

1968–69, AFSCME was battling two other unions, the Teamsters and the independent Civil Service Employees Association (CSEA), to win the right to represent New York State workers. Governor Nelson A. Rockefeller clearly preferred to deal with CSEA. AFSCME's Wurf charged Rockefeller with "union busting" interference during the 1969 union election campaign and warned of "serious consequences" if the governor did not resolve AFSCME's complaints.[40] But when the votes were counted in late July 1969, CSEA came away with the right to represent the vast majority of state workers. The result, the *New York Times* concluded, was a clear repudiation of the "militant tactics" associated with AFSCME.[41] Hood, who felt the shops he had organized favored AFSCME, was surprised by the result. It taught him a lesson about the difficulty of gauging the militancy of union members.

Still, Hood acquitted himself well enough in this effort to rise higher in the estimation of union president Jerry Wurf, which in turn led to an important promotion. In January 1970, Hood became area director of the union's operations in Michigan, making him the first black area director in AFSCME history. A few months after arriving in Michigan to take up his duties there, Hood received yet another call from AFSCME's Washington headquarters. P. J. Ciampa, Wurf's director of organizing, barked: "We want you in Memphis, Tennessee, ASAP." Hood immediately departed on a trip that would change his union career.

Memphis Local 1733 was the most famous and symbolically important AFSCME local. It had led the fateful strike of sanitation workers against the administration of Memphis mayor Henry Loeb that provided the setting for the assassination of Reverend Martin Luther King Jr. on April 4, 1968. While making preparations for his Poor People's Campaign in the spring of that year, King lent support to the striking garbage workers, who symbolized for him the plight of the working poor. King went twice to Memphis to march on behalf of AFSCME. On his second trip, he was slain. King's death galvanized AFSCME strikers, who eventually won a contract.[42] Their strike in turn cemented an alliance between AFSCME and the civil rights movement.

The turbulent conditions in Memphis had scarcely subsided two years after the strike, however.[43] And Local 1733 never quite stabilized itself. Soon, the local descended into financial chaos. In part the union's problems stemmed from a failed strike for union recognition against St. Joseph's Hospital in 1969.[44] For five straight Mondays during that strike (dubbed "Black Mondays"), marchers took to Memphis streets to demand a settlement. The Black Monday protest of November 10, 1969, resulted in fifty-three arrests and diminished support for the union.[45] On December 26, 1969, the strike was finally ended when the Roman Catholic Diocese of Tennessee offered a compromise endorsed by Reverend Ralph Abernathy.[46] However, the battle deeply scarred Local 1733 and its well-known African American leader, Jesse Epps.

In the spring of 1970, disenchanted members of Local 1733 began communicating to AFSCME headquarters their concerns regarding what they saw as Epps's dictatorial control of the local and its finances. Unless the local was not soon "operated as stated in the International Constitution," they warned, "there will not be a union to operate."[47] So bad was the situation that Local 1733's board asked the international to place the local into trusteeship, which it finally did on May 3, 1970.[48] Within weeks, Jesse Epps submitted his resignation and the local's remaining officers were removed from their posts.[49] "I was responsible for cleaning up all of that," Hood recalls. On June 5, 1970, Wurf named Hood administrator of the union local in whose cause Martin Luther King Jr. had died. Hood was perhaps the only AFSCME staffer who could have taken on such a delicate assignment. Even Epps expressed his approval for the choice of a man "for whom I have the utmost respect."[50] Hood won the confidence of others, as well. "His idealism made a deep impression on me," one prominent Democratic politician noted.[51]

Yet from the beginning, Hood's tenure in Memphis ensnared him in controversy. In July 1970, several members of Local 1733 filed suit against the departing Epps, charging that he had misappropriated union funds. The action embarrassed AFSCME leaders and betokened a level of rank-and-file distrust that soon found another target: Leamon Hood.[52] By 1971, Hood was confronting increasing dissatisfaction from Local 1733 dissidents, some of which stemmed from racial tensions in the local, some of which was fed by a group of Epps loyalists. In 1972 a movement of Overton Park Zoo employees, most of whom were white, attempted to break from Local 1733 to gain their own "more confined and compact" bargaining unit with the city.[53] No sooner had Hood warded off that effort than he faced a challenge from a faction that wanted to restore Jesse Epps to leadership of the local. "Don't be mislead!" by Leamon Hood, proclaimed one leaflet distributed by a group called the Committee for Better Union Representation.[54] Only by packing a January 28, 1973, meeting with supporters could Hood defeat the Epps faction.[55] But that did not end the unrest. In March 1973, opponents circulated leaflets charging that Hood raised "$55,000 for politicians" and yet had done "nothing for our sick and disable[d] members."[56] Meanwhile, dissident James Jordan fumed that "the democratic principles of this trade union and the right to dissent is a thing of the past in this local union." Under Hood's leadership, Jordan claimed, "any voice of disagreement is declared to be the enemy of the union."[57]

The Memphis experience taught Hood that the tricky dynamics of union leadership and politics often transcended race. This was a lesson that he took with him to the major confrontation with black political and civil rights leaders that awaited him in Atlanta, Georgia, in 1977.

Race and Labor in 1970s Atlanta

Shortly after Hood took on his role as administrator of Local 1733's trusteeship, AFSCME president Wurf also named him to the position of area director for the South in 1971. In this position, Hood was responsible for the union's operations in Tennessee, Georgia, Florida, Alabama, and North Carolina, an area containing a membership of more than 20,000. With a black man leading AFSCME's southern staff, the union was poised for a strong push to organize the largely minority workforce of the region's largest cities. In 1973, Hood moved to Atlanta, which promised to become "the hub of activity in the South."[58]

Hood arrived in Atlanta just as Maynard Jackson was making his historic bid for election as mayor of the South's largest city. Born in 1938, Jackson was a child of Atlanta's black middle class, his father a preacher and his mother a Spelman College valedictorian. Jackson himself was a child prodigy. Graduating with honors from Morehouse College, Jackson briefly attended law school at Boston University, before dropping out, working as an encyclopedia salesman, and later securing a law degree from North Carolina Central in 1964. If Hood rose quickly in the ranks of AFSCME in the years after 1964, Jackson rose even more quickly in the world of Atlanta politics. In 1965, he became the first black attorney to work in the Atlanta office of the National Labor Relations Board. Four years later he ran successfully for the office of vice mayor, becoming the first African American to hold that post. As vice mayor, Jackson became a champion of organized labor. In 1970, he broke with Atlanta's white mayor Sam Massell, over Massell's handling of a strike of Atlanta sanitation workers. "I can no longer hold my peace," Jackson announced in the midst of a strike in which Massell took a hard line against the union. "I am firmly convinced that this dispute can be settled, and could and should have been settled, several weeks ago."[59] Jackson defended the demands of the AFSCME strikers and even rode on a garbage truck to show his solidarity with the workers. His support helped the workers win that strike.

It was in part his stand during the 1970 strike that earned Maynard Jackson the support of Atlanta's union voters in 1973. AFSCME itself played a key role in Jackson's election. Shortly after arriving in Atlanta, Leamon Hood and William Lucy, AFSCME's black secretary-treasurer, met with Jackson at his home and contributed $100,000 to his campaign.[60] With

the help of the unions and a strong turnout of Atlanta's black community, Jackson defeated Sam Massell to become Atlanta's first black mayor.
During Jackson's early months in office, relations between the mayor and
the union were cordial. In March 1974, Hood helped negotiate a contract
with the City that gained pay raises and a restoration of the dues checkoff
privilege that had been suspended by the Massell administration during
the 1970 sanitation strike.[61]

But Jackson's good relations with labor did not last long. Shortly after
he took office, a fiscal crisis of mammoth proportions began to affect the
nation's cities. The hardest hit was New York City, which nearly went bankrupt in 1975. Although Atlanta did not experience fiscal problems of such
disastrous dimensions, it nonetheless felt the budgetary squeeze. Jackson
quickly grasped the political implications of that squeeze. Speaking to
a group of labor lawyers in November 1974, the mayor warned that "the
nation's economic situation will get worse," and in response he predicted
that cities "will tend to be ultraconservative in budgeting." He feared that
this would only "intensify a cycle of more labor unrest and more pressure
from unions." And he urged lawmakers to work on "a settled procedure
by which we [can] resolve disputes in the public sector."[62] But even had
such legislation been passed, it could not have averted the coming conflict between a mayor determined to balance the City's budget (as the law
required) and a union determined to lift its members out of poverty.

By the end of 1974, relations between AFSCME and Jackson were growing ever more chilly. "I couldn't even get to his secretary," Hood recalled.[63]
Jackson was taking other calls, though. Months after his election, he began
a vigorous campaign to court the city's business elite. "I don't need the
business community to get elected," Jackson explained to one prominent
Atlanta banker, "but you know I need them to govern.'"[64] As the fiscal crisis
worsened, Jackson's interest in cultivating the business elite increased.

Although Jackson still battled the white elite on issues important to
the black middle class, such as access to city contracts for the building
of Hartsfield Airport, he retreated from his warm alliance with the City's
employees. The effects of the energy crisis, economic stagnation, and rising inflation so evident by mid-1974 only reinforced Jackson's determination to defend Atlanta's fiscal stability. "There will be no deficit while I
am mayor," he repeatedly proclaimed.[65] As inflation eroded the wages of
municipal workers, the stage was set for an inevitable confrontation.

Long and frustrating efforts to force the Jackson administration to address their grievances had preceded the march on city hall by sanitation
workers on March 28, 1977. Since 1975, the union had been pressuring the
mayor for a wage increase. By February 1976, the frustration of sanitation

workers with their mayor was ready to boil over, and their union threatened a strike.[66] On July 19, 1976, angry city workers declared a one-day holiday for what they called "City Employees Pride Day." "We will be missed Monday," their leaflet warned, "but not as much as our families miss that $500 the Mayor agreed to *in writing*."[67] At the same time, the union promised that it would take "stronger action" if it was required: "IF STRIKING IS WHAT IT TAKES, *THEN STRIKE WE SHALL!*"[68] The fall of 1976 brought no resolution to this conflict. By December, Mayor Jackson was promising an increase of only $381 by July of 1977. "Every time someone has to bite the bullet, it's always us," Leamon Hood noted bitterly.[69]

In December 1976, after nearly two years of nearly fruitless negotiations, AFSCME Local 1644 tried yet again to get talks going with the mayor's office.[70] Their initiative was rebuffed. Increasingly restive sanitation workers staged a wildcat strike in February 1977, refusing to pick up trash during a wave of bitter-cold weather. A mass meeting held during the wildcat strike considered calling a citywide walkout of all AFSCME members. Leamon Hood, feeling that the union was not yet prepared for such a strike, counseled patience. But, as one account of the meeting explained, his attempts to review the issues were seen by those willing to strike as an attempt by the International to avoid a strike and thus preserve the dues checkoff. With unrest rising among its members, the union made a final offer on March 10, 1977. When Jackson rejected it, the stage was set for the march on city hall that launched the strike on March 28.

When he decided to let the strike vote go forward without objection that afternoon, Leamon Hood was confident that the union had enough community support to win a battle with the mayor. Initially it appeared that the strike would shut down most city services, as Hood reported "75–99% support in the various units that have gone on strike."[71] But Hood was not quite prepared for the ferocity with which Mayor Jackson was prepared to battle AFSCME. Jackson immediately turned to racial politics to undermine support for the union, claiming that AFSCME's national leaders had targeted him because he was a black mayor of a major city, and therefore presumably amenable to pressure from labor allies. It was absolutely essential, Jackson argued, that he not cave in to pressure from national union leaders. "I see myself as only the first domino in [labor's] Southern domino theory," Jackson announced. "If organized labor makes the move on black political leadership," he warned, "I think it's going to have severe consequences for labor Southwide, particularly AFSCME."[72] As one scholar put it, Jackson "short-circuited the union's attempt to build community support for the strike by portraying it as a racial attack by the white-led" union on his black-led administration.[73]

Jackson's comments shocked Hood, who, having spent most of his adult life struggling for racial justice in the workplace, could not believe that he was being portrayed as a tool of those who hoped to undermine Atlanta's black political leadership. Moreover, as Hood knew better than anyone, AFSCME's national leaders had played no role in calling the Atlanta strike. Rather, the walkout grew directly out of Atlanta workers' years of frustration. As Hood later explained, AFSCME president Jerry Wurf "didn't know we were going to strike."[74]

Nonetheless, Jackson aggressively pressed his campaign, and his stance was warmly received by Atlanta's business community and mainstream press, which Hood believed worked "in joyous concert" to break AFSCME.[75] The *Atlanta Constitution*'s stand was clear. "Perhaps the time for being sympathetic to the union is over," the paper concluded. "The mayor now needs to show some sympathy for the taxpayers and notify the strikers they will be fired unless they return to work immediately."[76] Jackson issued just such an ultimatum to the strikers on March 30. Strikers would be fired and replaced, Jackson warned, if they did not return to work within forty-eight hours. At a news conference held to explain his stand, Jackson claimed he had "leaned over backwards so many times that I think AFSCME is walking up our back."[77] Jackson was true to his word: termination letters were sent out immediately as the forty-eight-hour deadline passed. Initially unfazed by these letters — many of the 1977 strikers had also been fired during the 1970 strike only to be rehired after it was settled— AFSCME members were soon stunned when the mayor authorized their permanent replacement. Hood vowed that AFSCME members would prevail.[78] But his tough talk could not hold back the tide of strikebreakers eager for jobs in what Maynard Jackson himself called "the worst national recession in 40 years, with an average city-wide unemployment rate of 12.6%."[79] On April 4, 1977, the ninth anniversary of the King assassination, more than 800 applicants lined up for the job openings created by the firings.[80]

What appalled Hood and the strikers even more was the lack of support they received from longtime allies in the Atlanta black community. From the beginning, most black leaders took the side of the city's first African American mayor. The black newspaper, the *Atlanta Daily World,* for example, characterized the strike as a "power grab by the Union" and wondered why the union would attack a black mayor "at this time, when we stand at the point of convincing the world that our people can lead . . . in the South."[81] Atlanta's NAACP branch went on record supporting the mayor, as did the city's Urban League chapter.[82] Reverend Joseph Lowery of the Southern Christian Leadership Conference also weighed in, expressing "deep concern for the current strike." Lowery summoned Hood to a meeting to which Hood took two strike leaders, sanitation worker James Malone and local president Cleveland Chappell.[83] In that meeting, Hood was amazed to see Lowery turn to the strikers and tell them that Hood was nothing more than an outside agitator. Hood, Lowery reminded them, was "an international union representative. He won't lose a day's pay. Y'all need to think about that." Recalling this painful incident years later, Hood remarked, "I felt like jumping across the table and putting my fingers around his throat. How dare you? You eatin' at the trough of these workers as long as you've been head of the SCLC and now you're telling them that standing up for their rights is somehow a betrayal of them and their families and all of their years of service. And it is people like this who have made your organization what it is." Hood held his tongue that day. But one of the strike leaders, James Malone, withdrew his support from the walkout following the Lowery meeting.[84]

Another painful blow was delivered on April 4, less than a week into the strike, when the city's best-known black minister publicly sided with the mayor. On the ninth anniversary of the assassination of his son in Memphis, as replacement workers lined up to take the jobs of Atlanta's striking sanitation workers, Rev. Martin Luther King Sr. appeared at a news conference with officials from the Urban League and the Atlanta Chamber of Commerce and announced his full support for Mayor Jackson. "If any group comes in to try to destroy our town, we are against it, with all the power we have," he announced.[85]

For their part, Hood and the AFSCME strikers fought furiously to retain allies in the civil rights community. By mid-April 1977, a number of civil rights leaders finally spoke out on the union's behalf. James Farmer, formerly of the Congress of Racial Equality, addressed a rally on the steps of city hall on April 11, 1977; the leaflet advertising his speech drew on the familiar slogan "We Shall Overcome!" The most poignant statement, however, was written on a picket sign carried by an African American boy. "I Am Hungry," it read. "My Dad Works For A Black Mayor."[86] AFSCME also sought to highlight Jackson's betrayal with advertisements in the *New York Times* aimed at liberals who had been "buffaloed into believing he is the friend of the poor man, working man, black man, and so forth" and letting readers know "It just ain't so."[87]

In the end, Jackson's ability to marshal support from Atlanta's black elite and municipal business leaders thwarted AFSCME's members. The majority of black civil rights and church leaders believed that protecting a black elected official as prominent as Maynard Jackson amid the fiscal pressures he faced was a higher priority than defending the cause of underpaid African American workers. The workers' grievances could always be addressed

later, many black leaders believed, once Jackson's political future was secured. Jackson's appeal to racial solidarity thus overrode Hood's defense of
the interests of black workers, and by the end of April 1977, Hood and Local
1644 had been beaten. Nearly half of the strikers had already given up and
applied to get their old jobs back. Reviewing these facts on April 26, Hood
recommended that the strike be ended. Local 1644 strikers still wanted to
fight.[88] But AFSCME headquarters saw no reason to fund a losing battle.
The decision of the international to terminate strike support on April 29,
1977, ended the conflict. It was simple, as Hood saw it: "the mayor won."[89]

The aftershocks continued. It took almost a year before nearly all the
strikers who desired to be rehired had regained full-time jobs on the city
payroll. Accepting defeat without having secured the immediate rehire
of all strikers had been a bitter pill for Hood to swallow. More bitter still,
Hood watched Maynard Jackson's popularity soar. According to one analysis, Jackson's stance against AFSCME "shored up his support among white
moderates and the business community in Atlanta." When Jackson stood
for reelection on October 3, 1977, he won handily, garnering 63.6 percent
of the vote (and 90 percent of the black vote).[90] Whereas Jackson's position was strengthened by the strike, within Local 1644, dissension roiled.
"Our union leaders have sold us out," proclaimed one leaflet circulated by
dissidents. "The AFSCME union misleaders sabotaged the strike from the
beginning and refused to fight the system." According to this line, Hood
and Wurf were nothing more than "Class Traitor Union Misleaders."[91] The
irony of being accused of selling out was not lost on Hood, who had spent
much of his life challenging injustice. It was yet another lesson in the complex challenges of union leadership.

Ultimately, the strike left a painful scar on Hood. "I was knocked for a
psychological and emotional loop for a while," he remembered. The experience of losing this strike—and watching longtime allies betray him—was
almost too painful to contemplate. "Sometimes you didn't know whether
to cry or whether to go do something silly," Hood continued. "You [were]
just kind of in a daze wondering . . . how could people like Maynard do
what he did? How could people who supposedly been our friends . . . end
up deserting us?"[92]

Carrying It On

The only relief that Hood found following the bitter 1977 strike came from
his constant contact with the members of Local 1644 through his efforts
to rebuild the union after the strike. "The workers was my salvation, you
might say," he explained. For AFSCME to retain its role as bargaining

agent for sanitation workers, Hood had to show by October 1, 1977, that a majority of sanitation workers were paying dues to the union.[93] Not only was Hood able to rally workers back to the union after its crushing defeat, he was also able to persuade them to raise the dues rate so that the union would be better prepared should it ever go toe-to-toe with the City again. Even Jerry Wurf told Hood, "you can't" raise dues after losing a strike. Hood not only did that, he successfully reorganized Local 1644. It still represents Atlanta's municipal workers.

AFSCME indeed survived in Atlanta, but things were never quite the same after the 1977 debacle. "It was a blow to the coalition," Hood explained. To Hood, the Atlanta strike symbolized the declining power of the labor-civil rights coalition that had made the reforms of the 1960s possible. By the late 1970s, it was apparent that labor was entering a new and more challenging period of struggle.

Nor were there many signs that the situation would soon improve, for the failed Atlanta strike was but one of several developments that signaled the end of public employee unionism's period of robust expansion begun in the early 1960s. The fiscal crisis of the mid-1970s wreaked havoc on unions in the public sector. In one signal event, the nearly bankrupt government of New York City instituted an austerity program in 1975, freezing wages, retrenching jobs, and weakening AFSCME's powerful District Council 37. The fiscal crisis and rising inflation in turn triggered a grassroots tax revolt across the nation. Beginning with the passage of California's Proposition 13 in 1978, dozens of states slashed taxes and began to trim government payrolls. Unions did not fare as well in this new climate. Indeed, the percentage of state and local government workers in unions began to trend downward between 1975 and 1982, falling from 50 percent to 45.7 percent.[94] The election of Ronald Reagan in 1980 worsened labor's plight. Specifically, Reagan's decision to break the strike of the Professional Air Traffic Controllers Organization (PATCO) against the Federal Aviation Administration in 1981 sent a threatening message to public employee unions. Although Reagan offered a forty-eight-hour ultimatum to these striking aircraft controllers, as Mayor Jackson had done in 1977, unlike Jackson, Reagan did not permit their rehiring after the strike was broken. His uncompromising action opened the door to aggressive anti-union tactics by a number of private-sector employers in the 1980s and to hard-nosed bargaining by government employers at all levels.[95] To be sure, public employee unionism survived the Reagan era better than did private-sector unions. By the end of the century, 40 percent of organized labor's members were in the public sector. But the optimism that had marked the rise of public employee unions in the 1960s had clearly waned.

Within AFSCME, the passing of this era of great promise coincided with the death on December 10, 1981, of Jerry Wurf, an event that held important consequences for Leamon Hood's future. Wurf's death triggered a power struggle within AFSCME between Wurf's heir apparent, the black secretary-treasurer of the union, Bill Lucy, and Gerald McEntee, the white leader of AFSCME's organization in Pennsylvania. McEntee narrowly prevailed in that contest, much to the chagrin of Hood, who had been a longtime ally of Lucy's. Although the victorious McEntee did not purge AFSCME's staff of Lucy's supporters (Lucy himself retained the position of secretary-treasurer that he had held since 1972), many of Lucy's close allies saw their union careers languish as McEntee's crowd took power. McEntee pledged to stand "shoulder to shoulder" with Lucy against any "racial discord" in the union, 25 percent of the membership of which was African American.[96] Hood had enjoyed Jerry Wurf's confidence and support over the years, but under McEntee he felt marginalized within the union to which he'd devoted his life.

Exacerbating his pain was the knowledge of just how much he'd sacrificed for the union. Union work had not been easy on Leamon Hood's family life. He relocated periodically and traveled constantly throughout his AFSCME career. For his wife, Gloria, these relocations could be jarring. Within days of moving his family to his first assignment in Columbus, Ohio, in 1967, Hood left Gloria and three small children (the youngest of whom was then only six months old) to visit AFSMCE locals in other parts of the state. Alone in a strange city, Gloria had to fend for herself. Nor did his subsequent transfer to New York City make her happy. Gloria was initially terrified to use the city's sprawling and confusing public transit system with her kids, and she felt trapped at home. She eventually did learn her way around the city, looked up some relatives there, and even grew to love New York. But no sooner had she adapted to the city than she was uprooted again when Leamon was sent to Michigan and Memphis. "How can they do this to you!" she cried.

For Leamon Hood, the memory of Christmas 1968 came to epitomize all of the hardship, sacrifice, and personal compromises that were demanded by a life in the labor movement. Although he was based in New York City that year, he had to make a quick trip to Buffalo on AFSCME business and barely made the last flight back on Christmas Eve. Upon landing at La-Guardia Airport, he ran to his car and raced to Gimbel's department store, where Gloria had placed the children's presents on layaway. He arrived moments after the store bolted its doors for the night. Frantic, he banged away on the plate glass until security arrived. Desperately, he pleaded, begged to be allowed in. Initially rebuffed, he refused to leave until he was finally let in to collect the presents. The children wouldn't be heartbroken the next morning, but Leamon had not been able to shop for the special present he'd wanted for Gloria. Christmas and Gloria's birthday were the times when he'd try to "make up for all the pain and loneliness" that she'd put up with during the year. But this Christmas, the only gift he had for her was a gold-plated manicure set. When she opened it, she burst into tears. "It was a time she didn't forget and I couldn't forget," he recalled more than thirty years later, his voice cracking. Leamon and Gloria held their marriage together for more than thirty years despite the strains of his work. Yet their time apart eventually took its toll. In 1991, with their kids grown and moved out of the house, the Hoods divorced. Leamon did not remarry.

Single and possessing slim prospects for advancement within the union, Hood's last decade in AFSCME was not easy. Nonetheless, Hood carried on. "I felt then like I feel now," he explained. "The union is a political organization." Still firmly committed to AFSCME, Hood put politics aside and continued to organize. He held the post of AFSCME's area director for the South until 1986. During this period, he traveled extensively through the region, servicing the union's locals, participating in negotiations, and organizing. Hood's work helped keep AFSCME's southern chapters vibrant during the increasingly anti-union climate of the Reagan years. In December 1985, however, McEntee asked Hood to relocate to serve as the Michigan area director (the same post Hood had briefly held nearly fifteen years before). Not enthusiastic about the move, Hood nonetheless consented to it.

His feelings of alienation would later worsen. Twelve years after he moved to Michigan, an AFSCME convention adopted a plan to trim the number of the union's senior staffers. Hood recalls: "Unofficially I was told that, of the 11 old timers they want to get rid of, you are at the top of the list." Yet Hood decided to reject the retirement package that was offered him. He enjoyed his work and resented being encouraged to retire after thirty years of loyal service to AFSCME.[97]

Instead of retiring, Hood applied for a promotion. His application was rejected by the union's organizing director. But the same organizing director shortly thereafter promoted people to two positions that Hood says had not been advertised and for which Hood would have been eligible. Feeling that he had been treated unfairly, Hood decided to file a grievance with union. A short time later, Hood was informed by AFSCME headquarters that the Michigan area director's office was being closed. He was asked to report to a new assignment in New Jersey. "I never got an answer to my grievance," he explained. "I tried to appeal it to the executive board, and they rejected it on the basis that it [the decision not to promote him] was an administrative decision and not a policy decision." After the union rejected his grievance, Hood filed charges of employment discrimination with the federal government's Equal Employment Opportunity Commission (EEOC). Conciliation efforts through the EEOC failed, and Hood decided to pursue his claim in federal district court. At the age of 63, Hood found himself in the unlikely position of suing the union he had devoted more than half his life to building. He worried that AFSCME might be going "back to being a union that is discriminatory."[98]

Toward a New Century

The courts never ruled on the validity of Hood's claim. He had hoped to use the legal process to force AFSCME to reform its internal hiring and promotion procedures. But after three years of discovery, depositions, and delay, Hood finally acceded to the judgment of his lawyer, who urged him to settle out of court. Hood negotiated an out-of-court settlement with AFSCME on the advice of counsel, the terms of which were to remain sealed. Shortly after Labor Day 2003, he signed that settlement, and three months later he walked out of his AFSCME office for the last time, and into retirement. He ended his union career with what he called "mixed emotions." He had won a fine settlement, his lawyer assured him. Yet Hood felt something was missing. "I was not happy," he explained. "I didn't feel vindicated."[99]

In a sense, Hood's discontent and his desire for vindication at the end of his career was symbolic of the position of African American workers within organized labor as the twentieth century ended. Born in an age when labor was just beginning to shed the legacy of segregation and racial exclusion that had so profoundly shaped American unionism, Hood himself had gone on to play a role in building a more inclusive and progressive labor movement. That struggle, which defined so much of Leamon Hood's life, unfolded in a manner that underlined the complex position of African Americans in organized labor in the late twentieth century. In his criticism of racially discriminatory power structures, Hood had been inspired by both his father's cousin, teacher Lovette Hood, and white journalist Ralph McGill. As a union organizer he had benefited from the early encouragement of both black union representative James Howard and Jerry Wurf, AFSCME's feisty white president. A militant defender of black workers, he had endured the attacks of a prominent black politician who had used race politics to undermine support for AFSCME. A loyal union man, he remained continuously wary of racial discrimination within his own union. A vocal opponent of undemocratic union practices since his early struggle with the Teamsters, he periodically drew fire from union dissidents (some of whom also appealed to racial politics) as he struggled to consolidate AFSCME's organization in the South.

In the end, Hood's lifelong relationship to organized labor was marked by a blending of identities as black man and a trade unionist that resists simplification. In his life's work as a union official, these identities informed and shaped each other. His loyalty to trade unionism placed him at odds with civil rights leaders when he felt that their priorities favored black elected officials at the expense of underpaid African American workers. By the same token, his sense of racial justice placed him at odds with union leaders—from his early encounter with the Teamsters through his lawsuit against AFSCME—when he felt those officials were dealing unfairly with him as a black man. His personal history was marked by two intertwined struggles: the strivings of a black man demanding racial justice in both his nation and his labor movement, and the strivings of a union loyalist struggling to advance workers' interests in an era during which organized labor as a whole suffered decline.

His road had not been an easy one to travel. Yet Hood looked back on his life's journey philosophically. "I have no regrets," he mused toward the end of his career. "I don't know any other area in which I could have had the experience, the opportunities to improve wages and conditions for workers, the opportunity to interact with people of all persuasions in our society. I don't know anything I could have enjoyed more than my life as a union representative." Despite the disillusionments he endured as an activist, Hood still believed heart and soul in the union cause to which he devoted his life. He also remained optimistic about labor's future.[100]

Hood's own career is enough to encourage such optimism. During his lifetime, labor had gone a long way toward shedding its vestiges of racism and done much to improve the lives of workers of color, especially in the public sector. Yet the sense of ambivalence and the desire for vindication that Hood felt at the end of his career reminds us of the challenges that unions will face as they appeal to an increasingly diverse workforce in the twenty-first century. As workers of color constitute an ever greater share of union membership while whites continue to exercise a disproportionate share of leadership, his story helps clarify the challenges that await organized labor in coming years. Will organized labor ultimately vindicate the lifelong labors of Leamon Hood and others like him by incorporating the next generation of men and women of color into the highest ranks of union leadership? On the answer to that question may hinge the future of the union movement itself.

Notes

1. Interview with Leamon Hood, September 30, 1999. Tape recording in possession of the author; *Atlanta Constitution,* April 4, 1977, 1–A.

2. *Atlanta Constitution,* April 4, 1977, 1–A.

3. Interview with Leamon Hood, September 30, 1999.

4. C. Wright Mills, *The New Men of Power: America's Labor Leaders* (New York: Harcourt, Brace, 1948), 9.

5. Memorandum from John Reuther to Bob Klingensmith, March 29, 1977, "Re: Strike Being Conducted by Members of Local 1644," Georgia Local 1644 1977 file, Box 143, AFSCME President's Office, Jerry Wurf Collection, Walter Reuther Library of Labor and Urban Affairs, Wayne State University (hereafter cited as Wurf Collection, WRL).

6. Interview with Leamon Hood, September 30, 1999; *Atlanta Constitution,* March 29, 1977, 1A.

7. Melvyn Dubofsky and Warren Van Tine, eds., *Labor Leaders in America* (Urbana: University of Illinois Press, 1987), xi. One recent labor biography that has attempted to deal with labor's decline is Nelson Lichtenstein, *The Most Dangerous Man in Detroit: Walter Reuther and the Fate of American Labor* (New York: Basic, 1995). Yet its narrative ends in 1970, at the very moment when public employee unionism was on the rise and before the crisis of the 1970s that so severely weakened the unions.

8. Among these outstanding recent biographies are David L. Lewis, *W. E. B. Du Bois: The Fight for Equality and the American Century* (New York: Holt, 2000); Nell Irvin Painter, *Sojourner Truth: A Life, a Symbol* (New York: Norton, 1996); and Linda O. McMurry, *To Keep the Waters Troubled: The Life of Ida B. Wells* (New York: Oxford, 1998). Although activists have provided the subjects of study for recent biographers of African America, labor activists have not received attention.

9. One recent autobiography that attempts to do this is Lee Brown with Robert L. Allen, *Strong in the Struggle: My Life as a Black Labor Activist* (Lanham, Md.: Rowman and Littlefield, 2001). And for one published oral history of an AFSCME organizer whose career overlapped Hood's, see Susan Reverby, "From Aide to Organizer: The Oral History of Lillian Roberts," in Carol Berkin and Marybeth Norton, eds., *Women of America: A History* (Boston: Houghton Mifflin, 1979), 289–317.

10. George Lipsitz, *A Life in the Struggle: Ivory Perry and the Culture of Opposition* (Philadelphia: Temple University Press, 1988), 9.

11. No recent literature on race, class, and labor has caused more of a stir than those works that have employed the concept of "whiteness." As yet it is unclear, however, how much that concept can illuminate the experience of workers in the post-1960s era. The seminal work in the literature is David R. Roediger, *The Wages of Whiteness: Race and the Making of the American Working Class* (New York: Verso, 1991). A number of the shortcomings of the literature are discussed in Eric Arnesen, "Whiteness and the Historians' Imagination," *International Labor and Working-Class History* 60 (2001): 3–32.

12. U.S. Bureau of Census, *County and City Data Book, 1949* (Washington, D.C.: Government Printing Office, 1952), 110–15.

13. U.S. Bureau of Census, *County and City Data Book, 1949,* 110–15.

14. Ronald H. Bayor, *Race and the Shaping of Twentieth-Century Atlanta* (Chapel Hill: University of North Carolina Press, 1996), 7.

15. Ibid., 134.

16. Ibid., 217.

17. Ibid., 222.

18. John Egerton, *Speak Now against the Day: The Generation before the Civil Rights Movement* (Chapel Hill: University of North Carolina Press, 1994), 334; interview with Leamon Hood, May 8, 2001. On McGill's stance toward segregation, see Barbara Barksdale Clowse, *Ralph McGill: A Biography* (Macon, Ga.: Mercer University Press, 1998), chapter 8.

19. Interview with Leamon Hood, January 3, 2001. Notes in possession of the author.

20. Abraham Schragge, "'A New Federal City: San Diego during World War II," *Pacific Historical Review* 63 (August 1994): 351.

21. Interview with Leamon Hood, January 3, 2001.

22. Ibid., September 30, 1999.

23. On discrimination in the airline industry, see Herbert Northrup, Armand Thieblot, and William Chernish, *The Negro in the Air Transport Industry* (Philadelphia: University of Pennsylvania Press, 1971).

24. Interviews with Leamon Hood, September 30, 1999, May 5, 2001. For more on the Teamsters and race, see David Witwer, "An Incident at the Statler Hotel: A Black Pittsburgh Teamster Demands Fair Treatment during the Second World War," *Pennsylvania History* 65:3 (1998): 350–67; and Witwer, "Corruption and Reform in the Teamsters Union, 1898 to 1991" (Ph.D. dissertation, Brown University, 1994).

25. David J. Garrow, ed., *Atlanta, Georgia, 1960–61: Sit-Ins and Student Activism* (Brooklyn, N.Y.: Carlson, 1989).

26. Interview with Leamon Hood, January 3, 2001.

27. Robert Zieger, *American Workers, American Unions* (Baltimore: Johns Hopkins University Press, 1986), 164.

28. Zieger, ibid., 163; Deborah E. Bell, "Unionized Women in State and Local Government," in Ruth Milkman, ed. *Women, Work & Protest: A Century of U.S. Women's Labor History* (New York: Routledge and Kegan Paul, 1985), 283; Kim Moody, *An Injury to All: The Decline of American Unionism* (London: Verso, 1988), 197.

29. Zieger, *American Workers, American Unions,* 163.

30. Moody, *An Injury to All,* 212.

31. Zieger, *American Workers, American Unions,* 163; Leo Kramer, *Labor's Paradox: The American Federation of State, County, and Municipal Employees AFL-CIO* (New York: Wiley, 1962), 26.

32. For background on AFSCME during these years, see Joseph C. Goulden, *Jerry Wurf: Labor's Last Angry Man* (New York: Atheneum, 1982).

33. Quotation from Zieger, *American Workers, American Unions,* 163. See also Kramer, *Labor's Paradox,* 1–27.

34. Interview with Leamon Hood, May 8, 2001. Notes in possession of the author.

35. Interview with Leamon Hood, September 30, 1999.

36. Ibid.

37. The transformation of AFSCME and its embrace of racial equality in the 1960s South has yet to be explored in detail outside of the experiences of sanitation workers in Memphis, Tennessee. But one suggestive treatment of this topic can be found in Erik Ludwig, "Closing in on the 'Plantation': Coalition Building and the Role of Black Women's Grievances in the Duke University Labor Disputes, 1965–68," *Feminist Studies* 25:1 (1999): 79–94.

38. Goulden, *Jerry Wurf,* 95–111, 125, 245; quotation from interview with Leamon Hood, September 30, 1999.

39. Interview with Leamon Hood, September 30, 1999.

40. *New York Times,* February 8, 1969, 27; March 11, 1969, 1; March 26, 1969, 58.

41. Ibid., August 11, 1969, 34.

42. Joan Turner Beifuss, *At the River I Stand: Memphis, the 1968 Strike, and Martin Luther King* (Brooklyn, N.Y.: Carlson, 1989), 191–210, 283–314; Michael Honey, "Martin Luther King Jr., the Crisis of the Black Working Class, and the Memphis Sanitation Strike," in Robert H. Zieger, ed., *Southern Labor in Transition, 1940–1955* (Knoxville: University of Tennessee Press, 1997).

43. When Jerry Wurf went to Memphis to join Local 1733 in a memorial for King on April 4, 1969, the event was marred by violence that erupted later that day. *New York Times,* April 5, 1969, 1.

44. *New York Times,* October 6, 1969, 30.

45. Ibid., November 11, 1969, 1.

46. Ibid., December 27, 1969, 17.

47. O. D. Adams to Jerry Wurf, n.d. [April or May 1970], "Memphis Confidential, 1970" file, box 135, AFSCME President's Office, Wurf Collection, WRL.

48. Terrell O. Aytchan et al. to Jerry Wurf, May 3, 1970, "Local 1733, 1970" file, box 135; and Jerry Wurf to Terrell O. Aytchan, President, Local 1733, May 3, 1970, "Tenn. Local 1733, 1968–70" file, box 109, AFSCME President's Office, Wurf Collection, WRL.

49. Jesse Epps to Jerry Wurf, May 27, 1970, file 16, box 135; dismissal letters in "Local 1733, 1970" file, box 135, AFSCME President's Office, Wurf Collection, WRL.

50. Wurf to Whom It May Concern, June 5, 1970, "Local 1733, 1970" file, box 135; and Jesse Epps to Jerry Wurf, May 27, 1970, file 16, box 135, AFSCME President's Office, Wurf Collection, WRL.

51. Frank L. White to Gerald P. Clark, November 4, 1970, "Local 1733, 1970" file, box 135, AFSCME President's Office, Wurf Collection, WRL.

52. *Memphis Press-Scimitar,* July 14, 1970.

53. Animal Keeping Staff to Leamon Hood, Executive Director, Local 1733, September 7, 1972, "Tenn. Local 1733, 1972–73" file, box 125, AFSCME President's Office, Wurf Collection, WRL.

54. Leamon Hood to Tom Fitzpatrick, January 23, 1973, "Tenn. Local 1733, 1972–73" file, box 125, AFSCME President's Office, Wurf Collection, WRL.

55. Organizational Department to Jerry Wurf, January 24, 1973, "Tenn. Local 1733, 1972–73" file, box 125; and Tom Fitzpatrick to President Wurf, January 30, 1973, "Tenn. Local 1733, 1972–73" file, box 125, AFSCME President's Office, Wurf Collection, WRL.

56. "These Are Facts!!!" Leaflet, file 72, box 125, AFSCME President's Office, Wurf Collection, WRL.

57. James Jordan to Jerry Wurf, March 23, 1973, file 72, box 125, AFSCME President's Office, Wurf Collection, WRL.

58. Interview with Leamon Hood, September 30, 1999.

59. Jackson quoted in Gary Pomerantz, *Where Peachtree Meets Sweet Auburn: The Saga of Two Families and the Making of Atlanta* (New York: Scribner, 1996), 393. Details on Maynard Jackson's biography are to be found in this book.

60. Interview with Leamon Hood, September 30, 1999.

61. Memorandum, Bob Klingensmith to Tom Fitzpatrick, March 15, 1974, "Re: Atlanta, Georgia Negotiations," Georgia 1974 file, box 141, AFSCME President's Office, Wurf Collection, WRL.

62. *Government Employee Relations Report,* November 25, 1974, B-10.

63. Interview with Leamon Hood, September 30, 1999.

64. "Banker Notes More Downtown Optimism," *Atlanta Constitution,* May 9, 1977, 12A; David Andrew Harmon, *Beneath the Image of the Civil Rights Movement and Race Relations: Atlanta, Georgia, 1946–1981* (New York: Garland, 1996), 284–85, 290–92.

65. "Statement by Maynard Jackson Re: AFSCME," April 6, 1977, Strike 4/77 file, box 37, Records of AFSCME Local 1644, Southern Labor Archive, Pullen Library, Georgia State University (hereafter cited as Records of AFSCME Local 1644, GSU).

66. Bill O'Kain to Leamon [Hood], March 21, 1976, Strike Committees file, box 32, Records of AFSCME Local 1644, GSU.

67. "Holiday for City Employees, Monday, July 19, 1976," leaflet, box 58, AFSCME 1644.

68. "Mass Union Meeting: All City Employees" leaflet, n.d. [1976], box 58, AFSCME 1644.

69. "Atlanta Mayor Fails to Keep Commitments," *The Public Employee* (December 1976), 6.

70. Cleveland Chappell and James Malone to Maynard Jackson, December 14, 1976, Strike 4/77 file, box 37, AFSCME Local 1644, GSU.

71. Memo, John Reuther to Bob Klingensmith, March 29, 1977, "Georgia Local 1644, 1977" folder, box 143, AFSCME President's Office, Wurf Collection, WRL.

72. *Atlanta Constitution,* April 10, 1977, A9.

73. Adolph Reed Jr., *Stirrings in the Jug: Black Politics in the Post-Segregation Era* (Minneapolis: University of Minnesota Press, 1999), 5.

74. Interview with Leamon Hood, September 30, 1999.

75. Statement by Leamon Hood, April 5, 1977, Georgia Local 1644 1977 file, box 143, AFSCME President's Office, Wurf Collection, WRL.

76. *Atlanta Constitution,* March 30, 1977, 4A.

77. Ibid., March 31, 1977, 18A.

78. "Statement: Leamon Hood, AFSCME Area Director," March 31, 1977, Strike 4/77 file, box 37, AFSCME Local 1644, GSU.

79. Position Paper by Atlanta mayor Maynard Jackson on Labor Relations in Atlanta, May 25, 1977, Georgia Local 1644 1977 file, box 143, AFSCME President's Office, Wurf Collection, WRL.

80. Interview with Leamon Hood, September 30, 1999; *Atlanta Constitution,* April 5, 1977.

81. *Atlanta Daily World,* April 3, 1977, 4; April 7, 1977, 4.

82. Ibid., April 7, 1977, 1; *Atlanta Constitution,* April 5, 1977, 1; *New York Times,* April 5, 1977.

83. Mailgram, Dr. J. E. Lowery to Lemon Hood, April 13, 1977, Strike 4/77 file, box 37, AFSCME Local 1644, GSU.

84. Ibid.; interview with Leamon Hood, September 30, 1999.

85. *New York Times,* April 5, 1977, 22; *Atlanta Constitution,* April 5, 1977, A2.

86. *Atlanta Constitution,* April 9, 1977, 3A.

87. Jim Gray of AFSCME quoted in the *New York Times,* March 30, 1977, 28.

88. "Statement of Leamon Hood," April 27, 1977, Strike 4/77 file, box 37, Records of AFSCME Local 1644, GSU.

89. *Atlanta Constitution,* April 29, 1977, 20A; Hood quoted in *Atlanta Daily World,* April 29, 1977, 1. See also Goulden, *Jerry Wurf: Labor's Last Angry Man,* 245–54.

90. *New York Times,* April 17, 1977, 26; October 3, 1977, 19; October 5, 1977, 24. Local 1644 endorsed Emma Darnell for mayor in 1977. "AFSCME Local 1644 Endorsements," Leaflets file, box 35, AFSCME Local 1644; Memo, Jerry Clark to Bill Welsh, October 11, 1977, "Georgia Council #000, 1977" folder, box 149, AFSCME President's Office, Wurf Collection, WRL.

91. "Fight Back!!," Leaflet, n.d. [April 1977], Strike 4/77 file, box 37, Records of AFSCME Local 1644, GSU.

92. Interview with Leamon Hood, September 30, 1999.

93. Jim Gray to William W. Hamilton Jr., August 5, 1977, AFSCME President's Office, Jerry Wurf, series III, box 61, AFSCME President's Office, Wurf Collection, WRL.

94. David Lewin, "Public Employee Unionism in the 1980s: An Analysis of Transformation," in Seymour Martin Lipset, ed., *Unions in Transition: Entering the Second Century* (San Francisco: Institute for Contemporary Studies, 1986), 244.

95. See Steve Babson, *The Unfinished Struggle: Turning Points in American Labor, 1877–Present* (Lanham, Md.: Rowman and Littlefield, 1999), chapter 5; Arthur B. Shostak and David Skocik, *The Air Controllers' Controversy: Lessons from the PATCO Strike* (New York: Human Sciences Press, 1986).

96. *Washington Post,* December 18, 1981, A12.

97. Interview with Leamon Hood, September 30, 1999.

98. Interviews with Leamon Hood, September 30, 1999; January 3, 2001.

99. Interview with Leamon Hood, March 8, 2003.

100. Interviews with Leamon Hood, March 8, 2003; May 8, 2001; September 30, 1999.

Contributors

ERIC ARNESEN is a professor of history and African-American studies at the University of Illinois at Chicago and is the author of *Waterfront Workers of New Orleans: Race, Class, and Politics, 1863–1923; Brotherhoods of Color: Black Railroad Workers and the Struggle for Equality;* and *Black Protest and the Great Migration: A Brief History with Documents.* He is also the editor of *The Human Tradition in American Labor History* and the multivolume *The Encyclopedia of U.S. Labor and Working Class History,* and coeditor (with Julie Greene and Bruce Laurie) of *Labor Histories: Class, Politics, and the Working-Class Experience.* His articles have appeared in *American Historical Review; International Review of Social History; Labor History; Journal of the Historical Society;* and *Labor: Studies in Working-Class History of the Americas.* He has received fellowships from the Charles Warren Center for Studies in American History at Harvard University, the University of Illinois at Chicago's Institute for the Humanities and Great Cities Institute, and the National Endowment for the Humanities. In 2006 he held the Distinguished Fulbright Chair at the Swedish Institute for North American Studies at Uppsala University in Sweden. He received his Ph.D. from Yale in history in 1986.

BETH TOMPKINS BATES is an associate professor of history in the Department of Africana Studies at Wayne State University and is the author of *Pullman Porters and the Rise of Protest Politics in Black America, 1925–1945.* Her articles have appeared in the *American Historical Review* and *Chicago History.* She received her Ph.D. from Columbia University.

CYNTHIA M. BLAIR is an associate professor of history and African-American studies at the University of Illinois at Chicago. She received her Ph.D. in American civilization from Harvard University in 1999. Her book *"Vicious" Commerce: African American Women's Sex Work and the Transformation of Urban Space in Chicago, 1850–1915* will be published by the University of Chicago Press. She has received fellowships from the University of Illinois at Chicago's Institute for Research on Race and Public Policy and Great Cities Institute, as well as from the Smithsonian Institution's National Museum of American History and the University of Virginia's Carter G. Woodson Institute for the Study of African American and African Studies.

TERA W. HUNTER is an associate professor of history and associate director of the Center for Africanamerican Urban Studies and the Economy at Carnegie Mellon University. Her book *To 'Joy My Freedom: Southern Black Women's Lives and Labors after the Civil War* received the H. L. Mitchell Award of the Southern Historical Association, the Letitia Woods Brown Memorial Prize of the Association of Black Women Historians, and the Book of the Year Award of the International Labor History Association. She is the coeditor of *Dispersal: Gender, Sexuality, and African Diasporas* and *The African American Urban Experience: Perspectives from the Colonial Period to the Present* and is the author of numerous book chapters and articles.

WILLIAM POWELL JONES is an associate professor of history at the University of Wisconsin, Madison, and a scholar-in-residence at the Schomburg Center for Research in Black Culture. The author of *The Tribe of Black Ulysses: African American Lumber Workers in the Jim Crow South,* he also published articles in *Left History, Labor History,* and the *Journal of Urban History.* He received his Ph.D. from the University of North Carolina at Chapel Hill in 2000.

BRIAN KELLY received his Ph.D. in 1998 from Brandeis University and is currently a senior lecturer in the School of History and Anthropology at Queen's University Belfast. His first book, *Race, Class, and Power in the Alabama Coalfields, 1908–1921,* won a number of prizes, including the Southern Historical Association's H. L. Mitchell Award and its Frances Butler Simkins Award. He has published articles in *Alabama Review, Labor History,* and *International Review of Social History* and is a contributing editor to *Labor: Studies in the Working-Class History of the Americas.* He has recently completed an extended introduction to the reprint of Bernard Mandel's classic *Labor: Free and Slave,* from the University of Illinois Press. Recently a Walter Hines Page Fellow at the National Humanities Center, he is director of a transatlantic collaborative research project, *After Slavery: Race, Labor and Politics in the Postemancipation Carolinas,* and is currently working on a book tentatively titled *Counterrevolution in the Lowcountry: Black Workers and the Overthrow of Reconstruction in Coastal South Carolina.*

ROBERT KORSTAD received his Ph.D. from the University of North Carolina at Chapel Hill in 1987. A professor of public policy studies and history at Duke University, he is the coauthor (with Jacquelyn Dowd Hall, James

Leloudis, Mary Murphy, LuAnn Jones, and Christopher B. Daly) of *Like a Family: The Making of a Southern Cotton Mill World;* coeditor (with William Chafe and Raymond Gavins) of *Remembering Jim Crow: African Americans Talk about Life in the Segregated South;* and author of *Civil Rights Unionism: Tobacco Workers and the Struggle for Democracy in the Mid-Twentieth-Century South.* He has served as a codirector and research associate on the project "Behind the Veil": Documenting African-American Life in the Jim Crow South" of the Center for Documentary Studies at Duke University since 1989. His articles have appeared in *Law and Contemporary Problems; International Review of Social History; Social Science History; International Labor and Working-Class History; Journal of American History;* and the *American Historical Review;* he has received fellowships from the W. E. B. Du Bois Institute for Afro-American Research and the National Endowment for the Humanities. His *Civil Rights Unionism* was a cowinner of the Phillip Taft Labor History Award and the Liberty Legacy Foundation Award and the winner of the Southern Historical Association's H. L. Mitchell Award and Charles S. Sydnor Award.

NELSON LICHTENSTEIN is a professor of history at the University of California at Santa Barbara. His books include *Labor's War at Home: The CIO in World War II; Walter Reuther: The Most Dangerous Man in Detroit; State of the Union: A Century of American Labor;* and *Who Built America? Working People and the Nation's Economy, Politics, Culture, and Society* (with Roy Rosenzweig and Susan Strasser), vol. 2; *State of the Union* received the Philip Taft Prize in 2003. He is the editor of *Imagining Capitalism: Social Thought and Political Economy in Twentieth Century America; Major Problems in the History of American Workers* (with Eileen Boris); *Ambiguous Promise: Industrial Democracy in America* (with Howell Harris); and *On the Line: Essays in the History of Auto Work* (with Steven Meyers). His articles have appeared in numerous books and in *New Labor Forum, International Labor and Working-Class History, Radical History Review, Dissent, Catholic University Law Review,* and the *Journal of American History.* He has received fellowships from the John Simon Guggenheim Memorial Foundation, Oregon Center for the Humanities, and the National Endowment for the Humanities; he has also held the Centennial Fulbright Chair at the University of Helsinki. He received his Ph.D. from the University of California at Berkeley in 1974.

JOSEPH A. McCARTIN is an associate professor of history at Georgetown University. His *Labor's Great War: The Struggle for Industrial Democracy and the Origins of Modern American Labor Relations, 1912–21* won the Philip Taft Labor History Prize. He is the editor of *American Labor: A Documentary*

History (with Melvyn Dubofsky) and *Americanism: Essays in the History of a Contested Ideal* (with Michael Kazin). His articles have appeared in *Willamette Journal, U.S. Catholic Historian, Journal of Social History, Journal of Policy History, Labor: Studies in Working-Class History of the Americas,* and *Labor History.* He has held fellowships from the Charles Warren Center for the Study of American History at Harvard University, the National Endowment for the Humanities. He received his Ph.D. from the State University of New York at Binghamton in 1990.

STEVEN A. REICH is an associate professor of history at James Madison University and is the editor of the three-volume *Encyclopedia of the Great Black Migration of the Twentieth Century.* His article "Soldiers of Democracy: Black Texans and the Fight for Citizenship, 1917–1921," which appeared in the *Journal of American History* in 1996, won the Organization of American Historians' Louis M. Pelzer Memorial Award. He received his Ph.D. from Northwestern University and was a Summerlee Research Fellow at the Clements Center for Southwest Studies at Southern Methodist University.

LESLIE A. SCHWALM is an associate professor of history at the University of Iowa. Her book *A Hard Fight for We: Women's Transition from Slavery to Freedom in South Carolina* was the recipient of the Willie Lee Rose Prize of the Southern Association of Women Historians, and her article in this volume, "Sweet Dreams of Freedom," received the Letitia Woods Brown Prize from the Association of Black Women Historians. Her articles have appeared in *Journal of Women's History, Annals of Iowa History, Prologue: Quarterly of the National Archives,* and *Civil War History.* Her fellowships include the University of Iowa's May Brodbeck Humanities Fellowship and the National Endowment for the Humanities Fellowship. She serves as an advisory editor to the "Blacks in the Diaspora" series of the Indiana University Press. She received her Ph.D. from the University of Wisconsin at Madison in 1991.

NAN ELIZABETH WOODRUFF is a professor of history at Pennsylvania State University. She is the author of *As Rare as Rain: Federal Relief in the Great Southern Drought of 1930–31* and *American Congo: The African American Freedom Struggle in the Arkansas and Mississippi Delta, 1900–1950,* which received the 2004 McLemore Prize from the Mississippi Historical Society. She received her Ph.D. from the University of Tennessee in 1977.

Index

Inland Steel Company, 215
Interchurch World Movement, 53
Interclub Council of Chicago, 214
Intercollegiate Club, 204
International Ladies Garment Workers'
    Union (ILGWU), 214
International Woodworker, 255, 258, 261,
    262, 263
International Woodworkers of America
    (IWA), 255, 257, 259, 261–62
interracial unionism, 157, 252, 265
iron and steel industry, 43
IWA. *See* International Woodworkers of
    America
IWW. *See* Industrial Workers of the
    World

Jackson, Elijah, 250, 251, 253, 254–55, 259,
    261, 264, 265
Jackson, Ella, 78
Jackson, Ga., 273
Jackson, Maynard, 271–72, 274, 285–91
Jackson, Tenn., 163
Jacksonville, Fla., 156, 276
Janiewski, Dolores, 5
Jaynes, Gerald, 12–13
Jessup, Mabel, 225
Jones, Jacquelyn, 12–13
Jones, Ruby, 226
Johnson, Charles H., 57
Johnson, Charles S., 253
Johnson, Henry, 214
Johnson, James P., 85
Johnson, James Weldon, 46, 158, 160, 165
Johnson, R. H., 105
Jordan, James, 284

Katzman, David, 124
Keithfield plantation, 17, 19
Kelley, Robin D. G., 212
Kelly, Brian, 157
Kennedy, David, 149
Kennedy, John F., 279
Kentucky Manufacturers Association, 48
Kessler, Sidney, 61
Key West, Fla., 62
King, Martin Luther, Jr., 223, 244, 278,
    283, 284, 288

King, Martin Luther, Sr., 289
King County, Washington, 55–56, 59
Kingsley, Reverend Harold M., 205, 207
Kirby, John Henry, 96, 154
Kirby Lumber Company, 112
Knights of Labor, 2, 55–56, 61, 110
Korean War, 234
Ku Klux Klan, 77, 99, 262
Kusmer, Kenneth, 125

labor education classes, 387; Brookwood
    Labor College, 210; Bryn Mawr Sum-
    mer School, 209, 210; University of
    Wisconsin School for Workers, 209
labor history. *See* historiography
"labor question," 2–4
laundry work and laundresses, 16, 74, 104,
    125, 140, 154
Lawson, Lulu E., 211
Leadership Conference on Civil Rights,
    235
League for Struggle for Negro Rights, 211
Leggett, Tex., 167, 168
Levee district, Chicago, 130, 133, 137–40
Levine, Lawrence, 72
Lewis, George, 169
Lewis, Jeems, 160
Lewis, John L., 224
Lewis, Jonnie D., 264
Lewis, Leah Betty, 264
Liberty Loans and Bonds, 181, 185
lien laws, 265
Lightfoot, Claude, 211
Lincoln, Abraham, 155
Lipsitz, George, 273
Little, Larry, 238
Little Rock, Ark., 93, 149, 154, 165, 183
Litwack, Leon, 103
Local 22 (FTA), 226–28, 235–38
Local 600 (UAW), 230–31, 233, 239
Loeb, Henry, 283
Logan, Rayford, 46, 64
longshoring and longshoremen, 43, 45, 47,
    49–50, 55, 158
Longview, Tex., 149, 156
Loving, Prest, 58
Lowery, Joseph, 288–89
Lowry, Henry, 188

Memphis, 159; middle-class members' conflicts with black workers, 164–65; in Mound Bayou, Miss., 183; in Nashville, 161; in New Orleans, 159, 160; in North Carolina, 228, 378, 389; in Okmulgee, Okla., 169; in Pine Bluff, 183; post–World War I repression of, 166–70; post–World War II era, 235, 237–41; railroad workers as members of, 163–64; in Sapulpa, Okla., 165; in Selma, 164–65; in the South, 147–48, 157–61, 166, 170; in St. Francis County, Ark., 188; in Vicksburg, 167, 182; in Winston-Salem, 228, 238; during World War I, 147–48, 157–70; during World War II, 222–23, 227–32

National Association of Colored Women, 123

National Federation of Colored Women's Clubs, 202

National Labor Relations Board (NLRB), 223, 224, 225–26, 230, 236–37, 258, 259, 285

National Labor Tribune, 60

National Negro Business League (NNBL), 102, 103, 104, 203, 205

National Negro Congress (NNC), 213–15, 252; Chicago Council of, 213–14; women's auxiliary, 215

National Negro Labor Conferences, 205

National Negro Voice (New Orleans), 112

National Urban League, 64, 214, 222, 237, 240; Community Relations Project of, 237. *See also* Atlanta Urban League; Chicago Urban League; Detroit Urban League

National War Labor Board (NWLB), 154, 226, 321, 233

Navy, U.S.; desegregation of, 275; racism within, 276

NCC. *See* National Negro Congress

Negro Labor Conferences, Chicago, 203–6

Negro Labor Council (Detroit), 241

Negro Thought in America (Meier), 6

Newcastle, Wash., 55

"New Crowd" and "new crowd networks," 206, 210, 212–15

New Deal, 178, 189, 195, 223, 228, 234, 251, 279

"New Negro," 17, 157, 183, 184, 200, 204, 228

New Orleans, La., 49, 50, 62, 153, 157, 184

Newport News, Va., 62, 108

Newport News Shipbuilding and Drydock Company, 108

New Republic, 148

New South, 47, 73, 96, 98, 103; labor relations in, 96–97, 109

New York, 152

New York Age, 150

New York Post, 103

New York Times, 45, 46, 283, 289

NLRB. *See* National Labor Relations Board

NNBL. *See* National Negro Business League

Norman, Okla., 276

North Carolina, 150

North Carolina Central University, 285

Northern Pacific Coal Company, 56

Northrup, Herbert, 5

Northwest Herald (Seattle), 64

Norwood, Stephen H., 69n51

NWLB. *See* National War Labor Board

Oakland, Calif., 224

occupations of black workers: agricultural field hands and sharecroppers, 11, 13–14, 17–28, 149, 181; artisans, 45–46; automobile manufacturing, 229; of black men in Chicago, 131; child-nurses, 74–75; commercial laundry workers, 77, 125; cooks, 16, 74–75, 128, 153; domestic servants, 125, 127–28, 140, 153, 172–77; dressmakers, 45; in entertainment industry, 77; farmers, 153; longshoremen, 49, 50, 62; in manufacturing, 77; oyster shuckers, 62; phosphate miners, 47, 62; prostitutes/sex workers, 6, 122–42; public employees, 279; Pullman porters, 6, 62, 110, 196–215; railroad workers, 47, 98, 165, 252; sanitation workers, 271, 272, 286–87; seamstresses, 127; sharecroppers, 6, 11, 13–14, 17–28, 47, 149, 178–79, 181, 183, 185–86, 189, 273;

tobacco stemmers and processors, 62, 224; washerwomen, 93, 125
Odd Fellows, 277
Ohio State University, 282
OIC. *See* Oregon Improvement Company
Okmulgee, Oklahoma, 169
Oliver, William, 240
Olivet Baptist Church, 199
Operation Dixie, 234, 254–58, 263
Opportunity, 64, 251
Oregon Improvement Company (OIC), 56
Osofsky, Gilbert, 124
Our Colored Fighters, 160
Owen, Chandler, 147
Owens, Solomon, 257

packinghouses, 224
packinghouses and packinghouse workers, 95, 196
Packinghouse strike of 1904 (Chicago), 43, 69n51
Packinghouse Workers Organizing Committee (PWOC), 63, 215, 253
Painter, Nell Irvin, 5
Pana, Ill., 42, 50
Parker, Bell, 137
Parker, Francis, Sr., 17, 18
Parker, Judge John, 206
Partido Independiente de Color, 94
Payne, Charles, 3
Penn, Nettie, 78
People's Church of Chicago, 199, 202
Perry, Dora, 138
Petersburg, Va., 167
Phillips, Kimberley, 125
Phillips County, Arkansas, 185, 187
Pike County, Georgia, 273–75
Pilgrim Baptist Church, 202
Pine Bluff, Ark., 183, 188
Pittsburg Courier, 228
Pittsburgh, Penn., 49, 152, 224
Pittsburgh Plate Glass Company, 277
Poles, 232
poll taxes, 256
Poor People's Campaign, 283
Popular Front, 234, 243. *See also* Communist Party

populism and Populist revolt, 61, 97, 98, 100, 101
Port Royal, South Carolina, 15
Proctor, Henry Hugh, 80, 82
Professional Air Traffic Controllers Organization (PATCO), 291
Progressive Era, 50, 79
Progressive Farmers and Household Union, 157, 178, 186
Progressive Party, 236
Proposition 13 (California), 291
prostitution and prostitutes, 6, 122–42; structure of sex trade, 130
public employees and employment, 7, 278–79
public-sector unionism, 272, 279–80, 282, 291
Pullman, George, 197
Pullman boycott/strike of 1894, 48
Pullman Company, 110, 196–97, 200, 201, 203, 204, 208, 215; paternalism of, 197, 199, 201, 206
Pullman maids, 198, 215
Pullman porters, 6, 62, 110, 196–215; images of, 198, 216–17n7; origins of occupation, 197; position in black community, 198; working conditions of, 198. *See also* Brotherhood of Sleeping Car Porters

"race question," 2, 4
Rachleff, Peter, 5
"racial capitalism," 96
racial division of labor, 45–47
racial uplift, 95, 103, 108
Radical Reconstruction, 13, 99, 100
Railroad Administration, U.S. (USRA), 154, 164
railroad industry and workers, 47, 98, 163–65, 252
Raleigh, N.C., 159
Randolph, A. Philip, 147, 199–203, 209, 211, 214–15, 252; and Communist Party, 212; and March on Washington of 1941, 252; and National Negro Congress, 213. *See also* BSCP
Rapp, A., 137

Southern Conference for Human Welfare, 234

Southern Lumberman, 259

Southern Lumber Operators' Association (SLOA), 111–12

Southern Pine Association, 111

Southern States Farm Magazine, 101

Southern Tenant Farmers' Union (STFU), 178, 189–90, 224

Southern Workman, 48

South Parkway Branch of Chicago YWCA, 208

Southside Citizens Committee, 214

South Side Garment Workers Club, 214

Southwestern Christian Advocate (New Orleans), 50

Spahr, Charles B., 47

Spear, Allan, 124

Spellman College, 285

Spero, Sterling, 5, 53

Spingarn, Joel E., 158

Sporting and Cub House Directory, 122, 123, 132, 133, 136

"sporting houses," 123

Star of Zion, 152

steelworkers, 196, 213, 265

Steel Workers Organizing Committee (SWOC), 214–15

Stein, Judith, 96, 158

St. Francis County, Ark., 277

STFU. *See* Southern Tenant Farmers' Union

St. Louis Argus, 51

stockyards. *See* packinghouses

St. Paul, Minn., 56

St. Petersburg, Fla. 62

strikebreakers: African Americans as, 6, 41–65; African Americans' motives for becoming, 44, 53–54, 57–61; arguments on behalf of, 50; as black working-class activism, 44–45, 63; critique of, by Richard L. Davis, 60–61; image of black male, 42–43, 49, 65n5; Italian, 41; in mining communities, 42, 55–59; in North Carolina lumber strike, 261; recruitment of, 56; on Seattle docks, 63; violence against black, 44, 57, 63

strikes: AFSCME Atlanta sanitation workers' strike of 1970, 285–86; AFSCME Atlanta sanitation workers' strike of 1977, 271–72, 287–91; AFSCME St. Joseph's Hospital Strike in Memphis of 1969, 283; Birmingham coal strike of 1908, 111; Black Diamond Coal Company strike (fictional), 41–42; Cartersville, Ill., miners' strike of 1899, 52; Chicago packinghouse strike of 1894, 43; Chicago teamsters strike of 1905, 43, 52, 69; Chrysler Corporation strike of 1939, 229; cotton pickers' strike of 1891, 110; Galveston, Tex., strike of 1877, 99; Muchakinock, Iowa, mine strike, 52; of 1919, 184; North Carolina lumber strike of 1948, 260–62; R. J. Reynolds strike of 1947, 235–36; Seattle longshore strike, 54–55; Sopkins Strike in Chicago, 209; steel strike of 1919, 74, 49, 51, 53; sympathy strike, 85; UAW Ford strike of 1941, 64, 229; UAW General Motors strike of 1945–46, 238; Washington state coal miners' strike of 1891, 44, 55–56

Student Non-Violent Coordinating Committee (SNCC), 190, 243

Students for a Democratic Society, 239

Supreme Court, U.S., 179, 186, 206, 222, 264, 274–75, 276, 278, 279

SWOC. *See* Steel Workers Organizing Committee

Taft-Hartley Act, 236, 238, 263

Tampa, Fla., 158

Tappes, Shelton, 230–31, 233, 239, 240, 243

Taylor, Phil, 58

team driving, 43

teamsters and team driving, 43, 45, 47, 49

Teamsters' union, 277–78, 283, 295

tenant farmers. *See* sharecropping and sharecroppers

Texarkana, 150

textiles and textile workers, 43, 46, 234, 254, 256

Thirteenth Amendment, 201

Thomas, Julius A., 64

Thomas, Richard, 125

The University of Illinois Press
is a founding member of the
Association of American University Presses.

University of Illinois Press
1325 South Oak Street
Champaign, IL 61820-6903
www.press.uillinois.edu